The Complete
OLD TESTAMENT STUDIES

Rudolf Frieling (1901–86) studied theology and philosophy and took his Ph.D. at Leipzig. He was among those who founded The Christian Community in 1922. Before becoming the leader of this movement for religious renewal in 1957, his work took him throughout Germany as well as to Vienna and New York. He was a prolific author of books on Christian thinking and his writings on the Old and New Testaments.

The Complete
OLD TESTAMENT STUDIES

RUDOLF FRIELING

First published in German as Volumes 1 and 2 of Frieling's
collected works on the Old and New Testament,
Studien zum Alten Testament (Vol 1) and *Psalmen* (Vol 2)
by Verlag Urachhaus, Stuttgart in 1983 and 1985
Some parts originally published in English
as *Old Testament Studies* and in *Hidden Treasures in the Psalms*
by Floris Books, Edinburgh in 1987 and 1967 respectively
This expanded edition first published by Floris Books in 2022

See Sources and Translators, p. 444 for details of translators

© 1983, 1985 Verlag Urachhaus
English version © 1967, 1987, 2022 Floris Books

All rights reserved. No part of this publication may be
reproduced without the prior permission of
Floris Books, Edinburgh
www.florisbooks.co.uk

British Library CIP Data available
ISBN 978-178250-789-5
Printed and bound by Gutenberg Press Limited, Malta

 Floris Books supports sustainable forest management by
printing this book on materials made from wood that
comes from responsible sources and reclaimed material

CONTENTS

Foreword   9

I
FROM CREATION TO PROMISED LAND

1. The Creation of the Human Being	13
2. Creation and Emanation	25
3. God and Gods	31
4. 'Numberless as the Stars'	37
5. The Sacrifice of Isaac	43
6. The Building of the Tabernacle and the Creation	49
7. Aaron's Blessing	56

II
REVELATIONS AND PROPHECIES

8. Balaam	63
9. Gideon's Encounter with the Angel	71
10. The Offering of Manoah	77
11. Leviathan	83
12. 'Not by might ...'	91
13. The Sanctus of the Seraphim	98
14. The Four Living Creatures and the Human Being	104
15. The Beasts of the Abyss and the Son of Man	111
16. 'The Sun of Righteousness'	118

III
TREES, WELLS, AND STONES IN THE LIVES OF THE PATRIARCHS

17. The Fairy-Tale Nature of the Stories of the Patriarchs	123
18. Abraham and the Trees	125
19. Isaac and the Wells	134
20. Jacob and the Stones	142

IV
FROM SABBATH TO SUNDAY

21. Sunday: A Christian Fact	157

V
PSALMS ABOUT THE WORLD

22. The Human Being Under the Stars (Psalm 8)	175
23. God in Nature (Psalm 104)	186
24. The Heavens Declare (Psalm 19)	201
25. 'I Lift up my Eyes to the Hills ...' (Psalm 121)	213
26. The Life Forces in Devotion (Psalm 119)	220
27. Gazing Upon the Cosmos (Psalm 148)	231
28. The Seven Thunders (Psalm 29)	241
29. A Summer Song of Praise (Psalm 65)	247
30. An Autumnal Song of Pilgrimage (Psalm 84)	254
31. The Song of the Three Men in the Fiery Furnace	260

VI
PSALMS ABOUT THE PATH OF LIFE

32. The World of Sin and the World of Grace (Psalm 36)	269
33. The Great Confession (Psalm 51)	278
34. In the Presence of Eternity (Psalm 90)	290

35. 'My Times are in Your Hands' (Psalm 31)	300
36. In Exile (Psalms 42 and 43)	306
37. Experience of God (Psalm 63)	319
38. A Glimpse into the Sanctuary (Psalm 73)	326
39. The Passion Psalm of the Redeemer (Psalm 22)	334
40. The Way of Life (Psalm 16)	344
41. The Lord is my Shepherd (Psalm 23)	354
42. Authority to Tread on Serpents and Scorpions (Psalm 91)	362
43. The Hymn of the Soul (Psalm 103)	369

VII
THE NEW SONG

44. The Future of the Earth (Psalm 37)	381
45. 'A Mighty Fortress is our God' (Psalm 46)	391
46. 'I Shall not Die, but I Shall Live' (Psalm 118)	398
47. 'Sit at my Right Hand' (Psalm 110)	409
48. The New Song (Psalm 96)	416
49. Advent (Psalm 24)	422

Afterword	435
Psalms in the life of Christ 435; Psalms in Christianity 436; Aspects of interpretation of the psalms 437	
Bibliography	443
Sources and Translators	444
Index of Biblical References	445
Index	451

Quotations from the Bible are usually the author's own translations.

FOREWORD

Throughout The Christian Community's existence I have been privileged to serve it also in a literary capacity. What I have been able to write has largely been published as separate articles in the journal *Die Christengemeinschaft*. This volume and its companion, *The Complete New Testament Studies,* compile essays concerned with biblical themes published through the years in various issues of the journal, together with the addition of a few longer studies.

Given this gathering and conclusion of the work, I would like to offer a few personal words. From my childhood on I felt myself drawn to the biblical content of both the Old and the New Testament. Later, at school I became familiar with liberal theology and biblical critique, which I found problematic. As a matter of curiosity, I will mention in passing that at the age of nineteen I wrote an essay with the strange title, 'The Gospel of John in the Light of Expressionism' – and, touchingly, this essay was published in March 1920 in the monthly periodical *Christentum und Gegenwart* (Christianity and the modern age), edited by Christian Geyer and Friedrich Rittelmeyer. I sought to aspire to the 'intellectual honesty' that Nietzsche had demanded, and, despite the seemingly irrefutable critique to which the Gospel of John was subject, I wanted to retrieve its higher truth.

My closer acquaintance with the worldview of anthroposophy brought me a form of release: entirely new perspectives on biblical themes opened before me. Besides this, I learned of Friedrich Rittelmeyer's experiences with John's Gospel, finding there a modern religiosity and solidly founded theological learning harmoniously combined with anthroposophical knowledge. Over subsequent years I witnessed the publication of successive volumes of Emil Bock's monumental work on the Bible, in which he strode with mighty steps through the history of human consciousness as this is reflected in the entirety of biblical scriptures, from the story of creation through to the Revelation to John.

In my own work I tried to preserve and substantiate this newly emerging world of insights and anchor it in the details of the texts. I hope that, given this common background, the variety and diversity of what is compiled here will nevertheless produce a harmonious whole.

The original study of selected psalms was first published in 1958, and has been revised and enlarged at various times since then. Reflections on Psalms 63, 91, 118 and 121, and the 'Song of the Three Men in the Fiery Furnace', were added. Reflections on psalms 31 and 119 were also added.

The translations of the psalms examined in each account seek to make the Hebrew text comprehensible but make no claim to be fully valid 'translations'. To give a rendering that does justice both to the content and the artistic form of the originals would require much further work. I owe thanks for the various insights I found in translations by Emil Bock, Martin Buber, Franz Delitzsch, Hermann Gunkel, Emil Kautzsch, Rudolf Kittel, Werner H. Schmidt and Willy Stärk.

In what follows, I have selected 28 of the 150 psalms. This does not signify that these psalms are to be regarded as the most important. The selection was more or less subjective, a point of departure for embarking on the subject.

In arranging the psalms I placed nature psalms at the beginning, then those relating to sin and mercy and to the sanctity of the individual human being. Finally come psalms that look forward in apocalyptic fashion.

For interested readers I have included a concluding account of my approach to interpretation ('Aspects of Interpretation').

I
FROM CREATION TO PROMISED LAND

I

THE CREATION OF THE HUMAN BEING

THE FIRST CHAPTER OF GENESIS

The first page of the Bible describes the creation. 'In the beginning God created the heavens and the earth.' The world comes into being over the course of six days, with the human being appearing on the last of them.

It is evident from the way it is told that the human being is not just the last in a series of creations but constitutes the final and crowning glory. As the supreme creation, therefore, human beings also have the potential of growing beyond mere 'createdness' and by virtue of their own being rising to become fellow creators.

The style of the first chapter of Genesis emphasises this special human quality. Even a superficial glance shows that no other day of creation takes up so much space in this concise chapter, but the distinction can be observed in subtler details. We are well aware for example that the account of each day of creation ends with a particular phrase: 'And there was evening and there was morning, the first day ... the second day ...' Closer study of the Hebrew shows that this almost liturgical, rhythmical repetition is not absolutely identical for the different days. The first day is referred to as 'one' day: 'And there was evening and there was morning, one day.' An organic cycle of time has been formed as something separate and unique. It is only with the second day that the ordinal numbers appear, and even then we do not find 'the second day', 'the third day' but simply 'second day' and 'third day'. This continues up to and including the fifth day. But then comes *the* sixth day' (1:31). This is more emphatic. The seventh day has no concluding formula like the others but has instead the distinction of being called 'the seventh day' three times (2:2, 2, 3). The solemnity of the divine rest it comprises, however, requires the uniqueness of the events of the sixth day.

On the other hand the sixth day is not wholly reserved for man. You would think the 'day of man' would be more striking if it had no other content. But the sixth day begins with the bringing forth of the creatures of the firm land, the warm-blooded mammals. This comes very close to the creation of humans, which is also in line with modern scientific views. Genesis, however, sees not only this closeness but at the same time the huge difference between man and animal. This comes out very clearly by virtue of the juxtaposition. The gradually advancing development of organic forms has come close to the human, but man's actual coming into existence occurs only as a result of the entry of a quite new element from above, which had to await this moment in evolution to make its impact.

Until now we read in each case that God said, 'Let there be': 'Let there be light ... Let there be a firmament ...' or, 'Let the waters ... be gathered together ... let the dry land appear.' It is quite different with man. A unique and most solemn prologue precedes the creation of the human being (Gn 1:26).

1. The prologue

> Then God said,
> 'Let us make man
> in our image,
> after our likeness;
> and let them rule
> over the fish of the sea,
> and over the birds of the air,
> and over the cattle,
> and over all the earth,
> and over every creeping thing
> that creeps on the earth.'

The 'Let us ...' is like an appeal of the divine soul to its own creative powers, which in their manifoldness are addressed in the plural and

1. THE CREATION OF THE HUMAN BEING

which, while within God, are yet beings in their own right. What is translated as 'God' is in the original *Elohim* – quite clearly plural. The related verb forms, however, are nearly always in the singular.* *Elohim* is therefore a unified body of sublime beings through which God himself works. The prologue is unique in that here the Hebrew verb takes into account the plural quality of *Elohim,* and that this is followed by the plurals 'us' and 'our'. Three times the plurality of the divine soul utters itself: 'Let us ... our image ... our likeness.'.

In this threefold utterance we receive, as if from the highest heaven, an intimation of the mystery of the Trinity in the Old Testament. Not only do the *Elohim* form the sevenfold entity of which ancient tradition speaks, but, in still higher regions, the Trinity itself.

It is significant that such a highlighting of the 'three' occurs just here in connection with the creation of man, for it is only in relation to the number three that man's true nature can be understood. Simply as a duality of body and soul man would be no image of a triune God. A human being has spirit, soul and body.

The translation 'make man' is correct inasmuch as the original has only 'Adam', meaning 'man', with no article before it. In Hebrew this word indicates neither singular nor plural; it is like a collective noun.

'Let us ...' Man has his origin in this great, divine first person plural. Then comes, 'in our image'. The Greek translation has *eikon,* the Latin, *imago* – the word used of Christ in a special sense in the New Testament. He is the 'image' of the invisible God (Col 1:15, 2Cor 4:4). The Son proceeding from the Father in eternity, who brings the incomprehensible into manifestation, is the original image of all images. Man was created also to fulfil that image. Man is one day to be raised to the likeness of the Son, changing 'from one degree of glory to another' (2Cor 3:18). Since man was created *'in* [literally] our image,' then in him there also came into being the potential for what had been determined by the original image of the divine Son.

The 'image' springs as it were directly from the Father who brings forth the Son. The following introduction of the word 'likeness' (Greek *homoiosis,* Latin *similitudo*) presupposes the existence of intelligent beings who can comprehend such a likeness. Whoever recognises the image that proceeded from the Father will find that it leads

---

* See Chapter 3, 'God and Gods'

beyond itself as image, from the visible up to the invisible. 'No one has seen God.' But: 'He who has seen me has seen the Father.' So the 'likeness' touches on a motif of recognition and anticipates the sphere of the Holy Spirit.*

This basic definition of 'image' and 'likeness' is connected with the prospect of the ruling (or dominion) to which human beings are called. This raises them above all creatures and places them beside the Creator as his earthly deputy, as one who may share in God's kingship. The living creatures of water, air and earth that are now mentioned represent different soul activities, and they reflect the whole complex of human emotions. This complexity has to be held together in harmony, ruled by the I. The dominion God intended for man over the animals is not merely part of a plan for the civilisation of the earth; man is not only to cope with the animals outwardly and tame them. Great saints have been able to influence animals with ease since they had previously gained command over the animal within themselves. Thus to a certain extent we already anticipate the realm of the New Testament.

2. The act of creation

> So God [*Elohim*] created man in his own image,
> in the image of God he created him;
> male and female he created them. (Gn 1:27)

Just as the 'we' occurs three times in the prologue, so here, where the transition of the divine thought into actual existence is concerned, the word *bara* (create), so rarely used in the Old Testament, also occurs three times.

---

* As an introduction to the genealogy from Adam to Noah, the beginning of Genesis 5 turns back once more to 1:26. The descent from father to son is thus linked with the creation of man and seen in the light of it. Of Adam (and only of him) it is said: 'he begat a son in his own likeness, after his image, and named him Seth' (5:3). 'Image' and 'likeness' have changed places, also 'in' and 'after'. Thus for all the similarity the difference from 1:26 is also meant to be indicated. The 'image' appears again for the last time after the flood, where the death penalty is laid down for the shedding of human blood in view of the great dignity of man made in God's image (9:6). The two terms 'image' and 'likeness' occur only in 1:26 and in the repetition, 5:3, that mirrors it.

In all, the word *bara* occurs seven times in the story of creation: Straight away at the opening: 'In the beginning God *created* the heavens and the earth' (1:1). Similarly at its close where the six days are finally summed up: 'God blessed the seventh day ... he rested from all his work which he had *created*' (2:3), and 'These are the generations of the heavens and the earth when they were *created*' (2:4). So *bara* is used when the whole creation is reviewed. This expression should be distinguished from 'made'. God 'made' the firmament, the heavenly bodies and the beasts of the earth. He also said: 'Let us make man ...' But there is an exception with the first mention of ensouled life that begins to multiply in the waters and which also takes the form of the great sea monsters: 'So God *created* the great sea monsters' (1:21). And then in connection with man *bara* occurs in three consecutive sentences (1:27).

'Make' somehow presupposes an already existing substance out of which something can be made. The making of man in the prologue takes place in the realm of divine thought out of which the creator forms his idea of man in his image. But now the thought is to take on its own existence, separate from the inner being of God, outside God. That there can actually be something that itself is not directly God, is an immense and mysterious fact, one which philosophers have struggled to understand. Perhaps we can come closest to the mystery through the idea of love. To grant other beings their own separate existence God has, as it were, to delve into his own substance and release and give away something of himself. That is an act of love, a sacrifice. Wherever there is creation there is sacrifice.

In the 'Let us' lies the free and sovereign resolve. But the *bara* that now actually produces man cannot be thought of except in the context of loving sacrifice.

'So God created [*bara*] man in his own image.' The second sentence seems to say exactly the same thing again: 'In the image of God he created him.' Even so it should make a profound impression on us; the pronouncement in the first sentence is so holy and so forceful that the text cannot easily proceed. But the repetition does not in fact say only the same thing again. The order of the words is different. The conclusion of the first sentence, 'in his own image,' becomes the opening of the second sentence. It is taken up again after a pause of reverent silence and now raised like a monstrance: 'In the image of God...'

Behind this second of the three sentences there again stands the Son, the original image of all images.

The third sentence shows the duality of man's nature with the mention of 'male and female'. It is old traditional wisdom that humankind originally androgynous, and that both sexes only separated later.*

Genesis describes the actual separation into man and woman only after the story of the creation, in the second chapter – where Yahweh-Elohim puts Adam into a deep sleep and fashions Eve out of his rib (2:21f). This division had therefore not come about till then. The apparent contradiction has traditionally been resolved by supposing that two completely different creation stories were carelessly linked together by the 'editor' of Genesis. The argument is supported by differences of language between the two accounts (Gn 1:1–2:4a, and 2:4b–25).

It is quite conceivable that the two accounts resulted from the vision and literary formulation of different Hebraic schools. One need not exclude this possibility. The first chapter is concerned only with a supersensory, ethereal form of the world's existence, although it has already proceeded from God. The second chapter is more concerned with the world of matter. It is noteworthy that 1:1 speaks of 'the heavens and the earth' while this changes to 'the earth and the heavens' in 2:4b. The element of the dust of the earth is now imprinted upon the hitherto still ethereal being of man. The 'deep sleep' indicates a change of consciousness: he is asleep to the supersensory. Only now comes the division into sexes. Only now is humankind in the condition to meet the serpent. In fact the two chapters depict two different planes of existence. And if these were originally the concepts of different sages whose insights complemented one another, the 'editor' of Genesis was no naive patchworker. Must he not deliberately have joined together the two accounts in the proper order as a result of comprehensive knowledge? Must it not have been clear to him that the original man, 'male and female,' was not yet 'Adam and Eve'?

Yet the text reads: 'male and female he created *them*.' Scholars have expressed the opinion that an original 'him' has been changed to 'them' to eliminate the old idea as incompatible with Jewish tradition. This is not impossible, but such a conclusion is not even necessary. We

---

* See abundant material on this in Benz, *Adam: Der Mythus des Urmenschen*. Rudolf Steiner has also corroborated this old tradition.

saw that 'Adam' is a collective noun. and 'man' can also be one. In this prototypal realm singular and plural are not so rigidly distinguished; the one ethereal prototype holds many other possibilities. Thus the archetypal man appears as a unity when it is a question of being the image of God. 'In the image of God he created *him.*' The third sentence throws light on another aspect of man's nature: the fact that he is also member of a human race. 'Male and female he created *them.*' The plural should still not here be taken as the duality of a man and a woman. At this point it is still the male-female within the one prototypal 'man' that shows its plural potentiality. Nor is the male-female polarity absolute even after the division into sexes; everyone still has the other pole within them, and is faced with the task of bringing about within themselves the 'mystical marriage' in which the spirit and soul permeate each other. Marriage can be a more or less real image of that mystical marriage. But even those who do not marry need to seek this inner harmony, and by doing so will fit in more easily with their fellow men.

So the third sentence, which introduces the male-female as well as the plural motif, ultimately indicates a realm that belongs especially to the Holy Spirit, for it is the Holy Spirit that fosters inner harmony and the faculties for living in community. In the afterglow of the Pentecost experience the first Christian community, consisting of different kinds and conditions of people, both men and women, was 'of *one* heart and soul' (Ac 4:32).*

3. The blessing

After the human being is brought into existence through the act of creation (*bara*), there is a special blessing as an additional spiritual endowment. A first blessing was already given to the animals: 'Be fruitful and multiply' (Gn 1:22). The fact that a living creature

---

* The beginning of the fifth chapter – as noted earlier – once again looks back to the creation of man. There again *bara* occurs three times. 'This is the book of the generations of Adam [man]. When God *created* man, he made him in the likeness of God. Male and female he *created* them, and he blessed them and named them man when they were *created*' (5:1f). This is like an echo of the first chapter and only here is the giving of the name introduced. In the story of creation God named only day and night, the heavens, earth and sea.

reproduces itself was felt to be the continuation of the miracle of creation. The blessing is an awarding of such real sharing in God's power that it remains henceforth with those blessed.

The same seems to be repeated for man: 'Be fruitful and multiply, and fill the earth' (1:28), but it is introduced in a different way. In connection with the animals we read: 'And God blessed them, saying ...' With man it is more explicit and more solemn: 'And God blessed them, and God said to them ...' So far the creative speaking of God went out into the world, but he had no one in this world 'to whom' to speak. This is something entirely new. The blessing of the animals was not in a real sense spoken to them.

The 'be fruitful and multiply' takes on a more profound meaning in relation to man, who is the image of God. As far as the animals are concerned it means a mere multiplication. Even this is marvellous enough, but what emerges are always new samples of the same species. Human biological fertility does not simply lead to a duplication of the parent. The species is the basis for the incorporation of new and unique individualities. Rudolf Steiner suggested that in comparing man with animals one should accord to each human individual the status of a species of their own if one regards their personality as something entirely their own. With human beings the mystery of singular and plural exists on a higher level, and the increasing of humankind is linked with the mystery of God's letting a host of invisible beings proceed from himself, 'the Father of spirits' as he is called in the Letter to the Hebrews (12:9).

So what is intended for man is not repetition of the same, but 'increase of the kingdom of God' by means of the development of different individualities incarnating on earth. Consciousness for those on earth in pre-Christian times was not yet fully awake. When in Old Testament times a man rejoiced in the blessing of children, his thoughts and feelings were chiefly concerned with the natural propagation of the species. The unrepeatable nature of the individuality was first brought to light by Christ. Therewith 'being fruitful and multiplying' also undergoes a profound spiritualisation in that it becomes the concern of the inner life of the individual. The parable of the talents forcefully preaches God's high demands; he is not content for things to remain as they are, but expects an 'increase'. If man lets his lower self decrease and allows Christ to increase within him, then he becomes more than he was before. Then he becomes 'fruitful'. 'I am the true vine, and my Father is the vinedresser. Every branch of mine that bears no fruit, he takes away, and every branch that does bear fruit he prunes, that it may bear more fruit ... He who abides in me, and I in him, he it is that bears much fruit.' (Jn 15:1f, 5). What was intimated in Genesis here reaches its fulfilment.

From this point of view 'fill the earth' also becomes something different. For the animals, too, it does not just mean utilising a space allotted for their physical existence. In every instance the animal is a divine and artistic component of the landscape, it belongs to it, completes it and 'fills' it, as a spring evening is filled by the song of a blackbird. Human beings, however, 'fill' the earth in a much higher sense. Anyone who is sensitive can feel the difference between uninhabited deserts and the ground where for centuries there has been culture and spiritual striving in art and religion.

So although the words of blessing sound the same, they carry different overtones for human beings. The difference becomes even more obvious in what follows, where humankind is awarded something for which there is no parallel amongst the animals. 'Fill the earth and *subdue* it' – literally, 'put your foot upon it'. But physically taking possession, owning land, is still not the final goal. And the divine command certainly does not mean that man should blindly exploit an earth he has subdued by his techniques, and senselessly ruin its life. Again it is only the gospel that finally shows what is meant. On the evening of the Last Supper Christ washes the feet of the disciples. One of the teachings that can inexhaustibly be drawn from that symbolic deed on Maundy Thursday is that human beings as disciples of Christ should walk upon the earth in a different way from humans bearing the mark of the Fall.

The blessing once more adds the motif of ruling or dominion already contained in the prologue. There it shone out in the realm of divine intention, whilst here with the blessing it is actually awarded to man as a power: 'and rule over the fish of the sea and over the birds of the air and over every living thing that moves* upon the earth.' The same realms are named as in the prologue: water, air and earth – except that this time in relation to earth only the 'creeping' creatures

---

* Literally 'creeps'. The same Hebrew word is used as in the prologue (1:21).

are mentioned, not the 'cattle'. Perhaps this is already an oblique reference to the serpent, through which at the Fall man will lose his royal dignity.

4. The feeding

> And God said, 'Behold, I have given you every plant yielding seed which is upon the face of all the earth, and every tree with seed in its fruit; to you it shall be food. And to every beast of the earth, and to every bird of the air, and to everything that creeps on the earth, everything that has the breath of life, I have given every green plant for food.' (Gn 1:29f)

From the Old Testament one hardly gets the impression that the ancient Hebrews were specially concerned about vegetarian food. All the more remarkable is the fact that Genesis first allows the eating of meat after the flood (9:3). Here at the beginning plants are clearly the original human food.

Once again human beings and animals seem to draw close to one another; there is the underlying necessity for them both to be fed. But again the differences are more telling. God turns first to human beings and speaks directly to them: 'Behold, I have given you.' The word 'give' has so far been used only once in the account of creation when God 'gave' sun, moon and stars to the firmament, though translations obscure this. Now it is used with the dative case (the 'giving' case) in the second person; the direct address to man is even emphasised by repetition: 'I have given *to you* ... *to you* it shall be food' (many translations do not bring out this second dative). In the following sentence the animals are not themselves addressed; food is allotted to them in the impersonal sentence: 'And to [them] ... I have given every green plant for food.'

How different in relation to human beings. The words directed to them begin with an appeal to consciousness: 'Behold.' The animals also have eyes but one cannot say to them, 'Behold!' Here for the first time in the Bible we meet this call to open our eyes and become aware. Man is not simply to go after his food instinctively like the animal. The taking of food is to lead the way to an act of higher religious perception. The animals also receive good things from God, but the response is missing – the lifting of the eyes in recognition, and acknowledgement of him in worship.

An anticipation of the great 'Take, eat ...' of Maundy Thursday pervades the divine words in Genesis. At the Last Supper Christ gives the disciples his body and his blood in the form of the Melchizedek offering of bread and wine, consisting entirely of plant substances: grain and fruit.

Daily nourishment is a basic fact of man's earthly existence, but everyday events can reveal the deepest mysteries. God rests in his own substance. The beings who have come from him, however, cannot exist out of themselves. From the divine Ground of the World there flows a continuous stream of life whereby everything in existence maintains itself. Thus on one occasion in the psalms 'the bread of angels' is spoken of (78:25). This experience of heavenly communion is reflected in man's eating and drinking, which is something between 'the bread of angels' and the food of the animals, and can become either. In the one direction it can become the mediator of higher experiences. It can become sacramental. Eating and drinking does not thereby lose its reality and become a mere allegory, but opens to a higher reality and takes it in. 'For my flesh is true food, and my blood is true drink' (Jn 6:55). One could also translate: '... is the truth of eating ... is the truth of drinking,' is what earthly nourishment 'means'. The sacrament is more real than mere material food. The path leading to the sacrament starts with the grace before food, in which man begins to respond to the divine 'Behold, I have given you'. Without the upward glance ('behold') human intake of food falls into the danger of sinking down to the animal level, where the image of heavenly communion is obscured.

Thus the creation of man on the sixth day is accomplished. Let us look back once more. First came the prologue, then the act (*bara*) itself, then the blessing, and finally the feeding.

The Christian Eucharist has always proceeded through four main stages: Gospel, Offertory, Transubstantiation, Communion. The renewed Eucharist of The Christian Community also takes this course; it is named the Act of Consecration of Man because the consecration for becoming a true human being in God's image can only be ours through union with Christ. Can the Act of Consecration of Man not open our eyes to the fact that the four holy stages also plainly appear in the creation of man, and correspond exactly?

The *prologue* in the creation story would then be the great *Gospel,* God's message about the nature and goal of man. Behind the threefold *bara* of the act of creation is hidden the sacrifice, the *Offering,* of the creating Godhead, who brings man forth from his own depths and separates him from the Godhead for an independent existence. The *blessing,* which lives on in human beings as the power of increasing and being fruitful and of ruling the earth, confers the capacity for *Transformation.* This blessing is only fulfilled through Christ in the transformation of the individual man who 'bears much fruit', and the transformation of the earth entrusted to him. The *Communion* finally appears in the fourth event where God *gives nourishment* for human life in his plant kingdom – 'Take ...'

2

CREATION AND EMANATION

In modern theological discourses we read how, as the Bible sees it, the world as mere creation stands separately outside its Creator. God is God and world is world' From this the conclusion is drawn that the world which exists outside God is basically a profane affair (*pro-fano* means 'outside the sanctum'). It is widely regarded as progress to engage with this view of the merely mundane world by applying the prevailing materialistic outlooks of today. In doing so, people feel themselves in accord with the general trend towards 'demythologising' and secularisation, which dispels all mystery and indiscriminately renders all phenomena in the world in terms of a straightforward mundaneness. They believe that they promote the Bible's intrinsic outlook by excluding, along with all mythology and nature mysticism, also certain older biblical Christian views which derived the world from a divine emanation. Emanation means that the existence of the world depends upon the Creator having let something of his own being flow into the world.

It is true that in the account in Genesis, the creation of the world is presented as a freely willed, personal deed of the sovereign Godhead. In the theological domain, there is an anxiety that this truth would be endangered by ideas of emanation. However, this danger would only arise if we coupled the concept of emanation with the idea of some natural compulsion – such as when a spider, for instance, in obeying blind necessity is unable to do anything other than spin a web from its own substance. But must emanation only arise from such natural compulsion? Must a free, sovereign deed and the sacrificing gift of one's own substance be mutually exclusive?

In this regard it is helpful to take a look at the ancient secret doctrine of Jewish tradition, the Kabbalah, which has long accompanied understanding of the Old Testament. The Hebrew seekers of wisdom knew that the contents of the Bible are framed by a comprehensive spiritual worldview that, while not systematically expounded as such in sacred texts, silently presupposed supersensible realities. They were convinced that without such an overall context, one could not take proper account of the Bible's profundities. They would not have been satisfied by such a simplistic formulation as 'God is God and the world is the world'. They still had a sense for distinctions, for differentiated thinking. What is today summed up in an all too simple generalisation as 'world' was in their eyes already a fourth condition, which had been preceded by three differing modes of relationship between 'God' and 'world'.

The Kabbalah acknowledged a *very first* phase of the relationship between God and the world that must be silently presupposed before the beginning of Genesis ('In the beginning God created the heavens and the earth'). This phase, *Atziluth,* means 'emanation'.

Only then does the beginning of Genesis follow as a *second* phase, *Beriah,* derived from the mysterious word *bara,* 'to create', which appears only seldom in the Old Testament and is then reserved for the Godhead alone. In the account of creation it resounds seven times. This creation stage still belongs to the supersensible realm. What later becomes our 'world' still resides very close to the Creator, albeit not as intimately close as in the phase of emanation.

The *third* stage is named *Yetzirah* – 'formation' – during which God is still shaping what has flowed from and been created by him, and when, under his creating hands, the gradually emerging world substance is still warm.

And only the *fourth* stage, *Assiah* – derived from the verb 'to make' – corresponds as something finished and elaborated to what we now call 'world'. Only now can we speak of a 'creation' that has to some degree separated from its origin.

Beriah, Yetzirah, Assiah. The words 'create', 'form', 'make' (fashion) are taken by the Kabbalah from the Old Testament. Apart from citing Genesis, ancient Hebrew scholars also pointed to a passage in Isaiah where these three words stand alongside each other: 'Each one who in my name is summoned to the glories I make manifest I have created, formed and fashioned' (Is 43:7).

For Kabbalists these three words stand under the sign of *Atziluth* or emanation. No reference is made to this in the Bible itself; Kabbalists have drawn it from this unspoken source and given it utterance. As the very first phase, in fact, it forms the precondition for the three words in the Bible. But its meaning is by no means exhausted by a merely temporally conceived precedence. As the truly first stage it is the beginning in the sense of the Latin word *principium:* the 'principal' and defining impulse for what succeeds it. It is not 'over' when what comes later arrives but continues to accompany this succeeding reality, streaming on under it in the depths.

One could illustrate the sequence of four worlds in the Kabbalah with a – naturally imperfect – comparison. Think of the creation of an artwork – let's say that an author is writing a novel. In a somewhat schematic way, we could say that the *very first* stage of what later comes to completion is not to be found anywhere except in the author's inner world; consequently we are here concerned with this author as a person. What will later become the book is at this point truly still a piece of the author, though even the word 'piece' is not quite appropriate here insofar as it already contains some kind of sense of separation from its originator. As yet, creator and creation are *one* entity.

As a part or a piece – though still 'of them' – it only gradually crystallises out of the rest of the author's diverse and fluctuating soul life to become a self-contained entity in their mind. Within the author's interior life it acquires a kind of independent existence. This would be the *second* stage.

The *third* begins when they start to write it down. What hitherto resided within them now passes into outer manifestation; but as yet all is in flux, everything is very pliable under their shaping hands.

Then finally the *fourth* stage arrives, when the shaping hands have put their finishing touches to the whole, which now slowly cools and hardens into a fixed shape. Henceforth it has acquired its own, separate existence. Having finished the novel, the author gains distance from it and becomes free for a new project. After a while they may have 'moved on' to a quite 'different place'. With their free and independent personality they are no longer directly involved in the book.

Nevertheless something of them remains within it. Anyone who reads it with loving care and attention will therefore pursue a path that leads back in reverse order to the previous stages of its genesis, and can eventually come to an intuitive sense of the author's intrinsic being.

With this analogy we are aware of course that the phases so distinctly identified in the creative process may well overlap in practice. Here too the same is true as in the four stages of the Kabbalah: that in fact the very first phase – emanation from an essential unity – has not ended with the following phases but remains active in them, in a sense grounding and underpinning them.

In his spiritual research, Rudolf Steiner came to results that were similar to those of the Kabbalists in their four-world teaching. He too saw creation as beginning within the divine 'being' itself, and only largely separating itself, at a fourth stage, as world-made-manifest, from the active powers of the Godhead.* At the same time he was able to show a deeper purpose in this diverging evolution of God and world: only in a world-made-manifest could human beings become aware of their own self without being overwhelmed by divine omnipotence, shielded, as it were, against this omnipotence, and so able to take hold of the freedom that lay in them as potential.

If we can find our way into this view of evolutionary stages then, without repudiating Christianity, we can give due respect to the older religions. The ancient pagans, drawing on an inherited, and sometimes much dimmed clairvoyance, were able to encompass in their visionary mythologies a last flickering light of long-past epochs of the cosmos. They retained fading memories of former world-eras in which the world stood in a far more intimate relationship with the powers of its origin.

A religious person of today will acknowledge the character of our natural environment as world-made-manifest but will not therefore consider it to be 'profane'. Although the living God is no longer encountered in his immediate, intrinsic person in a natural world that unfolds by its own laws, his traces can still be perceived there. We would not expect the author of *Faust* to appear in person within

---

* Rudolf Steiner, *Anthroposophical Leading Thoughts*, p. 131ff.

the pages of his play, yet, in reading it, we can intuit something of the author's concerns and character.

Reading the ancient gnostics and Kabbalists we find the metaphor of the box of precious ointment. They compared the world made separate and manifest to a box which, though it no longer contained the precious ointment, still retains its wonderful fragrance. The whole container is still impregnated with it. Those who can sense nothing of this fragrance can easily become atheists in relation to a merely manifest world. But if we can still perceive a trace of the divine we will see in the world of substance the purpose or 'end of the ways' of God, which is at the same time the beginning of the ways of human beings. Coming here to an awareness of our I, we can thereby find our way to the I AM of Christ, who sanctifies and perfects the human being. For the Christian, the author of the world who, after creating nature, pursued further paths, will become differently and newly apparent in the Christ become man.

Precisely by looking towards Christ and his sacrificial deed we can also see the creation of the world recounted at the beginning of the Bible in a higher light.

The Kabbalists spoke of that very first stage silently preceding creation as emanation – *Atziluth*. If we say that God created the world 'out of nothing', this 'nothing' holds true only in relation to some kind of world existence that was not yet present. The creating Godhead had no existence outside itself upon which it could have drawn. It drew from itself what it would create, 'bringing it forth' from its own being.

There is a rather outmoded phrase which to modern ears easily sounds sentimental, but nevertheless still contains a deep meaning. In past times people sometimes said that a poet had written his verses 'with his heart's blood'. But this means that we expect of true poets nothing less than that they give forth something of their own intrinsic being and let this stream into their works. Surely we cannot think any less of the creation undertaken by a divine being? Certainly, in Psalm 33:9 we read, 'For he spoke, and it was done. He commanded, and it stood fast.' But does a reader of the Bible today have an apt idea of what is said here about the speaking and commanding of God? Surely every 'speech' that is really worthy of humankind is actually inconceivable without an element of 'emanation'. Speech as expression – utterance, externalisation – of an inwardness is at the same time a self-divesting and self-imparting. Must this not be true in the highest sense when God 'speaks' and in 'commanding' allows his will to stream forth? Only a few verses previously in the same psalm, we read: 'The heavens are made through the LORD's word, and all their hosts through the breath of his mouth' (33:6). This picture of exhalation gives wonderful expression to the emanation mystery of divine creation.

At the Last Supper, by virtue of his words of enactment, we see Christ surrender something of his own being. 'Take, this is my body ...' Here too a new creation takes its beginning. It starts with divine self-surrender. In the light of this fundamental sacrifice can we not also find illumination about what occurred at the beginning of the creation of the world?

We mentioned at the outset that, in the interests of divine freedom and sovereignty, Christian theologians seek to avoid the idea of 'emanation'. In the deed of sacrifice of Christ, who surrenders his own being 'for the life of the world', it becomes apparent that such surrender of one's own intrinsic nature, where this appears in its highest form, not only does not exclude a free deed and resolve but actually requires it. 'No one takes my life from me – I give it of myself' (Jn 10:18). At the hour of Golgotha the curtain in the temple is rent to allow vision of the innermost sanctum. In the same way, Christ's self-surrender reveals to our gaze the secret of all divine creation.

3

GOD AND GODS

It is generally agreed these days in Christian circles that only heathens use the word 'God' in the plural. God is one. 'You shall have no other gods before me.' That settles the matter. Or does it?

It cannot escape a careful reader that the monotheistic Old Testament here and there mentions 'gods', and certainly not in a derogatory sense. Translations sometimes obscure this. If for example one consults the original text of Psalm 29, then it is not the 'heavenly beings' as many translations have, but 'sons of gods' (*bene elim*) who are called upon. Similarly Job 38:7 does not speak of 'sons of God' but 'sons of the gods' who together with the morning stars 'shouted for joy' at the beginning of creation.

One is inclined to say that these are highly poetical passages; one does not take a poet all that literally if, with artistic licence he falls back on certain obsolete forms of expression. On the other hand it is now time to know that these old poets were not just whimsical storytellers. Other possibilities of consciousness and fields of experience were open to them which are at present unattainable by modern people. The scholar Karl Kerényi speaks of the 'immediacy' with which the mythological pictures confront the soul. Slowly there comes a new understanding in this field, though the fundamental insights were expressed by Rudolf Steiner earlier. The 'sons of the gods' were not products of the imagination; people saw them: superhuman beings shining with light.

The following passage from the Book of Job conveys an impression of how consciousness in ancient times actually still had other dimensions:

> How I long for the months gone by,
> For the days when God watched over me;
> When his lamp shone upon my head,
> And by his light I walked through darkness. (29:2f)

In those early times the human soul had not yet entered so fully into the bonds of the body as today; people still experienced their soul reaching out over their head and receiving the divine into it from above. Over their head still shone 'the lamp of God'. In a similar way Plutarch was still able to speak of the star of genius visible over a person's head.* On the other hand the actual sense world was still strange and hardly known, a 'darkness' through which people found their way thanks only to the light from above. Job still knows of such experiences from 'days of yore'.

It was by virtue of such faculties of vision that 'gods' were once spoken of. People had encounters with 'shining ones', and in whatever manifold and varying ways these radiant beings always conveyed the divine.

Finally, such an original experience of the divine through a host of higher beings is also indicated by the word mostly used in the Old Testament for 'God' – *Elohim*. That is undeniably plural. The singular is *Eloah,* as for example in Job's 'God watched over me'. Otherwise it is almost always *Elohim*. It is an extraordinary fact that the word for God in the monotheistic Old Testament is plural. On the other hand it should be noted that the verb to which *Elohim* is subject is not in the plural but the singular: *Elohim* 'creates', *Elohim* 'speaks', *Elohim* 'blesses'. At the time of recording this text, then, *Elohim* was felt to be a unity. Originally experienced as many, the *Elohim* had united in Yahweh, their head, and together formed a single spiritual organism, an 'Elohimity', as it were. Nevertheless, *Elohim* is originally plural and means 'gods'. One cannot avoid that. How is it compatible with monotheism?

For ancient religious experience the plenitude existing in the one God – 'the fullness of God' – (which also later came to light in the Christian conception of the Trinity) revealed itself through a manifold range of spiritual beings that God called into existence. The Nicene

---

* *On the Genius of Socrates,* Ch. 22.

Creed speaks of 'all things visible' and also 'invisible'. People knew of the various choirs of angels, of the hierarchies up to Cherubim and Seraphim. The Letter to the Hebrews calls God 'the Father of spirits' (12:9). Within the realm of these hierarchies one would therefore also look for those beings originally experienced as the plural *Elohim*.

For the Bible such a rich and graduated world of spirits is an obvious fact. But, one may ask, is it therefore permissible to speak of 'gods'? Of highly exalted spirits, yes. But 'gods'? Supersensory experience is remote from people of our age and they easily think in their abstract way that angelic realms are bound to obscure our view of the one God. They want to deal directly with God and not with the 'heavenly servants'. This shows that people no longer understand the word 'angel'. Angel (*angelos*) means 'messenger', someone therefore whose mission it is to establish a connection, a contact. God uses the angel as a delicate spiritual organism through which he turns towards us. It would be foolish to refuse the proffered hand of a fellow human being because it is not the hand but the person we are interested in. The person approaches us through their hand; it is not an obstacle, but serves to make contact. In the same way we may represent the relationship of the higher spirits to God – they serve him as his limbs as it were. If a spiritual being stands in the way and hides God from us instead of revealing him, then it is no true angel but an adversary of God; obscuring the view of God is the mark of devilish powers. The angels, however, are what their name implies. God shines through them – in various ways, of course, according to their rank. The eye of a fellow being speaks to me in a different way from their hand, but what it reveals is still the person themselves.

So in ancient times people could behold higher spiritual beings in great diversity, but what came to them through these was always, one way or another, God himself. This experience therefore naturally led them to be spoken of as 'gods'. These were still not – in the very first stage – 'other gods before me'. Not 'other gods' but fundamentally always the One in many forms. Indeed the old religions, too, had more or less of an inkling of this ultimate divine unity. It was only later that confusion and decline set in. The true gods were in many cases lost sight of and less pure and less exalted spiritual beings were able to take their place. The intrusion of demonic, even devilish, powers into religion is perhaps most clearly recognisable in the horrible cult of human sacrifice amongst the ancient Mexicans. If one takes into account this decline, this movement in various ways towards a twilight of the gods, one can understand why the gods of the heathens were so severely denounced in the Old Testament. In its final stages the old power of vision had become caught in the lower reaches of the invisible world, and finally faded out. It was their own individuality that the ancient Hebrews were supposed to feel called upon by the Yahweh-God. Grasping the idea of unity within their own being they were accordingly to be mindful of the ultimate unity of the divine, even at the cost of a certain abstractness. It is therefore no wonder that speaking of 'gods' became rare. The original plural signification of the word *Elohim* was finally almost forgotten.

In a few places, however, it persisted. In the law of Moses the whole assembly of judges is spoken of (in the Hebrew) as 'the gods' (Ex 21:6, 22:8, 9 & 28). This is referred to in Psalm 82. There the unjust judges are presented with the fact that they have nevertheless been named by God, 'gods, sons of the Most High' – how serious therefore their failures. Behind this stands the conviction that a human being should not actually judge and punish others; higher beings must be called upon. The council of those pronouncing judgment was once such a closely knit group that it offered a temporary 'body' for higher beings to speak through. At such moments the people who judged were 'gods'.

In the same way the king can also be designated 'God' in the Old Testament. Psalm 45 celebrates a royal marriage and addresses the princely bridegroom as 'O God' (45:6). Is it oriental courtesy? It is, but that is no explanation. One must understand that such a courtly style, however empty and meaningless in its later stages, was in origin based on true experience. Once there were kings who were initiates through whom higher beings worked. The royal 'we' goes back to this. So the psalm can address the royal bridegroom as *Elohim*. In the New Testament the Letter to the Hebrews quotes this passage (1:8f).

In the Old Testament the word *elohim* can also be used for the dead. Saul goes to the witch of Endor, who works with what we would call dubious occult methods, and makes her conjure forth the recently deceased Samuel. It is not Saul but the witch who 'sees'. Saul asks: 'What do you see?' She answers (literally): 'I see gods [*elohim*] rising up.' 'What is his appearance?' 'An old man is coming up out of the earth; and he is wrapped in a robe.' (1Sm 28:13f). Thanks to

Rudolf Steiner we can now begin to understand afresh such strange statements. Human beings incarnated on earth bear within and about them the lower kingdoms of nature – mineral, plant and animal. This all works into them from below. When they excarnate at death, they are drawn in the opposite direction into realms of higher beings. The angelic realms above take them further and further into higher existence; they do not cease to be themselves, but they are permeated by angelic activities. We can imagine that not long after his death a spiritual person like Samuel appears in a divine light, which in its radiance far surpasses what would be expected simply from his own being. The dead man, still recognisable by his own characteristics, already appears as if woven into a higher supersensory life. Since he shares in this divine life, he can himself be called 'God' according to those times, indeed even 'gods' – just as one uses the Latin plural *manes* of the spirit of someone dead.

In relation to judges, kings and the dead there is an underlying original experience of 'sharing' in the divine. If one understands it rightly, it does not contradict monotheism. There is always basically the one God, but he shares his divinity because in the depths of his being he is love. This first comes fully to light in the New Testament; it is in John's Gospel that we find Christ's words, 'You are gods' (10:34). Christ quoted the above-mentioned Psalm 82:6 where God said to the judges: 'I have said, "You are gods".'

Christ recognises as right the use of the expression 'gods' for human beings. He thus makes his own the promise which had been conveyed to humankind in a misleading sense from a quite different source, from Lucifer in Paradise, 'You will be like God' (Gn 3:5). This end can never be rightly achieved by following Lucifer. That can only lead to the God-likeness as a result of which people become afraid. We should not forget that it is Mephistopheles who makes this statement about becoming afraid, which seems so applicable today.* But here, too, being afraid is of no use. Christ knows more than anyone about the fallen human nature, yet he does not make us afraid. Instead – by himself taking on human form – he redeems the original intention of creation, that human beings should be the image of God. 'Be perfect, therefore, as your heavenly Father is perfect' (Mt 5:48).

---

* Goethe, *Faust I,* iv, 520.

In their technical ability, which rushes so far ahead of their moral ability, people today experiences that dubious God-likeness which can indeed lead to fear. But salvation does not lie in going back, only in going forward to where, through Christ, human beings can be led into their true God-likeness. Christ confirms the saying, 'You are gods.' Potentially human beings are God-like, though obviously the potentiality is not yet fully realised. Nevertheless, Peter can say that we may 'become partakers of the divine nature [*theia physis*]' (2Pt 1:4), and in his epistle, John speaks of the 'seed [*sperma*] of God' in those reborn in the spirit (1Jn 3:9).

In view of the great distance that separates us from this great goal it is fitting to speak only with awed reticence about it. But the bold statement of Novalis is still a most profoundly Christian one: *'Gott will Götter'* – 'God wants there to be gods'.

4

'NUMBERLESS AS THE STARS'

GENESIS 15:5

Life repeatedly asks us wanderers to embrace new departures and embark on journeys into the unknown. This is an archetypal motif of being human. In the very first book of the Bible, this primordial theme takes shape in an incisive picture – in the story of the calling of Abraham. 'Depart from your land and your kindred and your father's house to a land that I will show to you,' says the voice of God to him around four thousand years ago in Chaldea. At the same time dawns the promise of a blessing, one that in a far distant future will be vouchsafed to 'all peoples of the earth' (Gn 12:1, 3). And without hesitation Abraham hearkens to the call.

The promise which he so trustingly embraces, also tells him he is to become the progenitor of a 'great people'. This refers initially to the future people of Israel that is to come forth from Abraham, who hitherto has been without descendants. But this is not the full extent of the prophecy. Out of his deeper knowledge Paul revealed that something higher is also meant. Above and beyond a physical progeny, Abraham is to give rise to a still greater, spiritual legacy. What he accomplished as one individual in loneliness and inner trust, is subsequently to spiritually reproduce itself ever anew, spreading from this first progenitor 'to the broad plane of humanity' in countless future destinies. Thus Paul calls Abraham the 'father of all who trust and believe' (Rm 4:11) and in doing so broadens the idea of progeny beyond the 'great people' of Israel to a future, universal Christ-humanity.

As he sets forth from his father's house, Abraham is taking the first step on the path known as salvation history: the first step on the destined path of the people of Israel which will culminate in the path which the God-become-man takes from the Jordan baptism to Golgotha. This continues in the spirit journey of the resurrected Christ, in whose footsteps, ultimately, a renewed humanity is to pass from transformation to transformation.

Abraham sets out unquestioningly when he hears the call of God. It takes a certain time and various battles with doubt for the strength which enabled him to do so to arrive at its full self-awareness. Only at the beginning of Chapter 15 of Genesis is this strength given its name – the power of *belief*.

The patriarch, who has been wandering for a while in the Promised Land, receives a divine revelation which is expressly described as a visionary experience. It is here that we first encounter in the Bible the phrase that is so familiar to us from the gospels, 'Do not be afraid.' Abraham, who had so unquestioningly hearkened to the call to depart, is seized by doubt. 'I continue childless': how is a great people to arise from him, who has no son? In ancient times people regarded a son as the tangible embodiment of a human future, of the 'continuance of the human being'. Since he is without son, he begins to question the divine prophecy. His power of faith is starting to fail. Being plagued with doubt in this way surely also has a preparatory significance: the pain of it helps opens Abraham's soul to the divine vision.

The biblical account here uses only very few words, yet they carry great import: 'The Lord led him out and said, "Look up to the heavens and count the stars, if you can count them ... So will your offspring be".' (15:5). In an earlier promise, the number of his descendants was compared with the 'dust of the earth' (13:16); later it will become 'like the sand on the seashore' (22:17). At 15:5, though, God speaks of the *stars* of the heavens. They are mentioned here for the first time since the story of creation (1:16). Abraham's progeny are to be numberless as the dust of the earth, as the sand on the seashore, as the stars in the heavens.

These three similes are not the same thing three times: they are not randomly chosen and interchangeable, for each has its own specific nuance. The first two refer to the number of future human incarnations which, from the perspective of human consciousness, are unquantifiable. Grains of dust and sand cannot be counted. The stars, as the Bible sees it, are likewise beyond human counting but God can certainly count them. Psalm 147:4 tells us: 'He counts the stars and calls each one by name'. This becomes still more incisive in the prophet Isaiah: 'Lift your eyes on high and see who has made these and leads their host forth by number? He calls each one by name. His power and his strength is so great that not one is missing.' (Is 40:26). The counting of the stars is clearly not meant here as the accomplishment of some super-intellect that numbers them with a computer-like accuracy beyond ordinary human capacity.

Something originally united has divided itself into numerous separate beings. If we focus on them as separate entities, the counting of them can only be an enumeration that adds one to the next and finally arrives as some enormous random sum or meaningless quantity. But if we sense the common, primordial ground of all these separate entities which, in their distinct existence, nevertheless resound together harmoniously to form a great and unified symphony, then God's counting of them produces an encompassing musical ordering as sacred number. That 'not one is missing' signifies more than a perfect and precise overview. In the Hebrew text, which, in its reverent vision of the stars above speaks of 'these', the single star that must not be lacking is not only a neutral thing but a being, a 'someone', a starry individual, for whom Isaiah uses the same word otherwise used to designate a masculine human being, *ish:* 'So that not *one* shall be lacking.' If one simply adds separate human beings together, such enumeration finally leads to each person being only a 'number'. But divine counting of the stars invokes the sense that, rather than being a 'number', each star expressly bears a 'name' accorded it by God.

This world of stars, that is beyond human counting but can be enumerated by God, is shown Abraham by the Lord. You might think that everyone with normal sight can gaze up at the starry heavens on a clear night, as long as it is not obscured by lights on earth, which in Abraham's time would not have posed a problem. In the dry air of Judea, surely the glory of the heavens would have sparkled brilliantly each night. But there is, after all, a difference between seeing and seeing. There are moments when we see something 'with new eyes', when someone draws our attention to it. We see something that, despite good eyesight, we have never seen before. A deeper form of such experience played a role in ancient mysteries, where great significance was given to showing and being shown, to the opening of eyes to supersensible realities: 'And behold.' The instructing and enlightening priest was called a 'hierophant', one who 'showed' a revelatory image. For Abraham the Lord God himself is the hierophant who shows him the stars.

Christian biblical scholars have always rushed to see this passage in terms that were of foremost importance for them: that Abraham 'believed' when shown the stars in this way, and that this was granted him because of his 'righteousness'. But it is worth dwelling a little first on this experience of God which he has, which is so succinctly indicated in the text. Christian artists have often had a deeper feeling for this than theologians who tend more to abstract thoughts. The illuminated manuscript, the *Vienna Genesis,* was created in the sixth century in Asia Minor, which was then Christian. At the left margin of one image we see a depiction of the house from whose open door Abraham has departed. The Bible says, 'The Lord led him forth.' Rationalists may take offence that God is spoken of here in such 'crassly' realistic terms. In a similar manner the account of the flood relates that the Lord himself closed the ark behind Noah (7:16). But such passages are especially precious, and can appear to us like erratic blocks from a primary stratum of religious geology – like memories from eras when experience of the divine was self-evidently tangible and real.

As far as the leading of Abraham forth from his dwelling is concerned, we can still relate to such an experience if we have ever felt the effect upon the soul of opening ourselves for a while to the twinkling stars on an absolutely clear night. At least to a small degree we can feel a sense of being lifted out of our everyday consciousness: 'At night when good spirits walk abroad / Wipe sleep from your eyes and seek / Moonlight, glimmering stars that wrap / You in eternity: and you will feel / Discarnate already and can dare / To make your way towards God's throne' (Goethe *Zahme Xenien* 6). The Emperor Julian, who wished to renew ancient mystery experience in the fourth century, describes the experiences he had beneath the starry heavens as a child: how, transported by its ethereal glory, he was no longer in himself at all but entirely lifted out of his body. The sixth-century painter showed the same thing when he painted Abraham 'going out' from his dwelling and finding himself in an emptiness which is then, however, torn asunder from above to reveal the heavens. A deep blue shines through from which blossom six-rayed stars. And amidst them is an arm, a pointing hand – the hand of God. This is a supersensible experience, outside the body.

In the same *Vienna Genesis* another picture precedes this: Abraham's encounter with Melchizedek. Again, Abraham stands on the left side. As in the starry painting he has extended his arms in receptive humility. His hands are covered in a cloth in reverence for the gift he is to receive. From the shining golden tabernacle on the right of the picture Melchizedek comes towards him in priestly and royal manner, bearing bread and wine. Within the tabernacle the star motif appears on a blue ground.

The painter had a fine sense for the fact that this mysterious meeting with Melchizedek precedes the great vision of the starry heavens. This too is recounted in sparse words in the preceding chapter of Genesis (14:18–20). Through the Melchizedek experience, the 'cosmic dimension' is invoked in the soul of Abraham, and it is by this power that he becomes open to the vision of the stars.

On two further occasions, the voice of God utters the star prophecy. Abraham again hears it after proving himself in the trial of the sacrifice of Isaac (Gn 22:17); and then we hear it once more from his son Isaac (Gn 26:4). Thus these words about the stars figure three times in Genesis. And they are recalled later by Moses (Ex 32:13).

'And Abraham *believed* the Lord' (15:6). It may be worth mentioning that this is the very first time in the Bible that the word 'belief' appears. Surely this first invocation of the word is like the striking of a note that reverberates through all other passages in both the Old and New Testaments in which belief or faith figure. Here it can become very apparent that 'belief' in the Bible does not signify a deficient prelude to knowledge. It is, rather, an act of trusting, committed affirmation. The Hebrew word for 'belief' is formed from Amen, a word that affirms a higher experience of reality. 'And Abraham believed' – can be literally rendered as, 'He made Amen,' or 'he did Amen' with his whole soul. From the worlds of the stars unborn futures shine down towards the patriarch and progenitor, and above and beyond all earthly doubts he grasps the evolutionary principle that approaches him as the 'father of all believers'. At this moment of the birth of faith, we ought never to forget the God-revealed starry heavens.

This 'making Amen' to divine future aims is 'accounted to the righteousness' of Abraham. Through the Fall, humankind introduced disorder into the cosmic harmony. Instead of being a priestly mediator between above and below the human being became injurious. In terms of an immediate repercussion from cosmic justice, human beings would have to be extinguished. But since, despite everything, they harbour the germ of higher existence, and since, with their inward 'Yes' and 'Amen' they can position themselves on the side of this futurity, God bears the burden of the disruptive and injurious human beings. God sees the prospect of what still seeks to evolve from them – and also can evolve from them after Christ came to humanity's aid. What occurs with Abraham as a prefiguring or foreshadowing will later ripen to mature fulfilment once the 'Amen power' of the human being, first emerging in the patriarch under the starry heavens, can be directed to Christ and his deed of redemption. This does not mean that the human being has been transformed in a moment, for permeation with Christ is a process of development. 'What we will be has not yet been revealed' (1Jn 3:2). But until then, alongside humanity's as yet so imperfect goodness, our 'Yes' and 'Amen' to Christ will be placed in the scales, our faith will be 'accounted to righteousness'.

5

THE SACRIFICE OF ISAAC

'He who did not spare his own son, but gave him up for us all' (Rm 8:32). Paul wishes to impress on the pious mind what occurred at Golgotha, and in doing so reaches back to an ancient formula which he takes from the Book of Genesis: 'did not spare his only son'. These words are found in that unique narrative of the sacrifice of Isaac, which Christianity has always seen as a prophetic antecedent to the events of Golgotha.

The narration is unique both in its content and form, and it is therefore worth examining in detail how the story is told.

> And after these things had happened, God tested Abraham and spoke to him, 'Abraham.'
> And he answered. 'Here I am.'
> And he spoke, 'Take your son, your only one, whom you love, Isaac, and go into the land of Moriah, and there offer him for a burned offering on a mountain of which I will tell you.' (Gn 22:1f)

At the outset is the encounter with the Godhead, who calls the human being by his name, thus invoking and awakening him in his deepest and most intrinsic being. Abraham answers 'Here I am' – literally in the original, 'Behold – I.'

Now follows the command. In the original, the name Isaac does not stand at the beginning or the middle, as it does in many translations, but at the end. First comes: 'Take your son.' One has to have read the preceding stories about Abraham to gauge what the birth of this son signified for Abraham, who was a hundred years old at the time. The words that follow make us aware of the immeasurable depth of feeling that is bound up for Abraham with this son. 'Take your son, your only one, whom you love.' Only now, at the end of the sentence, does the name Isaac appear. The name, when at last it comes, encompasses in a single word all these worlds of feeling that have been conjured. And now comes the command to sacrifice him.

Here ends the first act in the narrative. Its grandeur lies in what it does *not* say. No word about what went on in Abraham's soul: dismay and terror, doubt, rejection, submission, such as a modern narrator would try to express it. Nothing of that. God's pronouncement simply stands there as a higher reality, upon whose sublimity the curtain of this first act falls. There is nothing more to add.

The second act opens at dawn. We might conclude from this that the words spoken by God to Abraham took place during the night, when the soul is more open to supersensible impressions. Not until the morning do we hear Abraham's answer, which consists of a silent and unquestioning deed:

> Abraham rose early in the morning and saddled his donkey, and took with him two servants and Isaac his son, and he chopped wood for the burned offering and departed and went to the place of which God had told him. (22:3)

He 'rose early in the morning'. The first cool, grey dawn of a new day can have a somewhat sobering quality. Not infrequently great resolutions, made perhaps without reservation in the heat of enthusiasm, are unable to withstand the effect of the sober light of day. But not so for Abraham. The truth of the commanding voice of God loses none of the force of its reality at the transition to everyday consciousness. Without a word and as a matter of course Abraham sets about enacting on the earthly plane what he heard in a higher world. There is a down-to-earth, morning feeling about saddling the donkey and chopping the wood. In the middle of the sentence stands the name Isaac, directly before a reference to the wood for the burned offering. Isaac – burned offering: we are compelled to bring these two together; and so what has been uttered is to be enacted.

With as few words as the first act, the second act now comes to an end too. The ensuing interval is taken up by the journey.

Then, like a chime of mysterious bells, the third act begins with the words 'on the third day'. In the John Gospel the same words initiate the marriage at Cana. This is not only an outward indication of the passage of time. We can sense that this third day is to bring something decisive.

> On the third day Abraham lifted up his eyes and saw the place from afar. (22:4)

It is as if he has been journeying with a bowed head. Now he lifts his gaze. In the mode of expression of the Bible this raising of the eyes always also signifies something like beholding a vision. Abraham looks up and recognises the mountain of which God has said he would tell him. This 'telling' has clearly now occurred. It is the mountain of Moriah, which will later bear the temple of Solomon. To refined and enhanced perception, one mountain is not the same as another: there is also something like an etheric geography. Sacred sites have special qualities.

The Hebrew *maqom* (place) is a significant word. It is used for an earthly site where people could feel an invisible supersensible quality descending from above.

Abraham sees the place 'from afar'. It can happen that a person feels something like a premonition when he first sees from afar a place where something important will happen to him.

The moment of decision draws ever closer. The 'place' is in sight. A last stretch of the journey must still be completed. This last part of the way is still more momentous than the silent journey hitherto. There is a parting: the servants with the donkey remain behind. Only the participants in the sacrifice may climb the sacred mountain. The whole occurrence becomes more intimate, more esoteric.

> And Abraham said to his servants, 'Remain here with the donkey. I and the boy will go there and worship, and we will return to you again. (22:5)

This is the first time in the story since Abraham said 'Here I am' that we hear him say anything. He does not manage to utter what is to happen on the mountain, speaking only of worshipping and of returning, of 'we' who will return. The implacable decision to act lives in his inward depths but his inner emotions have not been able to keep pace with this. He cannot yet acknowledge that after what is to happen upon the mountain it is not 'we' who will return but only a lonely I.

> And Abraham took the wood for the burned offering and placed it on his son Isaac. But he took in his hand the fire and the knife. (22:6a)

It has often been remarked by commentators what an illogical love is shown in the fact that the father himself carries the knife and the fire lest the boy cut or burn himself, though soon the knife is to fatally strike him and the flame is to burn his tender body to ashes.

This journeying on together is interrupted by a brief dialogue, but it not a conversation that brightens their journey. It makes it still harder. It is part of the great artistry of this narrative that the phrase 'and the two went onward together' is repeated in the same words (verses 6 and 8).

> And the two went onward together. Then Isaac spoke to Abraham his father and said, 'My father.'
> He said, 'Here I am, my son.'
> And he said, 'Behold, here is the fire and the wood, but where is the lamb for a burnt offering?'
> And Abraham replied, 'God will provide the lamb for the burnt offering, my son.'
> And the two went onward together. 22:6b–8)

The boy feels the silence weighing on them. The way he suddenly breaks the silence, because he can no longer bear it, is shocking. The intuitive soul of the child senses something uncanny, and his question goes right to the heart of the matter. Precisely this question of the sacrificial beast is not meant to be uttered. It immeasurably increases the father's anguish. His reply is evasive, yet at the same time unconsciously prophetic.

Finally, after the interrupted silence has again enveloped the two, they reach the place and the preparations begin – without a word, in silence.

> And when they came to the place of which God had told him, Abraham built an altar there and set wood upon it and bound Isaac his son and laid him upon the wood on the altar, and Abraham stretched out his hand and took the knife to slay his son. (22:9f)

Whereas their arrival and the beginning of down-to-earth preparations could be felt almost as a passing relief after the tortuous journey, new tension is now summoned, the most intense in this whole story, which in those ancient times must have almost overwhelmed its spellbound listeners. This is done through the dramatic, inexorable sequence of six verbs: he 'built ... and set ... and bound ... and laid ... and stretched out ... and took the knife.'

Then, literally, at the very last moment, the saving intervention from above:

> Then the angel of the Lord called to him from heaven and said, 'Abraham! Abraham!'
> He answered: 'Here I am.'
> And he said, 'Do not lay your hand on the boy, or do anything to him. For now I know that you revere God and have not spared your only son for my sake. Then Abraham lifted up his eyes and looked, and behold a ram ... (22:11–13)

Twice the angel calls the name of Abraham. When God himself spoke to him at the beginning of the story, he spoke his name only once. The ministering angel does not possess the all-seeing, universal calm of God. It is as if the angel were drawn into the excitement of the critical moment, almost as if he feared that he might come too late: 'Abraham! Abraham!'

The one whose name is called lowers the raised knife and says, 'Here I am'. This is the third time we have heard this phrase from his mouth. The first time was when God called to him, the second when Isaac broke the oppressive silence, and now it comes again in the last, decisive moment. 'Behold – I.' There is a calmness about this recurrence. One is reminded of the words with which Goethe once characterised Abraham: 'Calm and greatness'.

This calm and greatness, which enables him three times to say 'Here I am', has its roots in Abraham's solidarity with God.

In its austere beauty, the story of the sacrificial journey to Moriah is a classic document of true religion in its earliest stage.*

---

* In this chapter we have restricted ourselves to the manner and style of the narrative. For further understanding of the content – how the enigmatic event may be understood – we refer to the account by Emil Bock in his *Genesis,* pp. 135f, 148–55.

6

THE BUILDING OF THE TABERNACLE AND THE CREATION

No true ritual is an arbitrary human creation; it has its origin in divine revelation. So, too, the building of the Old Testament sanctuary, the tabernacle, stems from the divine instruction imparted to Moses on the holy Mount Sinai. There the heavenly archetypes for the ritual were shown to him by the Godhead. 'And see that you make them after the pattern, which was shown to you on the mountain' (Ex 25:40, also 26:30 and 27:8).

The concluding chapters of Exodus (39 and 40) describe how what has been 'shown' finds its way into earthly reality, how the archetypes revealed 'on the mountain' take on material form and become visible to human eyes. What occurs here on a small scale happened on a vast scale at the creation of the world.

The biblical text indicates this connection very clearly. Expressions appear that are strikingly similar to certain words in the creation story in Genesis.

'Thus all the work of the tabernacle, of the tent of meeting, was finished' (Ex 39:32); 'And Moses saw all the work, and behold, they had done it, as the LORD had commanded, so had they done it. And Moses blessed them' (39:43); 'So Moses finished the work' (40:33).

One can hardly read these words without remembering Genesis: 'Thus the heavens and the earth were finished, and all the host of them' (2:1); 'And God saw everything that he had made, and behold, it was very good' (1:31); 'And on the seventh day God finished his work which he had done' (2:2).

There is no doubt that this similarity puts the erection of the tabernacle in line with the creation of the world itself. The outer world, then, is the great tabernacle, the macrocosmic temple, while the tent of meeting reflects on a small scale this divinely ordered world. Both worlds, however, reveal the eternal, supersensory archetypes.

It is possible to trace the correspondence of the two stories in greater detail. Like the creation of the world the building of the tabernacle is a work of seven parts. And this sevenfold nature of the work is made all the clearer by the use of the same expression seven times. It reads characteristically, 'as the LORD had commanded Moses' (Ex 40:19, 21, 23, 25, 27, 29, 32). It emphasises that what enters the visible world corresponds with the archetype and that according to the divine will it is a worthy copy on earth of what exists in heaven. This echoes the expression in Genesis: 'And God saw that it was good.'*

The sevenfold division also applies to the making of the priestly vestments.† There, too, is reflected the creation of the world, which Goethe calls 'the living garment of God'. However, we shall restrict ourselves here to the building of the tabernacle, where the relation of the seven stages of the building to the seven days of the creation is clearly discernible.

I

> And in the first month in the second year, on the first day of the month, the tabernacle was erected. Moses erected the tabernacle; he laid its bases, and set up its frames, and put in its poles, and raised up its pillars; and he spread the tent over the tabernacle, and put the covering of the tent over it, as the LORD had commanded Moses.
> (Ex 40:17–19)

On the first day of creation 'the heavens and the earth' come into being as a first great 'above' and 'below'. This is reflected in the

---

* Seven times, though not coinciding with the seven days: first day (Gn 1:40), third day (1:10, 12), fourth day (1:18) fifth day (1:21) sixth day (1:25, 31).

† Seven times 'as the LORD commanded Moses' (Ex 39:1, 5, 7, 21, 26, 29, 31).

microcosm of the building of the tabernacle. The pillars rest on the firm ground and hold the tent-roofing aloft. What is stretched over as a roof, sheltering and enclosing, is in its ritual significance the heavenly 'above', the tent of heaven.

II

The next stage in the building of the tabernacle is the separating off by a curtain of the Holy of Holies. In what could be called this 'occult' space, hidden from sight, is placed the ark with the mercy seat over which the two Cherubim spread their wings: the place of the presence of God (Ex 40:20f).

On the second day of creation God makes a 'firmament' in heaven and separates the waters above the firmament from those below it. Rudolf Steiner has pointed out that we should not envisage this 'firmament' as something material but as an area of supersensory controlling power, like a watershed, on one side of which the water falls down in dense, heavy drops, on the other side of which it floats as cloud in the realm of light and lightness, in the divine sphere borne by the Cherubim. In ancient times it was a fundamental human experience that the upper world of clouds instilled a special sense of the working of divine powers.

This 'watershed', discharging water below it into the world of gravity and letting it rise above it into the realm of weightless light and mysterious heavenly powers, is pictured by the curtain which divides off the Holy of Holies, in whose secret place he who rules the Cherubim is enthroned.

III

In front of the curtain, on the north side, the table with the bread is set up (to the right of those entering, since the Holy of Holies, in contrast to the Christian altar, was in the west, not the east).

On the third day of creation firm land emerges for the first time from the surging waters. Dry land and water are separated, and the land which appears is immediately covered with green plants. 'Let the earth put forth vegetation.'

This vegetation springing from the earth is then given to human beings for food. The earth becomes 'the table of the Lord'. On the communion table there is bread and wine, the noble emissaries from the plant kingdom which, as the body and blood of Christ, are to become the food for eternal life.

This table with the shewbread is both a harbinger of the communion table and a recollection of the third day of creation.

IV

The fourth day of creation does not further the development of the earth since it is concentrated on the heavenly spaces. God creates the heavens' lights – sun, moon and stars.

The ritual symbolism is wonderfully transparent in the fourth stage of the building:

> And he put the lampstand in the tent of meeting, opposite
> the table on the south side of the tabernacle, and set up the
> lamps before the LORD; as the LORD had commanded Moses
> (Ex 40:24f)

The table with the holy bread is the true image of the earth, the lamp stand with the seven lights (Ex 37:23), the image of the heavenly luminaries.

V

After heaven's lights have appeared, life-bearing plants are followed by soul-bearing living creatures on the fifth day of creation. A life of feeling stirs in the waters and moves in the air. 'Let the waters abound with an abundance of living creatures, and let birds fly above the earth across the expanse of the heavens' (Gn 1:20).

In these creatures the soul-element makes its first entry into the world. Essentially it is a stranger on earth. Its home is the heavenly world, which is why calling it 'astral' (*astra,* Latin for the stars) is fully justified. The human soul is still kept back in the heavenly world, which manifested itself in sun, moon and stars on the fourth day. It is to descend into the earthly only on the sixth day; on the fifth it still rests 'unspoken' with the Godhead. The animal kingdom, however, already takes on existence before man. Its doing so is like a great prelude for the life of soul that will later be in human beings on earth.

This stirring, moving animal world of the fifth day, which has its essence in travail and storm, in wave and flood, is a true image of 'astrality'. Such sensitive, freely moving phenomena intimate to us the subtle realm of the soul's activities.

Now humankind is called upon to transform the whole world of inner activities and desires symbolised in these animal forms, and so far spiritualise it that all their soul life is at the service of higher worlds. All inner activity is then suffused with a mood of devoted self-sacrifice. The symbol worthy of this mood of soul has always been the ascending smoke of fragrant incense.

In the ritual of the Old Testament the incense offering was made every morning and every evening so that again and again the soul's aim was clearly set before it. 'Let my prayer be counted as incense before you, and the lifting up of my hands as an evening sacrifice' (Ps 141:2) – words of which we are also reminded in the Offertory of the Act of Consecration of Man.

There was a special altar for the incense offering. Its setting up constitutes the fifth stage in the building.

> And he put the golden altar in the tent of meeting in front of the veil, and burnt fragrant incense upon it, as the LORD had commanded Moses. (Ex 40:26f)

VI

The sixth day of creation then proceeds with the creation of land animals and, finally, the human being.

Corresponding with this in the building of the tabernacle is the erection of the altar for burnt offerings.

This altar for burnt offerings is bound to make an even deeper impression than the golden altar for the offering of incense. On it flowed the blood of the vicariously sacrificed animals, the blood of the warm-blooded creatures closest to human beings that appeared on earth just before them on the sixth day. In the blood of the sacrificial animals that flowed there people experienced the sacrificial offering of their own blood to the divine world. In the burning of the animals they sensed the consuming of their earthly being by the intensity of divine fire.

In blood and fire are indicated the deepest mysteries of the human being. In a way different from that of ancient times, more spiritual but no less real, they are brought home to us in every Act of Consecration of Man in the closing words of the Offertory about the divine 'fire of love', and in the mystery of the chalice. The altar of the Act of Consecration of Man unites what was separate in the Old Testament ritual. It is the table with the consecrated bread, it bears the seven lights, it is the place where the incense is brought and, finally, it is the altar of burnt offering where the sacrifice of Golgotha and human offering meet.

There is a solemn significance in this correspondence of the creation of the human being on the sixth day and the altar of burnt offering.

VII

The day of man's appearance brings the work of creation outwardly to an end. The seventh day adds no new phenomena, but it enriches the world inwardly with the element of hallowed rest.

God rests, God has a 'holy-day'. It is as if the divine lives within its own unique mystery, as if the Spirit were immersed in the depths of its own spirituality.

One should not think of the word 'rest' negatively as if it were synonymous with 'no work'. Not working outwardly should release forces that can then turn inward with full strength. It is also worth remembering here Nietzsche's saying about freedom, that it is not so much a question of 'free *from* what' as 'free *for* what'. A day of rest epitomises for many people today a sort of sterile and joyless boredom. But the hands which rest from work are clean of the dust of working days, so that activity on a higher, divine plane is possible.

In the account of the making of the holy vestments there comes seventh and last the description of the plate of the holy crown 'of pure gold' engraved with the words, 'Holy to the LORD' (Ex 39:30). The seventh stage of the building of the tabernacle is also designed with this same idea of purification and consecration:

And he set the basin between the tent of meeting and the altar, and put water in it for washing, with which Moses and Aaron and his sons washed their hands and their feet. When they went into the tent of meeting, and when they approached the altar, they washed, as the Lord commanded Moses, (Ex 40:30–32)

7

AARON'S BLESSING

The blessing below, widely known in the King James version, is one of the loveliest and most venerable texts of the Old Testament:

> The Lord bless thee, and keep thee:
> The Lord make his face to shine upon thee, and be gracious
>   unto thee:
> The Lord lift up his countenance upon thee, and give thee
>   peace. (Nm 6:24–26)

These words stand in a significant context in Numbers, the Fourth Book of Moses. The preceding verse expresses a deep truth of religious life and worship: that such words, as spoken ritually in a service, cannot spring from ordinary human consciousness. They have their source, rather, in inspiration:

> And the Lord spoke to Moses, saying, 'Speak to Aaron and
> his sons, saying, "Thus you shall bless the people of Israel,
> saying to them..."' (Nm 6:22f)

And having given the sacred words to Moses, God says further: 'So they shall put my name on the people of Israel, and I will bless them' (6:27).

The act of blessing is conveyed here with a wonderful spiritual realism: the name of God is 'put' upon the community. The Yahweh name, which points to the mystery of the I, is placed over those who are reverently assembled: is placed, laid over and above their heads as something with potency for the future, to which they are to grow upward.

The sons of Aaron, as initiated priests, are to speak the blessing, but then, as it says at the end, 'I will bless them'. In the Hebrew text there is a special emphasis here on the I, as if writ large. In a true rite, God himself is the celebrant.

If we look at the words of the blessing first in a more outward way, at the form of the sentences, their threefold quality immediately strikes us. There are three lines, and each of them contains the word 'Lord'.

Biblical scholars have remarked on the blessing's growth from line to line. The first line has only three words. Its paucity of utterance is closest to the sacred silence out of which such a blessing emerges. That it is only three words in Hebrew comes about because the 'you' in 'bless you' is attached to the previous verb as if it were a single word: 'bless-you'. In the same way, the 'and' in each instance merges with what follows to form a single word, roughly 'and-keep-you'.

The second line in Hebrew has five words, and the third has seven. Three-five-seven. If we were to try to illustrate this unfolding from line to line, we could do it roughly as follows: using a hyphen we connect all the words that are a single word in the original:

> May-bless-you Yahweh and-keep-you
> May-shine Yahwe his-face upon-you and-grace-you
> May-raise Yahweh his-countenance to-you and-give you
>   peace

The Yahweh name, 'The LORD', does not come at the beginning of each line in the original but always follows the initial verb which as it were prepares the way for him.

We can be sure that this form of growth from three to five to seven is not a merely outward play of word groupings but an organic expression for inner unfolding and progression.

To approach this inward progression let us turn our attention for a moment to the manner in which the human being is invoked as the recipient of this blessing.

In the first line the word 'you' figures twice. 'May bless you the LORD and keep you.' As already mentioned, here this word does not stand separate and alone but is attached to the verb. In terms of prosaic grammatical analysis, this 'you' is an accusative-object form. Here the human being figures initially only as the 'object' of divine care and deed.

This changes in the second line. May the LORD shine his face 'towards-you' as we should literally translate it rather than 'upon you'. A sleeping child can also be blessed and protected. The blessing and keeping-safe is done to him, irrespective of his knowledge and participation. But the shining of the countenance, on the other hand, presupposes a recipient who is aware and awake: a 'face-to-face' encounter. The face now shines 'towards-you', its shining is personally intended for and directed to you. A light source such as a lamp does not expend its light in such an addressed way but simply shines forth. But for the LORD to make his face shine towards you involves a shining from I to I.

The line continues, 'and be gracious to you'. In Hebrew there is no 'to you'. The original again has a verb that includes the accusative-object 'you': 'and-grace-you'. In this, the second line still invokes the mode of the first, and yet here it also already heralds something different. We can be blessed and kept safe also when asleep. But to receive grace we need to be a little awake at least. Giving grace not only presupposes an object but also a receiving participant who values this gift.

In the third line, the 'you' as such, as accusative object, now disappears altogether. Again it says 'to-you': May the LORD raise his countenance 'to-you' (as the original literally has it) and give you (dative case) peace. Thus right at the end of the blessing the dative form of 'you' appears, now as a word standing on its own, bearing the full weight and expressive power intrinsic only to the 'dative', a word which expresses giving and receiving. Every gift requires conscious receiving from the one endowed. The dative case can express the sense of 'being there for each other', the mutual opening of two personal beings. At the end of Aaron's blessing, God addresses the human being as a receiving 'you': 'and give you peace'.

Whereas human beings in the first line were still embraced and kept safe, in the second line they were awoken to a face-to-face encounter, and in the third and last line are fully acknowledged in their own intrinsic and independent being.

Might this threefold progression not have something to do with the sublime mystery to which Christian terminology refers in the phrase 'three-in-one'? Let us once again consider the Aaron blessing in the light of the fulfilment which Christianity confers upon the Old Testament.

The first line speaks of blessing and protecting. Someone who wishes to bless has to give something of themselves, must be able to allow something of their own being to radiate from them. Someone who always only keeps to themselves cannot do this. The loving surrender of one's own being, allowing something other than only oneself to flourish – is a distinctive, revered mystery of the Father God.

Safeguarding, protecting is also especially intrinsic to him. If anything at all is to exist, if only for a second, this is ultimately only possible by virtue of being consciously and divinely held and sustained above the abyss of non-existence by the Father's hand. Thus the Father also desires to keep humanity safe in its intrinsic existence and allow its true nature to survive through all eternity.

Wherever someone blesses and protects another, a reflection of this fatherly nature of the divine appears. We experience this especially in childhood, or at least we ought to, at a time when we are wholly dependent on being encompassed and sustained by love in the slumbering, dreaming dawn of our life. This Father experience does not lose its significance even for adolescents as they start to stand on their own two feet. However wakeful and active we become, we must lie down to sleep and entrust our soul to the all-embracing power of God. Even the most self-reliant of people, if they are not to grow narrow and hard, require this piety towards the Father. They also need an ultimate protection that wraps them not only in sleep but also in death, and by which, during their lifetime, they know themselves to be sustained.

But to meet the tasks of active life, to make the right use of our freedom and independence, we must also be able to enhance a reverence for the Father with reverence for the Son and the Spirit. In the Son, the Father Ground of the World, sublime beyond all perception and knowledge – 'no one has seen God' (Jn 1:18) – becomes visible and tangible to the I-conscious, earthly human being. 'He who sees me, also sees the Father' (Jn 14:9). In Christ, God has turned his face to humankind; and in Christ, from whose face of solar radiance God regards the human being, the second line of the ancient blessing is fulfilled. In Christ, God allows his face to shine 'towards us'.

And the rest of that line is also connected with this: 'and give you grace'. Allowing Christ to appear on earth is *the* great deed of God's grace.

The third line speaks again of the face or countenance of God, but this time not of its shining but of its 'lifting'. It is like a sunrise where the first, overwhelming impression of emerging light is still further enhanced by the experience of the sun rising in the sky. The higher it rises, the more majestically does it hold sway over our field of vision. God 'lifts his countenance' – the Christ-sun rises to become ever more dominant in our human worldview. To bring this about within human consciousness is the work of the Holy Spirit, of whom Christ says, 'He will bring me to full revelation' (Jn 16:14).

This increasingly enables human beings to receive the peace which God wishes to give them. 'And give you peace.' Not the peace of the graveyard but something creative, positive. If the countenance of God rises ever more powerfully in the human field of vision, then it becomes possible to harmonise, to tune all soul forces with each other. Then their antagonism is transfigured in a chord of many tones. As human beings we receive the peace given by God into our inward life and can then gradually also emanate it more and more. We can become a participant in the building of the 'heavenly Jerusalem', the city of peace which is built entirely out of what we might call the substance of peace.

In this way, in Aaron's blessing, the human being can connect with the threefold God. The whole, mighty perspective of human evolution dawns: from safety and protection in the Father through to a distant perfection in the Spirit.

II

REVELATIONS AND PROPHECIES

8

BALAAM

The king's messengers

It was more than a thousand years before the wise men who beheld the star journeyed from the east. The people of Israel had pitched their tents near the Promised Land and were encamped opposite Jericho like a lion ready to spring.

Balak, king of the Moabites, knew that armed resistance would be hopeless. He may have sensed something of the spiritual force at work in this remarkable people who had crushed all opponents on their way out of Egypt, and whose camp fires now burned on the banks of the Jordan. In this situation the sword would be useless to check the irresistible advance. In this situation, Balak felt, only a different kind of weapon would serve: a spiritual sword, the magic word from the mouth of one who had the full powers of blessing and cursing. Spirit would have to be opposed by spirit. He therefore sent his elders to Balaam far away in the east.

The seer dwelt on the banks of the Euphrates. The mighty currents and movements of this broad mass of mighty river, the gentle dulling of the physical senses by its flowing and rushing, the calling up of inner vision by the magical play of the waves – all helped him to attain other states of consciousness. While he was deep in prayer, the spirit gathered up his soul from his body, carried it to higher realms, showed it hidden things, gave it words of magic power. So Balak 'sent messengers to Balaam the son of Beor at Pethor, which is near the River' (Nm 22:5).

He is to hold back this uncanny people with the sword of his powerful word: 'for I know that he whom you bless is blessed, and he whom you curse is cursed' (Nm 22:6).

But Balaam cannot give an answer immediately. In bright daylight the inner voice is silent. He has to wait for night with its invisible flow, and in the silence of the night God's voice speaks. He should not go with them, nor curse the people of Israel, for they are blessed.

King Balak sends a second embassage, and offers great honour and reward. Again the secret revelation of the night has to be awaited. This time the voice allows him to make the journey, but 'only do what I tell you' (22:20).

Balaam's donkey

In the morning Balaam saddles his donkey and sets off. On the way he has a singular experience which is veiled in the fable-like account of the talking donkey.

Balaam is making the journey in order to use the sword of his magic word. He should feel the immense responsibility. He should feel how fatally this sword threatens anyone who does not use it in pious obedience. A warning is given him. The reproving angel steps into his path and shows him the naked sword.

Balaam the seer does not see, but the donkey does. One should read the biblical account itself (Num.22:21–35) to feel its magic and appreciate the oriental narrative art – how it builds up – how the reproving angel three times stands in the road till finally there is no way of avoiding him and the donkey sinks to its knees – how Balaam three times beats it, having no idea why it goes off the path, why it kneels down. 'Then the LORD opened the mouth of the donkey.' The suffering dumb animal, which nevertheless knows a great deal that the man has no notion of, is for once permitted to speak – if we do not take this speaking too literally but more imaginatively, as a visionary experience of the prophet. The creature is permitted to open its mouth to answer the man who lays about it so uncomprehendingly.

But it does not indulge in violent accusation, furious protest, noisy lamentation. It remains quite humiliatingly matter-of-fact, and hits the nail on the head. 'What have I done to you, that you have struck me these three times?' The rider, however, responds with fury, even wishes he had a sword to kill the animal he thinks is mocking him.

He has no idea how fatally close is the threat of the flaming sword from which the donkey has saved him. But once more the creature speaks, immovable in its righteous matter-of-factness. '"Am I not your donkey, on which you have ridden all your life long to this day? Is it my habit to treat you this way?" And he said, "No".' How subdued is this 'No' after the previous thunderous outburst when he wanted to kill it! His rage has died down so that the eyes of his soul can now be opened to the angel with the sword.

The story has yet another aspect. The donkey was also always the symbol of human beings' physical nature, whose task it is to carry their higher nature on earth. St Francis called his body 'Brother Ass'. The prophet Zechariah foretells that the Messiah will come riding on a donkey, meaning that he would descend into the realm of earthly corporeality. Christ entered the holy city riding on a donkey.

Balaam the seer does not see the donkey because he is riding it. He is not on the riverbank, nor wrapped in the mystery of night, but in an ordinary state of daytime consciousness, and his visionary power fails. It is because his visions are usually only a result of a dimming of normal consciousness that his clairvoyance is a danger to the people of Israel, for whom the prerequisite for the coming of Christ is wide-awake, clear consciousness. But now the admonitory apparition of the sword-bearing angel comes flaming into his full daylight consciousness.

The seven altars

Warned by the vision of the heavenly sword, Balaam arrives in the land of the Moabites, where the king receives him royally.

The next morning he takes the seer up to the high place of Baal, to a holy mountain, from where he sees the people of Israel encamped. Like the rushing river, like the silent night, this bare mountain, high above the everyday world, favours prophecy. However, a special sacrificial offering is still necessary to enable the magic word to be received and pronounced.

Balaam orders seven altars to be erected there and a bull and a ram to be sacrificed on each of them. Animal sacrifice in ancient times was certainly not the butchery today's 'enlightened' arrogance often considers it. There was once a very vivid awareness amongst people that every physical phenomenon corresponded to something within themselves, that in each animal a condition or quality of the human soul was made manifest. The animal really provided an offering in a double sense: the man who brought it to the altar at the same time also dedicated with it to the deity the attribute of his soul represented by the animal.

Bulls and rams are sacrificed on the seven altars. These altars are to bring about the connection with different levels of the upper world, with the planetary spheres. The sevenfold sacrificial flames on the mountain and the sevenfold rising of incense are to transport Balaam's soul to the heights of spiritual vision.

> And Balaam said to Balak, 'Stand beside your burnt offering, and I will go. Perhaps the LORD will come to meet me; and whatever he shows me I will tell you.' And he went to a bare height. (Nm 23:3)

This 'going' of Balaam to a meeting with God is not to be taken merely physically; it is a 'going out' of his soul from his body through the power of the seven burnt offerings. Nor is the fact that meanwhile Balak is to 'stand beside' the burnt offerings without inner significance. While Balaam's soul is on the 'bare height', the king is to carry on the sacrifice from the earth and give it spiritual support.

Balaam's 'going' does in fact lead to a meeting, and the first words he speaks to the deity are 'I have arranged the seven altars and I have offered on each altar a bull and a ram.' This means that the seven altars were the last earthly impression he had taken with him, that it was by the power of this image that he knew he was carried into higher worlds.

> And the LORD put a word in Balaam's mouth and said 'Return to Balak and thus shall you speak.' And he returned to him, and behold, he and all the princes of Moab were standing beside his burnt offering.' (23:6)

The seer's soul returns from its ecstatic state, descends once more into his body. As if out of clouds the earthly surroundings take shape before his eyes. The earthly world gradually becomes clear again in the same picture with which it faded away; with the sight of this solemn ritual the soul feels its way back to earthly existence. There is Balak standing beside the burnt offering and all the princes 'standing beside' it are like the priestly assistants at High Mass; their hierarchical grouping is like a picture of the higher worlds.

Now Balaam speaks what has been revealed to him; the seer becomes the magician who speaks forth words of power. It is not a curse, however, but a blessing he delivers.

Thereupon Balak leads him to another high place, Mount Pisgah. The same thing happens again. Once more Balaam does not bring a curse but a blessing.

The pronouncements

Balak led the seer to three mountains, led him in three different ways into 'higher' states of consciousness, for each mountain reaches up into higher worlds in a different way. The word from above, the inspiration, is thus received in different ways.

The pronouncements Balaam makes become more substantial and more forceful each time. This corresponds to the fact that he increasingly becomes an instrument of good powers, and that his own magic practices, his 'sorcery', decrease more and more the clearer the revelation flows. It is part of the subtlety of this account that the experiences on the three mountains also become more impressive as they proceed: three times the same thing seems to happen and yet each time the apparent sameness has a different shading.

The first time Balaam has to 'go' to a meeting with God. The second time he simply waits, the third time 'he did not go, as at other times, to meet with omens ... And the Spirit of God came upon him' (Nm 24:1f). His own deeds become increasingly insignificant the more firmly he becomes an instrument of higher spiritual beings who lead evolution towards Christ, and who can transform evil to good and curse to blessing.

In his first pronouncement he recognises the special status of the people of Israel in that they cannot be reckoned among the other peoples.

The second points even more clearly to the coming Messiah: 'The LORD their God is with them, and the shout of a king is among them' (23:21). And after the golden clarion ring of the word 'king' there shines out with sunlike power the picture of the lion raising itself up – an anticipation of the sunlike conqueror and vanquisher of death spoken of by John in the Book of Revelation (5:5): 'Behold, the Lion of the tribe of Judah ... has conquered.' The third pronouncement begins with all solemnity. Balaam sees the twelve tribes encamped in the wilderness. They are like the constellations in heaven. As it is in heaven, so also on the earth. Thereupon his visionary power this time really takes fire. Heavenly mysteries are revealed to him. Before his visionary eye the wilderness becomes the garden of paradise. In this third pronouncement there lies an anticipation of how the Messiah will bring about the 're-enlivening' of the wilderness of 'dying earth existence', and from far off appears the picture of the heavenly 'gardener' who works in the garden of the Resurrection. The Water of Life flows through this third pronouncement. Immediately on sight of the wilderness (24:1) this prophecy comes to him: 'How fair are your tents, O Jacob, your encampments, O Israel!' The poor tents become the heavenly 'houses' of the zodiac.

> Like valleys that stretch afar,
> like gardens beside a river,
> like aloes that the LORD has planted,
> like cedar trees beside the waters.
> Water shall flow from his buckets,
> and his seed shall be in many waters.

Finally, after the sign of the lion once more, 'Blessed is he who blesses you, and cursed is he who curses you.'

Balak grows angry and refuses the seer the reward of honour since he has not cursed but blessed the enemy. But then Balaam is inspired to a fourth pronouncement, and in this he soars to the very heights. Again there is the solemn prologue, but nowmore far-reaching than in the third pronouncement (24:15f).

> And he took up his discourse, and said,
> 'The oracle of Balaam the son of Beor,
> the oracle of the man whose eye is opened,
> the oracle of him who hears the words of God,
> and knows the knowledge of the Most High,
> who sees the vision of the Almighty,
> falling down with his eyes uncovered.

The extent of spiritual vision depends upon the degree of reverence. Balaam falls to his knees and so has his 'eyes uncovered'.

And now there comes in this fourth pronouncement the prophecy of the 'star'. The shining star of grace, which the wise men from the east are to see when the time is ripe, Balaam sees already, more than a thousand years beforehand. The future already exists spiritually, though simply as something coming towards the present, more or less distant from it. Balaam feels that he now sees what belongs to a far distant future (24:17).

> I see him, but not now;
> I behold him, but not near:
> a star shall come out of Jacob.

What follows may sound violently warlike. We are still in the Old Testament. The seer is able to perceive above all how the coming of the Messiah will be a judgment, and shall 'break down all the sons of Sheth [chaos]'. He sees how the coming of the Messiah will bring about the defeat of all those who would like to make the earth a godless chaos, free of the divine jurisdiction, and who do not want the star of peace to descend to earth. The seer of ancient times cannot yet, however, discern how the Messiah will appear with no weapon other than the victorious power of inner sacrifice, how the power of the Lion will come in the form of the Lamb. The Revelation to John says: 'Behold, the Lion ... has conquered ... Then I saw a Lamb ...' The seer of ancient times has only the images of military conquests, but the mighty sunlike power with which they are invested is the same that at a later time will be revealed in the 'Lamb of God'. And above all the star is the same which will shed its light over Bethlehem.

> I see him, but not now;
> I behold him, but not near:
> a star shall come ...

In these words there reaches us from a dim and distant past a very early anticipation of what Christ said to John on Patmos (Rv 22:16): 'I am ... the bright morning star.'

9

GIDEON'S ENCOUNTER WITH THE ANGEL

A SUPERSENSIBLE EXPERIENCE

Over three thousand years ago, the Old Testament hero Gideon had an encounter with an angel, which is related in the Book of Judges (6:11–24) and still preserves there the shimmer of a gradually unfolding supersensible experience.

We are first presented with a war situation: the nomad bandit hosts of the Midianites have overwhelmed the land. In the village of Ophrah in Samaria, Gideon, a farmer's son, is threshing grain as fast as he can in order to hide it away in the winepress from the expected plunder of approaching enemies. Close to this winepress, not far from his father's farm, a mighty oak stands beside a slab of rock.

'And the angel of the LORD came and sat under the oak at Ophrah' (6:11). In the original text it does not say, as in the King James version, 'an' oak, but *the* oak at Ophrah', which is significant. Under this oak the angel appears to Gideon.

People in olden times could still be clairvoyant for the invisible world concealed behind nature's exterior, and found that the veil of sensory appearance is not woven everywhere of an equal thickness. At particular places it can become transparent in various ways. This was experienced, for instance, beside 'sacred trees'. The tree, pervaded by a cloud of subtle life forces, could serve higher inhabitants of the spirit world as a kind of 'alighting' place, and as entrance into the earthly world.

In the same way, the tree at Ophrah is important in connection with the angel who appeared to Gideon: literally, 'he was seen by him,' or he 'let himself be seen by him' (6:12). Gideon was no doubt prepared for such vision by the state of his soul, which we can imagine was loosened, lifted a little from mundane consciousness by the threat of the approaching enemy.

The angel 'came'. As a being of the invisible world of spirits, he made a movement towards the earthly plane in order to make himself known to a human being. In the same way that the Gospel of John tells of the angel who 'descended' at certain times to stir the water of the Pool of Bethesda, here too the 'coming' of the angel signifies a descent into the earthly sphere. In the house, within the confines of four walls, he cannot reveal himself to Gideon, but under the tree he is able to condense himself into a subtle body and so impinge upon Gideon's awareness.

The angel is able to make himself not only seen but also to inspire the hearing of words in an earthly human being. 'Yahweh be with you, you mighty man of strength' (6:12). Gideon, who at that moment is full of fear of his enemy and thoughts of flight, is not aware of being strong at all. However, the angel addresses not his mundane human nature but the still slumbering higher being of the young man, so as to awaken him to consciousness of it. This does not immediately happen. First of all the hard-pressed soul must broaden its scope. To Gideon the angelic greeting, addressing him 'far beyond his circumstances', sounds like mockery. In what way is Yahweh with us? He has left us in the lurch, has abandoned us to Midianites.

Responding to this outbreak of doubt and despondency:

> Yahweh turned to him and said, 'Go into this your strength.
> You are to save Israel from the hands of the Midianites. I have sent you.' (6:14)

Yahweh turns to him. And yet until now we have heard only of the 'angel of Yahweh' (angel of the LORD). Is there a mistake in the text here – have two different versions perhaps been conflated? But if, instead of approaching such texts in an externally literary way, we allow ourselves to consider that they convey real experience, we can say this: even if two different versions once existed, whoever combined them did so rightly. There is in truth no flaw in the account, but rather a development, a heightening of experience. In the world of spirits there is no spatial exclusivity as there is in the material world, where only one thing at a time can exist in one place. For the world of spirits one being can work and live in another, there is reciprocal interpenetration, mutual interplay. Thus Yahweh and 'his angel' do not stand alongside each other in a spatially separate way like incarnated people, but they interpenetrate. At the beginning, it is the angel primarily who appears to Gideon's vision. But as the experience intensifies, the angel becomes transparent for the higher divine being who is revealed by his mediation. God 'turns to him', makes a 'movement' towards him so that the angel temporarily vanishes from his mind and Gideon instead becomes aware that he is speaking with Yahweh himself.

But even with this intensification, the hindrance arising from Gideon's everyday consciousness is not banished. Having given expression in his first reaction to his doubt about God's power, Gideon now expresses what we might today call a sense of inferiority. Why me? Who am I after all?! I am without followers, 'the least in my father's house.'

At this he is addressed for the third time: 'But I will be with you.' Gradually the message sinks into the tremulous soul.

'If I have found favour in your eyes, then show me a sign that this is you.' Once again, this seemingly illogical account is in fact profoundly appropriate and right. Supersensible experience has various degrees, contains transitional states of 'knowing and yet not knowing'. I see you before me, I hear your words – but is that really you? Gideon seeks confirmation of reality. He undertakes, for his part, to help in this by making an offering. It is ancient religious knowledge that what may seek to reach the human being from the hidden world can 'come' in a stronger or weaker form depending on what the person concerned themselves bring towards it. Sacrificial surrender and offering by human beings strengthens the power of the invisible world to make itself manifest.

Gideon knows that this heavenly vision can disappear again at any moment – 'as a rainbow fades' it says in an ancient eastern scripture. He wishes to hold fast to the experience, to be able to grasp it with even greater certainty. And so he says, 'Do not depart from here until I come to you again and bring my offering and lay it before you.' It is clear to him that he cannot invite the being to enter his house: the visitation has its fitting place under the sacred tree, 'outside the door'.

His plea to stay is granted majestically in the words, 'I will remain [literally: seated enthroned] until your return.'

In Christian worship, the angelic message of the gospel is followed by the reply of the Offertory, the offering from human beings. Gideon's experience unfolds in the same pattern. He has heard the angelic message and now briefly goes back into his house to fetch from there what he himself possesses, the sacrificial offering.

> And Gideon came and prepared a kid and a measure of unleavened bread and placed the meat in a basket and put broth in a pot and brought them out to him under the oak and approached. (6:19)

For Gideon's soul, as a man of ancient times, outward and inward are a single indivisible whole. With his outer belongings he offers at the same time his inner attributes to the Godhead. Even the basket and the pot are not profane utensils in these ancient times of crafted artefacts, but have their dignity. Gideon returns to the oak with his gifts. And behold, the mysterious higher presence has not been extinguished in the meantime but is still present. Sustained by his impulse to make an offering, Gideon has preserved the intensity of his soul as he returned to the mundane world of his house. Now he 'approached'. This is not only a bodily approach but at the same time a reverent 'coming nearer' to the Godhead in a mood and stance of offering.

Now the mediating angel comes into the foreground again, this time called the 'angel of God'. Gideon receives from him more precise instructions about what should now be done. Once again, this is a primordial religious experience. Ritual enactment is not left to human caprice. Out of a higher consciousness, the angel shows how the rite must be performed. 'Take the meat and the unleavened bread and lay them on this rock, and pour out the broth.' And Gideon 'did so'.

Just as, in Christian rites, a human offering leads over into further intensification of the divine presence, into the transubstantiation, so here also Gideon's devoted offering meets with a stronger annunciation of the supersensible, embodied in the 'sign' as confirmation of its reality.

And a new aspect now informs the vision: the angel holds a staff in his hand. The outstretched arm and hand embody a will made visible. By the addition of a staff, this pictorial expression of the emanating will is intensified. By extending the staff, the angel sends out a ray of power. And with the 'tip' of the rod – where this power is most strongly concentrated – he touches the offered gifts. Fire springs up from the rock and consumes the gifts.

Amongst the four elements, heat or fire stands closer to the invisible world than solidity, fluidity and air. Experience shows how, precisely in the realm of warmth sensation, inner and outer can pass over into each other. In its accounts of the establishment of new rites – the tabernacle (Lv 9:24), the temple (2Ch 7:1) – the Old Testament on each occasion speaks of the descent of an unearthly fire. The same is true of Elijah's offering on Mount Carmel (1K 18:38). While such fire was surely as non-physical as the Pentecost flames on the heads of the apostles, nevertheless real supersensible events were involved. In reading accounts from those times we should remember that they sometimes pass almost unnoticeably from earthly occurrences to ones that belong to another level of existence.

With the flaring of the divine fire on the rock, Gideon's vision reaches its culmination and its end. The angel 'vanished from his eyes'. In a later angel narrative from the same Book of Judges, the offering of Manoah, 'the angel of the Lord ascended in the flame of the altar' (13:20). With Gideon, too, the vanishing of the angel figure seems to have been connected with the appearance of the fire. This wonderful vanishing is precisely what makes Gideon awaken from dreamlike reverie to full clarity about what he has experienced. 'Gideon saw that it had been the angel of the Lord' (6:22).

Along with this realisation he is overcome – and this too belongs to primordial religious experience – by a 'threshold frisson', the deep alarm of a soul living in an earthly body who, touched by a higher world, becomes conscious of its own inadequacy. He who sees God dies (Ex 33:20). 'Alas O Lord God, I have seen the angel of the Lord face to face.' But it is precisely a humble realisation of his own unworthiness that can carry him through this crisis, in the same way that, in the Christian rites, the phrase uttered by the centurion of Capernaum – 'I am not worthy' – precedes the receiving of communion. Thereupon, Gideon gains a last and essential enhancement of his experience. The vision has already faded from his gaze but within him he hears the voice of God. 'The LORD said to him, "Peace be with you. Do not fear. You shall not die".' These words reverberate so powerfully within him that he names the altar which he then built under the oak 'The LORD is peace' (6:24).

Over a thousand years later, Paul will take up these words in the Letter to the Ephesians and say, now of Christ: 'He is our peace' (Eph 2:14).

10

THE OFFERING OF MANOAH

DIFFERENT ANGELIC EXPERIENCES IN MAN AND WOMAN

In the previous chapter, 'Gideon's Encounter with the Angel', we tried to show that a biblical account of that kind can be recognised as a true description of a supersensible experience. Later, in Chapter 13 of the same Book of Judges, a similar angelic experience appears – the annunciation of the birth of the sun hero Samson at the time of the Israelites' subjugation to the Philistines.

Whereas Gideon hears the call when he is an adult, the higher world intervenes already at the time of Samson's birth, in a distinctive annunciation to his parents. Both parents, the father, who is called Manoah, and the mother, whose name is not given, participate in the angelic experience but in characteristically different ways. The difference arises from the essential nature of the masculine and feminine, and the singular quality of this story is that it offers a classic depiction of the harmonious interplay of the male and female elements.

The angel does not first appear to the man but to the woman. When the angel appears to her, her husband is not with her. She is alone. In brief terms the story suggests that she is outside the house in the open air, at a special place. Then we learn that there, in the fields (13:9), there is a rock seemingly regarded as a place of offering or shrine (13:19), like the offering stone under the oak outside the village in the narrative of Gideon. The woman has sought out this sacred place, and perhaps she has often lingered there alone. What she feels to be the grievous destiny of childlessness may have led her into this state of loneliness, to beg or pray for a child. Tarrying at this consecrated place, her soul is lifted out of mundanity, and she is ready to have an encounter with a being of the higher world.

The angel appears to her and announces the birth of a son who is destined for great things, and whose descent into earthly incarnation requires a special kind of conduct of mother and child so that he may be 'one consecrated to God from the womb'. The woman then 'came to her husband and told this to him' (13:5f). In her report of what has happened we learn more about the angelic appearance: 'A man of God ... his appearance like the appearance of an angel of God, very awesome.'

'Very awesome' – this conveys something of the terror which seizes a person incarnated in an earthly body in the encounter with a higher reality. After this, she recounts the angel's annunciation and instruction; but more than just repeating them, she also expressly first speaks of something that did *not* occur during this experience, out of a feeling that she omitted to do something. In her terror, she says, she was unable to question the angelic appearance 'from where he came', nor to ask his 'name'. While she had the impression, in her soul's direct power of apprehension, that this was a supersensible being, she felt her waking, conscious power failed her. She tells her husband this, and he, with the capacities of his masculine mode of consciousness, must now augment and enlarge on what has happened. We can be reminded here of the Samaritan woman at the well to whom Christ says at one point in their conversation, 'Call your husband to come' (Jn 4:16). In the case of the Samaritan woman, the husband cannot be fetched. The Manoah story, on the other hand, portrays the right interrelationship between them.

Her husband must now also be led into the angelic experience, but this necessitates certain preconditions. It is not by chance that women first behold the resurrected Christ at Easter, and the disciples only subsequently. Male incarnation takes the soul deeper into the earthly and material realm, but on the other hand it provides the foundation for stronger powers of consciousness of the self. 'Manoah prayed to the LORD and said, "Let the man of God you sent come once more".' (13:8). He 'prayed' – in Hebrew the word used for this also means 'to burn incense'. The request is reinforced by a deed of offering which can help loosen the soul somewhat from its strong earthly ties and make it receptive to supersensible experience. The Godhead 'listened to the voice of Manoah' and allows the angel to appear a second time.

But even then Manoah is not immediately granted vision. It is the woman who first sees the angel once more – and again not in the mundane constriction of four walls but out in the open in the fields, at the offering rock, at the consecrated place. And this encounter again occurs in musing loneliness. As she previously revealed her suffering there to the Godhead and prayed for a child, so she may now have gone there to ponder the angelic appearance and prophetic promise. 'The angel of God came again to the woman as she was sitting in the field, but Manoah her husband was not with her' (13:9). This time the narrator does not say that the woman then 'came' to her husband to tell him, but 'in haste she ran' to him. By altering the phrase the narrator might be gently suggesting that after the first experience the woman went more hesitantly to her husband to tell him something almost incomprehensible. Now, on the second occasion, she can rely on their common understanding. She leaves the angel at the sacred place, without herself entering into dialogue with him. Hoping that the vision will stay there long enough, she rushes home to fetch her husband. It is the woman, therefore, who leads the man to the angelic experience. She is ahead of him in this. 'Manoah arose and followed his wife' (13:11).

But having 'come' to the angel by following his wife, he now takes over and addresses the angel directly, as I to I: 'Are you the man who spoke with my wife?' The angel affirms it by saying 'I am'. (In Hebrew this is expressed simply as 'I').

At this, Manoah asks the angel again about the child who has been prophesied. The angel in turn confirms what he said to the woman when he first appeared. And then: 'Manoah said to the angel of the LORD, "Let us detain you, and we will prepare a young goat for you".' (13:15). He knows that supersensible appearances fade again without warning like a rainbow, but that an offering, devoted commitment from human beings, can make it possible for the heavenly visitor to be 'detained' longer. Manoah may remember how the patriarch brought sustenance to the three mysterious figures in the shadow of his tree. And so he asks the angel to remain, in the same way that the disciples at Emmaus will one day ask the risen one.

The angel replies that though he will not eat earthly food, Manoah may still bring an offering to the Lord. As with Gideon, we can notice here a curious vacillation between knowing and not knowing – which is seemingly illogical given what has so far happened. He finds himself hovering in a condition of vision that has not yet become full certainty – 'for Manoah did not know that it was the angel of the LORD'. Yet he is able to pull himself together enough to ask the question his wife was unable to. In his consciousness he is, as it were, 'man enough' to ask the angel his name, as from I to I. 'What is your name?' As the Bible sees it, a name is not an empty formality of no consequence but rather the spiritual 'form' which invests someone with an unmistakeable character and renders this discernible to another mind.

In the story of Tobias we read of this kind of revelation of the name of a heavenly being: 'I am Raphael' (Tb 12:15). And in Luke the angelic appearance says 'I am Gabriel' to the priest Zechariah (Lk 1:19). Manoah does not reach such enlightenment about the angel's name, and this itself can confirm for us the realistic truth of the narrative. If the tale were invented and imaginary, a name would surely be given at this point. Manoah is unable to fully take in the being's angelic nature. 'Why do you ask my name, which is wondrous?' The true name is veiled in the experience of something 'wondrous'. Here there is a sense of the entirely other nature of a being of a higher world, surpassing all earthly concepts. In the prophecy of the Saviour that comes in Isaiah, 'wonderful' is even one of the names of the Redeemer (Is 9:6) alongside other names that together utter the full scope and wealth of his being. Nevertheless, Manoah gains initial entry into the mystery of the name when this heavenly figure shines into his awareness as 'the angel Wondrous'.

After this, Manoah makes his offering upon the sacred rock. In Christian worship, the offering from humankind is followed by the 'answer', the grace of transubstantiation. We find the same sequence in the tales both of Gideon and Manoah. 'And he did wonders' (13:19); or, literally, 'he was wondrous in his deed'. Here the narrative becomes very reticent. In reverent awe it does not dare to clothe in human words this action of the angel 'whose name is wondrous'. Important here is the phrase following, 'But Manoah and his wife looked on.' This does not mean something as obvious as that the two followed the holy deed with keen attention. This express reference to 'seeing' signifies rather that here a higher seeing than that of the ordinary and everyday came into its own. Manoah and his wife saw something that would not have been visible for ordinary sight. 'As the flame sprang up to heaven from the altar, the angel rose upward in the flame of the altar' (13:20). Once more the narrator says that Manoah and his wife *saw* this. The fire shows itself to be the intermediate element at the threshold between material and supersensible worlds, mediating ascent and descent between them. Overcome by the incandescence of this vision, Manoah and his wife fall on their faces.

Here the text interrupts the immediate story to state that the angel did not appear again after this. Once again we can gain from this the sense that the tale is not fantasy but an authentic account. At the same time this interruption allows us to sense a certain interval of time between the vision of the flames in which the angel ascends and the gradual realisation of what has been witnessed: 'Then Manoah knew that it was the angel of the Lord' (13:21). It takes a while for the deeply shaken soul to gather itself again and for the strange state of hovering between 'knowing and not knowing' to give way to full clarity and certainty. As in the story of Gideon, this clarity brings with it the fear of dying in consequence. Manoah says to his wife, 'We must surely die because we have seen God' (13:22).

It is not accidental that this phrase is spoken by the *man*. He stands in earthly existence with greater self-awareness, the price of which is that he has become more distant from the super-earthly realm, and therefore, when this realm does so powerfully approach him, he will inevitably feel more shaken, disconcerted and closer to death. At such a moment Gideon is comforted by the merciful voice of God telling him he will not die (6:23). Manoah is comforted through his wife's mediation. Standing closer to the tree of life, the super-earthly is more natural and understandable to her: it has not yet become so alien to her that it draws her as strongly towards death as it does the man who is seized by a complete 'threshold frisson'. In his painting, *The Offering of Manoah* (1614), Rembrandt characteristically distinguished between the two, the wife and husband. The man turns away as if he cannot bear the vision. The woman remains calmly turned towards it, in prayerful stance. And so she is able to speak these words of comfort:

> If the LORD had wished to kill us, he would not have accepted a burned offering and a food offering from our hands. Nor would he have shown us everything nor let us hear everything as he now has. (13:23)

II

LEVIATHAN

THE DRAGON MYTH IN THE OLD TESTAMENT

Every autumn after the full light of summer the soul senses the renewed encroachment of darkness. It is confronted by the picture – formed as it were out of the deepening darkness – of the dragon, that most ancient of human nightmares, prototype of man's fear and horror when faced with the powers opposed to God. Out of the all-pervading darkness the soul sees the dragon arise; out of the refined spiritual light with which a supersensory sun radiates into this autumn darkening there takes shape before it the picture of one who conquers the dragon.

It is very ancient human experience that stirs in the soul when it beholds the dragon and its conqueror. This vision, however, has its proper place in the present age only if the old picture is seen in the light of Christ's deed – as it is in the last book of the New Testament, the Revelation to John. There in Chapter 12, the picture of the fight with the dragon is placed within the framework of Christian apocalypse, and is thus recognisable for the first time in its full significance.

The Bible is an organic whole. This is apparent when we see how the climax of apocalyptic imagery at the end of the New Testament – Michael's fight with the dragon – is not unprepared: it has its first elements in the Old Testament.

The dragon-myth in the Old Testament? Is not the Old Testament really unmythological in approach? This objection would not be without foundation. Consider for example the creation of the world. Genesis describes it in a manner appropriate to a people who were to be guided from a fading dreamlike picture-consciousness to clear thinking. In comparison with the creation stories of other peoples, mythological imagery recedes markedly in favour of a more intellectual element. The power of thinking draws clear boundaries and distinguishes for the first time between world phenomena. We see at work in the creation story of Genesis something like a divine, cosmically active thinking: it masters uncontrolled chaos and 'thinks asunder' the various elements of the universe so that an ordered cosmos can arise. Thus God divides light and darkness, calls the one 'day' and the other 'night'. Thus he divides the water above from the water below, the firm land from the waters.

Apart, however, from the Mosaic story of creation into which there plays such a conspicuous element of thought, other different kinds of description of the origin of the world were obviously prevalent, genuinely pagan in their mythological colouring and imagery, akin to certain Babylonian traditions.

While in Genesis we are presented so to speak with the 'official' line of Old Testament spirituality, we find the old mythology chiefly in the more poetic writings, not indeed as complete pictures, but in fragments from which something can be reconstructed. Traces of a long-past picture consciousness, dimmed by the approach of reasoned thought, turn up where the prevailing more abstract spirituality is temporarily relaxed – that is to say, in poetry. Here the old imaginative wealth often survives and radiates its mysterious soul-warming power even where, as being 'only poetic', it is not taken absolutely seriously.

Such 'erratics', remnants of a mythical consciousness, are found chiefly in the Book of Job, which seems to be remembered only for the wonderful saying about the world's beginning, 'when the morning stars sang together'. We have, then, in the first place to deal with the Book of Job if we want to pursue the dragon myth. Such research into the mythical has its special attraction and value in our time when people want to reach beyond a merely intellectual consciousness to the sphere of imaginative vision.

Two monsters, Leviathan and Behemoth, are described at the end of the book. The explanatory footnotes added in some translations are typical of an intellectual understanding of mythical imagery.

These invite readers to envisage a hippopotamus under the name of Behemoth and a crocodile under the name of Leviathan. Readers are thus rendered immune to any mythological thrill of horror, they feel at ease, and above all are left with the impression of how inaccurately nature was observed in those ancient, unenlightened times. They then take this chapter as a rather inexact poetical fantasy about animals that one can nowadays view at leisure in the zoo – where one certainly never sees a crocodile spitting fire, as Job describes Leviathan:

> His sneezings flash forth light,
> and his eyes are like the eyelids of the dawn.
> Out of his mouth go flaming torches;
> sparks of fire leap forth.
> Out of his nostrils comes forth smoke,
> as from a boiling pot and burning rushes.
> His breath kindles coals,
> and a flame comes forth from his mouth. (Jb 41:18–21)

Leviathan – a crocodile? Rather the other way round: the crocodile – a Leviathan! In other words the crocodile, like the ancient saurians before it, still calls up a remote reminiscence of the dragon. Faced by the terrifying form of the crocodile the sensitive soul still feels something of the dragon-fear of ancient times. Granted that in Job's time nature could not yet be observed accurately. That is undoubted. But perhaps certain 'inaccuracies' of ancient story-tellers should be explained by a resurgence of ancient clairvoyance which was then unconsciously woven into the physical observation. The sight of the crocodile could trigger off 'second sight' of the dragon, and the mythical vision settled like a cloud in front of what the physical eyes saw. Thus this passage, taken as a description of a crocodile, may be rated inaccurate throughout; nevertheless, as a vision of evil it is more firmly based in reality than a superficial zoological catalogue. It is the Lucifer qualities of the dragon that spit out at us from the description in Job, which ends with the words, 'He is king over all the sons of pride' (41:34).

The Book of Job does not speak of dragons only in Chapters 40 and 41. It mentions them earlier in reference to a myth that it assumes to be well known. In this case, though, the dragon is not called Leviathan but 'Rahab', in view of his terrible ferocity. As in Babylonian myth the helpers of the monster are mentioned.

The story is concerned with an event at the beginning of time. The universe would not have become an ordered cosmos if the God of the I AM had not put the forces of chaos in their place and wrested the world order from them.

> He is God; no one can stay his anger;
> beneath him the helpers of Rahab bow down. (Jb 9:13)

The same struggle is spoken of later:

> By his power in an instant he stirred the sea;
> by his understanding he shattered Rahab.
> By his wind the heavens were made fair;
> his hand pierced the fleeing serpent. (26:12f)

The God of the I AM* is at the same time the God of the power of thinking who, creating clarity, conquered chaos. By his 'understanding' he struck down Rahab. Cleansing the atmosphere, which in the ancient days of dragons was a seething vapour, making possible a clear heaven and a pure, spirit-bearing breeze (in Hebrew as in Greek the same word indicates both 'air' or 'wind' and 'spirit') – these are the consequences of the primeval victory of Yahweh over the dragon, preparations in the natural world for the appearance of the thinking human being.

The psalms also tell of this myth (89:9f);

> You rule the raging of the sea;
> when its waves rise, you still them.
> You crushed Rahab fatally.

Similarly in Psalm 74 the raging sea is the element of the dragon, whose fearful, multi-headed image emerges from the waters as in the Apocalypse.

---

* Hermann Beckh once freely rendered Yahweh as 'He who speaks the I in me'. Beckh was one time Professor of Oriental Languages at the University of Berlin, later priest of The Christian Community and one of its best Hebrew scholars.

II. LEVIATHAN

> You broke up the sea by your might;
> you broke the heads of the sea monsters on the waters.
> You crushed the heads of Leviathan,
> you gave him as food for the people in the wilderness.
> (Ps 74:13f)

The latter passage recalls the far-reaching prophecy of apocryphal tradition that one day at the end of time Leviathan is to serve as food for the chosen people – the enormous energy active in the ungodly is one day to be won back to the good, 'incorporated' in those associated with God. So something of the future shines into this remarkable sentence about the approaching feeding of the people in the wilderness, whilst it also refers back to a long past event. The singer of Psalm 74, who has had to experience the destruction of the temple, faces the question, how is it that the Adversary apparently seizes the earth? Then he remembers the great conquest of the dragon in the dim past and is bound to ask himself, where is this power of conquest today? He cannot yet perceive that this power is undergoing a lengthy process of transformation, that in the future it will conquer the dragon by human means.

The same question – in modern words, 'Is God dead?' – troubled the soul of the prophet Isaiah (51:9):

> Awake, awake, put on strength,
> O arm of the LORD;
> Awake, as in days of old,
> the generations of long ago.
> Was it not you who cut Rahab in pieces,
> who pierced the dragon?

This power once conquered the dragon, but the fight brought no final decision. The dragon is 'wounded' but not dead.

This is recalled in a story from the Edda about the fight by Thor against the Midgard snake. Thor rows out to sea with the giant Hymir. He uses the head of a black bull for bait. The Midgard snake bites, Thor draws it up and as its frightful head emerges from the sea he hurls his hammer – but the blow does not strike with fatal impact; at the last moment Hymir has treacherously cut the line. The stricken monster sinks, but now there is the uncertainty whether it is dead or still alive. Will it recover? Will another fight be necessary?

The myth, of which traces are found in the Old Testament, also shows an awareness that the dragon conquered in primeval times now lives hidden in the sea. This is clear from the book of the prophet Amos (9:3): 'and though they hide from my sight at the bottom of the sea, there I will command the serpent, and it shall bite them.'

The serpent lurks at the bottom of the sea. A mysterious passage in Job shows that this does not only concern the outer world; it makes it clear how such myths are relevant to the inner life. The sea is at the same time the soul. And as in the sea there are the abyssal depths into which no ray of sunlight falls, in whose unlit, black darkness a most sinister and fearful world of creatures has its existence (one thinks of the pictures deep sea exploration has given us), so there are also the unillumined abyssal depths of the soul-sea, in which fiendish and terrible monsters hide. They will not always remain 'latent' – the visionary John sees the future rising of the beast from the abyss (Rv 17:8) for a final conflict with the powers of light.

In the world past, the dragon was conquered; in the world present, it is latent in sinister, threatening manner. What yet sleeps in the abysses of the soul can become awake. Schiller described how the magic of song penetrates into the deeper levels of the soul and stirs them: 'And wakes the hidden power of feeling so wonderfully sleeping in the heart.' There the poet thinks of what is great and noble sleeping in the heart and waiting to be woken. But evil in its most terrible form is also still hidden. To awaken and call up these forces is a deed of black magic.

It is of this that Job speaks in the very obscure passage mentioned earlier. In his despair he would curse the day of his birth. But it is clear to him as a man of ancient times that if it is to work, the curse like the blessing is determined by certain soul conditions and has to be skilled. Just as a momentary flaring up of good will is not enough to be able to bless effectively, so a fit of anger has not the power of effective cursing. When now even the day of his birth is to be cursed, Job accordingly looks out as it were for someone who is skilled in cursing. Then a dark and sinister picture of earlier times arises in his darkened soul: the black magicians of submerged Atlantis.

Herodotus in one place writes about the Atlanteans, who were so wicked that every day they cursed the rising sun. One could imagine no more apt characterisation of black magic than this curse hurled against the sun every morning.

The passage in Job runs: 'Let those curse it [the night of his conception] who curse the day, who are prepared to rouse up Leviathan' (Jb 3:8). Here Greek and Hebrew tradition coincide. Those 'who curse the day' are the wicked Atlanteans of Herodotus, those who so vehemently hate the rising sun. They set themselves against the Christ principle of the sunlit day, which by grace illumines the meaning of earth existence. They are there when it comes to cursing human birth on earth. They are therefore also able to 'rouse up Leviathan' – to call up and awaken what sleeps dragon-like in the 'abyssal' bottom of the soul's sea.

It is characteristic of the marvellous contrapuntal style of the Bible that before the rising of the Christ-Day ('I am the light of the world ... Abraham exulted that he should see my day; and he saw it and rejoiced' Jn 8:12, 56) a soul seeking God has to probe these abysses of negation.

What is hidden will come to light; the beast will rise from the abyss. 'The sun brings everything to light.' Once again Michael will gain the victory over the dragon in a new way in the future. Isaiah prophesies it (27:1):

> In that day the LORD with his hard and great and mighty
> sword will punish Leviathan the fleeing serpent, Leviathan
> the twisting serpent, and he will slay the monster that is in the
> sea.

But it will not be possible for this apocalyptic battle to be waged apart from human beings and without their involvement, like the earlier one. That battle could not be concluded since it was only to secure the natural foundations of human existence intended for man at the creation. Indeed we already get in the Old Testament a distant hint of this future involvement of humankind. Human beings in association with the angels are to triumph over the dragon:

> For he will give his angels charge of you
> to guard you in all your ways.
> On their hands they will bear you up,
> lest you dash your foot against a stone.
> You will tread on the lion and the snake,
> the young lion and the serpent you will trample underfoot.
> (Ps 91:11–13)

These are words that play a very significant part in the New Testament (see also Chapter 42 on Psalm 91).

By regaining through Christ their connection with angelic realms above, human beings will be a match for the dragon. They find their strength by looking up to the starry heights of their heavenly origin. This makes possible the glorious appearance at the end of the New Testament of John's mighty vision of Michael's fight with the dragon – a primeval picture, but one that now proclaims something entirely new – a future of humankind with Christ.

12

'NOT BY MIGHT ...'

THE KINGSHIP OF THE MESSIAH

Humankind was prepared for the coming of Christ in manifold ways. As part of this preparation two complementary 'ideals' developed in the world of the Old Covenant. They served to direct awareness to the One expected. They were those of 'king' and 'priest' – the one concerned with the world, ruling with enlightenment, the other tending the connection with the heavens.

At the very beginning of the development of the people of Israel there appears the mysterious picture of Melchizedek, a king of peace who is at the same time priest of the Most High God. He represents the ideal blending of king and priest.

More than half a millennium after Melchizedek, in the time of Moses, the people of the Old Covenant saw the founding of a dedicated priesthood, with Aaron as the first high priest. A few hundred years later a first king was anointed. In Saul and Samuel, king and high priest appear together for the first time side by side. One can then observe how after that the two lines move apart, how they occasionally meet again, how antagonism arises between them, but also fruitful tension that prepares the possibility of a merging of a higher kind in the future.

The word 'Christ', Greek *Christos,* is originally the translation of the Hebrew 'Messiah' (*mashiach*), the anointed one. Both the king and the high priest were anointed.* Each can be called 'the anointed of the LORD'. Philo, the Jewish sage living in Alexandria, saw in the high priest the representative of the divine Logos. But every king too who bore the crown in Jerusalem as 'son of David' was felt to be

---

* Only the high priests, not the others, were consecrated by having their heads anointed with oil (Lv 8:12, 30). In Lv 4:3, the 'anointed priest' means 'high priest'.

holding the position of the greater One who was to come. In itself a prophecy, the series of royal sons of David following each other through the centuries seemed like the keeping alive of a permanently burning holy light.* In the eyes of the Jews the king could from time to time already come very close to that which he was meant only to foreshadow. In Psalm 45, which celebrates a royal marriage, the princely bridegroom is already seen as almost indistinguishable from his divine prototype. Later on, moreover, the rabbis thought that the Messiah should have been recognised as actually already present in King Hezekiah.

In the New Testament the evangelist Matthew has a special eye for how the long-prepared line of 'images' of the king moves towards the figure of Christ Jesus and finds its fulfilment in him. He begins his account with a genealogy in which – different from Luke – he expressly adds to the name David, 'the king' (Mt 1:6) and – again different from Luke – follows the ancestry of Jesus from David through Solomon and thence through the whole succession of kings who ruled in Jerusalem. These form the middle of the three groups into which Matthew subdivides the genealogy. The series of kings reaches up to the catastrophe of the destruction of Jerusalem in 586 BC. Then the Babylonians brought the Jewish kings to a terrible end, burnt the temple and led the people into exile. From that point Matthew lists the third group of his genealogy, which leads to Jesus.

In this connection Emil Bock pointed out that those belonging to this third group certainly lived on in the minds of the Jews as the 'uncrowned kings'. Near the beginning of this list appears one who represents an important turning point in the history of the Old Testament idea of the king – that is Zerubbabel.

We imagine ourselves back in the year 520 BC. Eighteen years have passed since the Persian king, Cyrus, overthrew the kingdom of Babylon and gave the deported Jews permission to return home to Jerusalem and rebuild the temple. Since this return they have gradually re-established themselves in the ruined city, to some extent already even quite comfortably – one stern prophet points out the wood-panelled houses that people have already acquired, while the

---

* 1K 11:36, 15:4, 2K 8:19 (also 2Ch 21:7), Ps 132:17.

12. 'NOT BY MIGHT ...'

temple is still not rebuilt. Those who have returned look to two leading men who since 538 have energetically taken the fate of the people in hand. The one is Zerubbabel, 'son of David'. The Persians have made him governor. Special hopes, however, are concentrated on him. He is the present 'uncrowned king' and it is believed he will reestablish the monarchy. Beside him stands the high priest who bears the name of salvation – Joshua. In the Greek tongue this name is Jesus.

As Providence placed these two figures like prototypes, so it now also calls up a further pair to give a spiritual impulse, two 'prophets'. First appears Haggai in the autumn of 520. He it is who reproaches the people for dwelling in warm, comfortable new houses and appeals to their consciences about the rebuilding of the temple, which is still not done. With words that are also relevant to our own age he depicts how unsatisfactory it is to strive only for material well-being, how that must finally leave the soul empty if the temple is not also rebuilt, the connection with the divine cared for.

> You have sown much, and harvested little. You eat, but you never have enough; you drink, but you never have your fill. You clothe yourselves, but no one is warm. And he who earns wages earns does so to put them into a bag with holes.'
> (Hg 1:6)

In exemplary manner this sentence captures the suffering from an unfulfilled existence that we call 'frustration'. The prophet calls the people away from this egoistical waste of energy in striving for material well-being and injects into their souls the burning impulse for building the temple. He turns in the first place to the two leading men: to Zerubbabel and Joshua. His appeal catches fire. 'And the LORD stirred up the spirit of Zerubbabel ... and the spirit of Joshua ... the high priest, and the spirit of all the remnant of the people' so that in the middle of September the building is begun (Hg 1:14f).

At the beginning of October, also in the season of Michael, prophecy goes a step further. Haggai's utterances become apocalyptic. Coming world-shaking events seek to find expression through him. 'For thus says the LORD of hosts: "Yet once more, in a little while, I will shake the heavens and the earth"' (2:6). Beyond this shaking shines final fulfilment. The Lord will dwell in this temple, in Jerusalem. 'And in this place I will give peace' (2:9).

We notice here a peculiarity common to consciousness reaching into the supersensory: it is clearly not altogether easy for the seer to observe accurately *when* the event he 'sees coming' will be, how near or far off this coming is. Once, in the time of Moses, the seer Balaam observed of the star his vision had revealed: 'I see him, but not now; I behold him, but not near' (Nm 24:17). Haggai in 520 belongs to a very much later time when the original, more instinctive faculty of supersensory vision has become more distant. So the 'but not now ... but not near' escapes him. Eight hundred years had elapsed since Balaam, but there were still to be five hundred years till the coming of Christ. And the last 'shaking of heaven and earth' that entered his clairvoyant field of vision still today belongs to the future, though it is again and again heralded by catastrophes running ahead of it.

We could well imagine that at the fateful time of the rebuilding of the temple the future flashed forth in the supersensory as if in a spiritual storm, so that what was still far off could seem near. The time-perspective gets lost, contracting into mighty condensation what in fact will be a much longer lasting, much more complicated series of events. It is therefore not even really the second temple built on earth under Zerubbabel and Joshua to which the promise applies; this temple simply stands for what in John's Gospel is called the 'temple of his body' (2:21). So we should not be surprised, or doubt the genuineness of Haggai's inspiration, if we notice another 'short cut'. The prophet has arrived at the mystery of the Messiah. But his vision is caught up as it were by the figure of Zerubbabel who stands so close to him and is associated with so many hopes; it remains attached to this figure in the foreground. Thus it happens that Zerubbabel is proclaimed Messiah-King of God's future kingdom (Hg 2:21–23).

While Haggai looks first and foremost at Zerubbabel, the other of the two prophets, Zechariah, who became active somewhat later, shows a stronger interest in the high priest Joshua. To Zechariah also were vouchsafed Messianic and apocalyptic revelations. For him too the distinction between the earthly Jerusalem and the future city of God, the heavenly Jerusalem of the Apocalypse, is not yet altogether clear. Even through the pictures of the material world, however, there breaks the supersensory picture of the perfection he divines when he announces that the future Jerusalem no longer requires walls: the Lord himself encompasses it as a wall of fire, and within the fiery circle dwells the divine 'glory' (Zec 2:5). Zechariah knows that God is already on his way towards dwelling within the human being. 'Be silent, all flesh, before the LORD, for he has roused himself from his holy dwelling.' (2:13).

Then Zechariah has a divine vision of the high priest, Joshua (3:1). He stands in a dirty garment before the angel of the Lord and has to suffer Satan's accusation. By a divine act of grace he has a clean new priest's robe bestowed on him. In other words his priesthood, sullied by the all too human way he has borne the office, is restored in the purity of its original form. At the same time, however, it becomes clear that this does not mean the final perfection. It will first be possible to speak of the immaculate high priest only when the other Joshua-Jesus has appeared. Joshua is therefore told he and his fellow priests are only 'men who are a wondrous sign', and the true Messiah is mentioned immediately after, separate from their prefigurement of him.

The 'Branch' is spoken of – in Hebrew *tsemach,* Latin *oriens.* The Greek word, *anatole,* means both the coming up of a plant and the rising of a star. 'Behold, I will bring my servant the Branch' (3:8). Then immediately another image: God prepares a stone over which watch seven eyes, and which he says he will engrave with its inscription (3:9). The seven eyes indicate the cosmic being of Christ, who uses the 'seven planets' as his eyes. The engraving on the stone is a wonderful image for the fact that by the divine Word's becoming flesh the Spirit intends to brings its influence right down into earthly matter and imprint itself there.

Zechariah's visions reach a climax in the fourth chapter. The prophet experiences the transition to supersensory vision as an awakening from deep sleep – so seems everyday consciousness in comparison, say, with an angel's. Being awoken he sees the golden lampstand with the seven lamps. The seven celestial lights seek their abode on earth, and become the seven lamps borne by the lampstand. This is also an image for the incarnation of the heavenly in the earthly. The sun quality of the Christ-being expresses itself in the golden sheen of the lampstand. But if the heavenly light is to appear on earth borne by a lampstand, it needs fuel; oil must flow to it so that the holy flame remains alive. Zechariah therefore sees to right and left of the golden lampstand the two olive trees as 'the two anointed who stand by the LORD of the whole earth' (4:14). The two anointed: they represent the kingly and the priestly elements which, by serving the heavenly being of Christ, contribute towards his appearance on earth.

Apparently very abruptly in the midst of all this, (and therefore suspected by critics of not belonging to this text), there now also appears in the Book of Zechariah – for the first time – the name of Zerubbabel. 'This is the word of the LORD to Zerubbabel: Not by might, nor by power, but by my Spirit' (4:6). This is the decisive moment. With these words of God – the two negatives so emphatically setting aside the element of external power which had hitherto been inseparable from the image of king – the idea of Messiah-King is set free from that of earthly dominion. What is so clearly said 'about Zerubbabel' is also applicable to the other members of the third group in Matthew's genealogy that ends with Jesus. The 'uncrowned kings' are thus now no longer only potential kings impeded by the adverse circumstances of the time, but since Zerubbabel they represent a radically transformed and spiritualised idea of kingship.

In a later chapter of the Book of Zechariah we then find the Palm Sunday lines about the gentle king who does not force entrance as a conqueror, but allows his entry to depend on whether he is freely bidden welcome (9:9f).

> Rejoice greatly, O daughter of Zion!
> Shout aloud, O daughter of Jerusalem!
> Behold, your king is coming to you;
> righteous and having salvation is he,
> humble and mounted on a donkey,
> on a colt, the foal of a donkey.
> I will cut off the chariot from Ephraim
> and the war horse from Jerusalem;
> and the battle bow shall be cut off,
> and he shall speak to the nations: Peace.
> His rule shall be from sea to sea,
> and from the River to the ends of the earth.

Zechariah is also not yet wholly free of the prejudice arising from a short-term view, speaking words in relation to Zerubbabel which obviously were not fulfilled (4:7–10). Here we notice a gap in the Old Testament record. After the enthusiastic and energetic commencement of the temple building, the name of Zerubbabel disappears without trace from the texts. On the completion of the building – achieved already in March 516 – he is not named. Some tragedy must certainly be concealed behind this lack of mention. Perhaps an illness carried him off? We do not know.

The Book of Zechariah comes back once more to the other anointed one, to Joshua. At God's command Zechariah takes some of the gold and silver that pious Jews coming from Babylon have given for Jerusalem, and makes from it a crown (Zec 6:11). The plural 'crowns' in the original text perhaps indicates that it concerns a double crown, one part of silver and the other of gold. Already in Haggai we read: 'The silver is mine, and the gold is mine, says the LORD of hosts' (2:8). Silver and gold direct attention beyond their material metallic existence to the great cosmic forces that work in moon and sun. From silver and gold, therefore, a crown is shaped, and in a kind of visionary symbolic act placed on the head of the high priest, Joshua. It is not a political act with political consequences. It is like a prophetic and sacred dream-play concerning the bearer of the name 'Jesus', the man who is 'a wondrous sign'. It is like a prophecy that one day another Jesus will carry in him the sun-being of Christ that makes the moon forces subservient. The crown does not stay on the head of the high priest Joshua – for he is not yet the one who can finally unite in himself both king and priest. The crown is taken from his head again and henceforth kept in the temple as a sacred token of the longed-for mystery. In direct connection with this Zechariah speaks for the second time of the 'Branch' that will one day 'branch out' (6:12).

Only Christ Jesus combines in the deepest sense sun-kingship with humble self-sacrifice. He is truly a king not *in spite of* but *because of* his offering of himself. When we sense the touch of his presence, then the old prophetic words of almost two and a half thousand years ago take on a new glory: 'Not by might, nor by power, but by my Spirit' (Zec 4:6).

13

THE SANCTUS OF THE SERAPHIM

If we see a shooting star suddenly appearing out of the darkness of the night sky and vanishing again into darkness after its brief, luminous trajectory, we know that such a phenomenon cannot be understood if we only think of its visible ray. What shines out for a moment has been underway beforehand, and afterwards continues, albeit unobservable by us.

The same is true in a higher sense of human life on earth. What unfolds between birth and death before our eyes is similarly only part of a further journey, a before and after invisible to our earthly senses.

Before Christianity allowed itself to succumb to materialism, it was a self-evident matter for it to regard the life of Jesus in this way. In the incarnation something became visible to earthly humanity that originated in a pre-existence unfolding in the supersensible. What was approaching in the supersensible realm could be discerned in the gaze of illumined spirit vision.

Three prophetic visions of this kind are especially striking in the Old Testament. Isaiah perceives the Lord within the circle of the worshipping Seraphim. Ezekiel beholds the Son of Man borne up by the Cherubim. And Daniel sees him coming in a cloud.

In this essay we will first consider the vision of Isaiah.

'I saw the Lord...'

The date can be determined – 740 BC, 'in the year when King Uzziah died'. At this auspicious time Rome was being founded, and a new era of human consciousness was beginning during which humanity was to mature sufficiently to encompass the I. What was developing at that time in Greco-Roman, as also in Hebrew culture, was destined to work its way from I experience to the 'higher I' by virtue of the God-become-man.

> In the year when King Uzziah died, I saw the Lord seated on a high and noble throne, and the train of his robe filled the temple. (Is 6:1)

He saw the 'Lord' (*adonai*), who is subsequently called 'Yahweh'. When we read in the Old Testament of 'Yahweh' (the LORD in most English translations) and of the 'Elohim' (a plural noun, though usually translated simply as 'God'), we are accustomed to thinking of the highest God, 'God Almighty', who in the New Testament is the 'Father of Jesus Christ'. But this is only true in a limited sense. For a spirit perception of specific beings of the world of spirit – as has become possible through anthroposophy – the Yahweh being, together with the Elohim, belongs to one of the nine orders of angels ('hierarchies'), dwelling in the higher worlds of the 'heavens' between the Three-in-One God and the kingdom of humankind. More specifically, these beings belong to the level of the Exousiai (Powers) above the Angels, Archangels and Archai (primal forces). But at the same time, Yahweh was for the Israelites a kind of window which, at special moments, granted them a view of the highest God. By the mediation of Yahweh and the Elohim, they were then able to experience a divine Father principle.

In the same way there are also occasions when the Son God, the Christ who has not yet descended to earth, can shine through Yahweh to be beheld by devout people of the Old Covenant. This is the case here with Isaiah's vision. The John Gospel refers to this explicitly, citing Isaiah's words and adding that the prophet heard this 'because he saw his [Christ's] glory of radiance; and it was of him [Christ] that he spoke' (Jn 12:41).

The Seraphim

The vision arises from an experience of the temple at Jerusalem. Seeing the temple with its architecture and its rites evidently kindled higher perception in Isaiah, drawing him into a different state of consciousness. The earthly temple broadens into a greater sphere. Above, a divine figure is enthroned, but in pious awe Isaiah speaks only of the flowing train of his robe which fills the temple. He casts his gaze downward in reverence then raises it again and is now drawn out to the wider reaches.

> Seraphim stood above it [the temple]. Each with six wings. With two he [the Seraph] covered his face. With two he covered his feet. With two he flew. (Is 6:2)

Christianity of the founding fathers, as recorded in the writings of Dionysius the Areopagite, assigns to the Seraphim the highest rank amongst the nine orders of angels, in immediate proximity to God. Their name, which means the 'burning ones', signifies that – as spirits of love – they blaze in the divine element of the holy fire of love. When Francis of Assisi received the mystical stigmata on Mount Alverno, he saw the Christ in the form of a Seraph. As the bearer of higher powers of love, Francis was a 'Seraphic' saint. During Faust's ascension, Goethe puts words about the food of the spirits – 'the eternal revelation of love' – in the mouth of Father Seraphicus.

In the different degrees of the hierarchies, the Seraphim are several ranks higher than the Exousiai, to whom Yahweh belongs. Nevertheless they pay homage to him, for here Yahweh is the bearer of Christ: the divine Son, high above, shines through him into the earthly world.

The three pairs of wings

Since the Seraphim stand closest to the highest Godhead their manifestation bears a reflection of the original Trinity in their three pairs of wings. It is clear that these are connected, respectively, with head, trunk and feet. In the head, conscious apprehension is focused, in the centre lives feeling in the pulse of heart and lungs, and in the lower body are seated the deep forces of the will.

With their upper pair of wings the Seraphim hide their countenance which – unveiled – would look directly into the Godhead itself. Thus even the highest beings of the hierarchies experience their power of cognition as unfit to behold the divine. God 'lives in unapproachable light' (1Tm 6:16). Only the once-born Son 'has seen the Father' (Jn 6:46).

With their lowest wings the Seraphim conceal their feet. They experience how, in relation to the primal will of the Godhead, they cannot allow the mighty forces of the depths of their will to be seen, as it were.

Only the middle pair of wings is unfolded fully. While unreachable in terms of its knowledge and power of will, in the element of love the Godhead entirely imparts itself. The middle pair of wings is assigned to the region of the heart.

The Sanctus

What began as beholding with spiritual eyes progresses further into hearing with spiritual ears, or Inspiration. The prophet hears the voice of the Seraphim and hearkens to their words.

> And one called to the other, 'Holy, holy, holy is the LORD of the heavenly hosts. All the earth is full of the glory of his being.' (Is 6:3)

Here again, a trinitarian quality comes to the fore through the direct proximity of the Seraphim to God. The 'three holies' was rightly seen by Christianity as one of the passages in the Old Testament that announces the mystery of the divine Trinity. Church Fathers used the word 'theology' for this praise by the Seraphim – 'the theology of the Seraphim'.* Here we can still sense the resonance which this word 'theology' once had, when it signified an utterance about the Godhead that was still entirely spiritually specific and tangible.

---

* Cyril of Jerusalem (*c.* 313–386), *Mystagogic Catecheses* 23.6; Pseudo-Dionysius, *Celestial Hierarchy* 7.4, *Ecclesiastical Hierarchy* 4.5.

It is specifically the spirits of love who announce the holiness of God. No doubt we human beings all experience 'love' as the very highest quality. But we cannot overlook the degree to which self-seeking is mingled with human love, and sullies it. The Seraphim live in love as it springs forth in purity from its primal fount – where it is indeed holy.

The thrice holy one is the 'Lord of the heavenly hosts', in Hebrew *tsabaoth*. This refers on the one hand to the hosts of the stars, but at the same time also to the spiritual beings of the hierarchies, whose luminous manifestation was originally clairvoyantly perceived in the shimmer of the stars. The thrice-holy one is discerned as immanent within supersensible worlds. This also underlies the formulation in the New Testament concerning the 'Father in the heavens'. And the returning Christ does not come without his accompanying retinue of holy angels.

The praise by the Seraphim not only celebrates heavenly things however. A light also falls upon the earth. 'All the earth is full of the glory of his being.' This glory is the radiance of his being, in which the earth is also to participate. The Christ of 'all the earth' is here announced.

'One to the other'

In the account by Isaiah, the 'Sanctus' is not really described as the singing of the choirs of the Seraphim. The text says that 'one called to the other'. This also conceals a mystery of love. Merely to 'become aware' of a significant spiritual thought is not yet sufficient. In the realm of higher discernment, the phrase 'I know that already' has little traction. Seekers of knowledge must continually let matters that they 'already know' pass again and again through the soul if they are to participate in a higher, spiritual vitality. Here it is of special value to hear from another again something that one 'already knows'. Having it said to us by another conscious witness can reveal to us what we already know in an entirely new light and in a previously unknown depth of experience. The communal life of the Seraphim is of such a kind. The three 'holies' are born ever and anew again in the uttering of it 'from one to the other'.

13. THE SANCTUS OF THE SERAPHIM

The commission

> And the doorposts and thresholds [of the temple] were shaken by the voice of their crying out, and the house was filled with smoke. And I said, 'Woe is me, for I perish.' (Is 6:4f)

Seeing and hearing, Isaiah is shaken to the depths of his human existence. Just as the beams of the temple quake at the power of the heavenly voices, so the prophet is convulsed by his experience. An ancient religious experience is renewed for him – whoever sees God must die. 'I am of unclean lips,' he says – something that he becomes directly aware of as he hears the heavenly words. At this one of the Seraphim approaches him and touches his lips with a burning coal from the temple altar to cleanse his speech, so that the words of the divine message can live upon his lips.

The prophet's experience has intensified from seeing to hearing through to direct encounter with a being, and now 'the Lord' himself speaks to him: 'Whom shall I send? And who will go for us?' Once again we are reminded of the mystery of the three-in-one, for the Godhead says both 'I' and 'we': 'whom shall *I* send' and 'who will go for *us*.' The 'we' of the wealth of being contained within God is first met in the Bible in the resolve, 'Let us create man.' We hear it also in the story of the building of the Tower of Babel – 'Come, let us go down there' (Gn 11:7). In the John Gospel 'I am' is, at certain culminating moments, superseded by a divine 'we' in which the Son becomes one with the Father (Jn 10:30, 17:11, 21f).

The Godhead asks, 'Whom shall I send?' And this gives the prophet the opportunity to respond to the call out of his own intrinsic being: 'Behold, here I am. Send me.' (Is 6:8).

14

THE FOUR LIVING CREATURES AND THE HUMAN BEING

THE VISION OF EZEKIEL

The evangelist John connects Isaiah's sublime vision of God with the pre-existent Christ who has not yet descended to earth (Jn 12:41). This is true also of the other great prophetic vision, granted to Ezekiel a century and a half after Isaiah. Ezekiel was a priest in Jerusalem and was sent away to Babylon in 597 BC in a deportation primarily affecting the Jewish 'intelligentsia'. There he lived with the other exiles in a settlement named Tel Abib beside the Chebar River, not far from Babylon. The city of Jerusalem and the temple of Solomon remained standing, but Ezekiel foresaw the disaster which then occurred in 586.

He had his great vision in June/July 593, in the open air beside the waters of the Chebar: 'The heavens opened and I saw visions of God' (Ezk 1:1).

The four living creatures

As in the story of Pentecost, the prophet's supersensible experience begins with a mighty storm and wind. His soul is loosened, drawn forth from everyday consciousness, and feels itself to be surrounded by the previously unknown powers of another world. Then a cloud appears, which brightens inwardly. His soul's eye opens to perceive a radiant region of fire. A supersensible 'space' has opened and out of its brilliance emerge figures. He more or less discerns four countenances: Human being – lion – bull – eagle. It should however be noted that these four living creatures as they are known, have a human quality,

14. THE FOUR LIVING CREATURES

'They had a human likeness' (1:5); and the human countenance precedes the others. With almost pedantic conscientiousness, Ezekiel's account emphasises the likeness, a resemblance that does not completely equate with reality. Despite the animal-like forms, we are concerned here with the 'human being'. All four creatures possess 'human hands' (1:8).

In these four figures people have recognised the four 'corners' of the circle of the twelve constellations of the zodiac: Lion (Leo), Bull (Taurus), Waterman (Aquarius, the human being) and Scorpion (instead of eagle). Together they form a cosmic cross of forces.

In the spirit vision of ancient times, the twelve constellations, through which sun, moon and planets travel, were experienced as force fields of creative beings. From this encompassing sphere people saw powers streaming towards the centre, their harmonious interplay enabling the human body to arise. The four 'corners' of this zodiac were felt to be particularly distinctive. Each of these creative realms emanates a particular power which – working alone – would be embodied in a one-sided grandeur. If the Eagle were active alone, the human being would become nothing but 'head' and thought. The Lion alone would make us into a feeling chest person, the Bull alone into a metabolic person weighed down by the earth. In the earthly creatures eagle, lion and bull we see a faint reflection of the magnificent one-sidedness of these different heavenly powers which, as they become embodied in the human being, have to be tempered and harmonised, as this is heralded already in the Waterman or Aquarius, the 'human' constellation. Thus the 'four living creatures' are the developing human being as formed and emerging from cosmic realms and powers.

The spirit beings who hold sway in this surrounding sphere of the stars are the Cherubim. Ezekiel notes precisely that it is on the occasion of his second vision, in the late summer of the same year, that he became aware, as if through inspiration, that the beings he perceived were Cherubim (Ezk 10:20).

In the angelic hierarchies, the Cherubim are the second highest after the Seraphim, who stand in God's immediate presence as fiery spirits of love. They are the wise spirits who harmonise the twelve one-sided realms of power. Ezekiel beholds them in connection with the evolution of the human being.

Dynamic world of forces

A characteristic of supersensible experience is the dynamic nature of what is perceived. A painter, even someone like Raphael, cannot capture this living movement.

The Cherubim move in a powerfully 'straight' manner. They 'ran back and forth like lightning' (1:14). At first their spirit-substance appears like 'burning coals of fire', then 'like torches', then like light moving with lightning rapidity (1:13f). Horizontal movement alternates with their occasional rising in vertical motion (1:19, 21). We can be reminded here of the words of the earth spirit in Goethe's *Faust:* 'I surge up and down, I weave back and forth.' The creative powers produce an etheric interplay of forces through a kind of eurythmy.

This weaving and hallowing in the highest sense is what, in Ezekiel's vision, the Cherubim are doing, hovering in the spiritual sphere that is to become the 'place' of human formation.

The motion and dynamic of the whole thing finds further and distinctive expression through the 'wheels' that become visible in connection with the four creatures. 'Behold, there was a wheel on the earth ... appearing like four wheels ... as if one wheel were within the other' (1:15f). These wheels are something like 'vortices' in the soul world, and at the same time organs of supersensible perception. The wheels are 'full of eyes' (1:18), which is a motif both of 'perception' and of 'stars', for just as eyes are stars so stars are also eyes. In his second vision, where Ezekiel learns that he is beholding Cherubim, he also hears in spirit the word *galgal* ('whirling wheel', 10:13). We know this word from the Gilgal stone circle, which was an image of supersensible circular movement, or gyres. In Novalis there is a picture of a 'wheel' in connection with a significant dream. Heinrich von Ofterdingen says, 'I feel that he acts in my soul like a broad wheel and drives it onward with mighty momentum.'*

It is clear from Ezekiel's repeated emphasis on the spirit of the living creatures being in the wheels that we are concerned here with a supersensible reality which the metaphor he uses can only very distantly convey to earthbound, mundane consciousness. The wheels move in

---

* *Heinrich von Ofterdingen,* Chapter 1

harmony with the Cherubim, who rise at the same time as they do when the upward motion occurs (1:19, 21). Everything in this vision is filled with a dynamic spiritual motion.

The human being

It is part of this spiritual dynamic, too – though this may initially appear paradoxical – that everything comes to an intermittent standstill. In the supersensible world, active movement is something higher than the stasis in which immobile material things 'simply exist'. In the world of substance we have the passive 'quiet of the grave' that is not to be found in the mobile world of soul and formative forces. Nevertheless, above this dynamic motion something like a sphere of tranquillity reigns, a peace of a higher kind, radiating from above from the self-contained I AM at rest within itself. This I AM is an eternal reality that endures through all change and transformation.

This sublime world of peace appears in Ezekiel's vision as the 'firmament of awesome crystal' above the figures of the Cherubim (1:22). In connection with the appearance of this in his field of spiritual sight, Ezekiel also perceives the 'standstill'. 'When they stood still, they lowered their wings. And in the firmament above them it thundered, whenever they stood still and lowered their wings.' (1:24f). In other words, these moments of stillness have nothing to do with our dull, material stasis, but instead convey a conscious suppression of motion for the sake of something even higher that descends from above and for which their deliberate immobility is a receptive organ. The stillness and lack of movement becomes an intent listening to what resounds from above.

With the cessation of movement, the roaring like a 'rushing of great waters' (1:24) which accompanies the 'back and forth' and the 'upward and downward' motions of their weaving and hallowing, also falls silent. This roaring is sound of a supersensible kind, but it ceases for the sake of a still higher, resounding influx from that firmament of tranquillity which is heard as the voice 'thundering'.

With this, Ezekiel's narrative reaches its culmination. Above the firmament, in sapphire blue, a throne becomes visible. 'And upon the throne sat a likeness with a human appearance' (1:26). The loftiest

Godhead to which the prophet's intuiting vision can raise itself, appears in human image.

> And I saw, as if luminous, and inwardly with the appearance of fire all around. From above and below his loins I saw it shining brightly like fire all around. Like the rainbow in the clouds on a rainy day, it shone and shimmered. Thus was the appearance of the likeness of the glory of the LORD. And upon seeing it I fell upon my face and heard a voice of one speaking.' (1:27f)

The four living creatures, as we saw, have an inherently 'human' quality. In the harmony of the diverse forces of the stars, the human body is formed out of the cosmos. But in the enthroned Godhead appears, once again, something 'in form like a human being' which, as higher, heavenly human being, is nobler than the four creatures of human aspect. It is as it were the divine archetype of the human being. The one who has apparelled himself in this sublime archetype is not God the Father but God the Son. He is the pre-existent Christ on his way to earthly incarnation, who has initiated his becoming human by clothing himself in the divine human archetype. Thus Ezekiel could have said: *ecce homo* – behold, the man.

Temple symbolism

In the fullness of time, the heavenly human being will assume flesh in the earthly human being, and then this earthly man will become the 'place' of God's habitation. Significant words of this 'place' of God sound forth in the hymn which the Cherubim now sing. Isaiah hears the Seraphim sing of the sanctity of the Lord. Ezekiel hears the Cherubim singing, 'Praised be the glory of the LORD from its *place*' (3:12).

The temple of Solomon in Jerusalem was the prophetic earthly image of this future habitation. It is this temple that is destroyed in the year 586 BC: Ezekiel experiences this 'telepathically' from Babylon. But before this happens, in the late summer of 593, he has his second great vision of the Cherubim. At the same time, however, he sees himself wrenched from his body and transported to far-off Jerusalem. What he beholds is the prelude to the destruction of the temple: the divine glory which had inhabited the temple from Solomon's time now departs from this place assigned to downfall.

> The Cherubim lifted their wings, with the wheels beside them, and the glory of the God of Israel was over them. And the glory of the LORD rose from the city and stood on the mountain that lies to the east of the city [the Mount of Olives]. (11:22f)

Ezekiel has a third great vision: in 572, fourteen years after the destruction of city and temple, he beholds an apocalyptic future image of a new Jerusalem and a new temple into which the divine glory re-enters, seated upon the chariot throne of the four Cherubinic creatures.

> The vision I saw was just like the vision I had seen when he came to destroy the city, and just like the vision I had seen at the Chebar River. Then I fell on my face. And the glory of the LORD entered the temple through the gate facing east ... and behold, the glory of the LORD filled the temple. (43:3–5)

Ezekiel remains within the world of images of Jewish tradition, yet the future Christ event already shimmers through. It will not be about the temple in Jerusalem but about the 'temple of his body' (Jn 2:21). Upon this body will fall the destiny of destruction and rebuilding. At Easter, Christ will finally and ultimately enter through the eastern, morning gateway into the temple of resurrection, into the human body that has passed through transformation, whereupon the being of humanity will become to the fullest degree the 'place of God'. In premonition of this future, Ezekiel hears the words, 'Son of Man, this is the place of my throne' (43:7). He hears the new Jerusalem receiving the name, 'There is the LORD' (48:35) – the concluding words of the Book of Ezekiel.

The Book of Ezekiel begins, 'In the thirtieth year'. No doubt this refers to the age of the prophet when he had his first great vision. It is also the age of Jesus when he received the heavenly human being into himself at the Jordan baptism. Both Origen and Augustine refer to a Jewish tradition according to which pupils of mystery knowledge needed to have reached the age of thirty before they were allowed to immerse themselves in meditation upon these visions of Ezekiel. For the Kabbalists, who sought the deeper meaning of the Old Testament, the four Cherubinic creatures, whom they called the chariot (the *merkabah*), were a central preoccupation alongside the story of creation, and many profound things were addressed in this context. But the most important thing of all is that Ezekiel was granted a vision of the approaching Christ, the *archetypal human being* seeking his place on earth.

15

THE BEASTS OF THE ABYSS AND THE SON OF MAN

THE NIGHT-TIME VISION OF DANIEL

Alongside the Seraphim vision of Isaiah and the Cherubim experience of Ezekiel, the night-time vision described in Chapter 7 of the Book of Daniel is the third great prophetic vision to announce the approach of Christ.

At the beginning and end of this account, as it were signing it with his own personal responsibility, stand the words 'I, Daniel'. This is a mode of speech that gives us a sense of the dawning of a new era of consciousness in the Bible. Isaiah and Ezekiel likewise recorded their experiences in a narrative written in the first person, which they themselves vouch for. With Daniel we enter an intrinsically 'apocalyptic' realm in which secrets of the future of humanity – its glory but also its terrible catastrophes – are revealed. The beholder of the vision requires a bright, strong awareness of self to encounter these pictures. Later, in the same way, the Revelation to John, the Apocalypse, is framed with the formula 'I, John' (1:9, 22:8). Like a mighty, breathtaking, waking dream, the images of Chapter 7 of Daniel pass before us, yet these pictures are borne by a powerful awareness of I: 'I, Daniel' (7:15, 28).

The first three beasts

Lion, eagle and bull in Ezekiel's vision are not in fact animals, but are called 'living creatures'. In the Septuagint, the Greek translation, this is rendered by the word *zōon*. These are stellar, cosmic powers that shine into human evolution from the high heavens, nobler and loftier than earthly zoology which can embody only a very distant and weak reflection of them. By contrast, the beasts which Daniel beholds rising from the sea are entities that come not from above but act from below. These beasts in Daniel are rightly translated into Greek not as *zōon*, but *therion*. The Latin retains the same distinction, between *animal* and *bestia*. This is true too in the Apocalypse of John where *zōon* is used for the Cherubinic beings of heaven (4:6) while *therion* is used for the abysmal figures (13:1). In Daniel's night-time vision, therefore, the word 'beast' is appropriate – a word resonant of demonic qualities that cast their shadow from beyond nature, from regions below it, into the zoological realm. Unlike the Cherubim in Ezekiel, these beings do not appear from above but rise out of the lightless depths of a storm-whipped ocean. A further distinction from Ezekiel is that they do not all appear at once but one after the other, so that the 'story' has a noticeable temporal sequence.

An intensification through this sequence is unmistakable – a gathering intensity of eerie bestiality. The first beast appears relatively harmless, and can even be rendered to some degree human again. This can no longer be said of the second beast, with its dull, brutal lustfulness. The third displays a panther-like aggression and a head-type alertness and supple energy. As higher capacities are subsumed into the bestial, and serve it, their danger grows.

Nineteenth-century materialism began by seeking the origin of humankind in the animal. In reality, the animal is not our starting point but it could become our future, evil potential. What is intrinsically human originates in the primordial light but has been darkened by a growing admixture of soul and spirit nature that contests the divine. The human face is, to put it in terms of the Cain narrative, threatened by distortion (Gn 4:5f – a 'fallen countenance' in many translations). Daniel saw evil future capacities of this kind rising from the abyss. Even if, in his day, interpretations of such perceptions were initially bound up with antiquity's succession of 'world ages' – to which they may also refer – such visions nevertheless contain a far broader scope of significance and cannot be confined to narrower temporal correspondences.

The fourth beast

Daniel's account makes a special distinction between the three preceding beasts and the fourth by once again introducing the repeating formula of the 'vision by night', which figures three times in the chapter (Dn 7:2, 7, 13). This time all zoological affinities would be too weak to give an apt impression of the beast. Instead a whole range of adjectives – 'dreadful', 'terrifying', 'exceedingly strong' – try to convey its uncanny and sinister nature. Only 'teeth' and 'claws' are still conjured, but otherwise the 'animal' qualities are negatively 'surpassed' in that the teeth are of 'iron' and the claws of 'bronze' (Dn 7:19). 'Iron and brass' are first mentioned in the Bible in the Cain chapter (Gn 4:22). Awakening earth intelligence thus constructs for itself its own, new world, from whose beginnings the world of technology will later emerge. The words spoken by the Godhead to Cain can also be related to this awesome yet dangerous force: 'But you must rule over it' (Gn 4:7). If such powers exceed a human scope, then terrible destructive potential will arise. These are evil future capacities announcing themselves in this combination of 'animal' and 'iron-bronze': animal drives appear combined with a high degree of intellectualism. Excluding the heart centre, head and lower body are coupled directly. Cleverly conceived and refined weapons serve hatred; a desire to torture and torment can, today, employ highly intelligent methods. The destructive power of this beast is described in drastic fashion: 'It devoured and broke into pieces and trampled what was left with its feet.'

'Iron and bronze' are important. Genesis calls Thubal-Cain, the son of Cain, 'forger in all instruments of bronze and iron' (Gn 4:22). It is a significant feature of the biblical account that the fratricide Cain is not punished or annihilated by divine judgment. The 'mark of Cain' that is laid upon him is in fact to make him safe 'so that no one would kill him' (Gn 4:15). In the power of Cain, even if this acts very destructively following the Fall, God sees a potency that can be important for the future. This power should not simply vanish from the world but should be preserved for future transformation and, until then, be endured.

In this context it may be significant that the power of Cain proves necessary for building the temple of Solomon. Through the master builder Hiram this power decisively benefits its construction. Hiram came from Tyre and was the son of a widow. The king of Tyre calls him his spiritual 'father' (*Huram-Abi,* 2Ch 2:13, 4:16). He was 'a master in bronze, full of wisdom, understanding and skilled in all works of bronze' (1K 7:14). It was he who created the two pillars of bronze, Jachin and Boaz, the bronze sea with the twelve bulls, and various other temple artefacts (1K 7:15–46). The Cain power can work in the service of the divine. In the Apocalypse of the New Testament, there are three references to the 'iron rod' which is now found in the hand of Christ (Rv 2:27, 12:5, 19:15). The power of iron, which of course also plays an important role in human blood, can be mastered in service of the divine, and this would signify Cain's redemption. But since the influence of Christ is entirely dependent on human free will, and is not imposed upon humanity, it is possible for the fallen power of Cain to continue to serve negative uses, and to increasingly act with destructive and fratricidal effect. This is the characteristic of the fourth beast in Daniel's night-time vision, with its 'iron teeth and brass claws'.

The Cherubinic figures of Ezekiel, despite their allegorical animal affinities, clearly bear the sign of being human. But with the fourth beast in Daniel's vision, by contrast, the wrongness implicit in the combination of animal nature and technology is further exacerbated into a sinister quality through certain traits drawn from the image of the human being. Here, in this context that is so far removed from the truly human, they not only seem misplaced but invoke a sense of dreadful alienation. Human eyes, human mouth, human speech – these appear as locked into this sub-human world and enslaved by it. The beast's mouth or muzzle 'speaks great things'. In the original Hebrew no distinction can be made between a human and an animal mouth, but a human mouth is surely meant, for it can speak. The gift of speech that gives humanity an affinity with the cosmic Word, the Logos, is misused in the service of the sub-human, through which it becomes 'grandiloquent' propaganda for anti-divine powers.

In the interpretation that follows the vision itself, a further element is added. The fourth beast, it is said there, 'intends to alter time and law'. It also acts in a culturally destructive way in that it intervenes in the sacred festival calendar that depends upon insight into cosmic laws.

The fiery throne

The evils deeds of the fourth beast finally call forth a reaction from divine cosmic justice. A scene of judgment appears before the seer's eye (Dn 7:9). 'Thrones are set out' as for a board of judges. But in the vision this recedes again before the One who now appears as the great master-judge. Here the text does not use one of the designations for God otherwise usual in the Old Testament – Elohim (God) or Yahweh (the LORD) – but instead the expression the 'Ancient of Days'. He is the primordial figure before whom have passed all world days there have ever been, all aeons of time. His clothes and hair are white as snow. This snow-whiteness of the highest, purest spirituality contrasts wonderfully with the red flame of blazing fire as revelation of the most sacred love united with the purest wisdom. This union of white and red points as if from afar to an unspeakably divine quality.

The throne of the Ancient of Days is pure fire, and the wheels of the throne – which can remind us also of the wheels in Ezekiel's vision – 'burned with fire'. Besides this, a long, fiery stream becomes visible, issuing from the throne (7:10). This fire streaming out from the throne of the Ancient One takes us back to the very beginnings of the world. The vision of Daniel coincides with the findings of Rudolf Steiner of the first beginnings of the world's creation. He describes an out-streaming of fiery will substance through the power of divine sacrifice. In this primordial sacrifice upon which all future cosmic existence is founded, the Godhead employs a sublime angelic realm which, together with Cherubim and Seraphim, forms an uppermost triad in the angelic hierarchies. These lofty beings are known in Christian tradition as 'Thrones', and, along with other angelic orders, are cited by Paul in his Letter to the Colossians (1:16). In a sense they 'carry' the Ancient One. What appears in pictorial vision as an object – the throne – is in the world of spirit, which knows no objects but only beings, a living spiritual being. From this throne being issues the fire stream of God's fundamental sacrifice.

Surrounding the throne the seer perceives innumerable hosts of angels (7:10). 'The court sat in judgment and the books were opened.' At the primal beginning what was subsequently done in the unfolding cosmos upon the given foundations of existence is measured and judged. The opening books are the divine, cosmic memory which preserves all records of everything that occurs for all eternity.

Into this festive scene, like a shrill disharmony, the grandiloquent speech of the fourth beast once more penetrates, but its vacuity is now inevitably revealed, and it must fall silent. In relation to the primordial power of creation, the beast can no longer perpetuate its existence, and is consumed in the primal fire.

The Son of Man

Now the gaze becomes free for something quite new. The seer, who has had to behold so much of a subhuman nature, has thereby become all the more receptive for true human value and authentic human dignity. If the clairvoyant gaze had not stood firm at the sight of evil, it would now lack what is necessary when it comes to discern the Christ appearing in the form of the Son of Man.

Daniel's account begins again, for a third time: 'I saw in this nighttime vision' (7:13). The Son of Man appears in the 'clouds of heaven'. The continually forming and transforming clouds are an image of possibilities still open in the encircling sphere of our otherwise fixed and finished earth. The atmosphere with its clouds also belongs to the entirety of the earth, as the part of this whole from whose mobile substantiality everything can still grow and develop, a realm that can still be infused with the rays and streams descending from heavenly worlds. Out of this sphere of still hovering future possibilities, Daniel beholds the Son of Man approaching.

The cloud bears the Son to the Ancient One upon his throne, who passes to him 'sovereignty, glory and kingdom'. Something of great significance occurs here within divine relationships: the Godhead can embark upon new revelations and modes of action once the human being, with his predisposition for freedom in the image of God, has entered upon world existence. By virtue of the existence of the human being, the Godhead acquires new possibilities, and finds 'new land' in the human kingdom. The ancient times of the world stood above all in the sign of the Father God; now the hour has come for the divine in the figure of the Son. The divine Son nature has embarked upon a close connection with the human being, appearing now both as God's son and the Son of Man.

The Ancient One passes to the Son of Man a share in the power of the throne. This vision becomes reality at Christ's Ascension; from then onward he is 'seated at the right hand of the Father'. In the Creed of The Christian Community, this picture is translated into more of a thought element: 'He lives as the fulfiller of the fatherly deeds of the Ground of the World.' Christ, who was initially active within human souls, is now also served by the Throne powers, the deeply concealed Father powers that extend right into the mysteries of body and substance. Everything that can be called transformation of substance in terms of 'transubstantiation' belongs here. The inwardness of Christ acquires the capacity to reach right into body and blood. In the Revelation to John, Christ says at the conclusion of the letters to the seven churches, 'as I also overcame and sat down with my Father on his throne' (3:21).

The kingdom of the Son of Man, as Daniel beheld it, allows a new, universal humanity to arise, beyond all divisions of race and language (7:14). Here a prospect unfolds of the future workings of the Holy Spirit. Daniel calls the human beings of this coming kingdom, which will finally supersede the kingdom of the beasts, the 'holy people of the Most High' (7:27). The first Christians also called themselves 'the holy people'. This was not meant in any supercilious way: they were fully aware of their deficiencies, but with this name they wished to express that by being Christians a higher humanity had at least begun to live in them.

The fully conscious spirituality of the seer, which enables him to speak the words 'I, Daniel', is also apparent in the fact that the beginning and end of his account are precisely indicated, for the capacity to start and conclude something consciously also derives from a person's innate power. The account begins, 'Beginning of the words' (7:1, literally, often translated as the 'main facts' or similarly), and ends accordingly, 'Here is the end of the matter' (7:28).

No greater esteem could have been accorded Daniel's vision of the coming Son of Man than it was by Christ, at the moment of his solemn self-confession before the Sanhedrin, when he used the very words first coined by Daniel, recognising himself in the figure of the Son of Man appearing in the clouds (Mt 26:64).

16

'THE SUN OF RIGHTEOUSNESS'

In John the Baptist the gospels see a fulfilment of the words, 'Behold, I send my angel [or messenger] and he shall prepare the way before my face.' This comes from Malachi, the last of the prophets cited in the Old Testament. The Book of Malachi ('Malachi' means 'my angel') concludes the writings of the prophets, and, in turn, at the end of this conclusion, we find a reference to the coming 'Sun of Righteousness' (4:2).

The prophet was writing in the fifth century BC. After the return from Babylonian exile, the temple had risen again from its ruins, albeit in far more modest appearance. Reading the Book of Malachi, which contains only a few chapters, we first see the prophet preoccupied with the distress and difficulties of that time. Above all he is calling upon the conscience of the priests who do not serve the rites in an adequate way. Their worship lacks purity. What rises from the altars cannot find favour with God. But this is not just a matter of affairs in Jerusalem at the time, of a particular historical context, but of the whole situation for humanity that weighs upon the prophet's soul. The connection with the heavens is increasingly fading. Earthbound humanity cannot draw from within itself the power of sacrificial offering to open the heavens.

It is this suffering that awakens the prophet's visionary perception and enables him to utter a magnificent prophecy. He intuits the descent of God, who will himself now become an earthly human being so as to reunite the realm below with the realm above through a divine-human deed upon earth. Since fallen humanity is no longer able to make sacrificial offering to the heavens in a way that opens and accesses them, God himself assumes human vestment, entering into the human realm so as to make this redemptive offering from the earth. As Christians we see how the pure and perfect sacrifice of Golgotha pours its active influences into Christian service at the altar. The service is not bound to time or place, but is to include all humanity in its offering. In the bread and wine of the Last Supper we find a fulfilment of what Malachi saw before his prophetic gaze:

> From the rising of the sun to its setting, my name will be great among the peoples of the world. And in every place incense will be offered in my name, and a pure food offering. (1:11)

All peoples – every place. In Christ, God will announce his 'name', will say who he is. Discerning recognition of this 'name' at the same time draws forth the soul's deeper powers, imaged in the rising incense of prayer and worship. It is significant that the sun motif appears here, at this annunciation of the universal 'pure food offering': *From the rising of the sun to its setting.*

Following words at the beginning of Chapter 3 about the angel or messenger which the Lord will send before him, and about the coming of the Lord 'to his temple' in a no longer distant future – which in fact points to his incarnation in an earthly body – the Book of Malachi then increasingly invokes apocalyptic prospects. The 'day' of the Lord will dawn. This culminates in that monumental sentence which seals the Old Testament with the power of the sun at the end of all its prophecies:

> But for you, you hold my name in reverence and awe, the |Sun of Righteousness will rise with healing in its wings. (4:2)

'Righteousness' does not mean 'correct conduct' here, acting in accordance with the laws; it is not to be understood here in the abstract but rather, as elsewhere in the Bible, as antecedent to all 'laws', as their precondition and firm foundation. Divine righteousness is the living harmony that permeates everything and makes all accord with everything else, makes possible the existence of a manifold universe of harmony. In the sun, which people still beheld in its spiritual nature in those days, they saw the most glorious manifestation of this righteousness. Christ, as God become man, bears this solar righteousness into the realm of earthly humankind.

'With healing in its wings.' Doing justice to such a phrase in the Bible requires more than a reference to the culture of antiquity, in which images existed of a winged sun-disc. We have to search for the truth underlying this mythological image. Perhaps we can come closer to such a truth if we go back to the roots of that word 'wing' and find in it something of its original relationship with 'blowing wind' and a swinging motion or oscillation, and with the mysteries of rhythmically dynamic cosmic substance. The Sun of Righteousness does not lay down abstract laws but breathes and pulses through all existence in the rhythms of higher life. Because of this it can exert a truly healing effect upon all that has alienated itself from the sacred order of the divine. The Hebrew word means 'healing' in its literal sense, reproduced in the Latin as *sanitas*.

With this reference to the mysteries of the Christ being as sun and life, the Old Testament grows beyond itself and points onward to the New Testament. The gospels show us the transfigured Christ whose countenance shone like the *sun* (Mt 17:2). As if in a deep, pictorial order, this Christ-sun is joined on either side by Moses and Elijah, between whom the Sun-Christ stands as centre and mediator. *Moses*, looking back to the creation of the world, gives the law as a conceptual embodiment of primordially divine life. He is the bridge to the past. *Elijah*, who was regarded as the inspiration presiding over all prophetic vision, opens an apocalyptic gaze towards all that will come, towards world end and world fulfilment. Thus the Sun of Christ stands as present between world beginning and world end.

It is this same archetypal triad that we find at the end of the Book of Malachi. The words about the 'Sun of Righteousness' are followed by a reference to Moses: 'Call to mind the laws of Moses, my servant.' And immediately afterwards, 'Behold, I will send you the prophet Elijah' (4:4f). In the Hebrew original, the word translated as 'I' is given in its emphatic and greater form, *anokhi*: I myself will send you Elijah. What is outwardly revealed in the 'sun' is heard here speaking from within in this mighty I.

Malachi, the last of the prophets, and Matthew, the first of the evangelists: the bridge that joins them is this revelation of the solar being of Christ.

III

TREES, WELLS AND STONES IN THE LIVES OF THE PATRIARCHS

17

THE FAIRY-TALE NATURE OF THE STORIES OF THE PATRIARCHS

The stories of the patriarchs in the Old Testament continually exert a very special magic. This is not only because, when we were children, they perhaps impressed themselves upon our still fresh soul and are now bound up with our memory of childhood. These tales become so dear and precious to us not only for reasons to do with our own personal sensibility, but because they also contain something of the memory of the childhood of humanity itself. Humanity today as a whole is more or less 'grown up', but it once had a childhood, a time when it was still close to the invisible realm in a naive and natural way. Something of this magic of dawn, of humanity's childhood, lives in the patriarch narratives of the first book of the Bible.

But it cannot be denied that there is no lack of human frailty and culpability in these stories. Besides the purity of dawn, the Fall of Adam already casts very dark shadows. But at the same time there is still so much of the legacy of paradise.

As modern people of the scientific age, it is impossible for us to take literally the accounts of the garden of Eden and the serpent which tempted Adam and Eve. But we surrender nothing of our scientific outlook by acknowledging that there are other and higher forms of consciousness, in which truths can be clairvoyantly perceived in images. In the same way as with significant dreams, one then needs to translate these images into a conceptual language. The picture alone cannot be regarded as sufficient: it is, rather, like a window through which we must gaze. The picture of the garden of paradise no doubt stood in luminous and vivid colour before the souls of those with whom the Bible originated – it was an authentic and direct revelation, but one embodied in a pictorial language whose meaning we first need to decipher.

We would be entering the realm of superstition if we were to assume that a material, zoological serpent entwined itself around a material, botanical tree. But we touch upon a significant and weighty truth the moment we realise the reality these images express: that humankind originally lived in intimate proximity to God, and that this close union was lost when, as it were, the germs of egoism were inoculated into the human soul by demonic influence. Before being thus alienated from our divine source, we were in a true state of human childhood. But the Fall did not occur all of a sudden. This revelatory, poeticised picture of the expulsion from the garden of Eden was, in its earthly reality, a process that took lengthy eras, passing through many stages and some relapses along the way. Thus an after-glimmer of lost paradise could repeatedly surface in the history of humanity. For this reason, we can still sense in these tales the early dawn of humanity's childhood – no longer fully and unsullied, but as a reflected gleam at least.

This shimmer of paradise can be experienced in the tales of the patriarchs, above all where nature is included in the sacred events they relate. It was implicit in humankind's original connection with God that nature was as yet transparent and permeable for divine influence. In the stories of Abraham, for instance, it is striking that trees repeatedly play an important role. Similarly, wells or springs are important for Isaac, and stones for Jacob. The stylised nature of the tales means that it becomes impossible to overlook these leitmotifs once we have recognised them.

18

ABRAHAM AND THE TREES

The ancient peoples knew about sacred trees. They knew of meetings with the unseen world which had taken place under such trees and in consecrated groves. The picture-vision of Genesis sees Adam, not yet separated from God, walking under the trees of the garden of Eden.

An old and mighty tree is venerable and marvellous. Its roots reach deep down into the dark earth. Its lofty stem towers high in kingly pride. This upward striving entity is not short-lived like the flame which darts up only to sink back into itself again; the tree stands steadfast and enduring. In it there is something of the long will of eternity. Decades and centuries have inscribed their rings inside its bark. This calm, steady, dependable being awakens trust, one puts faith in it. Its power to grow upward becomes a power to uphold. The branches spread on all sides, and form a vault over the piece of earth below. The tree's silent strength spreads over human heads – a rustling, whispering heaven, in which the wind celebrates the mysteries of its secret, invisible being.

The oak at Shechem

Such an ancient holy tree is at the consecrated place of Shechem (which is later called Samaria). Abraham's first stop in the Promised Land is at the 'oak of Shechem'.

He has obeyed God's voice, which has laid stern commands upon him. He has left behind him the temples of Ur and of Haran, the places of Chaldean wisdom of moon and stars. Now for the first time he treads the soil of the country which God has shown him, which is to become the scene of the events of Christ's life on earth.

Today we regard 'making a journey' purely from the practical point of view of getting from A to B; at most we might consider those travelling and the sights they are to see. But we could look at it from another point of view: what does it mean for the landscape that human beings walk through it. Not only does the visible, material part of a human being affect the surroundings, but those people's inner soul-spiritual being is connected through the fine ethereal life-forces to the whole of nature around them. There is an interplay between the invisible in humans and in nature of which we are usually quite unaware. Goethe's words, 'the place a good man visits is hallowed,' are much truer than we might think at first. A landscape is affected by the people passing through it: something is left in the 'aura' of that area. Thus there are sanctuaries where the fine ethereal 'footprints' of a great and good person can still be felt in the invisible weaving of forces for a long time afterwards. There are also places which are cursed.

The Holy Land is prepared for the coming of the Christ a long time before the event. Part of this preparation is the journeying of the patriarchs. The first who takes on this task of 'consecrating' the land is Abraham. His wanderings follow not only the necessities of a more or less nomadic existence, but follow divine command: 'Arise, walk through the length and the breadth of the land, for I give it to you' (Gn 13:17). His wanderings to the north and south, east and west describe a great cross which is spiritually impregnated into the land.

The way in which he walks there shows that his wanderings are determined by a hidden spiritual geography of the holy places. Conscious of his goal, Abraham passed on to Shechem without delay and made his first resting place in the Promised Land beside the ancient oak, which was already regarded as sacred by the Canaanites.

At this consecrated oak of Shechem he was permitted to behold God for the first time in the new land. In remembrance of it he built an altar there. The ritual of sacrifice would henceforth maintain and foster a living union with the divinity which had revealed itself there. The Bible tells of other altars built by the patriarch, but it is not unimportant that this building of altars began under the oak of Shechem, or that this first place of sacrifice made by Abraham was blessed by a sacred tree.

18. ABRAHAM AND THE TREES

> When they came to the land of Canaan, Abram passed through the land to the place at Shechem, to the oak of Moreh. At that time the Canaanites were in the land. Then the LORD appeared to Abram and said, 'To your descendants I will give this land.' So he built there an altar to the LORD, who had appeared to him. (Gn 12:5–7)

In Hebrew the word 'place' (*maqom*) has a special significance. It is not only a 'place' in the ordinary sense, but implies a special sanctuary. So 'the place at Shechem' is an ancient holy site. On closer research these ancient holy places are often found to have been special since time immemorial. Often the place of Christian pilgrimage was a heathen sanctuary. Such sites remain holy through the changes of time and religion. This can also be seen in the Bible. The holy places of the Israelites were Canaanite sanctuaries before, and were simply incorporated into the new religion. Abraham must have known of the sanctuary at Shechem when he came from Babylonia in the east and 'passed through the land to the place at Shechem, to the oak of Moreh'.

The oak of Moreh could be called 'the oak of the master teacher'. In this name lies the memory of a wise man who perhaps dwelt beneath this oak long before Abraham's arrival. People must have come to this hermit to seek his wisdom. But we should not imagine that the place became holy through this sage. He will have been attracted to the place because it was special before. His presence will have added to its atmosphere.

At this place Abraham stayed for a longer time. There he received his first divine revelation. The locality will have helped this experience, for a revelation can come closer in the fine atmosphere of a sanctuary. Abraham responds to the revelation by building an altar. In the offering ritual the connection to the divine is maintained. True ritual is originally always connected with divine revelation; it has grown out of it, and it seeks to re-establish the relationship to the divine.

Later we hear again, in passing, of the sacred oak. When, at the divine command, Jacob begins to build an altar at Bethel, he first makes his followers purify themselves from the images of the heathen cults, and buries statues of the gods and heathen amulets under the oak of Shechem (Gn 35:4).

Again, after the conquest of the Promised Land, when Joshua holds a great assembly of the tribes in Shechem, he knows of no worthier place for the stone pillar, which he sets up in remembrance of the renewal of the covenant, than 'under the oak in the sanctuary of the LORD' (Jsh 24:26).

The decadence of the Canaanite religion brought with it all kinds of magical arts. These were practised at this sacred place, and the tree of Shechem became known as the 'magic oak' or the 'oak of the diviners' (Jg 9:37).

The grove of Mamre

When he returned from his journey to Egypt, Abraham chose as his dwelling place for a considerable time the oak grove of Mamre by Hebron.

This grove also had been previously discovered by Abraham to be an ancient holy place. The Jewish writer Josephus, who lived in the first Christian century, tells of an oak of Ogyges which was pointed out there. Ogyges – this name points back to mythical ages. Phoenician tradition speaks of a mythical king of the Titans who bore this name. This connection is also indicated by the other name which Hebron bore, Kiriath-Arba, the town of Arba (Gn 23:2). Arba was said to have been the ancestor of the Titans. Thus this place is haunted by secrets of past races of giants, who did not yet feel themselves to be limited and enclosed by the skin of the compact, earthly, human body.

Mamre, the owner of the grove of like name, must have been a kind of guardian of this place of the mysteries. He was obviously the leader among three brothers (Mamre, Eshcol, and Aner). With these three brothers Abraham had made an alliance (Gn 14:13).

This taking up of his abode in the grove of Mamre was no casual event. Abraham built there an altar. That was done only in consecrated places,

> So Abraham ... settled by the oaks of Mamre, which are at Hebron, and there he built an altar to the LORD. (Gn 13:18)

18. ABRAHAM AND THE TREES

One of the most solemn events in Abraham's life was his meeting with Melchizedek, the priest-king of Salem, who gave him bread and wine, thus prophesying the institution of the Lord's Supper. So there fell upon the patriarch a ray from Christ's kingdom of the sun which was now drawing near (compare Hb 7:3). That this event occurs during Abraham's stay in Mamre is not without significance; for the place where one meets an important event is always significant, as is the place to which one goes after the event, when the soul is still filled with the experience. An experience needs a preparation for it, then, after it has occurred, it leaves its echo behind and works itself out to its fulfilment. The place where Abraham experienced the preparation for, and the sequel of, this visit of Melchizedek was the grove of Mamre.

Following the meeting with Melchizedek there are three significant revelations of God to Abraham during his fourteen years at Mamre. The first, while he was still under the influence of this visit to Melchizedek, was when Abraham had the wonderful revelation of the stars. God himself, 'brought him outside' and showed him the stars (Gn 15:5). One sees many things, and yet never really 'sees' them until they are shown. Such a 'showing', which opened the eyes and awakened them to see visions, was the especial duty of the priest who dedicated the pupil in the old mysteries. Here the Godhead itself is the 'mystagogue' who leads his pupil on to vision. 'He brought him outside', is a saying which, in its mysterious matter-of-factness and simplicity, is equal to that other which says that God himself shut the ark behind Noah (Gn 7:16). He led Abraham 'out'. He took him outside the four walls of narrow everyday life; he removed the constraint of a consciousness which was merely earthly and said, 'Look towards heaven.' In the glory of the starry heavens which God showed him, the patriarch received the promise of posterity. Overarched by the vault of heaven, he felt in his heart the power of faith. 'And he believed in the Lord' (Gn 15:6).

His sojourn in the grove of Mamre may well have helped the soul of Abraham to grow ripe for this revelation of the stars.

The cosmos sometimes appeared to people of ancient times in the vision of the mighty tree of the gods, in whose boughs the shining stars hung, like golden fruit. What heaven did in large, they saw the tree do in image and parable as it overshadowed the earth with its vaulted branches and blessed it. As the cosmos is in the organism of streaming life, so also is the tree, which draws the sap of life into its most delicate branches. As the divine breath of the spirit breathes throughout the cosmos, so does the whispering wind blow through the leaves of the tree.

Although it is not expressly mentioned, yet, by the whole context, we are led to conclude that the grove of Mamre is the place where, in the second great revelation, Abraham received the promise of a son, Isaac. There the rite of circumcision was performed, and his new, changed name was given him. Abram and Sarai are henceforth called Abraham and Sarah. In both cases, the name is enriched by the addition of the same sound, the 'h', the consonant which is furthest from earth and nearest to heaven. It is the sound of the breath. Under the rustling of the trees of Mamre this breath of the blowing wind, of the spirit's breathing, enters by inspiration into both names.

But the third revelation given at Mamre reaches the highest point with the divine apparition in the form of the three men who sit at table with Abraham. The divine Trinity has come to him as guest. They appear to him in his ninety-ninth year to proclaim the birth of Isaac. It can hardly be a coincidence that the divine Trinity is revealed to the lonely old man at that point in his life when he is on the threshold of an experience of 'the son'. This revelation allows us to sense the mystery that God is not the 'alone', the 'all-one', but that the Triune is 'I' and 'we' at once. The birth of Isaac is the precondition for the patriarchal trinity of Abraham, Isaac, and Jacob. This threefoldness is a clear image of the Trinity which is only fully revealed in the coming of Christ.

The objection could be raised that it was not really the Trinity, but 'the LORD' and two angels. After the meal Abraham accompanies them for a short distance and then 'the LORD' remains with Abraham while the two others go on to Sodom. However, a careful perusal of the text does not give the impression that two of the three are servants, though they are not always acting together: sometimes it is only 'the LORD'. Textual criticism sees the careless editing of two different sources. Rather than examining such a hypothesis, we would do better to look at the text. We see a rhythmic alternation between the singular and the plural:

18. ABRAHAM AND THE TREES

Singular	*Plural*
And the Lord appeared to him (18:1)	
	... and behold, three men stood in front of him. ... he ran to meet them (18:2)
'My Lord, if I have found favour in your [thy] sight ...' (18:3)	
	'Let a little water be brought and wash your [plural] feet, and rest yourselves under the tree ...' So they said ... And he stood by them under the tree while they ate. They said to him, "Where is Sarah ...' (18:4–9)
The Lord said, 'I will surely return to you ... and Sarah your wife shall have a son.' ... He [the Lord] said, 'No, but you did laugh.' (18:10–15)	
	Then the men set out from there, and they looked down towards Sodom. (18:16)
The Lord said, 'Shall I hide from Abraham what I am about to do ...' (18:17–21)	
	So the men turned from there, and went towards Sodom; (18:22a)
but Abraham still stood before the Lord.* (18:22b–33)	

* 'The men turned from there' does not imply only two. The Lord himself says, 'I will go down to see ...' It is as if the three depart together. When it goes on to say 'but Abraham stood before the Lord,' we must not forget that the whole description is a revelation, and these imaginative events do not obey the pragmatic logic of the everyday world. It may be that Abraham 'saw' the departure of the three and subsequently 'spoke' with the 'one'.

We have the impression of a breathing in and breathing out in the one, the three, the one ... in three times three parts. A breathing of the mystery of the Three-in-One.

Into this tale, the motif of the tree is significantly woven. Not only does it begin by saying: 'And the LORD appeared to him by the oaks of Mamre,' (18:1) but in the course of the story we find this emphasised. Abraham says to his guests, 'rest yourselves under the tree,' (18:4), 'he stood by them under the tree while they ate' (18:8).

The ancient tree spread its holy shade over the divine meal.

This meal which a human being prepares for the Godhead is a complement of the archetypal religious experience that humanity is invited to God's table. Human beings have something to give to God. This reciprocity is expressed in Christ's words in the Apocalypse: 'And I will come in and eat with him, and he with me' (Rv 3:20).

The tree-planting in Beer-Sheba

But Isaac was not born in Hebron. Before his birth Abraham left the grove of Mamre and went into the land of the Philistines, to the place which was to be specially connected in future with his son Isaac: Beer-Sheba, the city of the well. As Hebron and the grove of Mamre is Abraham's town, so Beer-Sheba is the town of Isaac.

A symbolic event lets us see very clearly that in entering Beer-Sheba Abraham entered the future world, the world of the son.

> Abraham planted a tamarisk tree in Beer-Sheba, and called there on the name of the LORD, the Everlasting God. (Gn 21:33)

Until then we see Abraham under ancient trees; now in the city of his son, he plants a young tree. Jewish legends went so far as to place Abraham's tree as a tree of healing beside the tree of paradise where man fell into sin. 'The wise men say that because Adam ate of the Tree of Knowledge, he brought death into the world. But when Abraham came, he healed the world again by another tree.'* One may say this in

---

* Gorion, *Sagen der Juden*, 2.273.

all truth only of the cross of the Redeemer. Of him alone that is true which is said about the tree of Beer-Sheba. The Jewish sages regarded as fulfilment what was only prophecy. But in so far as it was true prophecy, they came near to attaining deep knowledge. The young tree of new healing was planted in the city of the son, in Beer-Sheba. This son is a prefiguration of the eternal Son who brings again to humankind the power of the Tree of Life in order to heal. Abraham's offering of Isaac upon Mount Moriah is an annunciation of Golgotha, as Christendom has always understood. Beer-Sheba is the place of preparation for the offering up of Isaac and the place where its immediate effect was felt. From Beer-Sheba, Abraham and Isaac went out to Moriah, and to Beer-Sheba they immediately afterwards returned. So the planting of the tree is a prophecy of the Tree of Life, which by the sacrifice of the Son shall grow green for the healing of the world. Abraham is sometimes called a prophet (20:7); however, his prophecy does not lie in words, but in his deeds.

After this prophetic entry into the sphere of the Son, Abraham returns into his own world. He passes the last decades of his long patriarchal life at the grove of Mamre. There Sarah dies. There Abraham also dies. Their grave is the cave of Machpelah, which Abraham had brought from the Hittites, with the piece of ground belonging to it and 'all the trees that were in the field' (23:17).

19

ISAAC AND THE WELLS

While Abraham's real place of abode was the grove of Mamre, near Hebron, Isaac's abode is Beer-Sheba, the city of wells. 'Beer' means 'well'. Beer-Sheba means both 'seven wells' and 'the well of the oath'.

Beer-Sheba

After the birth of Isaac, Abraham dwelt for a time in Beer-Sheba where he had planted the tree. In so doing he came out of his own sphere of life and symbolically entered, as a prophet, the sphere of his son.

Just as the meeting with Melchizedek was enclosed by Abraham's stay in Mamre, so the journey to Mount Moriah and the sacrifice of Isaac was enclosed by his stay in Beer-Sheba. There in the night he received the call to sacrifice; there afterwards the experience continued its influence upon him. 'So Abraham returned to his servants, and they arose and went together to Beer-Sheba; and Abraham dwelt at Beer-Sheba' (Gn 22:19).

A remarkable scene precedes the events on Mount Moriah. Abraham makes a treaty with Abimelech, king of the Philistines. There has been a quarrel over the well at Beer-Sheba. Abraham wishes to prove that this well had been dug by him. He therefore sets apart seven ewe lambs and gives them to the king in confirmation of his oath. Incidentally, this is the only story of a well which is told of Abraham in Genesis, and it takes place in the town which may in a special sense be called the town of his son, Isaac. And, as the trees have a special significance for Abraham, so the wells have for Isaac. The delicate attention paid to details in the composition of Genesis is shown by this placing of the picture of the seven lambs immediately before the sacrifice of Isaac. As in a solemn ritual the words 'seven lambs' are impressed three times upon the ears of hearers.

> Abraham set seven ewe lambs of the flock apart. And Abimelech said to Abraham, 'What is the meaning of these seven ewe lambs which you have set apart?'
> He said, 'These seven ewe lambs you will take from my hand, that you may be a witness for me that I dug this well.' (21:28–30).

The New Testament gives the key to these hieroglyphics and shows the sublimity of these old pictures. Providence formed objective prophecies of Christ, which were far beyond the perceptions of those who took part in them. The seven lambs at Beer-Sheba are like a prophecy of the sevenfold eyes and powers ('horns') of the Lamb of God in the Apocalypse of John (5:6).

Between this picture of the seven lambs and the sacrifice of Isaac, the story of the planting of the young tree in Beer-Sheba is placed.

> Abraham planted a tamarisk tree in Beer-Sheba, and called there on the name of the LORD, the Everlasting God. (Gn 21:33)

Here we find the Everlasting God, or God of Eternity, El-Olam. Genesis shows us how at that time different aspects of the Godhead were perceived at different holy places. The attributes of God, which can be found tabulated now in a primer of dogmatics as a series of more or less abstract concepts, were in earlier times living experiences. At each holy place the hidden Godhead revealed another side of his nature to the pious worshippers. And so every name which was given to the Godhead had local 'colour', the colour of the consecrated place. Thus at the 'well of him who lives and sees' they met El-Roi, the God of Seeing (Gn 16:13). At Jerusalem El-Elyon, the 'Most High God', was revealed by Melchizedek (14:18). In Bethel El-Bethel, the 'God of Bethel', was revered, the God who will build his House of God upon earth (35:7).

This city of wells, Beer-Sheba, with its young tree, gives to this name of God the 'local colour' of a concrete experience far removed from any abstraction. In the green of the young tree the God who renews the world reveals his power to rejuvenate. This is he who in the power of his eternity brings on the new 'for ever', the new aeon, the new cycle of time; who also, out of the divine wells that are never dry, draws 'the re-enlivening of the dying earth-existence' as it is expressed in the Creed of The Christian Community. El-Olam: the name throws its radiance over the chapter which immediately follows that of the sacrifice on Mount Moriah. One might also say: this name of God reveals in what follows even greater depths of its own mystery. The God who reveals his eternity in the cycle of time is the God of death and resurrection.

The offering of Isaac is the most sublime of the prophecies of the sacrifice of Christ contained in the Old Testament. In the Letter to the Romans, Paul cites the word of God which was spoken on Mount Moriah in order to express the mystery of the Father 'who did not spare his own Son' (Rm 8:32, Gn 22:12).

Jewish tradition shows with what tremendous force this story could act upon the soul, how near one could come, under its impression, to the sphere of Christ, to the Son's secret of death and resurrection.

> When the sword came to Isaac's neck, his soul flew away from him. But when the voice of the Lord came from among the Cherubim, 'Do not lay your hand upon the boy,' his soul came back into Isaac's body, Abraham unbound him and set him upon his feet. Then Isaac learned that there is a resurrection of the dead and that all the dead shall arise one day. In this hour he opened his mouth and said, 'Praised be the Lord, who raises the dead.'*

Similarly, the Letter to the Hebrews says of Abraham, 'He considered that God was able to raise the dead; hence, figuratively speaking, he did receive Isaac back' (Hb 11:19).

Perhaps it has to do with this experience of death that in connection with Isaac a strange name of God is used: 'the God of Abraham

---

* Gorion, *Sagen der Juden* 2.292.

and the Fear of Isaac', and Jacob swore 'by the Fear of his father Isaac.' (Gn 31:42, 53). The Hebrew word *pachad* may well indicate the fear of death, the shuddering of Isaac as he approached the threshold of death.

Isaac's destiny was to awaken the idea of death and resurrection. Out of death new life wells up.

To find life in death — is not that really the experience by a well? Turning from the bright sun of day, and bending over the edge of a well, one looks down into nocturnal dark depths, but out of the darkness comes the silvery reflection of life.

> How strangely solemn and different from everyday life is one's mood on looking down into the depths, along the blackened, dripping sides of the well, down to the rippling mirror at the bottom. Suddenly one is no longer on the surface of life, but is gently touched by its depths. In the midst of the bright, sunny day one meets the eye of the dark and solemn night.*

Let us reflect how penetratingly people of ancient times experienced such pictures, how symbolic the well must have been to the desert people especially. Life upon the surface of earthly existence was condemned to thirst and parch in the searing heat of the desert, unless the wells opened up that other kingdom. There would be no life above in the light, in the white glow of midday without the beneficence of its depths, dark as a vault, cool as a grave.

The Isaac chapters are distinguished by their emphatic repetition of the motif of the well, of life and death. In his *Hymns to the Night*, Novalis, expresses this intimate relationship.

> By death, eternal life was given.
> You are death, and make us whole again.

---

* Kurt von Wistinghausen, *Die Christengemeinschaft* 1931, p.167.

Beer-lahai-roi: the Well of Him who Lives and Sees

Isaac's wife Rebekah is also specially connected with the mystery of the well. Abraham had sent his faithful old servant Eliezer back to his home in Mesopotamia to seek the right wife for his son. One of the most poetical stories of the Old Testament tells how Eliezer rested with his camels by a well at the gate of the city and how, in the cool of the evening, the women came out of the city with their water jars to draw water. Rebekah holds out her jar for the old servant to drink and, unasked, also gives water to the camels. In this gesture Eliezer recognises the bride whom providence has indicated. She follows him to Beer-Sheba. One evening Isaac meets the returning caravan.

> Now Isaac had come from Beer-lahai-roi [the Well of Him who Lives and Sees] ... And Isaac went out to meditate in the field in the evening. (Gn 24:62f)

The Well of Him who Lives and Sees – in this mysterious name the two gifts of the two trees of paradise seem to be united – life and knowledge. Whoever sees God dies, but the one who rises out of this dying may unite his seeing of God with a higher life in God. That this well was really a place of higher experience is shown also by the meeting which Hagar, the Egyptian, had there with the 'angel of the Lord' (Gn 16:9, 14).

Isaac led Rebekah into his mother Sarah's tent (his mother had died three years before). Thus 'Isaac was comforted after his mother's death.' Genesis presents Isaac as the 'son' who feels himself united in filial love to the mother. This small detail is characteristic of the delicate manner of the description. Genesis speaks in this way only of Isaac.

Isaac lived for a long time by this well. Three and a half years after Isaac's marriage, Abraham died.

> After the death of Abraham, God blessed Isaac his son. And Isaac dwelt at Beer-lahai-roi. (25:11)

19. Isaac and the Wells

In the land of the Philistines

Unlike Abraham and Jacob, Isaac does not undertake great journeys. He never visits Babylonia or Egypt, but remains in the Promised Land. Only once, during a famine, he journeys to the land of the Philistines which is not far from Beer-Sheba. Here enmity is roused against him, but he ultimately overcomes it, not by force, but by the quiet power of blessing which proceeds from him.

We see Isaac's intimate connection with the plant world. It is a fact that some people have 'green fingers' and plants flourish under their hands. In ancient times it was known that hands folded in prayer were hands blessed with the power over forces of life. It can be a blessing for the land when a farmer walks over it in reverence. We remember the words as Rebekah arrived, 'Isaac went out to meditate in the field in the evening' (Gn 24:63).

Isaac is so strongly in league with the etheric forces of living things that the crops in his fields bear a hundredfold under his careful hands and eyes. 'The LORD blessed him' (26:12).

The Philistines became jealous, and

> So the Philistines had closed off and filled with earth all
> the wells which his father's servants had dug in the days of
> Abraham his father. (26: 15)

It is again characteristic of the style of these stories that we have heard nothing of those wells in the stories of Abraham, except the one in Beer-Sheba. It is in connection with Isaac that we hear of wells. (Neither do we hear anything in Genesis about Jacob's well, which is mentioned in John's Gospel).

> And Isaac dug again the wells of water which had been
> dug in the days of Abraham his father, which the
> Philistines had closed off after the death of Abraham.
> And he gave them the names which his father had given
> them. (26: 18)

Isaac brings to life again what was dead. He awakes to new life the ruined wells of his father.

As he has shown himself to be filial to his mother, so now Isaac shows himself to be filial in a special way to his father. He not only opens up again his father's wells, he gives them their names again. He 'gave them the names which his father had given them.' This name-giving is a solemn ritual act. Isaac also causes new wells to be dug. But he has no joy because of the enmity of the Philistines.

'But Isaac's servants dug in the valley, and found there a well of living water' (26:19). Yet the herdsman of Gerar dispute with them saying, 'The water is ours.' And the same thing happened by another well dug by Isaac's servants. Therefore Isaac called the wells 'Esek' and 'Sitnah' – 'contention' and 'feud'. In perfect tranquillity he caused a third well to be dug, and there was peace with the brawlers. This well he called 'Rehoboth', 'broad places' or 'room'. The narrow, oppressive strife is over. Unrestricted and untroubled now, his men can draw the water of this well.

Beer-Sheba again

From there Isaac returned again to Beer-Sheba. In the night he received a divine revelation at this holy place. In remembrance of it he built an altar at which he solemnly called out God's name (26:25). Genesis tells of only one altar which Isaac built – it is this altar at Beer-Sheba. The special connection of Isaac with this sacred place is shown much later. When Jacob, in very old age, goes down to Joseph in Egypt, he breaks his journey. at Beer-Sheba, and there sacrifices 'to the God of his father Isaac', who blesses him 'in the visions of the night' (46:1f). The God to whom Isaac builds his altar is El-Olam, who reveals his eternal nature in the dying and rising again of the cycle of time.

After the building of this altar Isaac 'pitched his tent there', and this pitching of a tent is followed immediately by the digging of a new well (26:25). The beginning of this digging and the crowning of the labour by the finding of water enclose significantly a scene of reconciliation and contentment. Abimelech, the king of the Philistines, who was before too jealous to bear to see Isaac in his land, whose subjects quarrelled with Isaac's servants about the well – this very king appears with two of his great men in Beer-Sheba to change enmity into friendship.

He has been deeply impressed by the quiet but great power of blessing which proceeds from the patriarch. To the latter's wondering question: 'Why have you come to me, seeing that you hate me and have sent me away from you?' they are constrained to reply: 'We see plainly that the LORD is with you ... let us make a covenant with you ... You are now the blessed of the LORD' (26:27–29).

Isaac prepares a solemn feast for the three; next morning, at the hour of the early sacrifice, they swear a covenant and they depart from him in peace.

> That same day Isaac's servants came and told him about the well which they had dug, and said to him, 'We have found water.' (26:32)

Thus the whole story of the reconciliation, in which the power of Isaac's love overcame jealousy and enmity, is inserted into the account of the digging of the well (26:25–32). This is not because the Bible wants to give a strict chronological account of it, but in order that the secret of the power of love, which brings peace at last, may be felt to be a 'secret of the well'.

In *Poetry and Truth* Goethe describes Abraham's 'calm and greatness', and Isaac he characterises by a subtle change of description: 'quietness and devotion'.

'Calm and greatness' like the nature of God himself. Calm and greatness comes to Abraham under the boughs of ancient, venerable oak trees.

'Quietness and devotion' is the mark of those who have looked into the cold well of death and found a higher life.

20

JACOB AND THE STONES

It is characteristic of the third patriarch that stories about stones are told of him. In connection with Abraham and Isaac we hear nothing about stones. Jacob had his first great experience of God by the stone of Bethel.

The stone of Bethel

Jacob is fleeing from his brother Esau towards Haran and the east. 'And he came to a certain place [*maqom*], and stayed there that night' (Gn 28:11). In the original text the words are more mysterious: 'he came to *the* place'. The essential quality of a 'place' is that it is a place of 'presence', that something is experienced as being present there. In this sense every being has its place somewhere or other in the cosmic being, whether in a higher or a lower sphere. The primal picture of all these experiences of presence is the presence of the divine being; the place where one meets the divine being is *the* place.

That here in Genesis the word 'place' has a special meaning is shown by the repetition of the word three times in the first sentence of the story.

> He came to a certain *place,* and stayed there that night,
> because the sun had set. Taking one of the stones of the *place,*
> he put it under his head and lay down in that *place* to sleep.

This refers to an ancient group of stones, which had been set up in this 'place' like cromlechs. In the Holy Land, as in other countries, such stones were set up as memorials in prehistoric times. At this 'place' there still hovered something of the solemnity and magic of the ancient cosmic celebrations of the priests. Here, without knowing it, Jacob fell into a kind of temple sleep. This sleep in the consecrated place was illuminated by the gentle, lucid light of clairvoyant dreams.

For his pillow Jacob took 'one of the stones of the place' – so there were several stones marking the place. The sacred text speaks of this stone in no trivial sense; it is not calling the attention of the reader to the hardness of this Spartan pillow so that the poverty of the homeless fugitive may be emphasised. If we contemplate the picture quietly for a little, we find that this juxtaposition of head and stone begins to speak. Head and stone. The 'cool' head, ruled by the mineral element of its bony structure, is it not related to the stone? The 'place of the skull' in which the intellectual thought has its abode, which understands only what is dead, which celebrates its triumphs only in the kingdom of dead matter, is leant against a stone. Stone upon stone! Is it not this head of clever Jacob in which the force of the 'clear head' has been awakened to an uncanny degree? This force which is so tragically strangled by lower egoism. And is not the awakening of the calculating, intellectual thinking of the head the sign that in Jacob heaven has been lost, and the last downward step into the earthly world has been taken?

It was not said of Abraham that he laid his head upon a stone, nor was it said of Isaac. But this picture 'looks like Jacob'. A more minute study of destiny may lead one to see that what happens to someone is always 'what is like them'. One has perceived the hidden configuration of a human life in grasping the fact that all the events are 'like' the person whose destiny it is to live it.

Those who, like Jacob, develop the forces of the head lose paradise. Jacob is far from the trees of Eden, which still cast their shade over Abraham. He is far from the waters of Eden which still spring up in Isaac's wells. Jacob, the most earthly of the patriarchs, lays his head upon a stone.

Here a special relationship is expressed. This is a sacred stone. On the one hand a stone can embody to an overwhelming extent the stark deadness of matter; in its hardness and coldness it marks the lowest point of the descent. But since it is this lowest point it may also become the foundation stone of a new ascent to the heavens. Just because it is the very lowest, it may point upwards to the very highest: it may support the ladder which reaches upward to the stars again. In this way, Jacob experienced the stone which he had laid for his head as the foundation stone of this whole vision of the ladder which reached upward to heaven. Observe the reverence with which he treats this stone when he awakes. But we anticipate, and will first let Jacob's experiences by night pass before us in detail.

The 'sun had set' when he placed the stone under his head. The day-consciousness disappears and the mysterious night-consciousness opens its starlike eyes.

> And he dreamed, and behold, a ladder set up on the earth, and the top of it reached to the heavens; and behold, the angels of God were ascending and descending on it. And behold, the LORD stood above it and said, 'I am the LORD ...' (28:12f)

The supersensory experience begins with the picture interwoven with light, with the *Imagination* which shines out before the eye of the soul (*behold* a ladder. ... *behold* the angels of God), then it proceeds further to the perception of the divine words, revealed spiritual hearing, to *Inspiration* (the LORD said ...)

Imagination, Inspiration. In the place of the third and highest stage, there is *Intuition,* the complete union of the knower with the known, in this case the dread with which Jacob, being awakened in the night, becomes conscious of the *presence* of God.

> Then Jacob awoke from his sleep and said, 'Surely the LORD is in this place; and I did not know it.' And he was afraid, and said, 'How awesome is this place! This is none other than the house of God, and this is the gate of heaven.' (28: 16f)

This shuddering at the nearness of God belongs to the night. The following verse tells what happened next morning.

> So Jacob rose early in the morning, and took the stone which he had put under his head and set it up for a pillar and poured

> oil on the top of it. He called the name of that place Bethel. (28:18f)

He set the stone up for a pillar – the stone which perhaps had been set up a long time previously, when the old worship of heaven was at its zenith in this place, before it sank down into decay over the course of hundreds, perhaps thousands of years. The upright stones, the menhirs of prehistoric worship, were a great and unique proclamation of the forces which raise bodies upright. The weight of earthly things, the dull heavy resistance of matter, is overcome by this force which morning by morning makes human beings stand upright, raises them from the position of a corpse. The mystery of 'setting up', which so intimately touches humankind, was the message proclaimed with simplicity and power by this upright stone.

In the morning we stand up from sleep. In the morning Christ rose again from the grave. Standing upright is a mystery of the early morning. In the sacred morning hour, after the night of divine illumination, Jacob set up the stone.

In order to consecrate it he 'poured oil on the top of it.' In the original this is 'on the *head*' of the stone. Here again we have the motif: stone, head. The golden oil is specially the bearer of consecration. 'Christ' means 'anointed'. The 'head' of this stone which has been lifted up is 'anointed with oil', the hard is blessed with the soft, the earthly is made golden with light.

To the onlooker this event seems like a prophetic hieroglyph. Because such a thing is told of Jacob who had descended most deeply into earthly things we can surmise that the lowest and most earthly thing may, just because it is so, become the foundation, the base and the support of a new ascent. He who has reached the bottom of the valley is in a sense nearer the heights than he who has not yet descended so low but is still coming down the slope. In this earth world, which is very far from paradise, the clear awakened head, the activity of the intellect which one acquires 'at the stone', is intended to find its way back again to the divine. What Jacob did in subconscious prophecy when he set up this hieroglyph may perhaps be expressed more abstractly thus: it is the spiritualising of intellectual thought, the hallowing of the strong forces of earth, which humanity can acquire in the region of the dead material world. It is a prophecy of the time of the Holy Spirit, when the way will be found again from the stone to the stars.

In the trinity of the patriarchs, Jacob is the representative of, or to put it more modestly, he stands for the Holy Spirit. This may at first seem strange. But, if we may speak so humanly, it was comparatively easy for Providence to fill the roles of 'father' and 'son', to find in Abraham and Isaac worthy representatives of these sublime divine principles. But on the other hand it was much more difficult to find a worthy representative for the third. That one cannot yet be found who fits this role completely shows that this third divine principle is by nature connected with the future. Only through Christ will the Holy Spirit be able to enter into human beings. It is no chance that in the third patriarch we feel especially the discrepancy between the representative and what he represents.

It is noticeable that the word 'head' is a keyword in the whole narrative. Jacob placed the stone 'under his head'; the 'head' of the ladder (literal translation) reached to heaven; he took the stone which he had put under his 'head', and he poured oil on the 'head' of it. Emil Bock reminds us of the Babylonian expression 'the elevation of the head'.*

With the anointing of the stone is connected the *giving of the name*. In solemn ceremony Jacob calls out the name of the place: 'Bethel', 'the house of God'.

The end of the sacred morning service is the vow which Jacob vowed. If what has been promised in the vision by night should be fulfilled, if Jacob is guarded on his way and returns home in peace, if he has food and raiment, then here he will build a house of God and give him tithe.

Abraham gave tithe to Melchizedek. The tithe was given in order that consecrated and sacred persons should be able to have an existence upon earth. Jacob was to give to the 'God of Bethel' his tithe.

In this is mirrored a great truth. After human beings have got a firm footing upon earth by the unfolding of their egotistic power, after they have built an earthly house for themselves, then there must be awakened in them devotion to the divine. When earthly humans turn in sacrifice to the Godhead, then the Godhead can find through human beings an entrance into the 'earthly world', which before was

---

* *Genesis,* p. 170.

possessed only by egotism. Earthly human beings when they turn to sacrifice help to build 'Bethel', the house of God upon earth.

In contrast to the mood of Buddha, who feels that earth must be renounced and that the work of the 'housebuilder' destroyed, the conception of the 'house of God' contained in the Bible, is very important. It finds its fulfilment in the Christmas mystery of the incarnation of the divine.

So we find a deep meaning in the fact that the sacred place of the most earthly of the patriarchs is Bethel, the house of God. The descent to Jacob's level was also necessary to prepare for the descent of God into an earthly body.

The stone on the well

Immediately after the story of Bethel we have the story of the well in the east.

> Then Jacob went on his journey, and came to the land of the people of the east. As he looked, he saw a well in the field ... The stone on the well's mouth was large. (29:1f)

After the holy night in Bethel, Jacob continues his way to the place from which Abraham had once come. 'In the east' lies the garden of Eden. The way to the east, is the way to the rejuvenating, life-giving forces.

At the well he meets Rachel. Like Rebekah before this, and Zipporah, the bride of Moses afterwards, Rachel appears first beside the well, in union with its ethereal life-forces. But this story of a well (the only one told of Jacob) contains also the characteristic of the experiences of Jacob: upon the well lies a *great stone*. It is Jacob's destiny to be obliged always to struggle against obstacles. Thus he must overcome obstacles in winning Rachel also. For her he must serve twice seven years. This picture also is 'like him'. By *his own strength* he must *roll the stone* from the well.

The herdsmen want to wait until they have all assembled. Only by a common effort, out of the power of their collective force, can they open up the well.

> Now when Jacob saw Rachel ... Jacob went up and rolled the stone from the well's mouth. (29:10)

The man whose strength is increased by the resistance of the stone, so that he overcomes its weight, can find access to the water of life which flows from the well towards the morning, and he wins the bride.

The stone of Gilead

During the twenty years at Haran in the east Jacob became rich. After that he returns home, now no longer a poor fugitive, but a patriarch, with Rachel and Leah and the children, a train of servants, and large flocks and herds. Laban, his father-in-law, pursues him, hunts the wanderer who is returning home; but in a vision he is warned not to act against Jacob in an unfriendly manner. He makes a covenant with him upon the mount of Gilead, where he has caught up with him. Again it is characteristic of Jacob that he sets up a pillar of stone as testimony to the compact. The like is never told of Abraham or of Isaac.

> So Jacob took a stone, and set it up for a pillar [*matsevah*]. And Jacob said to his kinsmen, 'Gather stones,' and they took stones and made a heap, and they ate there by the heap. (31:45f)

Just as Abraham was priest under the sacred tree, so Jacob celebrated the ritual of the stone. He set up the stone and surrounded it by a circle of stones. It is easy to see that this stone had a sacred significance. There the covenant was sworn by Jacob and Laban. It is also clear that the eating is not merely a meal, but a sacramental repast. Then

> Jacob offered a sacrifice on the hill country and called his kinsmen to eat bread. They ate bread and spent all night in the hill country. (31:54)

At the stone circle upon the height of the sacred hill, the ritual of sacrifice was celebrated, and in connection with this the sacramental meal of peace was held. That they also remained there *all night* denotes again an experience of a 'temple sleep'. This time, however, we are not told of any clairvoyant dreams at the consecrated spot, but immediately afterwards we are told of the meeting with angels.

> Jacob went on his way, and the angels of God met him. And when Jacob saw them he said, 'This is God's camp.' So he called the name of the place Mahanaim. (32:1f)

The sacramental act performed beside the sacred stone on the mountain, the sacrifice and ritual meal, and the sleep under the stars, had all combined to lay open Jacob's soul to a vision of the angels, like that which he had before at Bethel. This time it was not a dream, but as he was on his way it came into his clear day consciousness, the consciousness of the man who has just set up a sacred stone.

The return to Bethel

After the vision of the angels at Mahanaim, Jacob meets the angel at the Jabbok ford and wrestles until dawn to extract a blessing. He calls this place Peniel, 'the face of God'.

Following the meeting with Esau, Jacob settles at Shechem. He buys some land and builds an altar there which he calls El-Elohe-Israel, 'God who is God of Israel'. Israel (he who strives with God) is the name he is given by the angel at Peniel. The changing of his name shows, as with Abraham, an inner development. He has become another, or one could say, more 'like himself'. Now, as an individual, he carries the name of the whole people who will be his descendants.

We see in the third patriarch again a connection with the Holy Spirit. At Pentecost the Holy Spirit founds a new community, the Church. Jacob here becomes the founder of the people Israel, who are made up of twelve tribes, as the Church is founded on the twelve apostles.

Later Jacob is told by God to go to Bethel. What he had experienced as he set out upon his journey on that holy night remained for him the fundamental experience of his life. The stone of Bethel had become for him the foundation stone of his religious consciousness. Just as the grove of Mamre may be called Abraham's place, and the city of the well, Beer-Sheba, Isaac's place, so Bethel may be called the place of Jacob.

Even into a foreign land he had been accompanied by the memory of it. While he is still dwelling with Laban in the east, he speaks to Rachel and Leah of a dream in which the voice of God says: 'I am the God of Bethel, where you anointed a pillar' (31:13). So we can understand why after his stay in Shechem he again seeks a place which is so important to him. A special call from God points the way.

> God said to Jacob, 'Arise, go up to Bethel, and dwell there.
> Make an altar there to the God who appeared to you when
> you fled from your brother Esau.' (35:1)

This journey to Bethel, which is a kind of pilgrimage, is preceded by an act of ceremonial purification. The 'foreign gods' and earrings (a kind of amulet) which his servants had, were removed and buried under the old oak by Shechem.

In Bethel, Jacob now builds an altar, which is in a special sense *his* altar. This is the last of the seven altars built by the patriarchs of which we are told in Genesis. Four of these were erected by Abraham: at the oak of Shechem (12:7), upon a mountain near Bethel (12:8), in the grove of Mamre (13:18), upon Mount Moriah (22:9). Isaac's altar stood at Beer-Sheba (26:25), Jacob built an altar in Shechem (33:20), and now, completing the number, he builds the seventh in Bethel (35:7): 'and there he built an altar, and called the place El Bethel; because there God had revealed himself to him when he fled from his brother.'

This ritual of sacrifice at the altar of Bethel was the response to the new revelations of God.

> God appeared to Jacob again, when he came from
> Paddanaram [Mesopotamia], and blessed him. And God
> said to him, 'Your name is Jacob; no longer shall your name

> be called Jacob, but Israel shall be your name.' ... Then God went up from him in the place where he had spoken with him. (35:9, 13)

The objection has been raised that we have already been told of this change of name from Jacob to 'Israel' in the story of the wrestling with the angel by night at Peniel, at the ford of the River Jabbok (32:28); and it has been said that here we have another 'reading', according to which the change of name took place not at Peniel, but at Bethel. But we must understand this passage in the sense that the experience by night – the struggle with the angel – has an inward connection with the experience at Bethel, which is the most important among all of Jacob's experiences. Many and varied spiritual experiences may exist side by side in the soul; it needs time to let them grow together into an organic whole. Until now the mysterious experience of that struggle by night was as it were isolated in Jacob's memory; it had not been integrated in his soul with the earlier experience of Bethel. Now, when Jacob is back in Bethel, this unifying of his inward revelations occurs: the two great meetings with God. The gift of the name Israel, God's warrior, received for the first time at dawn at Peniel was strengthened and confirmed at his own place, Bethel.

Similarly it may be a mistake of modern biblical interpretation to speak of a 'doublet' when it finds a repetition of sacred acts: setting up a stone and anointing it. It is true that the same thing occurs again which had previously occurred on the morning after the night when Jacob dreamed of the ladder which reached up to heaven.

> And Jacob set up a pillar in the place where he had spoken with him, a pillar of stone. He poured a drink offering on it and poured oil on it. So Jacob called the name of the place where God had spoken with him, Bethel. (35:14f)

This doing of the same thing again is in reality the recurrence of the experience that lay three times seven years behind him. Jacob performs this act of repetition as a concrete 'in memoriam' of the original act. And by doing so he brings the act back again out of the past into the present. So he has really returned to Bethel. One might almost say he has returned home.

The fact that the place is three times solemnly named Bethel, as in a solemn baptism, gives the name a quite special importance (28:19, 35:7, 35:15).

To the last hours of Jacob's life this experience echoed in his soul. The dying patriarch calls his twelve sons to his death-bed and prophesies to them. As he blesses Joseph he calls the Godhead by a unique name, he calls it the 'Stone of Israel' (49:24). God is for him connected with the stone, the 'foundation stone'.

The stone on Rachel's grave

The first experience at Bethel was followed by the meeting with Rachel at the well. The second story in Bethel was followed by Rachel's death. The relation of Jacob to Rachel, among all the relations between husband and wife in the age of the patriarchs, is the most personal and individual. Rachel was not brought to him by the servant as Rebekah was brought to Isaac. He had chosen her personally, had worked for her and won her. She was taken from him by an early death. She died when Benjamin was born.

> And Jacob set up a pillar upon her grave; it is the pillar of Rachel's tomb, which is there to this day. (35:20)

When he met Rachel at the well towards morning, he rolled the stone from the well. Now that gracious gift, which then had entered his life, disappears from it again. Jacob's life is a prophecy; it is not yet fulfilment. For only a short space of his long life could he be united with Rachel, the mystical 'bride' who came from the well in the east. The most earthly of the patriarchs, he who descended most deeply into incarnation, must taste the bitterest tragedy of earth. The last stone he sets up is a gravestone. It is as if the well were covered again by the stone.

Upon Rachel's grave stands the stone – fit expression, in its implacable hardness and frigid silence, of the tragedy of human destiny. But the stone is not only a heavy, dead mass; it is set up as a memorial pillar. It is an anticipation; it is a beginning of the conquest of the 'stone' by the forces which set things upright.

In this story of Rachel's death we have a special prophecy: Rachel died upon the way 'to Ephrath (that is, Bethlehem)' (35:19). How marvellously the lines of destiny are intertwined! Bethlehem: there the boy Jesus will be born one day, and through him God will enter this earthly world. There the prophecy of Bethel, the 'House of God', will be fulfilled. And Mary will take the place of Rachel, in whom the 'eternal feminine', the morning forces of the tree of life, enter Jacob's life for a time.

IV

FROM SABBATH TO SUNDAY

21

SUNDAY: A CHRISTIAN FACT

This chapter was written as a little book in 1965, when there was much talk of creating a simplified world calendar that would make a date fall on the same weekday each year. Such a reform requires a 'blank day' every year to match the length of the actual year (and a second blank day every four years). This would interrupt the flow of the seven day week. The clamour for such reforms seems to have died down since then.

If our solar year had only 364 days it could be divided exactly by seven, which is the number of days in a week. In that case the dates of every year would have the same day. For example Christmas Day would always fall on the same weekday. As it is, the year has an extra day with the result that each year the days of the week move on from the date. If your birthday is on Monday this year, next year it will be on Tuesday or in the case of a leap-year on Wednesday.

This rotation of the days of the week in the course of the years is anathema to certain would-be calendar reformers who would like to make the year's cycle correspond once and for all with the week's cycle. The extra (365th) day would be 'neutralised'. As the year cannot be shortened by a day, these so-called reformers would like to remove the surplus day from the week, giving it a non-weekday name. They would wait until a year comes when December 30 is on a Saturday. They would then make January 1 a Sunday for all time, and declare December 31 a blank day with no weekday name and instead call it a 'world-holiday'. In a leap-year they suggest doing the same at the end of June.

For thousands of years Sunday has followed Saturday. This rhythm of our lives would be broken. It is difficult to understand why every single person in Christendom has not risen to defend themselves against this proposition which touches the very nerve of Christian religious practice. Apparently there is no real sense of what such a break in the rhythm would mean. Hitherto the Christian Sunday has been week after week the exact and uninterrupted 'octave' of the Easter Resurrection Day, but now it would no longer be a 'true' Sunday. Is that so very important? One cannot answer this question until one understands how the seven-day week and the Christian celebration of Sunday have come about.

The Chaldean planetary week

The names of the weekdays are familiar and well known from olden times. Few people think anything of it. But let us just ask ourselves, what sort of names are they? With Sunday and Monday the connection to Sun and Moon is immediately apparent. Tuesday is harder to recognise. It bears within it the name of the Germanic god of war Tiw. In Wednesday the god Wodan (Odin) can be found, in Thursday we find the god Thor, in Friday the goddess Freya. Saturday, however, originates from the Roman god Saturnus, the Greek Kronos. In spite of the Germanic names of the gods the seven-day week is in all probability not an indigenous Germanic institution, but was taken over from the Romans. Through the western tribes of the Franks and Alemanni it was brought further east and north, while the old gods were worshipped before Christianity became dominant.

The week, then, was a pre-Christian planet-god week, which spread by way of the Rhine and the Danube. Seven ancient pagan gods gave their names to the days of the week: Sun-god, Moon-goddess, Mars, Mercury, Jupiter, Venus and Saturn. In Greek: Helios, Selene, Ares, Hermes, Zeus, Aphrodite and Kronos. The Germanic peoples applied the names of their own corresponding gods, thus Tiw for warlike Mars; Thor and, further south, Donar for Jupiter. Donar is still to be found in the German *Donnerstag*. In the Romance languages the Latin names survive: the French *jeudi* comes from *Jovis dies*, *vendredi* from *Veneris dies*, *mercredi* from Mercury, the messenger god.

The worship of these seven gods of the days seems to have flourished particularly in the Romano-Germanic border areas during the third Christian century. A considerable number of monumental stones representing the seven has been found east and west of the Rhine.

21. SUNDAY: A CHRISTIAN FACT

But the origin of the week is not even to be found with the Romans. The ancient Romans themselves had a kind of eight-day week whereby the farmers, after seven working days, brought their produce to the market on the eighth. The seven-day week first found its way into the Roman Empire shortly before the beginning of the Christian era, coming by way of Egypt, though Egypt was not its cradle. The planetary week originated in the eastern centre of culture which in the ancient world had the reputation of possessing the deepest knowledge and wisdom of the stars: Chaldea. It began with Saturday in the sign of Ninib which corresponded to Saturn. Then followed Shamash–Sun, Sin–Moon, Nergal–Mars, Nebo–Mercury, Marduk–Jupiter, Ishtar–Venus. Romans and Greeks and later the Teutons applied their own corresponding names.

Was this Chaldean star-wisdom perhaps rather primitive? Modern people are inclined to remark that Sun and Moon are not 'proper' planets, and that Uranus, Neptune and Pluto are missing, not to mention the planetoids. We should however arrive at a more just appreciation of these ancient cultures if we would accept the idea that people of those days did not think and pursue their research in our modern, scientific way, but that they used quite different faculties of perception which have since been lost; for should we not also allow that human consciousness itself has undergone a variety of transformations and developments? Of course the seven planets of the Chaldeans do not coincide with what we today regard as the planetary system. What is important here is to note that the ancient septuary of the planets was a result of direct visual observation. The way in which phenomena present themselves to the senses is important, for the senses are in fact designed in accordance with the reality of the world. The seven celestial luminaries present themselves to the eye as planets which move against the background of the fixed stars. Yet to the deeper contemplation of the ancients their individual 'qualities' were revealed.

It is not surprising that a great deal of superstition has attached itself to the number seven. But we should not throw out the baby with the bath-water. In connection with the number seven several observations from different fields of existence could be adduced, and these must give us food for thought. In fact, its function is to bring things into order in many different ways.

The order of the seven 'planets', or spirits of the stars, in the days of the week is remarkable, as the spatial arrangement is not just projected into time; for the spatial ordering would make Jupiter and Mars follow Saturn in order of distance, and then the other three, Venus, Mercury and the Moon, whose periods of revolution are shorter than the sun's year, would also be together. But in fact near and far planets follow each other alternately. The order goes from Saturn via the Sun to the near Moon, then back out to Mars and in again to fast-moving Mercury; from Mercury to distant, slow Jupiter, and in again to Venus, and from this slowest of the inner planets out again to the slowest of the outer planets, Saturn, whose period of revolution requires as many years as the Moon's requires days. It is like an in and out-breathing between near and far.

This ordering of the week spread through the Roman Empire in the first century BC. In Roman literature of that time the Saturn-Day appears. The poet Tibullus (54–19 BC) mentions the observance of the hallowed Saturn-Day as a possible obstacle to leaving his home place. In the first two Christian centuries the planetary week completely established itself. The famous magician Apollonius of Tyana (first century) placed a different ring on his finger for each of the seven days. At the excavations in Pompeii and Herculaneum inscriptions and pictures have been brought to light which name and represent the seven day-gods, and which must have been created before AD 79, the year Vesuvius erupted. Dio Cassius writes about AD 210–20 that 'the custom of referring the days to the seven stars called planets ... is now found among all peoples, though its adoption has been comparatively recent ... it is now quite the fashion ... even with the Romans themselves.' (37.18). That was during the reign of Septimus Severus who thought highly of Chaldean astrology and who built a temple to the seven day-gods on the Palatine.

The Jewish week

It is a remarkable fact that during these same centuries the seven-day week was spreading in another form, namely through Judaism. There were Jewish congregations everywhere in the Roman Empire. It was just at that time that the Diaspora Jews who had been scattered abroad were involved in successful missionary work. Many gentile seekers, no longer content with the decadent pagan cults, were attracted by the strict monotheism and by the ethical nature of the Ten Commandments, and approached Judaism as sympathisers or as proselytes. The Sabbath as a day of rest after every six working days was adopted in many circles.

Philo of Alexandria, a Jewish mystic and philosopher of the Logos, who lived at the time of Jesus Christ (20 BC to AD 54) wrote: 'The Sabbath is held in honour by the foremost Hellenes and Barbarians' (*De Opificio Mundi* 43). And the Jewish historian Josephus (AD *c.* 37–100) expressed with pride: 'Also much enthusiasm for our religion is to be found among the masses, and there is no nation, no Greek or Barbarian city, where our custom of resting from work on the seventh day has not gained entrance.' (*Contra Apionem* 2.89). In his biography of Tiberius (Ch. 32) Suetonius tells of a grammarian Diogenes, who at that time lived on Rhodes, that he was in the habit of holding his disputations 'only on the Sabbath'.

Still in pre-Christian times we encounter the Sabbath in the writings of the poet Horace (65–8 BC). In his *Satires* (1.9,60–74) he mentions an amusing episode which, however, can also be regarded as symptomatic. Horace wishes to free himself from an importunate companion who has joined him in the street. He hopes to be relieved by his friend Fuscus Aristius who happens to cross his path at just the right moment. 'Could not the two of us discuss an important matter privately?' But his friend lets him down sharply. 'Another time!' This friend is a Roman like Horace, but he says: 'Not today. Today is the Sabbath.' Horace replies that *he* does not feel himself constrained on religious grounds, whereupon his friend retorts: 'But *I* do! I need something to support me – I'm one of many.'

The Sabbath has left further traces with Ovid (43 BC–AD 17), Martial (AD 38–102) and Juvenal (AD *c.* 47–130). The latter sees in the celebration of the Sabbath only a reluctance to work and condemns the Romans for adopting such a custom. 'But the father is to blame for always being lazy on the seventh day and for not touching the least thing of his business.' (*Satires* 14.105). The biting vituperation of a man like Seneca the Younger (4 BC – AD 65) proves how far the observance of the Sabbath had already penetrated Roman circles. He maintains that the Jews lose a seventh part of their lives through idleness: 'In the meantime the custom of this wretched people has become so prevalent as to be adopted in all countries, and this means that the vanquished are imposing their laws upon the victors.' (quoted from Augustine *De Civitate Dei* 6.11). He wrote: 'Let us put a stop to this lighting of the Sabbath lamps by all kinds of people.' These protests were fruitless.

In contrast with the Chaldean, the Jewish week does not begin with Saturday but with Sunday leading up to the Sabbath as the crowning of the week. It was known that the Jewish Sabbath coincided with the Saturn-Day of the Chaldean week (Dio Cassius 37.17), but for the rest the Jewish week had quite a different character.

Providence had given the Jews the task of developing a wakeful consciousness of the I. This consciousness was to be the preparation for the Christ, for the I am spoken in clear, calm self-awareness. In Judaism there arose an intellectual thinking capable of protecting the developing free personality from the incursions and domination of obscure dreamlike soul states. Abraham, the initiator of this new spirituality, by his wandering forth, freed himself from the womb of the Babylonian-Chaldean culture, which had centres of moon and star-worship in Ur and Haran (Gn 11:28, 31).

The star-wisdom of the Chaldeans, founded upon ancient powers, and fallen into decadence, could not lead into the future. Progress necessitated the transition to a consciousness of the I which, although primarily abstract, was nevertheless firm in itself and pure fundamentally.

We cannot be surprised then that the Jewish week, though looking back to Chaldea in its aspect of a seven-day rhythm, bears no more trace of the planetary character of the individual days. In the Jewish week Sunday is not the day of the Sun, but the 'first day after the Sabbath'. Monday is then 'the second', and so on.

The numbering of the days, which appears to us so dry and calculating, had still in those days a last echo of 'quality', because for the ancient world the numbers were not so external and colourless as they are today. In the story of creation in Genesis the seven days of creation are numbered with a certain solemnity. The Jewish week stood in the afterglow of this exalted archetypal week, but we cannot deny that in comparison with the powerfully pictorial day-gods the Jewish week has become abstract.

Apart from the creation itself, the soul's rhythmic experience of the seven days appears early in the Old Testament. One week before the beginning of the flood Noah receives the last warning from God

(Gn 7:4, 10). Towards the end of the flood the seven days again play a part with the sending out of the dove (Gn 8:10, 12). At Jacob's wedding the seven days are kept (Gn 29:27f), as later with Samson (Jg 14:12, 17). We find them also in the observances of a death. Joseph mourned for his father for seven days (Gn 50:10). Several centuries later, seven days' lamentation were made for King Saul (1Sm 31:13).

In the law of Moses the Sabbath is not introduced but re-emphasised: 'Remember the Sabbath day, to keep it holy' (Ex 20:8). At the time of the Passover unleavened bread is eaten for seven days (Lv 23:6). For seven days the Feast of the Tabernacles is celebrated (Lv 23:34). Seven days were needed for the consecration of Solomon's temple (1K 8:65). A culmination of the experiencing of the week came every year between the Passover and the Jewish Feast of Weeks. The latter pertained to the ingathering of the harvest and also to the celebration of the Ten Commandments, which were given to Moses on Mount Sinai seven weeks before the exodus from Egypt. This Old Testament Pentecost was called Shavuot meaning the 'seven-ness', the 'weeks'. Admittedly that does not prove that the seven day week has rolled on without interruption from earliest times. The scanty sources do not allow that to be established with certainty. But what does stand assured is the fact that at least since the exile in Babylon, that is since the sixth century BC, the continuation of the seven day week has not suffered any interruption. Thus the Sabbath today is irrefutably the exact octave of the Sabbath of at least two and a half thousand years ago. With its innate tenacity Jewry has preserved its Sabbath through all kinds of calendar situations obtaining among its host nations right up to the present day. With that the 'genuineness' of our present-day Christian Sunday as the repetition of the Day of Resurrection is guaranteed.

The Christian Sunday

From the background of divine worlds Christianity entered earth history through the event upon Golgotha. The institution of the seven-day week can be regarded in all earnestness as an act of Providence relating to the appearance of the divinity upon earth, for the 'Incarnation of the Word' does not merely mean that the invisible revealed itself in an earthly body, visible in space to the human eye, but also that it entered the course of time. From the supra-temporal it entered the sequence of the temporal and thus became a historical fact. Thus the eternal entered the course of the three years from the Baptism in Jordan. Thus it entered the format of the seven day week when it enacted the central deed of Death and Resurrection. The Holy Week, as a 'form' in time, receives the great mystery into itself, whereby Palm Sunday with its rejoicing is like a pre-octave to the Sunday of Resurrection, which in its turn initiates the seven weeks that lead to Pentecost.

The day which hitherto in Judaism only bore the name of the 'first after the Sabbath' now received a decisive accentuation. Thenceforth for Christianity it is inseparable from the Resurrection.

A student of history must constantly ask the question, how was it possible for the early Christian communities who were so deeply rooted in the Old Testament to make the transition from the celebration of the Sabbath to that of Sunday. We hear of no decree by the apostles whereby the commandment given upon Sinai to keep the Sabbath holy is to be applied to another day. The Sabbath was kept at first, but it gradually lost its importance as the new Christian day prevailed as a matter of course. The Council of the Apostles (held in Jerusalem around AD 50) laid down the minimum obligation to the laws of the Old Testament to be demanded of non-Jews adopting Christianity. They are enjoined to abstain from the flesh of animals that have not been slaughtered, but of an observance of the Sabbath we hear nothing (Ac 15:20).

Only by taking into account the all-powerful impress of Easter can we understand how the 'first day' gradually superseded the Sabbath in importance. God did not proclaim a new law for Sunday through a new Moses, but he let Christ rise from the dead – on Sunday. A deed spoke. From that day, Sunday was 'the day which the Lord had made'. Sunday as a recurring octave made itself felt in religious experience with compelling power. The genius of the Russian language gives a wonderful expression to this experience by calling Sunday *Voskresenye*, 'Resurrection'.

John's Gospel tells us of the first octave experience. The Risen One reveals himself to doubting Thomas 'eight days later' (20:26) and indeed so realistically that Thomas has to confess: 'my Lord and my God'. And just as after the week of weeks, the seven times seven days after the Passover the Jews celebrated Pentecost, so now the fiftieth day (*Pentecoste* in Greek means the fiftieth), the seventh octave of the Easter event, becomes the Christian Pentecost, Whitsun. Thus Sunday is also anchored in Christendom by the Festival of the Holy Spirit.

The Lord's Day

In the New Testament the Jewish nomenclature of the 'first day after the Sabbath' is at first retained. We find this 'first day' in the Easter chapters of all four evangelists (Mt 28:1, Mk 16:2, Lk 24:1, Jn 20:1, 19), and Paul also uses this form. In the First Letter to the Corinthians 'the first day of every week' (16:2) is implied as the usual day for the assembly of the Christian congregations. That would be about the year 54. The Acts of the Apostles tells how the congregation of Troas were gathered together with Paul by night on the first day after the Sabbath, which of course ended at sunset on Saturday evening; and the rite of the 'breaking of bread' was celebrated early on Sunday morning before the first rays of the rising sun (20:7–11).

At the end of the New Testament, however, in the Revelation to John, a new name with greater content is introduced. John, now an old man on Patmos, beholds the all-powerful sun-filled appearance of the Risen One on the 'Lord's Day' (1:10).

The new name now becomes general. About AD 107 Bishop Ignatius of Antioch, the martyr, in his *Letter to the Magnesians* (Ch. 9) warns the congregation there against back-sliding into the Sabbath cult which he calls *sabbatizein,* 'to Sabbathise'. He exhorts them rather to live *kata kyriaken,* according to the Lord's Day, 'on which our life has sprung up again'. Ignatius shows that he is filled with the knowledge that the Lord's Day is something quite new and quite distinct from the Sabbath. It is not the 'Christian Sabbath'; it has in fact nothing to do with the Sabbath; it is quite different altogether.

The word *Kyrios* played a part in the cult of Caesar. Domitian called himself officially 'Lord and God'. However, there is abundant material showing that the word *Kyrios* was also used particularly for the Sun-god.*

---

* Dölger, *Sol Salutis.*

The day of the sun

In harmony with that, in AD 150 Justin Martyr the philosopher presented a defence, an *apologia,* to the Roman Emperor which was addressed at the same time to the educated Greco-Roman world. For the first time – in the documents we know to date – the expression 'Day of the Sun' is used (*First Apology,* 65). In broad outline Justin describes the course of a Christian service as celebrated 'on the day of the sun'. He adds: 'For that is the first day on which God transformed the darkness and the original matter and created a cosmos.' According to Justin's worldview a kind of original substance, wrapped in darkness, already existed at the time when the creation, described in Genesis, began and the Word resounded: 'Let there be light'. Justin builds a wonderful bridge from this 'Let there be light' to the Easter event: 'On the selfsame first day our Saviour Jesus Christ rose from the dead. On the day before the Kronos-Saturn Day they crucified him, and after the Kronos Day, on the day which is the day of the Sun, he appeared to his apostles.'

It should not be forgotten that the *Apology* is not directed to those within Christian circles, but is intended to be understood by outsiders. Nevertheless such a dedicated Christian as Justin Martyr must have considered it permissible to use the cosmic names Saturn-day and Sunday. His allusion to 'Let there be light' stands in harmony with the 'day of the sun'.

Early Christendom did not by any means exclude the content of other pagan, non-biblical world-views, for Christianity was not felt to be just the continuation and sublimation of the Old Testament, but the rightful heir to all the true spiritual possessions of humanity. That is implicit in the words of Paul: 'For all things are yours' (1Cor 3:21). A Christianity which cherishes Paul's words that follow, 'You are of Christ,' regards as justified that 'the glory of the nations'* should be included in the heavenly Jerusalem, as the Revelation to John envisioned (Rv 21:24–26).

A link with the sun-character of the Resurrection Day is already inherent in the gospels. Mark says of the Easter morning: 'Very early on the first day of the week, when the sun had risen' (16:2). The

---

* The 'nations' in the Bible refers to the gentiles, the heathens.

sun-nature of the being who could say: 'I am the light of the world' (Jn 9:5) appears in important places in the New Testament. At the Transfiguration upon the mount his countenance shone 'like the sun' (Mt 17:2). He appears to Paul before Damascus at the midday hour as a light 'brighter than the sun' (Ac 26:13). John on Patmos sees his countenance 'like the sun shining in full strength' (Rv 1:16). For early Christendom the appellation of the Lord's Day as the 'day of the sun' was directly illuminating.

Jerome (*c.* 347–420) writes: 'When the day which the Lord has made, that is the Day of Resurrection, is called the day of the sun by the heathen, we may gladly accept this designation; for today [Easter Sunday] the Light of the World, the Sun of Righteousness has arisen' (*Commentary on Psalm 118*). Likewise Maximus of Turin (around 460) writes: 'The Day of Resurrection is for us so to be honoured, because on this day the Saviour, after overcoming the darkness in the underworld, shone forth like the rising sun in the light of the Resurrection. Therefore this day is called the "day of the sun" by the people of the world (*homines saeculi*) because Christ, the Rising Sun of Righteousness illuminates it with his light.' (*Homily* 61). The expression 'Sun of Righteousness', comes from the Old Testament. Significantly, it is to be found at the end of the last book of the prophets, Malachi (4:2). Christian preachers and writers repeatedly refer to this passage.

Noteworthy is what Tertullian (*c.* 155–220) in two of his writings has to say (*Ad Nationes* 1.13, and *Apologeticus* 16). 'Others [of our antagonists] believe with more humanity and probability that the sun is our God. If we are accounted to be Persians ... I believe that this comes from our well-known custom of praying towards the east.' He reminds the heathens: 'It is you who have taken the sun into your calendar of seven days.' He complains that they improperly observe the Day of Saturn through Jewish influence.

On March 7, 321 the Emperor Constantine promoted a memorable law, raising the 'worshipful Day of the Sun' to a legally protected holy day. Coming as he did from an ancient sun-cult he thought to satisfy therewith both Christian and heathen sun-worshippers.

Shades of confusion

We can observe how Christianity in the first centuries had largely adopted the planetary week, not only with regard to the sun's day. We remember how Justin quite freely speaks of Holy Saturday as the day of Kronos-Saturn. Likewise Clement of Alexandria calls Wednesday and Friday the day of Hermes-Mercury and the day of Aphrodite-Venus (*Stromata* 75.2). Christian inscriptions discovered from the time between 269 and 473 show that even in Christian circles the planetary names were sometimes used.

This obviously caused reservations. The established Church, with its strong Old Testament colouring, shied away from this cosmic connection, even retreating from the 'Sun-Day'. The strictly orthodox Emperor Theodosius recommended the return to the earlier usage when 'our forefathers rightly called the "day of the sun" the "Lord's Day".' In the times following, the 'day of the sun' was no longer approved. The Romance languages have adapted themselves to this. They have dropped the 'day of the sun' and have returned to the 'Day of the Lord'. The derivation from *dies dominica* is clearly recognisable in the French *dimanche,* Italian *domenica* and Spanish *domingo*. It may be because of a stronger feeling for the natural and cosmic that the northern peoples, in contrast to the usage of the Latin Church, have held fast to the sun. German *Sonntag,* English *Sunday,* Dutch *zondag,* Norwegian *søndag.*

We can feel an unmistakable unease in Augustine when he speaks of the planetary week. He asserts rather vexatiously: 'The first day after the Sabbath is the Lord's Day. The second day after the Sabbath is the Second Day [*secunda feria*], laymen [*saeculares*] call it the Day of the Moon. They call the third, Day of Mars. The fourth is called Mercury's Day by the heathen – and even by many Christians. But we should not do so. They should correct it and not speak thus!' (*Expositions on the Psalms* 93). Apart from the 'Lord's Day' Augustine favours the old Jewish number names, which is still what holds today in the liturgical language of the Catholic Church.*

An extreme example of the struggle against the cosmic day-names is provided by Martin of Braga, a sixth-century Spanish bishop. He

---

* Portuguese, unlike Spanish, keeps to this practice.

goes as far as declaring the planetary gods of antiquity to be ordinary, even criminal, human beings who in former times lived in Greece. Thus Jupiter was an adulterer, Mars a ruffian, Mercury a thief, Venus a prostitute, Saturn a child-eater. They were 'the worst of men and rogues among the people of Greece' (*De Correctione Rusticorum*) This representation is indeed a nadir in the lack of understanding of, or the determination *not* to understand, ancient mythology and its pictorial language.

While the resentment in these voices was narrow-minded and restricted, we must also try to understand the opposition by Christianity to the adoption of the planetary names. 'All things are yours', but 'you are of Christ'. If the second sentence loses its force, and the real Christ-element becomes ineffective, then in reaching for 'the glories of the heathen' one becomes alienated from one's own glory. If in the sense of the Apocalypse the glory of the nations is to be brought into the heavenly Jerusalem, it must undergo a rebirth through the Christian element.

The exalted mystery-wisdom of the ancient Chaldeans had assumed a very decadent form when it was being spread through all sorts of murky channels in the Roman Empire. Juvenal complains in his *Satires:* 'But there is even greater confidence placed in the Chaldeans. Everything told by the astrologers is taken as valid ... for now the Oracle at Delphi is silent and mankind is tormented by the darkness of the future' (6.554). People were thereby made unfree. They held the stars responsible for their own misdeeds. The Church Fathers had to concern themselves at times with such views. Against the turbid after-effects of a once exalted star-wisdom Tatian the Assyrian (AD 170) was assuredly right when he said: 'We Christians stand above fate and instead of planetary daimons we know the one unerring Lord' (*Oratio ad Graecos* 9). Christians are 'above the compulsion of destiny': a glorious saying.

Even so the 'all things are yours' remains. Christ said, 'The Sabbath was made for man, not man for the Sabbath. So the Son of Man is Lord even of the Sabbath' (Mk 2:27f). Becoming fully human is the meaning and goal of creation. People may not surrender their freedom to what has been created for them. Once freedom is assured through their attachment to the Christ, then they can and ought to avail themselves of all that can help them towards their development. In the deepest sense Sunday also exists 'for man' as the 'day which the Lord has made' for the good of humankind.

In this sense the Son of Man is also lord of the cosmic forces. On Patmos, John sees the Risen One holding the 'seven stars' in his right hand. They are the seven genii, the seven world-qualities. In this connection we can also consider what the seven day-gods were for the Chaldeans. In the decadence of the ancient wisdom a stage was reached when people felt themselves to be without freedom 'in the hands of the seven stars'. John sees it the other way round: the seven stars in the hand of the Son of Man. They are subordinated and integrated to his higher working: they must serve him. Under this sign is set the task of future Christianity, that is to bring the cosmic wisdom to a baptism whereby it can be reborn as Christian wisdom. That applies particularly to Sunday, whose sun-character is confirmed and strengthened by Christ's Resurrection, and which is ready to be grasped with a new consciousness by Christians.

Of that there is little to be seen in the history of the representative churches. From the fifth century onwards in Greco-Roman Christendom the use of the cosmic week day names began to decline. The residue of ancient wisdom was cast out, no effort was made towards its rebirth within Christianity, no attempt was made to bring this wisdom into the New Jerusalem: a Christianity bereft of wisdom was all that was desired.

A consequence of this was that in the sixth century a 'Sabbathisation' of Sunday began. Ignatius of Antioch had warned against confounding the Sabbath and Sunday, but already the sense for the difference in spirit of the two days was lost. There was no longer any feeling for the Saturn character of Saturday and the sun quality of Sunday. And so the mood of the Jewish Sabbath began to be implanted on Sunday, which was being turned into a Christian Sabbath. Theodor Zahn, a scholar of early Christianity, wrote: 'It never occurred to the Christians of the first three centuries to consider Sunday as a continuation of the Jewish Sabbath or even to call it the Sabbath, and even in the fourth and fifth centuries only uncertain beginnings of such an outlook are to be found'* By the time of Charlemagne the blurring of the difference was in full swing.

---

* *Geschichte des Sonntags,* p. 128.

The Reformation, having no knowledge of any Christian wisdom, brought no return to the original usage. Here the only consideration was social and educational. It was decided that there should be a day free of work for religious instruction, and in the interests of good order a special day had to be agreed upon. 'Because from former times Sunday has been assigned to this purpose we should leave it at that, that it may continue so in good order by common consent' (Luther in the *Large Catechism*).

Calvin's Protestantism, bearing the strong imprint of the Old Testament, almost completely transferred the Sabbath mood to Sunday. An amusing picture of this puritanical strictness of the Sabbath is given by Bismarck in an address to the Reichstag (May 9, 1885), when he tells of his first journey to England in the 1840s: 'I had just landed ... on a Sunday, and was glad to have survived a bad crossing, so that I was involuntarily whistling a tune, not very loudly, and a fellow-passenger accompanying me said to me rather anxiously, "Please sir, do not whistle." I said, "Why shouldn't I? I'm happy!" "It's Sunday," he explained to me benevolently, and that I was in danger of being exposed to some unpleasantness.'

Nowadays for many people Sunday has become more and more externalised and submerged completely in the idea of the weekend. We have almost completely forgotten that Sunday should not end the week but should be the beginning of the week, shining into it with the power of Christ's Resurrection. Because the 'true' Sunday is threatened by a calendar reform – and also because the movable Easter festival is even more acutely threatened – we should take this as a signal for Christendom to rouse itself and think about its Sunday. We stand now at a time when it is imperative to attain a wisdom and knowledge of the workings of cosmic powers and their intimate rhythms, and this through the 'freedom of a Christian' as Luther rightly puts it, and in the sense of those words 'All things are yours, but you are of Christ'. In Rudolf Steiner's anthroposophy we see such a modern wisdom, which has as its centre Christ and the Deed of Golgotha.

Appendix: The week and calendar reforms

We shall now deal expressly with an objection that is often heard. The 'genuineness' of Sunday depends on whether the weeks have flowed without interruption since the first Sunday. Many people believe that this 'genuineness' must have been affected by former calendar reforms.

At the time of Christ the Julian calendar was in force. This had been introduced by Julius Caesar with the help of an Alexandrian scholar in the year 45 BC. In 1582 it was replaced by the calendar of Pope Gregory XIII, because it had become apparent that the Julian Calendar, with its 365¼ days, was not accurate enough, the year being actually 11¼ minutes shorter. This discrepancy, small at first, accumulated over the course of centuries until finally it was noticed clearly that the calendar was falling behind the real sun year. In autumn 1582 the calendar was turned back to the position it held at the time of the Council of Nicaea (AD 325) by removing ten surplus days from the year. October 4 was followed immediately by October 15. But the course of the weekdays was not affected. October 4 was a Thursday, and the next day, 15, a Friday.*

The order of the days of the week in fact has not been altered since the time of Christ, and even before that it goes back undisturbed to the sixth century BC. This order has remained constant both in Jewish communities, who were well practised in preserving their holy times amid whatever calendars obtained in their surrounding world, and in the Christian Church, which whether it was persecuted or recognised, has held to its Sunday.†

---

* The adoption of the Gregorian calendar followed later in some countries, for instance in 1752 in England. Some Orthodox Churches, including Jerusalem, Russia and Ukraine, still use the Julian calendar.

† There have been temporary interruptions, for instance during the French Revolution with its calendar of ten-day 'weeks' which was in force from 1793 to 1805. Similarly, after experiments with a five-day and six-day week, the Soviet Union returned to the old week in 1940.

V

PSALMS ABOUT THE WORLD

22

THE HUMAN BEING UNDER THE STARS

PSALM 8

In the season of autumn we can come to ourselves more readily than at other time of the year. During the summer, sun and heat often threaten to oppress us, in winter cold and darkness cast their spell. In spring the fresh new life tends to carry us away. But in the cool of autumn we return to our self. In the sign of Libra, the scales – the zodiacal sign of autumn – we find our balance.

Psalm 8 is an autumnal contemplation. Very likely the Hebrew text suggests as subtitle 'a song at the winepress', not 'a song on the Gitthit' (a musical instrument). The Septuagint, the Greek translation of the Old Testament made in the third century BC, also interpreted the instruction as referring to wine-making, an activity well-known to the Greeks and traditionally accompanied with special songs and hymns. The picture of the ripe green and golden grapes forms the background of our psalm, in which the mysterious position of the human being is weighed, poised between heaven and earth.

Valuable discoveries are made if we observe how each language has its special designation for the human being or man. Thus, for instance, the English *man* and the German *Mensch* are both connected with an Indo-Germanic word indicating *thought, thinking*. Here man is recognised above all beings as the bearer of the spirit. *An-thropos* in Greek means 'the one who looks upward'; it is felt essential that they are capable of looking upward to heaven, that they can lift their eyes to the stars. *Homo, humanus* in Latin (from which we have 'human') is related to *humus*, 'earthly', hence they are the terrestrial, the earthly,

> **Psalm 8**
>
> *O Lord, our Lord*
> *how all the earth shines forth in the magnificence of*
> *your Name!*
> *You have set your glory into the heavens.*
> *² Out of the mouths of children and infants,*
> *you have founded strength in view of your oppressors*
> *to silence the enemy and the avenger.*
>
> *³ When I look at your heavens, the work of your fingers,*
> *the moon and the stars, which you have set in place,*
> *⁴ what is man that you are mindful of him,*
> *and the son of man that you care for him?*
>
> *⁵ Yet you have made him lack but little of the dignity of*
> *heavenly beings*
> *and crowned him with light of revelation and splendour.*
> *⁶ You have given him dominion over the works of*
> *your hands;*
> *you have put all things under his feet,*
> *⁷ all sheep and oxen,*
> *and also the beasts of the field,*
> *⁸ the birds of the heavens, and the fish of the sea,*
> *whatever passes along the widths of the seas.*
>
> *⁹ O Lord, our Lord*
> *how all the earth shines forth in the magnificence of*
> *your Name!*

they who stand in a distinct and important connection with the earth. The Hebrew agrees here with the Latin. In the language of the Old Testament the human being is fundamentally characterised through the earthly relationship. *Adamah* is the earth, *Adam,* the human being. Human beings are thus felt to be ones who are unthinkable without the specifically terrestrial earthly element. They are closely connected with the whole evolution of the earth, they are its crown and completion.

This earth-aspect of humans is of greatest significance. Human beings are the goal and meaning of the earth. They bear in them-

22. THE HUMAN BEING UNDER THE STARS

selves the extract of its finest forces. Only under the quite special and peculiar conditions of earthly existence can human beings evolve to an independent personality endowed with consciousness of their self. Yet, however justifiable the Roman-Hebrew name for man may be, it needs completion. It can lead to the one-sidedness of materialism if only the human relation to the earth is stressed. The other aspect is wonderfully brought into play through the Greek aspect: *anthropos,* the one looking upward.

On the one hand it is true that no independent consciousness of self is possible without passing through the hard sphere of the terrestrial. But on the other, it must not be forgotten that what penetrates through to self-consciousness against the resistance of earthly conditions originates from above. And when people look up to the stars they lift themselves to the sublime worlds of their heavenly origin. Here too there is the danger of one-sidedness, dramatically expressed in the story of the philosopher who contemplates the heavens and falls into a ditch because he has paid no attention to his path on earth.

It is only in harmony between above and below, between heaven and earth that the true human being is achieved.

'What is man?' In Psalm 8 this question is formally posed, and in a wonderful assessment of his heavenly and earthly importance, the nature of man is set forth and extolled.

> O LORD, our Lord
> > how all the earth shines forth in the magnificence of
> > > your Name!

The earth is a realm of divine manifestation. 'How is your name visibly inscribed in all earth-existence!' The earth is thus not only dull heavy substance, blind and deaf. It is not only anonymous matter, an accidental assembly of nameless atoms. On the contrary, it is filled with the divine Name. The 'Name' is the inner nature, the essence, lifted into consciousness of what is known of a being. So the 'Name of God' is the tenor and purport of what the Godhead gives of itself to be known. In the individual works of creation, the letters of this divine Name are, as it were, the open secret. Hence the Name shines forth out of earth existence.

In the same breath the psalm passes over from the earthly to the heavenly, and so our eyes are raised to the upper world:

> You have set your glory into the heavens.

The earth, weighty with the secrets of the great Name, is overarched by the spheres of heavens. *Shemaim,* 'heavens' in Hebrew, is plural. At that time people still knew of the supersensible worlds ranging upward one beyond another and turning to us their 'outer side' in the firmament of stars. St Paul, for instance, speaks of being 'caught up to the third heaven' (2Cor 12:2). The reflection of the Name in the earth guides our gaze upwards to the heavens in which the Godhead is revealed in eternal radiance. This raising and lowering of our eyes to heaven and to earth continues, as we shall see, to be characteristic of Psalm 8.

From the outspread radiance in the heavens let us turn again to earth. Now, for the first time, human beings appear in the field of vision, and first in the stage of childhood:

> Out of the mouths of children and infants,
> you have founded strength in view of your oppressors
> to silence the enemy and the avenger.

From the modern intellectual point of view, children are just not yet fully-grown adults – 'not yet'. In contrast to this, the grown-up people, measured by children, represent in many respects a 'no longer'. They are by no means only the goal, the attainment of which 'devalues' the preceding stages. No; childhood has its own intrinsic worth. From the purely earthly point of view, children, as still young inhabitants of earth, are imperfection, immaturity. However, adding the heavenly standpoint, childhood is highly significant. For children are not yet completely incarnated human beings, ones who still belong in a great measure to the higher worlds. 'Their angels always see the face of my Father who is in heaven' (Mt 18:10). It is significant that in Psalm 8 the words about children are placed between verses 2 and 4, both of which contemplate the starry heavens.

If we recognise the heavenly in addition to the earthly we no longer see in the child merely the still unfinished adult. We are no longer tempted to 'offend these little ones'. Indeed, we recognise in the nature of the child a powerful factor in the conflict which is fought around human beings by good and evil spirits.

Infinitely much spirituality would be lost if human beings came into the world at once clever and grown-up, fixed and finished, without first being children. Few people have any idea how much they have to thank the dawning years of childhood for those moments when they were gently touched by a higher world. Powerful divine forces continuously enter earthly existence through the experience of one's own childhood, or the childhood stage of others. How much light and warmth has been shed by the picture of the Child in the crib into a grown-up world which has grown cold. So we can take quite seriously the psalmist's words, that for the Godhead the stage of human childhood represents in its own right a factor of strength in the conflict with the opposing powers. These are the forces of the Adversary, who tear from the heart of earthly humans the memory of their heavenly origin and thus turn them into mere creatures of earth. Mere earthly intellectuality is in its very nature unchildlike. It makes one precocious and so plays into the hands of the powers of death.

'Strength in view of your oppressors.' The oppressors (this is the literal translation) are in fact the beings who drive the divine element on earth 'into a corner'; they wish to deprive it of room to live and air to breathe. This passage in the psalms once falls also from the lips of Christ. The chief priests and scribes take offence at the hosanna which the children in the temple cried out to him on his entry. Christ answers them with the words of Psalm 8:2 (Mt 21:15f). With the Christ, the lost and forgotten heaven draws once more into the human world, and it is the childlike element in the people which, in contrast to the inwardly fossilised chief priests and scribes, recognises the One who is entering and hails him with cries of joy.

From the sphere of childhood the gaze of Psalm 8 turns upward again:

> When I look at your heavens, the work of your fingers,
> the moon and the stars, which you have set in place,

Here the Greek aspect of man is most beautifully shown: *anthropos,* the one who looks upwards. Above all earthly needs and riches we look with deep awe into the splendour of the star-set night sky. The psalms do not often speak of the stars. The word 'star' (*kokhab*) is not to be found again until towards the end of the Book of Psalms. In Psalm 136 the works of creation are enumerated, each sentence being followed by the response: 'His loving devotion endures for ever.' All the separate acts of creation in Genesis are brought once more to consciousness and extolled as proofs of mercy, communications of divine spiritual life. 'He made the great lights – his loving devotion endures for ever; the sun to rule the day – his loving devotion endures for ever; the moon and the stars to rule by night – his loving devotion endures for ever.'

Then in Psalm 147:4: 'He assigns the number of the stars; he calls them all by name.' The numbering does not signify mere calculation. Its purport is that God carries them all in his consciousness, and indeed as organism of a totality, as a complete choir. But this entirety (the number) consists again of purely separate star-individualities, as St Paul says, 'for star differs from star in glory' (1Cor 15:41). So this choir is truly a symphony, a harmonious consonance of all the single individualities, all of whom God calls 'by name'.

And finally the stars are mentioned once more in Psalm 148:3, in the grand hallelujah of the universe. Just as in Psalm 136 the words of the eternally enduring loving devotion are added to each sentence, so Psalm 148 contains the ever-repeated exhortation to join in the great chorus of praise. It begins with the heavens and the higher worlds, passes on to angels and heavenly hosts, and only with the sun, moon and stars passes over from the invisible into visibility. 'Praise him, O sun and moon, praise him all you stars of light.'

These three passages supplement one another. In Psalm 136 the stars come forth from the merciful self-communication and revelation of the eternal Godhead. In Psalm 147 the stars appear as multiplicity and yet unity, a symphony of individualities. In Psalm 148 the stars are clear mirrors which radiate back to the Creator his splendour, in that they 'praise him'. This is like a reversal of Psalm 136. These three passages which refer to the relation of God to the stars and of the stars to God, contrast with our Psalm 8 where the relation is shown between the stars and humanity. 'When I look at your heavens ... the moon and the stars.' We must pause a while and feel the quietness of contemplation, how everything falls away around us, and only the starry heaven remains, which in the land of the psalmist shines with brilliant clarity and radiance. Let us feel for a while the calm peace – all self forgotten – of this contemplation, 'When I look at your heavens ... the moon and the stars.'

But now this forgetting of self flows into the question about humanity. A deep inner logic lies in the fact that this experience of the stars, which carries us out into the infinite universe, turns back to the human. A deep contemplation of the stars does not imply getting lost in the far spaces, but coming in connection with the eternal powers who work together from the periphery into the centre, in order to bring forth the human being. We sense in the stars the cosmic dwelling-places of the higher beings who take part in our human evolution. The macrocosm without stands in intimate relation with the microcosm, the human being. This is the inner logic of the transition from the contemplation of the stars to the question about the human being. Again we observe the upward and downward movement between heaven and earth, peculiar to Psalm 8:

what is man that you are mindful of him ...?

One must not hear this question with the ears of the modern 'enlightened' scientist. For them it would mean, 'What indeed is the speck of human dust in the face of these giant astronomical dimensions!' What indeed can human beings signify in the universe? Less than nothing. To consider the world from the point of view of materialism is far from the mood of the psalm. Incidentally, this 'speck-of-dust' sentiment no doubt has the appearance of praiseworthy humility; it is, however, rather lazy; through a purely quantitative view human beings are reduced to nothingness, and then in non-committal irresponsibility one can lead a morally inferior life. If the starry heaven is understood again as the revelation of creative spirit-powers, then the question, 'What is man?' is raised once more in all earnestness.

The human being is not yet completed. Called to grow in the image of God, we are still in process of becoming. For the sake of our evolution to this distant goal we go through a 'history'. An integral part of this history is the Fall, presented in the Old Testament in hieroglyphic images. This event severed human beings from the world of their origin, and enabled the power of death to draw near them. There is an echo of this in the text of our psalm, where for 'man' the usual *adam* is not used at first, but the word *enosh*. This denotes the 'transitory', 'perishable', similar to when we speak of humans as 'mortals'. Thus: 'What is a mortal that you are mindful of him, that you bear him in your divine consciousness?' In the next lines, however, the word 'adam' appears in *ben-adam,* the 'son of man'.

    and the son of man that you care for him?

Man is absorbed in the contemplation of the starry heavens. This could not happen if human beings were made only of what is transitory. Beholding the stars they become conscious of the riddle of death, which has been added to their nature: 'What is mortal man that you cherish him in your thoughts?' Then the gaze passes from the human being of today into the future. 'The son of man.' Again *adam* is used in the Hebrew, which stresses the relation to the earth, but without implying material transitoriness. The 'son' of man – this is the human being growing into the future, striving towards new possibilities. It is the figure which, out of the Old Adam marked by death and the Fall, is to come forth one day as something new. In the New Testament, 'Son of Man' appears significantly as characterising Christ, for he alone can overcome the powers of the Fall and make the human being capable of a divine future.

Note too the polarity of the elements of thought and will in the words 'mindful of' and 'care for'. God is mindful of mortal humans, he carries them in his consciousness. He cares for, takes charge of, the son of man. He lets his vigorous help stream to him. The Hebrew word is sometimes also rendered by 'visit' in the positive sense of attending. The Godhead unites itself with the future form of human beings and inclines to them with strength of being. Here the mysteries of Christ are touched upon from afar, as in premonition. Only in the light of Christ does the question of human beings and their future find its answer. Only, too, in the light of Christ as the one who reinstates and perfects true humanity, do the following verses that speak of human glory and honour receive their full meaning.

Before we pass on to these, let us look back once more and see how the human being meets us in three forms, shown in Psalm 8 with the three names: the child – the mortal – the son of man. The 'child' is the human being still enveloped in the divine forces of their origin. The 'mortal' is the adult of the Fall, who has bought consciousness at the cost of being permeated with the powers of death. The 'son of man' stands as the figure of the future in the glory of Christ.

That the psalm does not answer the question that arose from contemplation of the stars in the sense of a speck of human dust, is shown in the way it continues. The glory of the origin and the glory of future perfection of human beings lie in these words:

> Yet you have made him lack but little of the dignity of
> heavenly beings
> and crowned him with light of revelation and splendour.

Human beings – 'lack but little of the dignity of heavenly beings' – almost as gods. In this 'almost' lies the drama of their evolution and their problem. They feel themselves called to divine status. Lucifer was able to ensnare them through this noble urge for perfection. 'You will be like God' (Gn 3:5). But only Another will truly redeem this promise – 'you are gods' (Jn 10:34).

A crown was an image in ancient times, indicating that humans were not 'closed' above, but reaching upwards into the divine light. Here the human being is spiritually crowned with 'glory and majesty', with *kabhod* and *hadar*. The former word often stands in the Old Testament for the aura of the Godhead when the tabernacle, or later the temple, is filled with the shining traces of its presence. The second word means 'radiating splendour', 'sublimity', 'majesty'. Certain early rabbis saw in this crowning with *kabhod* and *hadar* a reference to the endowment of the 'higher soul' (the *neshamah alyonah* in the works of David Kimchi and Salomon ben Melech); and rightly so. This mysterious event finds its full consummation again only through the Christ. The Book of Revelation (2:10) speaks of the 'crown of life', which is given to him who goes with Christ through death, and the warning is uttered 'that no one take your crown' (3:11). For the Adversary would snatch the higher spirituality from human beings and thrust them down into animal nature.

The psalm, which in the image of the crown of light looked up to the heights, now turns once more towards the earth. After having considered that which is above man and descends as a crown upon his head, it passes on to what is beneath humans:

> You have given him dominion over the works of your hands;
>   you have put all things under his feet,

The created world is put in subjection to him who is crowned with spirit. Human beings participate in both worlds. Upwards they extend to the Godhead, downwards they shares in the creature through their body. Mediating between the visible and invisible world, they are called to be the representative of God on earth. Should they permit the opposing powers to rob them of their crown, they become tyrants, exploiters of the earth. That they should subdue the earth is a divine commission (Gn 1:28). But they must not forget that they may only rule the earth as bearer of the spirit crown, and that the world beneath them is 'the works of your hands'. Herein lies the whole programme for human work and civilisation on the earth.

And now the animal world is especially mentioned as subjected to human beings, not in the order of creation as in Genesis, but in the reverse order. The text begins with the higher animals, those nearer to the human being, and then advances to those further removed, the creatures of air and water. First the domestic animals, then the wild animals (beasts of the field), then birds and finally fish.

> all sheep and oxen,
>   and also the beasts of the field,
> the birds of the heavens, and the fish of the sea,
>   whatever passes along the widths of the seas.

This rulership of human beings over the beasts has another aspect, a more inward one. There exists something like an underground connection between the animals and the various aspects of the human soul. Fairy-tales and dreams make known to us in manifold ways that the animal world represents the totality of human emotional nature. Certain soul-forces are made into objects in the animal forms. To rule over the animal, including the animal in one's own inner being, through a connection with the higher realm of spirit, is the task which lies before human beings. They stand between angels and beasts. In

Psalm 91 this finds classic expression: 'For he shall command his angels to guard you ... they will lift you up in their hands ... you will tread on the lion and the adder, you will trample the young lion and the serpent underfoot' (91:11–13). Not in the proud Luciferic sense is the majesty of the human being intended here.

The psalm concludes with the same sentence with which it began:

> O Lord, our Lord
>   how all the earth shines forth in the magnificence of
>   your Name!

The same sentence as at the beginning. But it has grown richer. The human being has been built into this song of praise. When human dignity is fully established, the Name of God can truly reveal itself on earth. Dedication to being human is humanity's true divine service.

23

GOD IN NATURE

PSALM 104

Psalm 104 is like an echo in human form of the story of creation in Genesis; the events recorded in the succession of the days of creation resound in the psalm, which is composed of seven sections.

1. The heavens

> Praise the LORD, O my soul!
> O LORD my God, you are very great.

This expression 'very great' is more than a merely edifying turn of phrase. It holds the key to an understanding of the creation of the world. 'Great' – in ancient times – is a term for a spirituality of such overflowing force that it can pour itself creatively into an outer world. A spirituality which from inner abundance can become 'spiritual-physical'. The pre-eminence of the purely spiritual as the original beginning is not infringed, but we must think of a spirit capable of creating a world.

Psalm 104 traces the path that leads from the essential being, the inner existence of God, to the becoming of the world. In this progress several stages may be distinguished. It begins with the 'spiritual-physical' quality of the state of 'greatness'. What then proceeds out of this quality of the Godhead is designated by words that in the original Hebrew text have a mantric power: *hod we-hadar*.

> You are clothed in radiance-of-being and splendour-of-majesty.

Psalm 104

*Praise the L*ORD*, O my soul!*
  *O L*ORD *my God, you are very great.*
You are clothed in radiance-of-being and splendour-of-
    majesty.
  ² *You cover yourself with light as with a mantle,*
    you stretch out the heavens like a tent.
³ *You build your lofty abode by the waters.*
You make the clouds your chariot.
    You rush forth on the wings of the wind.
⁴ *You let your angels work in winds,*
    your lofty ministers in flaming fire.

⁵ *He set the earth on its foundations*
    so that forever it shall never be shaken.
⁶ *You covered it with the flood of the deep as with a garment;*
    the waters stood above the mountains.
⁷ *At your rebuke they fled;*
    at the voice of your thunder they hastened away in terror.
⁸ *The mountains arose, the valleys sank down,*
    to the place that you set for them.
⁹ *You have set a boundary that they may not pass,*
    so that they might not again cover the earth.

¹⁰ *You send the springs flowing into the valleys,*
    running between the hills.
¹¹ *They give drink to every creature of the field,*
    the wild beast quenches his thirst.
¹² *Beside them the birds of the heavens dwell*
    they sing among the branches.
¹³ *You water the hills from your lofty abode,*
    you satisfy the earth with the fruits you create.

¹⁴ *You cause the grass to grow for the cattle*
    and grain for man to cultivate,
that he may bring forth bread from the earth
    ¹⁵ *and the wine to gladden the human heart,*
oil to make his countenance shine,
    and bread to strengthen human heart.

^{16} *The trees of the* LORD *are fully sated,*
   the cedars of Lebanon which he planted,
^{17} *where the birds build their nests.*
   The stork has her nest on the tree top.
^{18} *The high mountains are the realm of the wild goats,*
   the rocks are a refuge for rock badgers.

^{19} *He fashioned the moon as a sign for the times;*
   the sun knows its setting.
^{20} *You make darkness, and it is night,*
   when all the beasts of the forest creep about.
^{21} *The young lions roar for their prey,*
   praying for their food from God,
^{22} *When the sun rises, they come together*
   and lie down in their dens.
^{23} *Man goes out to his work*
   and his labour until the evening.

^{24} *O* LORD, *how manifold are your works!*
   In wisdom you have made them all;
   the earth is filled with what is yours.
^{25} *Here is the sea, great and wide,*
   which teems with creatures innumerable,
   living things, both small and great.
^{26} *There go the sea-monsters,*
   and Leviathan whom you made to play in there.

^{27} *These all wait upon you;*
   that you give them their food in due season.
^{28} *When you give it to them, they gather it up;*
   when you open your hand, they are filled with goodness.
^{29} *When you hide your face, they are filled with fear;*
   when you take away their breath, they die,
   and return to their dust.
^{30} *When you send forth your breath, they are created,*
   and you renew the face of the earth.

^{31} *May the glory of the* LORD *endure forever;*
   may the LORD *rejoice in his works.*

> ^{32} *He looks on the earth and it trembles,*
>   *he touches the mountains and they smoke.*
> ^{33} *I will sing to the* L*ord* *as long as I live;*
>   *I will sing praise to my God while I have being.*
> ^{34} *May my meditation be pleasing to him,*
>   *for I rejoice in the* L*ord*.
> ^{35} *Let sinners be consumed from the earth,*
>   *and let the wicked be no more!*
> *Bless the* L*ord*, *O my Soul!*
> *Praise the* L*ord*.

Radiance-of-being and *splendour-of-majesty* – the meaning, but not the sound of the two words, may perhaps be thus distantly reproduced. They are unusually impressive, both in consonants and vowels, and particularly in their sequence. The first word *hod* appears in the Greek translation of the Septuagint as *exomologēsis,* Latin *confessio*. 'Confession' would suggest that in the acknowledgment, something inward is turned outwards and made manifest.

The two words express a streaming out from the unmanifested into the manifested. There is as yet nothing externally physical, we are still in a region of etheric light. Only in what follows do we enter the realm of the visible world, even though 'light' is not actually 'visible', but only renders the world visible for us. However, compared with *hod* and *hadar,* light is a step further into external existence.

> You cover yourself with light as with a mantle,
>   you stretch out the heavens like a tent.
> You build your lofty abode by the waters.

Only now we have reached the 'Let there be light' of Genesis. The radiance-of-being and splendour-of-majesty belongs to a still earlier, preceding stage. Now the heavens appear together with the light. Then 'the waters'. As yet this is no earthly water, nor is it water existing in cloud-form, but it is the 'water above the firmament', a heavenly ocean of etheric fluid forces.

Let us look again at this succession. Being very great – radiance-of-being – splendour-of-majesty – light – waters. It is the path into ever denser forms of existence, the path from within to without. This becomes very evident when we set the other series beside it; the words of comparison which express the relation to the Godhead: clothed – mantle – tent – lofty abode. 'Clothed' lies closest – and the psalm compares it with the radiance which precedes the light. The 'mantle' is a degree more external. Removed still further from the origin is the 'tent' though it is not so far from the mantle as, finally, the 'lofty abode'. With the 'being very great' at the beginning we are still within the very person of God. Then begins the manifestation, and the resulting world detaches itself more and more from the immediacy of the Creator, it clothes him, concealing-manifesting, manifesting-concealing as garment, as mantle, as tent, as house. But this house of the heavens is at the same time the temple of his direct presence.

From this high radiant heaven we now descend to the atmospheric heaven nearer to earth. We pass over at the same time from a world of tranquil being and tranquil radiance into the dynamic spheres of active forces.

> You make the clouds your chariot.
>   You rush forth on the wings of the wind.
> You let your angels work in winds,
>   your lofty ministers in flaming fire.

Clouds and winds bear the Lord in his movement, when he leaves the temple of his heavenly peace, and 'goes out of himself', (*ek-stasis* in Greek) into the storm.

Finally, contemplation passes from the divine Person himself to the forces which have detached themselves from him, as independent spirit-personalities. There are the 'messengers', the 'angels' who can embody themselves in the wafting winds; there are the 'lofty ministers' of God who can embody themselves in the flaming fire, in lightning. The Hebrew word *meshoreth* does not mean a slavish servant, but one who from free will serves as 'minister', as server in the highest sense. The ninefold order of the heavenly hierarchies has as the lowest degree the messengers, the angels. They can embody in the wafting winds. The highest hierarchy is the Seraphim, which means the 'burning ones'. They reveal themselves in the fire of lightning. The prophet Isaiah sees them in his great temple vision as the heavenly celebrants who begin to sound the hymn 'Holy, holy, holy', the Sanctus (Is 6:1–7).

2. The earth

Through the elemental spheres of clouds, storms and lightning, we descend to the solid earth.

> He set the earth on its foundations
> so that forever it shall never be shaken.

In order to characterise in its stages the gradual detachment of the world from the Creator, Rudolf Steiner used a series of four concepts: being – manifestation – activity – finished work. 'You are very great' – here we are still in *being*. With the light-heaven, *manifestation* began to issue from the being, but it still remained intimately linked with it. The world of clouds and winds, of lightning and thunderstorms – this was the sphere of *activity,* where the being is represented by the forces sent out, but the being himself remains far in the background. With the solid earth the stage of the *finished work* is reached; it is accomplished, finished, released, henceforth set free from the Creator. The end product is as hardened lava.

In its stony hardness the earth has an important function in human evolution. Human beings are to come to independence. To this end they must be withdrawn for a time from the direct life of divine being, in order to become aware of their own power of initiative in a world of death. It is precisely in the rigid element of earth, isolated from the immediate life of the higher worlds, that human beings can awaken to consciousness of themselves as individuals. Moreover the solid earth holds fast human work and lays out impressively before their eyes the results of their deeds, whether constructive or destructive.

Bringing about this solid earth was a special work of God in creating the human I, the self.

> You covered it with the flood of the deep as with a garment;
> the waters stood above the mountains.
> At your rebuke they fled;
> at the voice of your thunder they hastened away in terror.

The deep, *tehom,* appears often in the Old Testament as a sinister demonic being, as a kind of dragon of the pre-world chaos. The evolution of the firm earth, with its solid ground for the developing of human self-dependence, was God-willed design. In the ever-recurring floods the 'dragons', the Luciferic beings, who were servants of chaos, were active. In the Babylonian myth, Marduk, the Babylonian Michael, subdues Tiamat, the dragon of the primeval world. So here, the I-creating God 'rebukes' with a voice of thunder the powers of chaos and frees the earth for human activity.

So now at length the earth emerges from the primeval waters.

> The mountains arose, the valleys sank down,
>   to the place that you set for them.
> You have set a boundary that they [the waters] may not pass,
>   so that they might not again cover the earth.

Psalm 95 says still more plainly how the surface of the earth is shaped by God: 'And his hands have formed [*eplasan* in Greek] the dry land' (95:5). Thus mountains and valleys are the scene prepared by divine Providence for the unfolding of human destiny. We remember many sacred mountains upon which people received divine revelation, and think of the deep Jordan valley, lying far below sea-level, where at the Baptism by John, God entered into existence on earth.

3. The life of the earth

A boundary is set to the flood. In the solid element the earth is for the first time truly earth. But if the earth consisted only of earth it would become a wilderness of death. While Lucifer worked in the floods of chaos, in the hardened earth the Lord of Death appears: Ahriman, as the Persians called him. The earth must be kept living. The water-element, no longer as *tehom*, the dragon of the primeval deep, but now as a servant helps the earth to maintain life.

Now the earth is rescued from sclerotic death by water in the form of rivers, streams and rain. Without water there would be no plants. Water itself is not life, but it is the necessary medium of life, the vehicle of the etheric life-forces, which cannot work into the hard earth directly but which can be active in the liquid. There can be no life upon earth without water. And just as the moulding of the earth in hill and dale is no accident but the work of the divine 'potter', so too are the streams and rivers in the landscape, which flow from the springs, the result of organising divine action.

> You send the springs flowing into the valleys,
>   running between the hills.
> They give drink to every creature of the field,
>   the wild beast quenches his thirst.
> Beside them the birds of the heavens dwell
>   they sing among the branches.

Many commentaries have pointed out the poetic beauty of this description. The vivifying water not only appears in brooks and streams. It also falls upon the earth as rain. By falling in drops the water is prevented from being destructive and is wonderfully suited to the needs of the plants. Moreover in ascending and evaporating, water has been enriched with certain forces which it now brings down with it in the rain as a blessing. The ancients rightly believed that something came with it from God. Its etheric quality is a gift from heavenly spheres. It is a blessing from above.

> You water the hills from your lofty abode,
>   you satisfy the earth with the fruits you create.

Then the psalm describes in detail the fruitfulness of the earth:

> You cause the grass to grow for the cattle
>   and grain for man to cultivate,
> that he may bring forth bread from the earth

Cattle can eat the grass as it grows. But grain must be worked for; human effort must be added to the natural process in order to cultivate grain and bake bread. Working grain – *agri-cultura* – is the origin of 'culture', 'cultivate' and also of 'cult'. The words are derived from the word *colere,* to till the soil. Here, in connection with the preparation of bread, the human being is mentioned for the first time in Psalm 104.

> and the wine to gladden the human heart,
> oil to make his countenance shine,
> and bread to strengthen human heart.

The trinity, wine-oil-bread, points also to the sphere of worship. Bread and wine are both brought into connection with the human heart. The bread 'strengthens' our heart in steadfastness, the wine 'gladdens' it. In the service of Christ, these two become his body and his blood.

In addition to bread and wine with their relation to the heart, oil is mentioned, which is likewise a sacramental substance. 'Oil to make his countenance shine.' Oil is related to light. It is used in the Anointing Service and in the Ordination of priests as the agent of a spiritualising process. It is not connected with the heart, but with the countenance in which our human spirit nature is revealed.

The psalm then passes from the cultivated plants to nature in the wild. Linking up again to the words, 'You water the hills from your lofty abode,' it now reads:

> The trees of the LORD are fully sated,
> the cedars of Lebanon which he planted,
> where the birds build their nests.
> The stork has her nest on the tree top.
> The high mountains are the realm of the wild goats
> and the rocks are a refuge for rock badgers.

The manner in which the 'trees of the LORD', of Yahweh, are spoken of here, the cedars of Lebanon which he himself planted, is magnificent. Primeval forests stood on Lebanon, nature untouched by human beings. Time and again the Old Testament witnesses to the wonder and awe with which those mighty cedar trees were observed. The presence of God himself was felt in the midst of such forests. ('Cedars of God'* are also mentioned in Ps 80:10.) In view of the peculiar lack of sense for natural beauty in later Judaism, one is glad to hear such words in the Old Testament. In the stories of the patriarch Abraham, sacred groves and the planting of sacred trees play an

---

* *Arze-el,* literally 'cedars of God', is often translated as 'mighty cedars'.

important part. But the cedars of Lebanon were felt as if planted by God himself.

The rock badger or rock hyrax of the Middle East and Africa (the dassie in South Africa) is a mammal living high in rocky hillsides. It is a world of untouched solitude, far from humans and civilisation. In the psalm's devotional contemplation of nature this remote world is also included. It is as though the psalmist felt that the sphere of human activity required a zone of undisturbed nature around it belonging to God.

4. Sun and moon

In the account given in Genesis, the celestial bodies, sun, moon and stars only became visible on the fourth day of creation, even though the light-heaven had been there for some time. Similarly, this psalm, following the events of Genesis in a free manner, comes to speak of stars, moon and sun in its fourth section.

The psalm began with a descent out of the spheres of light to the waters of heaven and the clouds, and then down to the firm earth. In considering the earth, this way was reversed: first the earth as 'solid land', then the earth in so far as it is kept living by water. Now the earth is described with the great variety of emotions of which its inhabitants are capable, and which form an 'astral' relation with the celestial lights. For sun and moon do not appear here on their own, but in their relation to soul life on earth. The stars, the *astra,* influence 'astrality' on the earth.

> He fashioned the moon as a sign for the times;
>   the sun knows its setting.
> You make darkness, and it is night,
>   when all the beasts of the forest creep about.
> The young lions roar for their prey,
>   praying for their food from God,
> When the sun rises, they come together
>   and lie down in their dens.
> Man goes out to his work
>   and his labour until the evening.

First, the moon. The moon stands in the evening sky as a 'sign'. It marks the divisions of time, according to its phases. The significance of the lunar cycles is far-reaching for life on earth. Even the date of the Passover (and the Christian Easter) is fixed by these cycles. The sun 'knows its setting'. It 'knows' that earthly creatures may not be uninterruptedly exposed to its effects. So in going down it makes place for the kingdom of night, ruled by the moon.

Darkness and night, as in Genesis, are living beings. They are not merely absence of light. With the night the 'astral' world of the moon comes to life, to which the animals belong. Lunar astrality, not yet penetrated by full waking consciousness of self, under the spell of dreams, makes the beasts stir in the dark forests, makes the lions roar. The roaring, the cries, the bellowing of the beasts by night arouse a clear feeling in us of how remote the human world is from the animal soul-world of the world's primeval ages.

It has been thought touchingly naive that the psalm implies a prayer to God in the roaring of lions. But often the naive view is nearer to the original fact. The stirring of the animal souls is still close to the divine worlds. These primal instincts are no longer so innocent in human beings as in beasts, but are poisoned through the contact with an egotistic selfhood which has not yet achieved a selfless I. This direct proximity to God has been almost entirely lost among human beings.

The lunar world is overcome by the rising of the sun. The nocturnal beasts of prey hide in their dens. In human soul life something similar occurs. Nightmares, bad dreams, anxiety, spectres – all vanish when the sun comes up. It helps to kindle spirit-consciousness in the I, it brings human beings to themselves, helps them to be themselves. In a sacred, solemn mood it is said: 'Man goes out to his work'. It is the sunlit day with which human beings are most deeply united. Their work belongs to the light of day, they 'labour until the evening'.

The fourth section closes with this archetypal picture of the worker who 'labours so long as it is day'. The contemplation of the earthly world has reached its climax. At first it is simply hard ground; then enlivened by water and adorned by plants; then the souls of the beasts begin to stir; and finally human beings, related to the sun, go about their work on earth. Here the psalm rises to words of wonder:

> O Lord, how manifold are your works!
>   In wisdom you have made them all;
>   the earth is filled with what is yours.

Literally, the earth is full of your property or possessions. God, the Creator, has laid something of his own into the earthly world.

5. The sea

Just as Genesis has the swarming animal life in the sea (fifth day) follow the appearance of the celestial lights (on the fourth day) so too does Psalm 104 turn once more to the sea and its living creatures.

> Here is the sea, great and wide,
>   which teems with creatures innumerable,
>   living things, both small and great.
> There go the sea-monsters,
>   and Leviathan whom you made to play in there.

Here *tehom,* the primeval flood, still lives, but within the bounds given to it. The sea is like a memory of primeval stages before the earth had hardened into solid form. Indeed, everything alive has had its beginning in the sea. The composition of our human blood shows a mysterious relationship with seawater – memory of far-distant stages of the evolution of our body.

According to an illuminating conjecture it should not read 'There go the ships' but instead of ships: 'sea-monsters'. Leviathan is then mentioned directly in connection with this. The mythical sea-dragon is an echo of long-banished worlds of the saurians. 'To play in there' – the play points to artistic activity. In all the changes of form among the living and ensouled plasma, divine formative force is at work – comes into play. It comes into 'play' on the infinite possibilities of form in organic substance, until after this great prelude the human form finally appears. The fantastic prehistoric shapes, sea-monsters and dragons lie, too, on the way to the final human form.

6. The mystery of sustaining the world

> These all wait upon you;
> > that you give them their food in due season.
> When you give it to them, they gather it up;
> > when you open your hand, they are filled with goodness.
> When you hide your face, they are filled with fear;
> > when you take away their breath, they die,
> > and return to their dust.
> When you send forth your breath, they are created,
> > and you renew the face of the earth.

In a sweeping view at the totality of living creatures, the Godhead is acknowledged and honoured. Three images express what God continuously means for the world, even after the creation has come to an end: the opening hand, the face turned towards or away, the ingoing and outgoing breath. These pictures harmonise into a wonderfully organic trinity. They are known in anthroposophy as the nerve-sense system, the rhythmic system working in pulse and breath, and the metabolism-limb system.

In our countenance where our principal senses operate, our consciousness is awake. The basic condition for the existence of the world is that God turns his face towards it. If he should turn his face away, the fear of annihilation comes over all living beings. The world remains in existence as long as it is beheld and affirmed by the divine consciousness.

Breath lives in the rhythmic sphere. The world exists so long as the divine breath permeates it. If God draws in his breath, the world falls into nothingness. Similarly in Job (34:14f), 'If he gather his spirit and breath into himself, all flesh would perish.' This view is reminiscent of ancient Indian wisdom. The world is dependent on the breath of God. He breathes out: worlds arise; he breathes in: worlds perish. And so it goes on in exalted rhythms, incalculably long. Manvantaras and pralayas, cosmic days and cosmic nights, are the result of this divine rhythmic breathing. In the creating exhalation, the breath of life (the Hebrew *ruach* is both 'spirit' and 'breath') is still directly God's – 'your breath'. When God withdraws the breath, it is observed that meanwhile it has become the individualised breath of separate beings, for it now reads: 'their' breath. 'When you take away their breath.' The life of God becomes the life of the individual beings. But inasmuch as he takes back the world into himself, 'their' breath returns to its source.

To close or open a hand is a voluntary movement. The divine hand opens, the beings are filled with 'goodness'. 'Good' is a word that ultimately belongs to God alone. God gives of his own being, his own substance, so that something can come into existence. Nothing would be there, if this mystery of divine self-imparting, self-surrender did not exist. The whole world is fed from divine substance. The reception of nourishment is again only a picture, an image. Even without eating, a being 'lives' from the Godhead in every moment of its mere existing. Apart from the taking of nourishment, there is the great communion of all creatures in the substance of God himself. 'When you open your hand, they are filled with goodness.' In the original text 'good' is the same word as 'goodness'. In a wider sense every good thing, all goods, even the everyday consumer goods are dependant on the divine self-imparting, the original goodness. This mystery is acted out in the Last Supper. The opening hand is the gesture of the great divine 'Take this' (Lk 22:17). Psalm 145:16, offers a parallel to this: 'You open your hand and satisfy the desire of every living thing.'

Different aspects of the relationship of God to his world are set forth in these three images. In order that the world may be, God must turn his face to it, he must breathe his breath into it, he must open his hand and distribute.

The face of the earth is renewed. The earth has already passed through manifold forms; each time the face of the earth was coherent, formed according to a definite 'style'. These ancient worlds passed away when their hour had struck and gave place to new epochs. The face of the earth has thus already been renewed many times. This is true too for the succession of civilisations. All these events are associated with the taking in and giving out of breath by God. The world is not only sustained; in greater or smaller rhythms it is continuously renewed by the living breath of the Spirit, which ever and again sends out new waves of becoming, as *Creator Spiritus*.

7. Closing verses

> May the glory of the LORD endure forever;
> > may the LORD rejoice in his works.
> He looks on the earth and it trembles,
> > he touches the mountains and they smoke.
> I will sing to the LORD as long as I live;
> > I will sing praise to my God while I have being.
> May my meditation be pleasing to him,
> > for I rejoice in the LORD.
> Let sinners be consumed from the earth,
> > and let the wicked be no more!
> Bless the LORD, O my Soul!
> Praise the LORD.

The closing lines admit that there is also dissonance in the symphony of creation. The wonderful symphony is disturbed through the evil in human beings. The psalmist knows of no other solution than to desire that the evil-doers be exterminated from the earth.

The Fall follows the creation of the world. Since the song of praise is honest and realistic it cannot pass over this fact. It calls for a sentence of punishment in order that the creation may be purified and re-established. The mystery of redemption through Christ has not yet been revealed. Nor can it yet be evident that the permitting of evil was only a withdrawal, preceding a new creation which was to go beyond nature. Human beings were set on their evolutionary path in order that they may redeem themselves in future times by placing their independence freely into the service of the divine.

But this dark shadow, this unresolved discord, cannot really disturb the impression that Psalm 104 is altogether a great hymn of joy. Joy and gladness is the real character of this song of praise. In the final verses this is said in so many words. God rejoices in his work. Without joy there can be no creation. In response comes the human rejoicing in God. The sight of nature and its beauty turns into joy in God: 'I will rejoice in the LORD.'

The psalm ends as it began, with the exhortation to our own soul to join in the song of praise.

24

THE HEAVENS DECLARE

PSALM 19

1. The starry heavens

Psalm 19 opens in a mood of marvelling contemplation of the starry sky. Its first words are 'the heavens' and the whole psalm is dedicated to this subject and pours forth from it. Whilst the psalmist remains absorbed in selfless contemplation of the shining worlds they begin to sound and speak to his inner ear.

> The heavens recount the glory of God
> and the firmament proclaims his handiwork.

For the ancient world the 'music of the spheres' was a definite supersensible experience. The heavens not only shine: to the opened spiritual ear they sound, ring and finally even speak. There is an echo of this in the opening words of Goethe's *Faust:* 'The sun-orb sings in emulation, / 'Mid brother spheres his ancient round.'

The heavens 'recount' – the Hebrew word is of the same origin as the word *sepher,* the 'book'; the book in which things are entered, enumerated, recounted, declared, 'booked'. The starry heavens are the archetypal book, the book of books. The heavens were the first holy script. The Holy Scripture is a mirror, an image of this. Even today, the Bible and ritual book on the altar are not only a memory aid for the celebrating priest, but represent the Book of the Heavens.

The content of this cosmic proclamation is the 'glory of God'. 'Glory' is, however, too superficial a rendering. It is the splendour of revelation to which the psalm refers.

Psalm 19

*The celestial spheres recount the light-manifestation of
the eternal,*
  the firmament proclaims the work of his hands.
² Day to day pours out the word of revelation,
  night to night brings knowledge to life.
³ These words and this speaking
  are not inaudible.
⁴ Their sounding brings order into all earth-existence.
  *To the ends of the earth's cycles their speaking resounds
mightily.*

His tent, he pitched it in the orb of the sun.
  *⁵ And he – as a bridegroom comes out of his bridal
chamber,*
  rejoicing as a mighty hero to run his course.
⁶ His going forth is from the end of the heavens,
  and to the ends again he closes the circuit.
  Nothing is hid from his fiery glow.

⁷ The ordering of the world of the Lord is without flaw,
  making the soul peaceful.
The testimony of the Lord creates spirit-confidence,
  making wise the simple.
⁸ The statutes of the Lord are righteous,
  rejoicing the heart.
The ordained goal of the Lord is clear,
  enlightening the eyes.
⁹ The fear of the Lord cleanses through and through,
  enduring forever.
The precepts of the Lord are grounded in truth,
  uniting in righteousness all with one another.
¹⁰ Nobler than the noblest gold;
  sweeter than the sweetest honey.

¹¹ Moreover by them is your servant enlightened,
  and he who keeps them in his soul reaps God's reward.
¹² Hasty actions – who is aware of them?
  Cleanse me from unknown faults,

> ^{13} *preserve your servant from the powers of arrogance,*
>   *let them not gain dominion over me;*
> *then I have part in the eternal*
>   *and am purified from great transgressions.*
> ^{14} *May my words find echo in the heavens,*
>   *may the meditation of my heart reach you,*
> *O*L<small>ORD</small>, *rock-foundation and redeemer of my self!*

If the first sentence speaks of the divine revelation in the splendour of light, the second sentence refers to the divine power: 'And the firmament proclaims his handiwork'. The firmament (*firmus* means fixed) is for modern people an outdated scientific concept. To scientists of today the tranquillity of the firmament is an illusion; space for them is full of movement and tensions.

Yet the ancient word 'firmament' is somehow true. It conveys to us the spiritual experience of a divine world, resting deeply in itself despite all creative activity – a world eternally founded upon its own being. This spiritual experience was released through the sight of the stars. It is not for nothing that the fixed stars in their stability appear to the human eye as resting in their places. It is just as little accidental as the blue of the sky, which indeed is also 'only' an optical phenomenon. The pictures in which the universe offers itself to the human eye are not merely accidental. They have their own picture-value, their own intrinsic justification, upon quite a different plane from their purely physical existence. As pictures which the cosmic artist has allowed to appear thus and not otherwise before human eyes, they have their own laws independent of the purely physical nature and condition. To this extent it is justified if we contemplate the firmament, to feel face to face with a world of immovable calm, eternally founded upon itself, one which fills us with inner stability, assurance and harmony.

The psalm touches the roots of eternity. It rests at first in the contemplation of the highest spheres. Then it gradually descends. It is as though it traverses at the same time the path of incarnation, the way the super-earthly takes when descending to earth to become flesh. From the eternal world of the immovable stars we descend gradually into the sphere of time. We have not yet reached the spatial and bodily nature. But the soul which was surrendered to the timeless and eternal, surrounds itself now with the fine web of the *temporal*. Before it enters the spatial body it assumes, as it were, the time-body as a fine sheath:

> Day to day pours out speech
> and night to night reveals knowledge.

We have entered the world of rhythmic time. This is shown impressively in the original text, *yom le-yom ... laylah le-laylah*, 'day to day ... night to night'. Quite literally, it reads, 'Day lets word arise to day, night makes knowledge living to night'. Here a fine differentiation is made between day and night. The day brings to light the 'manifestation', it proclaims the word, it brings it 'to the light of day'. But this 'bringing to light' is only one side of the process of learning to know. When we sleep, mysteriously in the depths of the soul, all that we have acquired by conscious experience by day is further worked upon throughout the night. Everyone is aware how a thought can live and develop further when we 'sleep on it'. What the day makes evident to us is permeated by higher life in the night. Life is added to light. In Hebrew, *yom* is masculine, *laylah* has a feminine character. In the clear concept of the day a male element is active; the night, however, is a mother of life.

Only now does the psalm reach our earth and its spatial, material existence. But it does not see the earth with ordinary, everyday sight; descending from heaven, it hears the word of the stars resounding in the corporeal element. The terrestrial shows itself to be ordered, fashioned, 'sounded through' by the celestial.

'Their line has gone out through all the earth.' This 'line' is the measuring line, the tape measure. Inasmuch as the chaos of earthly substances comes to life in manifold forms, our enlightened eye now beholds the heavenly forces at work 'measuring', setting a standard. Just as in the well-known experiment of the Chladni figures, a fine powder on a glass plate takes on forms from resonating tones, the sound-figures of the stars work into formations on the earth.

> There is no speech nor language
> > where their voice is not heard.
> Their line has gone out through all the earth
> > and their utterances to the end of the world.

We can now review the first part of the psalm. It leads us through three worlds. First, the eternal in eternity. The fixed stars radiating in the firmament. Then, the eternal entering into time. The temporal, rhythmic world of day and night stands as mediator between the eternal light of heaven and the darkness of the earth. Finally, the eternal working into space, the working of the stars in earthly substances, the sound-figures of the celestial spheres in the dust of the earth:

> The celestial spheres recount the light-manifestation of the eternal,
> > the firmament proclaims the work of his hands.
> Day to day pours out the word of revelation,
> > night to night brings knowledge to life.
> These words and this speaking
> > are not inaudible.
> Their sounding brings order into all earth-existence.
> > To the ends of the earth's cycles their speaking resounds mightily.

2. The sun

The first part of the psalm has led us down the path from the heights of the stars into the depths of matter. When we find ourselves again in earthly existence, the splendour of the stars grows pale. We hear it still echoing in earthly substances. Then all this vanishes before the glow of sunrise. The deeper foundations of existence are concealed behind the veil of the senses. The rising sun deprives us of the sight of the stars but it shows us instead the earth as the field of our labours, the scene of our actual human life.

> Which comes like a bridegroom out of his chamber,
> > and, like a hero runs his course with joy.

> Its rising is from the end of the heavens
> and its circuit to their other end,
> and there is nothing hid from its heat.

In Hebrew the sun is masculine. It is ensouled by a 'sun-spirit', the 'sun genius'. Here in the psalm it becomes a manifestation of the Son God, while behind the stars the Father God appears as the eternal Ground of the World.

People of ancient times did not yet possess the independent consciousness of our self that we have today. They were dependent on the sun for this: they were only truly themselves in the shining light of the sun. With the setting of the sun the contours of their personal consciousness became indistinct, and with the dimming of that consciousness the supersensible – both the divine and the demonic – appeared to them. The further humanity receded from its divine origin, the more night became the realm of spectres and ghosts, instead of being the holy night of revelation. In Christ, the Godhead appeared as the great I AM in the bright day-consciousness, in order to sanctify the awakened human self and to unite it again with the divine world. In pre-Christian times something like a promise of Christ shone down to people out of the sun. Even today we still feel how the sunrise can rescue us from the horror of an uneasy night and make a different person of us. The sun gives fresh vital energy, new joy and a holy soberness. It drives away the phantoms of the night.

The psalm depicts the lofty sun-spirit in two images: as hero and as bridegroom.

The *hero* is the outstanding person who shows others what it really means to be a human being, pursuing a path and completing its course. The stronger the personality, the more strongly marked is the line of this course. Most people idle away their time straying to right and left of the path, like Little Red Riding Hood when she met the wolf. The higher a person develops towards the divine, the more they are a 'hero', and the more a certain path and significant form appear in that life. In the ancient mysteries a particular grade of initiation was called Sun Hero – *Heliodromos,* literally 'Sun Runner', who, like the sun, runs his course sure of his goal and full of strength. St Paul said in old age, 'I have finished the race' (*ton dromon teteleka,* 2Tm 4:7). In its sublime, unswerving path the sun daily displays the image of a glorious 'course'. In his commentary on the psalms, Professor Kittel has a beautiful description of how the Israelites experienced this daily course of the sun:

> Behind the eastern mountains, the ranges of Moab or Bashan, and further back behind the infinite eastern desert, the sun rises for the inhabitants of the Holy Land from the scented mist of the horizon in red and golden brilliant splendour ... It moves along in its majestic course over the land, to dip down once more in the evening into the blue waves of the western sea, behind the cliffs of Joppa or on the dunes at the foot of Mount Carmel, again in red-gold haze wrapt as in a purple mantle. (p. 370)

The course of a hero reaching his goal was a prophecy of the earthly path of Christ. The Gospel of Mark, in particular, describes the life of Christ on earth as an unswerving sun-path that must take this course and no other. Again and again one finds in Mark the word 'immediately' (or 'straightaway', the exact rendering of the Greek word *euthys*). The 'immediately' which appears so often in Mark has no hint of haste or breathlessness. It indicates that all the deeds of Christ lie on the direct path of his course as a Sun Hero.

But Christ is not only the great example of a runner on the path, he is more: he is the archetype of our true being working creatively within us. The archetypal plant does not stay outside the plant but is present in it, concretely active and creative. So does the Christ draw into us and work within us as creative archetype. At this stage our relation to him passes over into mysticism: he is the *bridegroom*. This word echoes from the mysteries. John the Baptist 'rejoices at the bridegroom's voice' (Jn 3:29) and Christ frequently describes himself as the 'bridegroom'. The sun-spirit is called the bridegroom because he is to receive the full surrender of the human soul, with which he will unite himself in the innermost communion of the mystical marriage.

The Hebrew text in the next line ('In them he has set a tent for the sun' 19:4) is somewhat uncertain. If one single letter is altered, it would read, 'in the ocean he has set a tent for the sun'. This sounds like an echo from ancient myths. People saw the sun in the evening dip down into the sea and thus arose the mythological picture of the bridal chamber of the sun-god in the depths of the ocean. A higher truth is revealed in this image. The depths of the ocean become a genuine allegory for the depths of the soul. The Christ who is experienced in bright day-consciousness unites at night with deeper regions of the soul's life. The ancient mystical image only becomes true and real in Christianity.

But it is a question whether the original Hebrew text read differently after all. How otherwise would the Septuagint, the Greek rendering of the Old Testament, put: 'In the sun he [God] has pitched his tent'? It says that God has chosen the sun as his tent to dwell in, and not that he has given to the sun a dwelling at the ends of the world, that is in the ocean. The Greek word for tent (*skēnē*) is of the same root as that used in the prologue of John's Gospel: 'The Word became flesh and dwelt [literally, pitched his tent] among us' (1:14). John implies that the place where God dwells – which in the wandering in the desert had been the tabernacle (tent) of the Covenant – has been moved into Jesus of Nazareth. His human body is now the sacred 'tabernacle of God among men'. It appears that the Greek translators of the third and second century BC worked from a Hebrew text in which the sun was declared the tabernacle of God, in accordance with ancient 'cosmic' religion.

It is quite possible that the later Jewish orthodoxy altered this text, because it struck the orthodox rabbis as too 'pagan'. This surmise is confirmed, if one observes that the Greek translation of Solomon's Prayer for the dedication of the temple contains a line (1K 8:12; 8:53 in Septuagint) which is completely missing in the usual Hebrew bibles of today. Are we to believe that the translator simply invented that line? The usual Hebrew text says: 'The LORD has said that he would dwell in a thick cloud. I have indeed built you an exalted house to dwell in.' The Greek Septuagint reads: 'The Lord has given the sun in the sky for our knowledge. He said that he himself would dwell in the darkness.'

It seems that these remarkable words testifying to an age-old sun worship have simply been excised. It was for Solomon to realise that the time was at hand when the spirit of the sun would transfer his dwelling place into the interior darkness of the human soul. Solomon's temple was a prophecy of the body of Jesus, in which the glory of God should dwell. In his prayer of dedication Solomon proclaimed the crucial transition from an epoch which observed the divine presence radiating into human beings from without, from the cosmos, to a new epoch which would receive God as a presence, indwelling in human beings.

Psalm 19, which is described as a Psalm of David, belongs still to the time *before* Solomon. Thus the second section of the psalm, which is inspired by the recognition of the mysterious relationship between the Son God and the sun, could be rendered as follows:

> His tent, he pitched it in the orb of the sun.
>   And he – as a bridegroom comes out of his bridal
>   chamber,
>   rejoicing as a mighty hero to run his course.
> His going forth is from the end of the heavens,
>   and to the ends again he closes the circuit.
>   Nothing is hid from his fiery glow.

3. The holy book

After these verses, full of the powers of nature, the psalm takes on a quite different tone. It turns away from stars and sun and becomes a hymn to the Mosaic law. It loses in colour, in elemental force that overwhelms the heart; it becomes paler, more abstract. Thus biblical criticism is of the opinion that this praise of the law was added to this powerful psalm of nature in a later period. However the matter may stand, this hymn to the law is part of Psalm 19, and we may find that it is nevertheless truly complementary to the preceding part.

In the starry heavens – God the Father; in the sun – God the Son. With the holy book we enter, as it were, into the future sphere of the Holy Spirit. And since the working of the Holy Spirit is something that is still to come, we cannot be surprised if the third part of the psalm is more abstract, less vigorous and natural. Yet this part, too, possesses its distinct beauty.

At the beginning of the psalm the heavens and stars are extolled as the great manifestation; there the heavens are the book. In the third part of the psalm this is reversed and in the book the heavens are discovered. 'And when your hands unroll some parchment rare, all heaven descends and opens out before you' – even if that dry and dusty bookworm, Wagner, speaks these words in Goethe's *Faust*, they are nevertheless a kind of reflection of genuine joy of the mind, genuine delight in knowledge given through the opening book of wisdom. This dried-up scholarship of Faust's amanuensis can be seen in the old Jewish rabbi's study of the law. But the words of the psalm, which speak of the blessedness which springs from the meditative study of the inspired holy texts have nevertheless something valid for all time, quite apart from the 'scribe' element. Thus in Christianity they can become alive and true for us. So, for instance, the Gospel of John can become a book for us today in which 'all heaven descends' to us.

This eulogy of the Holy Scriptures is cast in a form which divides into exactly twelve sentences (six double sentences). Something of the ordering of the starry heavens lies in this twelve-ness. The soul surrendered in devotion to the law feels the harmonies of the world of the stars stream into it, bringing peace.

> The ordering of the world of the LORD is without flaw,
>   making the soul peaceful.
> The testimony of the LORD creates spirit-confidence,
>   making wise the simple.
> The statutes of the LORD are righteous,
>   rejoicing the heart.
> The ordained goal of the LORD is clear,
>   enlightening the eyes.
> The fear of the LORD cleanses through and through,
>   enduring forever.
> The precepts of the LORD are grounded in truth,
>   uniting in righteousness all with one another.

These twelve statements are followed by a comparison which once more gathers the whole mood together, and in its forcible imagery would make us feel that the joy of the spirit does not yield to the joy of the senses, but can surpass them in intensity of happiness.

> Nobler than the noblest gold;
>   sweeter than the sweetest honey.

Gold was seen at all times as the transitory symbol of the sunlike light of wisdom. Honey in ancient times was something like the food of the mysteries. The Risen One, according to Luke's account, partook of honey as well as fish. According to this psalm the Holy Book mediates the gold of wisdom and the most exquisite blessedness.

4. The human being

Having touched upon the three spheres of manifestation of the Father, the Son and the Spirit, now at the end the psalm leads to *human beings,* who turn back to themselves out of the depths of their contemplation of the divine mysteries. Just as the first verses spoke of the resounding of the stars, of the Word of God sounding out from the heavens, which is heard by devoted human beings, so the psalm ends with the desire that similarly the inner word of human beings may be heard above in the heavens. This is not presumption, but a presentiment of the dignity to which human beings are called, in which they can only be fully established through Christ, that is, that they may not only 'hear' but may also 'speak', as spirit to spirit, to God.

Just as in the Lord's Prayer, the petitioner passes from selfless absorption in the great wish of the divine ('your name ... your kingdom ... your will'), to then come to their own needs and necessities, so at the end of Psalm 19 human beings enter the sphere of their own life. From being absorbed in contemplation they emerge again and come to themselves. But they have themselves become a different being. They have come to know the bliss of the higher life. At the same time, however, they have acquired deeper insight into their own inner nature and the perils and threats confronting it. They know that much of our wrong-doing never enters our consciousness. They know of much that wanders by night through the labyrinth of the soul, unknown and unheeded. They have gained impressions of the working of the opposing powers; for the old saying holds good, that the devil always draws nearer to us when we take a step towards God.

Finally, let it be repeated once more: the words of the psalm reveal their full and right significance only through Christianity.

Moreover by them [the statutes of the Lord] is your servant
    enlightened,
  and he who keeps them in his soul reaps God's reward.
Hasty actions – who is aware of them?
  Cleanse me from unknown faults,
preserve your servant from the powers of arrogance,
  let them not gain dominion over me;
then I have part in the eternal
  and am purified from great transgressions.
May my words find echo in the heavens,
  may the meditation of my heart reach you,
O Lord, rock-foundation and redeemer of my self!

25

'I LIFT UP MY EYES TO THE HILLS'

PSALM 121

I

The words 'I lift up my eyes to the hills' express a primal religious experience. They form the opening of Psalm 121, which in all its simplicity is a classic religious document.

It belongs to a group of psalms each headed: 'A Song of Ascents', pilgrim songs that were sung when people went up to the holy hill-city of Jerusalem. Physical and spiritual pilgrimage were inseparable in people's experience of those days. Outwardly as well as inwardly it meant a going upwards, an 'elevation'. The pious uplifted gaze of the distant pilgrim quite naturally began to 'see' in a higher sense.

'I lift up my eyes ...' The animals also have eyes; some animals are even superior to humans in the penetrating keenness of their vision. The animal, however, cannot so unselfishly give itself up to pure 'looking' as we can. This is expressed physiologically in the fact that animal eyes have a stronger blood supply, are more part of the actual life processes. An animal's seeing is always somehow determined by its biology. Its looking always has something to do with its own interests and is concerned with its main task of survival. The human eye enables us simply to look with absolute objectivity and thus we can get quite free of ourselves and the needs of our own organism. We are able to raise our eyes to the distant hills.

In the original text the second line does not follow in the way that is so familiar from the Authorised or Prayer Book versions of the psalm: 'from whence cometh my help.' It is a question: 'From where does my help come?' This question arises from looking at the distant hills. Looked at aright they point beyond themselves and allow a sense

> ## Psalm 121
>
> A Song of Ascents
>
> ¹ *I lift up my eyes to the hills.*
>   *From where does my help come?*
> ² *My help comes from the L*ORD*,*
>   *who made heaven and earth.*
>
> ³ *He will not let your foot be moved,*
>   *he who keeps you will not slumber.*
> ⁴ *Behold, he who keeps Israel*
>   *will neither slumber nor sleep.*
>
> ⁵ *The L*ORD *watches over you;*
>   *the L*ORD *is your shade on your right hand.*
> ⁶ *The sun shall not strike you by day,*
>   *nor the moon by night.*
>
> ⁷ *The L*ORD *keeps you from all evil;*
>   *he watches over your soul.*
> *The L*ORD *watches over your going out and your coming in*
>   *from this instant and for eternity.*

of the divine. It is by no means superfluous to draw attention to the fact that the order of the sentences is not reversed. It is not, 'From where does my help come? So I lift my eyes and look for help from God above.' The starting point for true religion is not the need for help that causes people to seek for help, or a danger that makes one pray. The starting point of Psalm 121 is the religious experience of the divine that follows from looking up to the holy hills. This lies a plane higher than merely needing help; it is the selfless sphere of altruistic worship. If, then, as a result of this devoted gaze, the question arises, 'From where does my help come?' it is not connected with individual needs but the basic, primal need that arises from our human nature in the presence of the divine: in looking up I first become aware that I am not as I should be, that my humanity is incomplete. This calls for decisive help which can come to me only from above. The chief thing is not that this or that wish is fulfilled, but that I myself am fulfilled.

This insight grows in a true and legitimate way in the very act of striving. Only someone who makes a great effort comes to the point where they know the indispensability of grace, the 'love from above'.* The question born out of looking up to the hills, 'From where does my help come?' is asking for that love from above. 'From where does that come that is *the* help for my innate being?' If as Christians we adopt the psalm, we may complete it by affirming that this decisive help for our human nature has come to us in Christ. The name Jesus even means God's help. In Christ Jesus *the* help descends to us which alone can do enough for the primal need of our destitute humanity.

Since the question about help first arose from looking up to the divine, it quite naturally penetrates into higher regions where it answers itself. As if it were an inspiration from those distant hills, the questioner hears something like what they say to themselves out of a higher self, 'My help from the LORD!' (literal translation)

The LORD – *Yahweh* in Hebrew, *Kyrios* in the Greek translation – already indicates the sphere of Christ. But the looking up to the hills that enlarges the soul makes it at once clear to the singer of the psalm that this Lord is not only the ruler of our soul but at the same time is the universal world self or essence. He it is who 'made heaven and earth'. The vision of the help-bringing God therefore broadens into the one who encompasses the whole universe.

> I lift up my eyes to the hills.
> > From where does my help come?
> My help comes from the LORD,
> > who made heaven and earth.

II

The pious inner dialogue leads on to hearing a 'voice' that reaches the ear of the soul from the spiritual world itself – in a higher sense 'from without to within'. The answer to the question was experienced as arising within the questioner's own self, so that they spoke to themselves, 'My help comes from the LORD.' Now comes the step from

---

* A phrase from Goethe's *Faust* often used by Rudolf Frieling.

talking to oneself to being spoken to from a higher world that begins to disclose itself. 'He will not let your foot be moved.' Earlier it says, *my* eyes ... *my* help, now suddenly it says *your* foot ... keeps *you*.

Now the singer of the psalm is no longer so obviously in their own body as to consider it a personal possession, but they look at their earthly being from the opposite direction, as if from the spiritual world.

> He will not let your foot be moved,
> > he who keeps you will not slumber.
> Behold, he who keeps Israel
> > will neither slumber nor sleep.

With our feet we walk our life's path. Once we have learnt to walk we are normally no longer conscious of it. Our feet go downstairs correctly, they even find their way over dark uneven ground, they are often in advance of our conscious attention with the sureness of the sleepwalker. But then there can be an unexpected stumble or slip that brings unimagined consequences in its train. All this does not lie entirely in our conscious control; the unconscious plays a part in it. In this case the ever-wakeful divine consciousness must help to complement inadequate human awareness; it is awake where we are asleep.

God does not sleep. What does this really mean? What does 'sleep' mean? The usual attitude today is that someone asleep is in some way diminished, deprived of the something that makes them conscious and capable of action. They have shrunk as it were. In reality their soul has gone out of the body to dwell among higher beings who now strengthen, heal and renew the sleeping soul given into their care, as well as the body left without consciousness. We sleep only because there is something higher into which we enter and immerse ourselves. We need something 'into' which we can sleep. God is the highest being. He does not sleep – for into what should he sleep? He is himself the all-embracing. He has his rest and support within himself; he does not need to immerse himself in another, but can ever receive all other beings into himself so that they take rest from their separate beings in him, so that they find new life, new creation in him. One can only truly rest 'in God'. In order that he who sleeps can rest in God,

God must be awake for him. What goes on partly in the sleeping-unconscious even while we are awake, like the movement of the feet, is also in the psalm entrusted to this being who is awake for everyone. 'He will not let your foot be moved'. From mysterious depths he will grant a safe journey through life and prevent 'false steps'.

Again those who pray are led beyond the personal to the general: he who keeps them also keeps Israel. He certainly has his personal relation to each individual, but one should never lose sight of the fact that over and above this, he is the guardian of much wider circles. In Christian terms he is the keeper of humankind.

III

In its characteristic way of linking thoughts together our psalm again takes up the 'keeper' motif in the third stanza:

> The LORD watches over you;
> > the LORD is your shade on your right hand.
> The sun shall not strike you by day,
> > nor the moon by night.

To those of us who live in northern countries where the sunlight is not so strong, 'shade' suggests something negative, a looming of the realm of darkness into the brightness of day. If we have done harvesting on a hot summer's day, we can appreciate what a blessing it can be if only for a moment a cloud takes away the merciless heat. We can then understand how the overshadowing clouds with their refreshing coolness were experienced in the lands of the Bible. In this sense Luke speaks of the overshadowing of Mary by the Holy Spirit. In this sense the psalm speaks of the overshadowing of our hand by the divine. It is the right hand, with which every day we have to engage in shaping our earthly existence. God watches over the traveller, he shades the worker. Our creative hand needs this protection so that its activity can be beneficial.

This positive aspect of shade also enables us to understand the next verse, which speaks of the warding off of harmful influences. Just as at high noon the intense rays of the sun can harm us, so too, we are told, can the full moon shining with unclouded brilliance from the zenith at midnight in biblical lands. For us sunstroke and moonstroke can stand for all harmful influences that threaten destruction by day or by night.

IV

The psalm has spoken of the eyes, the foot, the hand. It is as if it went through the whole threefold human organization: the thinking head – the earth-treading foot – the hand whose creativeness comes from the middle region, the heart. In a fourth stanza the theme is taken up again and, in three final sentences, drawn to a grand conclusion.

First, the protection from 'all evil'. As with the seventh request of the Lord's Prayer it would be too superficial to think only of being protected from misfortunes that come to us from without. In the deeper Christian sense it is not only the evil that is done to us, but above all the evil to which our soul is prone insofar as we are possessed by egoism. The dark possibility of doing evil is also always connected with the wonderful possibility of being aware of our own individuality, of saying I.

From here we proceed to the 'soul',* which with its whole range of feeling is submitted to the divine protection, and lastly to the 'going out and coming in', which again refers us to the earthly journey, this time considered in its rhythm of going and coming, of setting out and returning home. We find this rhythm throughout life, in small things and in greater ones. We find it in the morning departure and the evening homecoming, in breathing out and breathing in, in sleeping and waking, in being born and dying. Coming into the world is seen from above as going out of a higher world, and death as the homecoming. From the earth, incarnation is seen as coming in, and death as going out, the *exitus*.

These life rhythms afford at the end of the psalm the far view into the timeless, the eternal: 'from now and for evermore.' In order to appreciate the meaning of this ancient religious expression anew perhaps instead of 'now' we could try using the word 'instant' for its more immediate effect. Between the past and the future stands the 'instant' – which can be seized only by real 'presence' of mind. For whoever

---

* Some translations have 'life' for the Hebrew *nephesh*.

grasps the instant in spiritual awareness, will at the same time find a window into the timeless: 'from this instant and for eternity.'

As in the first stanza looking up to the hills leads out into the distances of space, so in the last the grasping of the rhythmical world leads towards the distances of time, and thence into eternity.

> The LORD keeps you from all evil;
>   he watches over your soul.
> The LORD watches over your going out and your coming in
>   from this instant and for eternity.

26

THE LIFE FORCES IN DEVOTION

PSALM 119

I

If it is really to come to life, religious life needs practice. Everything that can be called 'practice' – and the phrase 'practice of religion' is not insignificant – requires a will that does not momentarily kindle but establishes itself ever and again, and repeatedly anew; it might be called an 'enduring will'.

In such efforts to cultivate a serious religious practice, more important than ever today, we can gain a certain stimulus from an ancient text, Psalm 119, which in its own way – before Christ's appearance – announces this long-enduring will, or we might also say the sustained breath of piety and devotion. This psalm is little known or valued, at least in part because of its unusual and easily off-putting length. It has 176 verses (whereas the well-known psalm, 'The Lord is my Shepherd,' is only 6 verses altogether).

And yet the remarkable number of verses is precisely what can give us a first insight into this unusual text. These 176 verses can be divided into 22 times 8. There are 22 stanzas, each of whose 8 verses begin with the same letters; and 22 is the number of the Hebrew (consonantal) alphabet. Thus each of the first 8 lines begins with *aleph,* each of the next 8 lines with *beth,* and so on.* Mostly this has been regarded only as a kind of devout playfulness. But we can learn to bring a quite new, intuiting respect to bear upon the Word and its various speech sounds. We gradually learn to honour in each sound the diverse creative forces of the universe whose totality forms the

---

* In most English translations, the letter appears in the heading of each stanza.

active organism of the divine cosmic Word, of which John speaks as the Logos. And therefore we can understand that reverently dwelling upon each letter of the alphabet was, for ancient Hebrews, a systematic quest for experiencing the Word.

This alphabetic structure of Psalm 119 can scarcely be reproduced in another language without artificiality creeping in. But gaining a sense of this secret of the alphabetic characters in Hebrew can help us to see that the Word, the Word of God, is in fact the great content and theme of the text. Written in a pre-Christian era, the psalm is as yet unaware of the Word become flesh in Jesus Christ. It therefore adheres to the prophetic revelation of the approaching Word, as this appears in the sacred Jewish texts – above all in the Torah, the five books of Moses. The soul of Psalm 119 is a continuous religious practice – one that informs, shapes and sanctifies the whole of life – in engaging with this revelation of the Word.

However, Psalm 119 lacks the original, primary poetic element, the fresh energy and character of David's psalms. It clearly belongs to late Judaism and cannot compare with various other passages of the Old Testament. But this need not prevent us from noticing its special strength – which lies precisely in the domain of an unshakeable, enduring will, of a religious practice cultivated with ultimate seriousness, and here and there breaking through to tangible supersensible experience. Where this happens, we can see the otherwise prosaic text blossom into a remarkable and sublime beauty.

'I bear my soul continually in my hands and I do not forget your law' (119:109). A classic expression of self-education and mental discipline. In the original text it is put still more succinctly: 'My soul in my hollow hand continually.' Here the energetic endeavour is not to become a volatile plaything of inner stirrings and moods. From a higher perspective, the soul is brought under control, 'taken in hand'. This persistent spirit-will also wages a continual battle against 'forgetting'. From myths and fairy-tales we know this motif of forgetfulness, repeatedly surfacing as an admonition. It is hard to maintain the inward connection with a higher consciousness, to preserve it, as it were, as an eternally burning lamp. The danger of tiring repeatedly threatens – of relinquishing the endeavour, of letting go, of losing touch with oneself. In Richard Wagner's *Parsifal* we hear: 'I forgot my own mother! What else did I also forget?'

Forgetting is not merely a natural and intrinsic process in us, though this is true to a certain extent. From self-observation we all know the role which feeling and will play in our forgetting or not forgetting. Thus the pious author of Psalm 119 makes clear that words of divine 'instruction' (Martin Buber used this word to translate 'Torah') are something not to be forgotten, never to be forgotten: 'and your Torah I do not forget'. The impulse of seeking not to forget comes no less than eight times in this psalm.

Connected with this is the fact that words such as 'protect' and 'preserve' often recur. One of these words is *natsar* in Hebrew, and reminds us of the Nazarites – seekers who endeavoured to 'nurture' the life of spirit and religion. At the very beginning we hear the beatitude, 'Blessed are they who nurture and preserve (*natsar*) his testimonies and seek him with their whole hearts' (119:2).

This systematically conducted nurturing or cultivation of the sacred scriptures is not merely a learning and reciting of texts, although that also has its place. Devoted engagement with God-revealed truths does not remain in the intellectual sphere but also deepens into 'pondering'. The Latin translation understandably renders this as *meditari* – meditation. This meditative 'pondering' is likewise a key word in the psalm, recurring no fewer than eight times. Precisely through such repetition it impresses itself on us as an ever-recurring activation of patient, enduring will. It is also the same word that we encounter so strikingly in the patriarch stories. Of Isaac it is said that he went out in the evenings to 'meditate' (Gn 24:63). This signifies a weighing and fathoming that self-evidently encompasses a pious and prayerful mood. Both by day (119:97) and by night (119: 55, 62, 148) the psalmist makes divine revelation the subject of this pondering contemplation.

Such devotional activity, faithfully sustained, leads to inner experiences of a higher kind. The psalm is aware of certain light experiences. The nature of 'illumination' is wonderfully expressed as 'the unfolding of your word gives light' (119:130). In the original one has a sense of a tangible experience directly fashioned into words: 'The self-opening of your words shines forth.' The words of a sacred text have repeatedly been taken into pious, contemplative pondering, but one day a moment arrives where they open inwardly like buds, and their light dawns in the soul in a light process of the highest order. Words that have, sadly, become something of a worn-out cliché – 'Your word is the lamp to my feet and a light upon my path' (119:105) also contain a mystical light experience. 'Way' and 'path' are ancient, true figures for progress in inner transformation. Just as we do not find our way outwardly in the darkness, so this supersensible path is in even greater need of the illuminating light of grace.

With an awakening to perception of divine light, something like a new dimension enlarges the human being. We experience a *broadening* of our whole being. The image of broadening is not an accidental one but apt and precise. In *The Brothers Karamazov*, Dostoevsky describes how the young Alyosha has a supersensible experience beside the coffin of his revered *starets,* expressed by the author writing, twice, that Alyosha felt as if the room had expanded.

Our ordinary, mundane consciousness is bound up with the coarser, material body of earth, and initially is unaware that other 'bodies' of a much subtler nature also belong to us. This finer aspect of our nature, in Rudolf Steiner's account, involves far less seclusiveness than the material body. The latter is something like an 'isolation cell', whereas the organism of etheric life forces is far more open to the influx of cosmic forces. If the soul develops conscious experiences of itself within this subtler organism, it enters upon the 'path into the open': bright expanses open before it, which are pervaded by the great breath of the cosmos.

'Constriction and breadth', 'fear and release' into light-filled breadths are archetypal motifs of religious life, which originate in very particular experiences. Fear is connected with a sense of constriction, and the word 'anxiety' has its roots in the Greek word 'to choke'. In a Psalm of David we read, '[The LORD] led me out into the broad expanse' (18:19). And in Psalm 118: 'From the constriction of fear I called to the LORD, and the LORD answered me in the far breadths' (118:5). In Psalm 4:1: 'When I call, answer me, God of my righteousness! In my narrowness you make me broad.' In the Isaac narratives of the Book of Genesis, a well is given the name Rehoboth – 'the breadths'. Around other springs and wells, altercation had arisen. Earthly human possessiveness and egoism, connected with the constriction in a coarse, material body, reached out with its unhallowed hand towards the life-giving divine gift of a well. Now, at last, there was a well 'over which they did not quarrel' and which could therefore embody its wellspring-mystery in unsullied form. This experience led people out of 'constriction' and helped them to sense 'the breadths' or Rehoboth (Gn 26:22).

Psalm 119 also arrives at this experience: 'And I walk in the breadths; for I seek your precepts' (119:45). 'Breadths' is characteristic here. Divine order, which finds its expression in the law, is not felt by the pious as something which constrains or constricts their existence. As it becomes apparent to their 'pondering' as divine, living reality, it leads them 'into the breadths'. Likewise in verse 96, 'I have seen the completion of all things, but your commandment is abundantly broad.' We have to sense how this 'breadth' is not only outward but how living feelings implicit in a supersensible state bring with them a sense of breathing more deeply and 'emerging into the open'.

At one place the psalm uses the word 'breadth' also in relation to the human *heart*. The original text says, 'The path of your commandments will I run; for you make broad my heart' (119:32) This image has even found its way into the Koran. At the time of Muhammad, various emigrants lived in Arabia who had come from unorthodox, Christian-Jewish-Gnostic circles. These people may well also have held the 'Nazirite' Psalm 119 in special esteem; and no doubt the motif of 'making wide' the heart or the breast reached Muhammad in this way. Ultimately it appeared in Goethe's *Faust*. Goethe was very familiar both with the Bible and the Koran. That the Moon Goddess is addressed as 'You heart-broadener' (*Faust II*, Act 2) must surely be attributable to these sources.

In Psalm 119, this 'broadening of the heart' is connected with the motif of 'running', or 'taking one's course' rather than, as elsewhere, with 'walking'. Only here do we read, 'the path of your commandments will I *run*.' We may be reminded of Psalm 19 ('The Heavens Declare'), whose verse 6 also refers to 'running', there in relation to the sun which 'runs' like a hero. This does not signify a hasty or restless 'hurrying'. The Sun Hero's advance is a stately progress, a moving forth born of an excess of mighty life energies. In the same way, after the divine judgment on Mount Carmel, Elijah 'ran' all the way to Jezreel as if transported by an excess of divine power (1K 18:46). In the Mithras mysteries, a certain degree of initiation was designated

Heliodromos or Sun Runner. In Psalm 119, in the time of late Judaism as we have said, the mood is quiet and inward. But it may not be accidental that precisely in a passage concerning the heart, which is after all the sun organ in the human being, something of the Sun Runner of the ancient mysteries sounds through. The heart, 'made broad', fills with sun forces, and by this means human beings can progress on their way in harmony with the divine order. This inner progress is then like an image of the mighty motions of the sun itself, the Sun Hero running on his way from one constellation to the next.

II

The spatial realm with which we are concerned when speaking of constriction and breadth was by no means void of soul for people of earlier eras, but pervaded by inner experience – so that the experience of 'breadth' seamlessly led over from spatial to supersensible dimensions.

The same holds true for *time*. In our era we have grown far more abstract, so that time, like space, has become something external and alien to the supersensible domain. Even for contemporaries with a religious outlook, the 'temporal' appears strictly separate from the 'eternal' – like two entirely different, unbridgeable worlds.

But we must recognise that the term 'eternity', in the abstract and absolute meaning assigned to it nowadays, does not exist anywhere in the Bible. What does figure is the word 'aeon' in various forms: into the aeons – the aeons of aeons – aeonic. But this cannot simply be equated with what we understand by eternity today. The word 'aeon' so often used in the New Testament designates a time cycle, founded on the underlying experience that time does not simply run on in endless linearity. Rather it has the quality of coming full circle, as in the daily or annual round. In this return, the temporal allows us to sense a higher, sublime principle at work above all temporal things, yet shining in from above into the circling time sphere. It is the sense of this shining in that gives the word eternity its religious resonance. Rather than a boundlessly proliferating, unending time, this points us to the divine and sublime world belonging to a fundamentally different plane by contrast to all that is temporal, a plane which nevertheless deigns to shine out mercifully and mysteriously within the circling rounds of time.

This time-sphere or time-cycle through which we intuit eternity is the 'aeon' of the New Testament, and in Hebrew *'olam*. We meet it no less than eight times in Psalm 119.

In many translations verse 152 is: 'Long ago I have known from your statutes [or testimonies], that you established them forever.' Here *'olam* is translated as 'forever'. But the reader can scarcely be aware that the words 'long ago' render a significant Hebrew word, which, like *'olam*, conveys an eternal quality. This is the word *qedem*. It signifies the east, in spatial terms the cardinal direction where the sun rises. In terms of time, it signifies the dawning of creation, the morning of the cosmos. As if to the dawn of the universe, *qedem* points back to something primordial. It is therefore translated sometimes as 'once', 'of yore', 'in the beginning' 'of old', 'before' or 'in ancient times'. But none of this quite renders the specific, unique nuance of *qedem*. Despite its relation to the past, one should avoid using words such as 'old' or 'ancient' for it, since *qedem* points precisely to the youthfulness of the world that emerged from God. For us, looking backward, the long-gone days when life began are 'the ancient times' in so far as this dawning was still connected with a past eternity. In his poem 'In Spring', Eduard Mörike speaks of 'ancient, unnameable days'. The adjective 'unnameable' here preserves the quality of mystery and relieves the word 'ancient' of the sense of something grown old and grey.

In Psalm 77:6 – 'I considered the days of old, the years long ago' – the two words signifying eternity come together: 'the years long ago' in Hebrew are 'the years of the aeons' (*'olamim*) while the 'the days of old' is 'the days from the dawn of time' (*qedem*). The word 'old' or 'ancient' does not do justice to the quality of *qedem*.

Another example is in Psalm 78:2: 'I will utter dark [or hidden] sayings of old.' Once again 'of old' distorts the original, in which *qedem* again figures. It could be literally rendered as, 'I will utter words of wisdom, and in inspiration will announce enigmatic sayings springing from *qedem*, from the divine morning of the universe.'

If one thinks – as is wholly justifiable – in terms of endeavours leading to far-off goals, one may sometimes run the risk of conceiving of the prior stages leading to such goals as of lesser importance, and in consequence may fail to do them justice. For instance, we might then think of a child only as a preliminary stage towards a mature individual. Yet childhood itself can shed wonderful illumination upon the nature of humanity. A prior stage can allow something to shine forth that has its own value and significance and can no longer be found in the same way at a later stage. Thus the dawning of a day, as preliminary to a day's full brightness, is only a passing transition, yet possesses its own distinctive quality. It can reveal a certain something, a delicate, spiritual transparency which is then lost as the more robust brightness of day succeeds it. As sacred dawning, *qedem* has its special quality by virtue of relating back to the mystery of the night, and, in the shining of dew drops and the shimmer of dawn's rosy hue, allowing us to feel and sense something of divine origins. We also find the word *qedem* in Adam *qadmon,* a term known in Hebrew esotericism. This does not signify the 'old Adam' but Adam in the sacred dawning of the morning of creation, as yet unsullied by the Fall.

Returning to Psalm 119:152, 'Long ago I have known,' therefore means, 'By the power or virtue of *qedem,* I have known,' We bear within us a share in the morning of the cosmic creation. By virtue of this we can draw forth from the depths of our being an eternal knowledge, in the truest sense an a priori knowledge. We can draw it from the divine dawning of the universal morning.

In the same way as this mystery of the morning, of *qedem*, still stands in special proximity to the eternal and super-temporal realm from whose womb it has only just been born, so the same is true of the *future* when, towards the end of the world, in the gathering dusk of evening, everything transient allows eternity to shine through more clearly again. Thus the awoken gaze penetrates to the future also, from which, as from primordial day, eternity shines upon it. 'Your statutes [or testimonies] are my heritage forever: for they are the joy of my heart' (119:111). Through prayerful pondering on sacred texts, the worshipper has grown so intimate with the contents of divine revelation, has absorbed them so deeply, that the direct certainty arises, 'I bear *this* with me into the furthest future, and *this* bears me with it into eternity.' These contents of the scriptures brought to inner life can become assurances of eternity because we have not only appropriated them rationally but have invoked the depths of our being to do so – have let them be the 'joy of my heart'. The same holds true of verse 98 ('for they are always with me') where the original text has 'for this belongs to me in eternity'.

Being open to the eternal that reveals itself from the future also allows Psalm 119 a prospect of coming 'salvation'. In the centuries leading towards the Christ event, a hope repeatedly surfaces here and there in the humanity of antiquity of a great, world-redeeming occurrence. In Greek it is the *sōteria,* the great salvation, in Hebrew the *yeshuah,* the great succour of God. Pious believers await this event (119:41, 81, 166, 174). The words used there sound like an intimation of the fact that this salvation is one day to stand visibly before human eyes: 'My eyes long for your salvation' (119:123). 'Blessed are the eyes that see what you see,' the Christ will one day say to the disciples (Lk 10:23). The Old Testament worshipper of our psalm has a sense that human history is ripe for the redemptive intervention from above. 'Time it is for the Lord to act' (119:126).

From our Christian perspective we may say that in this psalm, despite its strong Old Testament quality, a vision of the approaching redeemer is apparent. It is true that this Psalm 119 also contains an unmistakable element of scriptural orthodoxy, a tendency towards scholarly rigidity, but at certain places in the text we can also gain a sense of the warmth of the approaching Christ-sun. For instance, we can note how often the verb 'love' appears. This devotee is far from being only subservient. On twelve occasions in his psalm he feels the urge to say that he 'loves' the directives that come from God. While he adheres strictly to his ordered day of seven times of prayer (verse 164), this is no mechanical lip-service on his part. In a wonderful phrase he speaks of the 'freewill offerings of my mouth' (119:108). His endeavours do not seek reward, for he has come to the point of tasting eternal reward already in the very act of such worship itself – the true meaning, surely, of verses 33 and 112. 'I have inclined my heart to perform your statutes for ever to the very end.' The laws, the imperatives of the divine world acknowledged in love, are not something merely followed in obedience. They become wings for the loving soul and awaken its creative power. 'Your statutes are songs to me in the house of my pilgrimage' (119:54).

What was law becomes for him song: a higher artistry awakens in the soul and imbues ethical life with creative energy. The divine will that is inwardly recreated anew in love becomes a song of praise.

The love of God, which announces itself at such culminating moments, does not, however, lack a sacred awe. There is a strong feeling here of the inadequacy of human beings in relation to the divine, bearing as they do a splinter of the adversarial powers within them. Shattering threshold experiences underlie the psalmist's words when he says, 'my flesh trembles in fear' (119:120); and 'before your words my heart trembles in fear' (119:161). Against this background, the expression of God-belonging must have all the more authenticity, in the inward and plain phrase, 'Yours I am' (119:94).

This sense of God within helps the psalmist to avoid a danger, one that so easily surfaces when someone exerts themselves to do their very best: we can easily succumb to Pharisee-like self-satisfaction. It is moving to see how, at the end of the psalm, the seeker who has made such strenuous efforts and can no doubt recognise a degree of achievement in his worship, rediscovers himself in the picture of a straying and lost sheep, ending with the prayer, 'Seek your servant' (119:176). It is highly significant that precisely in someone of such religious activism, a primary awareness breaks through that all quest for God by the human being, however fervent, will fail if the deity does not mercifully and lovingly incline towards the seeking worshipper from above. This insight is not a comfort blanket for human beings, who with their love of ease might relinquish their endeavours, because, after all, everything depends upon God's mercy. Rather, our striving efforts alone, if genuine, lead us towards the experience of divine grace. Such endeavour can create in us the state in which we can first value grace and allow it to encompass us.

Thus at the end of Psalm 119, which originated in late Judaism, the insight is clearly expressed that human beings are lost without help from above. This is all the more striking for being uttered by a pious and devotional seeker. The Christian view of this is that humanity, however it may strive, would fail to find salvation without the Christ, who is the redeeming 'love from on high' become man. Without him and his deed humanity could never work itself free from its 'lostness'. There can be no end of our admiration for the insight of the author of Psalm 119, which leads him, despite all his experiences of an eternal world, despite his flights of selfless love for God, to see himself in the picture of the lost sheep that needs God to seek him. With this image we come very close to Christ's parable of the shepherd who goes to seek the lost sheep.

And yet this grace, the 'love from on high', has to find a means to engage with the human being. We are conscious, responsible, personal beings, and respected as such by God himself. For this reason we cannot simply be saved without our involvement. We would be, and remain, lost if the good shepherd did not set out to seek us 'at our place', but we also have to be willing to be found. 'Seek thy servant.' In the last words of this psalm – which is 'activist' in the right sense and so vigorously appeals to the energies of consciousness – our contribution to our own salvation is summed up thus: 'for I do not forget thy commandments'. Once again we are urged to begin in all earnestness the battle with powers which seek to make us forget that our true being originates in eternity and is oriented to it.

27

GAZING UPON THE COSMOS

PSALM 148

The Book of Psalms concludes in final hymns of a mighty *Te Deum*. In Psalm 150, the orchestra of musical instruments is invoked in God's praise – 'Praise him with trumpets, praise him with psalters and harps.' In Psalm 148, it is the orchestra of the world itself. Heaven and earth join in harmony together for the glory of God.

This psalm – like Psalm 150 – receives its special resonance from the 'hallelujah'. Besides sounding at the beginning and end, it sounds wherever most English translations have the word 'praise'. This is a rendering of the Hebrew *halal,* which is contained in hallelujah' (*halelu-yah* means 'praise Yahweh'). The whole psalm resounds with it. Rather than 'praise' we can also render *halal* with 'ring out', 'resound' or 'reverberate'. We could therefore roughly reproduce the first part of the psalm as:

> Hallelujah!
> Ring out to the LORD from the heavens.
> > Ring out to him in the worlds of the heights.
> Ring out to him all his angels.
> > Ring out to him all his shining host.
> Ring out to him sun and moon.
> > Ring out to him all stars of light.
> Ring out to him heaven of heavens
> > and you heavenly waters.
> Let them all re-echo the name of the LORD.
> > For he commanded: and they were created.
> He established them for enduring aeons.
> > He made a decree: they do not transgress.

Psalm 148

Hallelujah!
*Ring out to the L*ORD *from the heavens.*
  Ring out to him in the worlds of the heights.
² Ring out to him all his angels.
  Ring out to him all his shining host.
³ Ring out to him sun and moon.
  Ring out to him all stars of light.
⁴ Ring out to him heaven of heavens
  and you heavenly waters.
*⁵ Let them all re-echo the name of the L*ORD*.*
  For he commanded: and they were created.
⁶ He established them for enduring aeons.
  He decreed order: they do not transgress.

*⁷ Ring out to the L*ORD *from the earth,*
  dragon-monsters and all abysmal depths,
⁸ fire and hail, snow and thick vapours,
  the spirit roar of wind, his word's fulfiller.
⁹ Mountains and all high places,
  fruit trees and all cedars,
¹⁰ wild creatures and cattle,
  creeping things and flying birds,
¹¹ kings on earth and all their peoples,
  princes and all judges on earth
¹² young men and maidens,
  old people and children –
*¹³ let all ring out the name of the L*ORD*.*
  For his name alone is sublime;
  his confession shines forth over earth and heaven.
¹⁴ He raises the ray of thinking's power of his people.
  He is a song of praise to all the devout,
    to the sons of the fighter of God, Israel, the community
      close to him.
        Hallelujah!

It begins with an upward gaze to the *heavens* and the *heights*. These are not mere words for the psalmist, but they raise his soul to the tangible multiplicity of higher worlds above us.

The psalmist does not first invoke the visible heavens – sun, moon and stars – in these heavenly worlds but rather what is invisible to us. In lofty spirit vision the tangible phenomena of the heavens pale while spirit beings of the higher spheres – 'all his angels' – are revealed to the opening inner eye.

The angels order themselves together into a mighty organism of spirits, into the heavenly host. This is not simply a naive transference of military concepts to the higher worlds of the heavens, but the reverse is true. In the strict regiment of an earthly army one can see the reflection of cosmic orders.

'Host' is *tsaba* in Hebrew, *tsabaoth* in the plural. (The same word is in the name 'Lord of Hosts'.) The underlying verb from which the word is derived means 'shining'. *Tsaba* signifies the shining ranks of the heavenly host, in the Old Testament sometimes called a 'host of stars'. But originally it is a host of spirits that the stars only make manifest. Seen inwardly, they are angelic beings, outwardly they are stars. When we read in the book of Job (38:7), 'When the morning stars sang together and all the children of God rejoiced' (literally 'sons of the gods', *bene elohim*), this is not only highly poetic but at the same time true for ancient vision.

The great Greek philosopher Aristotle also still called the stars the 'visible aspect of the divine', the 'most divine of all phenomena'. He confessed that 'It is a beautiful thing to be able to say that these ancient teachings of the patriarchs are founded on truth.'

In Psalm 148, therefore, it makes sense that the 'shining hosts' lead over into the visible lights of heaven, 'sun and moon', and 'all stars of light'. Through the preceding invocation of the angels, they have acquired a spiritual quality: they are not material masses in mechanical motion, but the translucent light bodies of the spirits that express themselves in them. They shine forth into sensory appearance.

From this gaze upon the stars arises the subsequent 'heaven of the heavens'. We should take this quite literally. Higher and ever higher supersensible realms rise one above the other, one heaven above another, in the same way as Paul speaks very factually of a 'third heaven' (2Cor 12:2).

But what are the 'heavenly waters'? Today people are dismissive of the 'primitive' ideas of the ancients, who, it seems, thought of heaven as a giant water tank and the firmament as its solid base with some kind of outlet for the rain. This is roughly how they understand the creation story of the terra firma dividing the waters above from the waters below.

But we can see this differently. When water evaporates and rises as vapour, in a sense it dematerialises or de-terrestrialises itself. Goethe says of the cirrus clouds dissolving into the blue, 'Thus flows at last what easily formed below, quietly into the lap and the hand of the Father above.' What has dematerialised itself in this way unites above with the etheric forces of the heavens, apparent to the ancients in their vision of the 'heavenly ocean'. When it descends again, and water at last falls to earth in heavy drops, it brings with it something like a heavenly blessing from above. 'Rain is God's blessing,' says an old proverb. The 'solidity' between the waters is in truth an invisible field of forces that brings about the separation between heavenly and earthly forms of existence, as Rudolf Steiner has shown in his lectures on the story of creation. As ancient powers of clairvoyance faded, these original perceptions no doubt materialised themselves into earthly concepts.

Having soared aloft into the 'heaven of heavens', the psalm now descends earthwards again with the 'heavenly waters', following the path of rain falling from the sky. Here too, therefore, ends the invocation of the diverse heavenly beings. One last time they are encompassed together: 'Let them all re-echo the name of the LORD.'

The *name* of God is the epitome of what God divulges of himself, what can be known about him. All hymns of praise are a celebratory unfolding and revealing of the divine name. Well may the heavens let the great name re-echo and reverberate, for they issued from God. He created them through the commandment of his Word – which is wilful and dynamic, and yet as Word also signifies utterance and self-imparting.

Creation – and here, as in the story of creation, the sacred word *bara* is used – is joined by the further wonder of *enduring existence*. He placed them into existence for the duration of aeons. The heavenly world is not obsolete and short-lived. In its resilient permanence through all cycles of time it is a reflection of eternity, of God himself.

A third aspect is *ordering*. Eternal divine thoughts are implanted in the celestial order. Schiller expresses a deep truth when he speaks of order as 'the heavenly daughter full of blessing'. And in this celestial world there is no *transgressing*: sacred order is in its undisputed element.

Here at the end of the celestial part of the psalm, a Trinitarian note sounds. In the creative Word lives the Son, in the preservation of existence, the eternal Father, and in order lives the bright thought-world of the Spirit.

The second part of the psalm leads us into a quite different world, one that turns towards the earth:

> Ring out to the LORD from the earth,
>   dragon-monsters and all abysmal depths,
> fire and hail, snow and thick vapours,
>   the spirit roar of wind, his word's fulfiller.
> Mountains and all high places,
>   fruit trees and all cedars,
> wild creatures and cattle,
>   creeping things and flying birds,
> kings on earth and all their peoples,
>   princes and all judges on earth
> young men and maidens,
>   old people and children –
> let all ring out the name of the LORD.
>   For his name alone is sublime;
>   his confession shines forth over earth and heaven.
> He raises the ray of thinking's power of his people.
>   He is a song of praise to all the devout,
>   to the sons of the fighter of God, Israel, the community
>   close to him.
> Hallelujah!

What first strikes us here is that the 'ringing out' which resounded in nearly every line of the psalm's celestial part now comes only sparingly. In the first part it was accorded to each group of entities: angels, sun and moon, stars of the light etc. Here, in the 'earthly' stanza of the psalm, it only frames the rest, at its beginning and end. Is this accidental? Surely not. The psalmist feels that the pure and pious reverberation of the divine is truly at home in celestial realms, and that things are different in this respect in the earthly world.

The celestial stanza ends by surveying the sacred order, 'they do not transgress'. The motif of transgression leads over to the earthly world in the next stanza. Above, in the heavens, the will of God is self-evident. Below on the earth he must struggle to establish his will. We might say that he allowed hindrances and resistance to him to arise on earth so that he might demonstrate his profoundest power in their eventual and ultimate overcoming. Thus the earth is on the one hand dark and problematic, but on the other, it encompasses what to us may seem a fearsomely vast scope, leading to still greater divine glories that can be born into light only from the dark womb of the earth.

As the first representatives of the earthly realm *dragons and abysses* appear, in utter contrast to the celestial world. This immediately strikes a fundamental tone for terrestrial things that is dark and uncanny. The *taninim* of the Hebrew text should not lead us towards zoology but mythology. Zoological creatures only appear later in the psalm as we will see. Here, rather, we are offered a terrifying picture of mythic vision, a nightmare image perceived by the clairvoyant human spirit.

The God-willed archetype of the human being has its home in heaven, in the bright, ideal world of creative, divine thought. It seeks to become reality within earthly substance, but to do so it must first laboriously wrestle its way to embodiment through resistant matter. Adversary powers seek to thwart this intention and so earth evolution throws up grotesque, uncanny forms. Instead of the self-realising pure archetype, a monstrous misformation appears that must be overcome. Dinosaurs, in so far as we can reconstruct them, show a bodily form that has some of these characteristics. In a sense we can say that the monstrous and uncanny forms of dinosaurs were dragon-like. But we should not put it the other way round and say that the dragons of myth were in reality dinosaurs. Dinosaurs embody only a zoological reflection of the dragon principle and certainly do not encompass the true meaning of dragonhood. The demonically thwarting will that tries to corrupt the archetype and make of it a degenerate form, is also at work in the intrinsically human realm of inwardness, of soul nature. Here the dragon appears as the monstrous form towards which sub-human aspects of the soul incline. For this reason the dragon belongs primarily in the domain of clairvoyance, of a visionary or dreamlike perception of soul truths.

Alongside the dragon monsters the psalm sets the 'abysmal depths' – *tehom* – the same word, albeit here in the plural, that is familiar to us from the story of creation: 'and darkness was upon the face of the deep (*tehom*)'. Once again, this is a word resonant of mythology, more vision than geographical designation. Just as the upper world in the 'heaven of heavens' is immeasurable, an 'abyss of light' in Nietzsche's phrase, so in the terrestrial realm too we can intimate abysses that sink into ever deeper, immeasurable depths.

Following this mythic-visionary prelude, one that reflects in a grandiose way the motif of earthly existence, the psalm gradually approaches a more 'naturalistic' earth-world. Yet we are not entirely in the ordinary, mundane realm – the psalm first invokes the *atmosphere,* that transitional boundary zone where the earth is not yet fully earth but is still open to celestial influences. 'Fire [here, given the context, no doubt the fire of lightning], hail, snow and thick vapours.' The heavenly world still plays into these elemental powers of the atmosphere. This is especially true of the wind, the offspring of heaven. What could be rendered here as the 'spirit roar of wind', is also expressly related to the divine Word. Old languages, after all, have the same word for 'wind' and 'spirit', out of a primordial clairvoyance, an original spiritual-physical form of experience.

Only after passing through the atmospheric and elemental zone still permeable by higher influences, do we reach the earth itself, but firstly only where it extends beyond or above itself and seeks to remain close to the heavens. Descending from above we 'land' as it were upon the peaks of *mountains* – 'mountains and all high places'. We may be reminded here of all the mountains revered as sacred by a humanity seeking the heavenly realms.

Then, descending further we reach the region of *plant* growth: 'Fruit trees and all cedars.' From there we go on to *creatures,* described in their polarity of wild and domestic creatures, that is, hostile to human beings and inclined to them, as well as in the other polarity of creeping and flying.

The psalm proceeds in a precise sequence from stone to plant to animals and thus finally arrives at the *human being* as the earthly creature of culminating importance.

In the human kingdom, the kings come first; in the understanding of ancient initiation, they were seen as spiritually elevated, rising into a realm higher than the human. This is also true of the 'princes and judges'. In the Old Testament, judges are sometimes even called 'gods' (*elohim*). People still had a sense that one person cannot judge another without further elevation. The council of judges was intended to be an instrument of higher powers.

Even the 'peoples' assigned to the 'kings' do not yet lapse from the super-human context. Rather than individual human beings, the psalm is referring to blood ties superordinate to the individual, which in olden times were still truly the bearer of a divine group-spirituality. Rather than the 'masses' spoken of today, they were still a sacred people who as such embodied and gave abode to a higher spirit.

Finally, we take the last step into a mundane and universal humanity, apparent here in the polarity of the sexes and of the old and young: 'Young men and maidens, old people and children'.

With the 'children', the invocation of a sequence of earthly beings comes to an end. In the prophecy of Isaiah, the 'child' figures as the form of a promised messianic redemption, which will enter a humanity grown old and rejuvenate it. 'To us a child is born, to us a son is given' (9:6). The wild animals will live in peace with one another, and 'a little child will lead them' (11:6).

The earthly part of Psalm 148 begins with the dragon and ends with the child. In thus encompassing both monsters and the dangerous abyss, as well as the promise of a redemptive future, it offers a succinct panorama of earthly existence – from the dragon to the Christ child.

As towards the end of the celestial stanza, so here too, a general, summarising exhortation is offered: 'Let all ring out the name of the LORD.' Even the monsters of the depths, once vanquished, must ultimately contribute to the higher revelation of God.

Here in the earthly part of the psalm, something more is added to the motif of the name. 'For his name alone is sublime' – he rises in a sense into the unreachable and unapproachable realm where he is 'alone with himself'. There is something of the very highest nature concealed within this name of God, still unrevealed, like a mountain peak shrouded in cloud. Here the psalm awaits the fulfilment by Christ, who will say, 'I have revealed your name and will continue to reveal it' (Jn 17:26).

The revelation of this name ascending into the unapproachable heights spans 'earth and heaven' (verse 13). What many translations render as glory, majesty or splendour, is more accurately translated in the Greek text as 'confession'. We need not think here only of a confession of sins or confession of faith. A confession exists wherever something inward is outwardly made manifest. In the name of God which reveals itself, the divine is confessed. And this confession shines forth over 'earth and heaven' (the sequence in the original). Here *earth* takes precedence, rather than, as in the usual phrase, 'heaven and earth'. Behind this dawns a distant intuition that the name ascending into the unapproachability of its unique aloneness will eventually be able to fully impart itself to the earth as well. The old creation follows the sequence 'heaven and earth'. The new creation, beginning with Christ at Golgotha, is initiated in the earthly domain and from there shines back into celestial worlds.

Only when seen from the perspective of Christ's fulfilment does an inspired pre-Christian script such as Psalm 148 reveal its full light. Then, behind the chosen people of Israel, to whom the last gaze of the psalm is turned, the true people of God become visible, the community of Christ Jesus. The Christ event seeks, after all, to live on and bear ever more fruit in a renewed, transformed humanity upon earth.

In place of the community or Church, the psalm still looks upon the people of Israel. 'He has raised up a horn of his people.' What does this curious image of the 'raised horn' signify? The Hebrew word *keren* means both 'horn' and 'ray'. The horn is a ray of energy that has become visible. The 'horns' of Moses are originally the rays issuing from his head, a manifestation of the power of his inspired thoughts. Thus the 'raising of a horn' in our psalm no doubt means that the power of thought should be directed upward. The powers of intelligence should not act only upon earthly and material things, but also be directed towards the supersensible.

This is significant in connection with the name that has not yet been fully revealed, that still ascends into unapproachability. The more the ray of thinking power acquires an upward direction, the more the content of the great name will be able to dawn within human awareness.

Then the people of God on earth, or as we would say, the 'Church of Christ', will increasingly become 'the community close to him' as the last verse of the psalm has it. Through Christ and his works, implicitly also through the ray of thinking's power being raised to the divine, the unapproachable God will become approachable and the unknown will become known. He will live with and in human beings. At the end of the psalm, therefore, in a kind of apocalyptic prospect, there rises from the eerie darkness of the earthly world a new humanity characterised by intimacy with God – 'the community close to him'.

Psalm 148, if we study it more closely, is therefore far more than a mere listing of whatever happens to come to the psalmist's mind. As we have seen, rather than the random accumulation it might appear to be at first reading, it is in fact a truly illumined sequence. In this selection and arrangement, in a few words only, a 'world in miniature' emerges in which the 'greater world' can be rediscovered; in which key aspects of fundamental truths of heaven and earth are faithfully reflected.

28

THE SEVEN THUNDERS

PSALM 29

I

A heavy storm is approaching over the sea. The devout person of the Old Testament lets their gaze rest upon the threatening masses of cloud in solemn and anxious expectation, as befits the reception of some great revelation.

Then comes a flash of lightning, flaming over the whole sky. It rends the clouds. It rends, too, a curtain before the searching eye. The soul knows that it is carried away from the earthly world. Vanished are earth, sea, thunderclouds. In mighty visions the ritual in heaven appears, divine worship as it is solemnised by those who dwell in the higher worlds.

> Bear to the LORD, O sons of God,
>   bear to the LORD revelation and power!
> Bear to the LORD the reflection of his name!
>   Offer the LORD worship in holy vesture of light!

II

The vision of the heavenly high mass fades. Among deepening rolls of thunder the curtain closes again. The soul returns from its ecstasy to the earthly body, sees again earth, sea, storm-clouds and hears the thunder, which now follows the forewarning lightning. But now, sanctified by the vision, the soul is able to give the thunder its right name – 'the voice of the LORD' (*qol Yahweh*). For the Hebrews this

Psalm 29

*Bear to the L*ORD*, O sons of God,*
    *bear to the L*ORD *revelation and power!*
[2] *Bear to the L*ORD *the reflection of his name!*
    *Offer the L*ORD *worship in holy vesture of light!*

[3] *Thunder-voice of the L*ORD *over the sea.*
    The God of glory thunders;
    *the L*ORD *over the great waters;*
[4] *Thunder-tone of the L*ORD*, full of strength,*
    *thunder-tone of the L*ORD*, full of majesty.*

[5] *Thunder-tone of the L*ORD *breaks the cedars;*
    *the L*ORD *breaks the cedars of Lebanon;*
[6] *he makes them leap like a calf,*
    the mountains of Lebanon and Sirion like young unicorns.

[7] *Thunder-tone of the L*ORD *breaks forth fiery flames.*
[8] *Thunder-tone of the L*ORD *shakes the wilderness.*
    *He shakes, the L*ORD*, the desert of Kadesh.*
[9] *Thunder-tone of the L*ORD *makes the deer give birth,*
    and strips bare the forests.

    And in his temple – all that is his, cry: Gloria!
[10] *The L*ORD*, above the flood sat enthroned,*
    *enthroned is he, the L*ORD*, a king in eternity.*
[11] *The L*ORD *will give strength to his people.*
    *The L*ORD *will bless his people with peace.*

was a name for thunder. Seven times the rolling *qol Yahweh* occurs in the psalm. It may perhaps be rendered 'thunder-tone'.

> Thunder-voice of the LORD over the sea.
>   The God of glory thunders;
>   the LORD over the great waters;
> Thunder-tone of the LORD, full of strength,
>   thunder-tone of the LORD, full of majesty.

The storm moves slowly over the leaden sea. The voice of Yahweh over the waters – memory arises of the beginnings of creation, how once the Spirit of God brooded over the waters like a cloud. It was pregnant with creative lightning-thoughts and powerful thunder-words; below it the expectant elements yielding in obedience.

III

The thunderstorm moves towards the land. It takes its way over the hills of the coast to the desert of Kadesh.

> Thunder-tone of the LORD breaks the cedars;
>   the LORD breaks the cedars of Lebanon;
> he makes them leap like a calf,
>   the mountains of Lebanon and Sirion like young
>   unicorns.
>
> Thunder-tone of the LORD breaks forth fiery flames.
> Thunder-tone of the LORD shakes the wilderness.
>   He shakes, the LORD, the desert of Kadesh.
> Thunder-tone of the LORD makes the deer give birth,
>   and strips bare the forests.

From the sea to the land – the solid land is the realm of human existence. All that in primeval beginnings was still pliable and heaving ocean is hardened and solidified in the earthly element. The world trembles before the creative Word of the Highest. What has taken shape on earth feels itself called in question when the eternal speaks new words of power. The sons of God in the heights solemnise the high mass, earthly human beings feel themselves brought to judgment.

What is mortal groans in its foundations. The psalm shows this in its manifold pictures. Age-old cedars, towering trees, are struck by lightning and split asunder. Who can behold this and not be gripped by the gravity of the Last Judgment? The mountains tremble, rocked by an earthquake. In rich metaphor the psalm compares them to skipping calves. Branches and leaves are torn from the trees by the tempest. The elemental pressure of what is taking place seizes the beasts of the forest, penetrating them through and through.

In seven mighty thunder-claps, three over the sea, four over the land, the storm passes over. One is reminded of the seven thunders of the Apocalypse of John, 'The seven thunders sounded their voices' (Rv 10:3).

IV

On earth there is excitement, shock, shuddering. What is mortal groans in its foundations. The seven thunders have sounded. The soul, which had trembled in its mortal part, turns from the picture of the groaning uprooted forests, and lifts itself to the eternal. In Novalis' words, 'But what is immortal begins to shine more brightly, and know itself.'

> And in his temple – all that is his, cry: Gloria!
> The LORD, above the flood sat enthroned,
> enthroned is he, the LORD, a king in eternity.
> The LORD will give strength to his people.
> The LORD will bless his people with peace.

The psalm ends where it began: in the heavenly sanctuary. There the *Gloria in excelsis* of the heavenly hosts resounds. The eternal is throned in tranquillity above the flood – with the mention of which the earthly, catastrophic storm once more appears, dying away in violent downpour of rain as in the days of the flood itself.

In the Apocalypse of John it is impressive to observe how, in the midst of the visions of disaster chasing each other, the picture of the heavenly throne appears over and over again, giving us the assurance of an eventual guiding of events. So here, too, the tranquil enthronement of the eternal over the storms is presented in magnificent contrast.

The last word of this psalm of storm is 'peace'. The storm is followed by the rainbow, the divine token of the covenant. This peace is not weak or cowardly. Human beings who have passed through the storms and have become conscious of their immortal being feel their passage through the tempest as an increase of inner strength. So, too, their journey through the apocalyptic catastrophes effects an increase of powerful spirit-will. 'The Lord will give strength to his people.' The word of peace follows upon this word of strength. *Gloria in excelsis* is answered by *et in terra pax* – and peace on earth. Throughout the storms human beings knows themselves to be united with the one throned in eternal majesty. The divine tranquillity throned above becomes a peace full of strength in the human heart below.

Appendix: the heavenly ritual

Those taking part in the heavenly worship are, in the original text, called *bene elim,* sons of God, not just 'sons of the mighty' or 'mighty ones'. The gods of the ancient religions are beings from the ranks of the heavenly hierarchies, the angelic ranks of a ninefold order.

They are also spoken of in Psalm 89 (5–8): 'And the heavens shall praise your wonders, O Lord, and your faithfulness in the assembly of the holy ones. For who in the clouds can be compared to the Lord? Who can be likened to the Lord among the sons of God? God is awesome in the assembly of the holy ones, great and revered by all who are about him. O Lord God of Hosts, who is like you?' Thus the vision of ancient times saw the God who speaks the great 'I am' in the midst of numberless hierarchical beings, for it is these that are meant by the 'holy ones' in Psalm 89. It does not refer here to righteous people who have reached perfection, but to high beings from the ranks of the angels. Those standing in his presence partake in his holiness, as for instance the Seraphim whom Isaiah hears intone the great 'Holy, holy, holy' in his vision (Is 6).

The sons of God bear to him the light of revelation (*gloria, kabhod*) and power. God has graciously poured forth his being into the world and they reflect it back to him in gratitude. Divine thoughts and divine will-forces are reflected, as it were, in the world, and the beings of the angelic ranks mediate this divine reflection.

In Psalm 96, which extols apocalyptically the coming of the divine, almost the same words are to be found.

There is, however, the difference that people and indeed the whole of humankind are considered worthy to enter into this heavenly act of worship. Psalm 29 does not yet take this human possibility into consideration. It sees only the worship of the angels.

In the last two psalms the 'holy vesture of light' is mentioned. The one who turns to the Highest in prayer and sacrifice is clothed in light. Ancient wisdom spoke of the fact that the one who worships receives a reflected splendour of the One who is worshipped. The light-garment of holiness is the heavenly prototype of the priestly robes.

29

A SUMMER SONG OF PRAISE

PSALM 65

I

An inner mood of peace and relaxed, joyful calm, and outside the ripeness of nature in all its fullness: these two are woven harmoniously together in Psalm 65.

'Praise awaits you, O God' – literally 'Quietness is a song of praise to you, O God'. The soul turns towards the divine in the silence of devotion.

'To you the vow shall be performed'. The full range of this second sentence is perhaps not immediately apparent to the modern reader. What sort of religious feeling lies behind it?

We regard it as an offence when someone promises something and fails to fulfil the promise. We are willing to allow that small children cannot be expected to make binding promises. But it is different with adults, for a truly grown-up person is not at the mercy of changing moods and feelings. The more the individuality develops in human beings, the more reliable and constant they will be in all the changes of life. If human beings were only of a passing temporal nature, they would neither be capable of faithfully remembering the past nor of carrying out with firm will their aims for the future. Anyone who is able to fulfil a promise given perhaps a long time before, has built out of the powers of eternity a bridge across the changing waves of time. A religious vow was a means of education in the perception of these powers of eternity. Whoever fulfilled a promise had, in that moment, a meeting with themselves as a being of eternity, above and beyond all that is temporary and passing. They felt confirmed and strengthened

Psalm 65

Silence towards you is a song of praise, O God in Zion.
  The vow fulfilled, unite in peace with you.
² *You hear prayer.*
  To you shall all flesh come.
³ *If our failures overwhelm us,*
  our transgressions – you cover them.
⁴ *Blessed is the one you choose, to whom you grant*
     your presence,
  who will dwell in your courts.
We may be satisfied with the goodness of your house,
  with the holiness of your temple.

⁵ *By awesome earnestness you answer us with*
     righteousness,
  O God, our Help,
the hope of all the ends of the earth
  and of the farthest seas;
⁶ *who by his strength established the mountains,*
  being girded with might;
⁷ *who stills the roaring of the seas,*
  the roaring of the waves,
  the tumult of the peoples.
⁸ *They are in awe at your signs*
  who dwell in the extremities
You make rejoice the going out
  of the morning and the evening.

⁹ *You visit the earth and water it,*
  enriching it greatly.
The river of God is full of water.
  You prepare the grain,
  indeed you strengthen it.
¹⁰ *You water the furrows abundantly,*
  press down the ridges,
you soften it with showers.
  You bless its sprouting.
¹¹ *You crown the year with your goodness,*
  your tracks drip with abundance.

> ^{12} *They drip on the pastures of the wilderness,*
> *the hills are girded with joy,*
> ^{13} *the meadows are clothed with flocks,*
> *the valleys are covered with grain.*
> *They shout for joy and sing.*

in the timeless core of their own being. And they felt accepted by God through this fulfilment.

Thus the psalmist felt that his vow returned to the realm of eternity, and drew with it into that realm him who had fulfilled it. 'To you shall the vow be fulfilled.' The Hebrew word for 'fulfil' is the same root-word which also means 'peace' (*shalom*).

A further experience grew out of the fact that human activity in the sphere of eternity finds its way to God, that God hears prayer. Our endeavours towards the eternal sphere are not lost. They are taken up, accepted. Whether our prayers are 'answered' is a secondary matter. 'You hear prayer.'

Just at this point the psalm does not stop at the self. It recognises the fact that every experience of the divine openness to our prayers lifts those who pray above their own personality into the universal human sphere. 'To you shall all flesh come.' The ear of God is open to all souls incarnated in an earthly body and suffering from the limitations of material existence.

The thought of the 'flesh', the temporary sheath of our being, suggests the further thought of human failure and guilt: 'You purge away our transgressions'. A power comes from the divine world which can overcome them. Something is dimly perceived here which was only realised in Christ.

This premonition of a future redemption from sin gives rise to the saying which follows: 'Blessed is the one you choose.' This 'choosing' should not be thought of in the sense of an abstract theory of predestination, any more than the saying in the gospels which seems to give precedence to those who are 'chosen' over those who are 'called' (Mt 20:16). All higher experience has two aspects. 'I shall know fully even as I am known fully' (1Cor 13:12). 'I will eat with him, and he with me' (Rv 3:20). In the living experience of a devout soul, the one side of the truth 'I want God' is far outshone by the other side 'God wants me'. So also the fact that the devout soul has made a decision for God is completely overshadowed by the overpowering impression that God, for his part, has chosen the soul.

A further experience is linked with the sense of being 'chosen'. It is the feeling that God is near. Certainly God is everywhere, but his nearness is capable of a strengthening, an intensification. This feeling of nearness can be enhanced until it becomes more and more a sense of being at home in divine realms. Or, as the psalm expresses it, whoever is near to God may 'dwell in your courts'.

Again the psalm does not remain caught in self-centred mysticism, but presses on to a higher social consciousness, in the sphere of community. Just where the first section of the psalm rises to its height, to unity of being, to communion, the 'we' appears over and above the individual.

This first part might perhaps be rendered:

> Silence towards you is a song of praise, O God in Zion.
> > The vow fulfilled, unite in peace with you.
> You hear prayer.
> > To you shall all flesh come.
> If our failures overwhelm us,
> > our transgressions – you cover them.
> Blessed is the one you choose, to whom you grant
> > your presence,
> > who will dwell in your courts.
> We may be satisfied with the goodness of your house,
> > with the holiness of your temple.

II

The second part leaves the inner world of mystical and sacramental life and turns to the destiny of humankind, to world history. In the otherwise peaceful psalm, an apocalyptic thunder becomes audible. 'Awesome' is the divine judgment which 'answers' from above the human deeds and misdeeds. Eternal righteousness cannot do otherwise, it must react. The Godhead appears in history as the guiding power in the life of nations over the whole earth. The signs of the times are its beckoning gestures.

But just as in Beethoven's *Pastoral Symphony,* the storm casts only a passing shadow over the bright summer day, so in this second part the mood of gratitude and joy breaks through again.

> By awesome earnestness you answer us with righteousness,
> > O God, our Help,
> the hope of all the ends of the earth
> > and of the farthest seas;
> who by his strength established the mountains,
> > being girded with might;
> who stills the roaring of the seas,
> > the roaring of the waves,
> > the tumult of the peoples.
> They are in awe at your signs
> > who dwell in the extremities.
> You make rejoice the going out
> > of the morning and the evening.

III

The third part turns to nature, giving us one of the most beautiful pictures of nature in the Bible. It describes how God visits the earth in the fructifying rain. It was not foolish superstition when the people of ancient times saw in rain the fructification of the earthly world by the heavenly. There was a time when the divine still revealed itself to people directly in nature. Expressions like 'trees of God' or 'river of God' were still meant quite literally. The inner and outer world were not yet separated from each other in human consciousness. So people still saw in the flowing river the very life-stream of God.

Through this ancient power of vision the year was also regarded as a living spiritual being, which revealed itself in time, and at the climax of its life was crowned by God. It stands before us in spiritual, ensouled embodiment, and not merely as an abstract concept of a calendar.

What is experienced in the first section as inward and sacramental, the divine goodness which offers itself in communion, comes again in the third section as mythical greatness in the life of nature seen as though from outside. The Authorised Version says: 'thy paths drop fatness'. But the literal sense is 'wagon tracks', the underlying visionary picture being the wagon of God which travels through the land bestowing fruitfulness wherever it goes.

'You bless its sprouting.' Whoever can really bless is able to set free from his own soul a power which remains henceforth with the one who is blessed. A blessing is not a 'mere word', but the real passing on of inward power. God has spoken as it were a part of his divine soul into the being of the plant, so that it can grow.

The hills and meadows are also seen in this religious way as living beings. 'The meadows are clothed with flocks.' The animals add yet another covering to the green vesture of the plants. A flock of grazing sheep is like a garment drawn over the earth. And just as the green grass lays a covering of life as a fine etheric garment over the otherwise bare earth, so in the soul-life of the grazing flocks another, a soul-sheath, is woven above it. Lastly, the shouting and singing for joy of human souls also enters the landscape. To the etheric life and the soul-activities of the animals is added human soul-life which is open to the divine spiritual world. 'The little hills are girded with joy.'

This religious joy in nature unites beautifully with the inward silence of the temple at the beginning of the psalm. The three kingdoms of divine revelation have now been traversed: the sphere of the Holy Spirit in the mystic-sacramental inner life, the realm of the Son in the drama of world history, the kingdom of the Father in the natural world. Thus in each of the three sections the word 'God' is spoken once. In this psalm it is not the stern name of Yahweh, but Elohim, the name which bears within it the whole rich fullness of the divine powers.

> You visit the earth and water it,
>   enriching it greatly.
> The river of God is full of water.
>   You prepare the grain,
>   indeed you strengthen it.
>   You water the furrows abundantly,
>   press down the ridges,

29. A Summer Song of Praise

    you soften it with showers.
        You bless its sprouting.
You crown the year with your goodness,
    your tracks drip with abundance.
They drip on the pastures of the wilderness,
    the hills are girded with joy,
the meadows are clothed with flocks,
    the valleys are covered with grain.
They shout for joy and sing.

30

AN AUTUMNAL SONG OF PILGRIMAGE

PSALM 84

I

When summer comes to an end, cold and darkness slowly come to mind again, unnoticed at first, but with gradually increasing penetration. Human beings feel more strongly the need of a home as shelter for the winter. 'Woe to him who has no home,' Nietzsche wrote in his autumnal poem 'Vereinsamt' (lonely).

The more people today feel uprooted and homeless in their outer life, the more they should feel called upon to seek a true home in a higher world. If they succeed to inwardly settle there, this homecoming will help them take on with new courage the uncertain destiny of their earthly pilgrimage.

These two things, the finding of a home in the eternal and courage for the earthly path, are wonderfully expressed in Psalm 84. Its designation 'a song over the wine-press of the sons of Korah' marks it as a song for autumn, for, as has already been explained in connection with Psalm 8, the Hebrew text does not indicate 'a song on the Gitthit' (guitar, zither?) as in many translations, but 'over the winepress'. Thus an autumnal mood is indicated, though in a different way from that in Psalm 8.

Psalm 84

A song over the winepress of the sons of Korah

How beloved is your dwelling place,
  O Lord of the shining Hosts.
² *My soul longs and even faints*
  for the courts of the Lord.
My heart, my whole body, cries out in joy
  to God who is life itself.
³ *Even the bird found a home,*
  the swallow her nest where she may lay her young
at your altars, O Lord of the shining Hosts,
  my King and my God.
⁴ *Blessed are they who dwell in your house,*
  ever singing your praise.
     Selah.

⁵ *Blessed are those who have their strength in you,*
  their heart is set on the raised ways,
⁶ *they pass through the vale of tears*
  and they turn it into a valley of springs,
    full of blessings pointing the way.
⁷ *They go from strength to strength,*
  until God appears in Zion.
⁸ *O Lord of the shining Hosts, hear my prayer,*
  give ear to me, O God of Jacob.
     Selah.

⁹ *Behold us O God, our shield, send us your ray of light,*
  illumine the countenance of your anointed.
¹⁰ *One day in your courts is more precious*
  than a thousand others.
Rather would I stand at the threshold of the house
     of my God,
  than live in the tents of wickedness, far from him.
¹¹ *Yes, sun and shield is the Lord God,*
  grace and glory does he bestow.
No good thing does he withhold
  from those who walk uprightly.
¹² *O Lord of the shining Hosts,*
  blessed the one who trusts in you!

> How beloved is your dwelling place,
>   O Lord of the shining Hosts.
> My soul longs and even faints
>   for the courts of the Lord.
> My heart, my whole body, cries out in joy
>   to God who is life itself.
> Even the bird found a home,
>   the swallow her nest where she may lay her young
> at your altars, O Lord of the shining Hosts,
>   my King and my God.
> Blessed are they who dwell in your house,
>   ever singing your praise.
>   *Selah.*

These verses may still be a valid expression of ritual worship for us. We too know that wherever our altar stands is 'home' for us. Certainly God is everywhere. But it is a fact of the most ancient and fundamental experience that the earthly environment may become especially open and transparent for the presence of the supersensory world in places that have been set apart for worship. Earthly space is enclosed in a higher spiritual space. The psalmist is conscious that the whole human being is affected by this sensory-supersensory event; not only the soul, but also the heart, the actual centre of self, and even the 'flesh'. The earthly body also shares in the stream of life that can be felt issuing from God.

Several commentators have noted how beautifully a trusting feeling of being at home with the divine is interwoven with a reverent humility in this psalm. The idyllic, peaceful picture of the swallow which has found a place for her nest, is followed by a glimpse of the greatness and majesty of the divine: 'my King and my God'. The Lord *tsabaoth* means literally the Lord of the 'shining hosts', by which we may think of the visible world of stars as well as of the heavenly hosts of the angelic realms which belong to them.

The first section of the psalm ends with the word 'selah'. It is not quite clear what this means. The Greek translation says *diapsalma*, which would indicate a musical interlude echoing the mood of what had gone before.

II

The first part closes with a blessing promised to those who live continually near to God. The blessing is taken up again at the beginning of the second section. (The Greek version uses the word *makarios*, which we know from the beatitudes in the Sermon on the Mount.) But now it applies to anyone who goes courageously forward on pilgrimage. Here a strong Michaelic note comes into the psalm.

> Blessed are those who have their strength in you,
>   their heart is set on the raised ways,
> they pass through the vale of tears
>   and they turn it into a valley of springs,
>   full of blessings pointing the way.
> They go from strength to strength,
>   until God appears in Zion.
> O Lord God of the radiant Hosts, hear my prayer,
>   give ear to me, O God of Jacob.
>   *Selah.*

Whoever has found the 'ways upwards' in their heart (Greek, *anabaseis,* Latin *ascensiones*) does not shrink from the necessary path of destiny through the vale of tears. This description of earthly life has not always had a healthy effect in religious circles. It may lead to a certain escapism. But the psalm itself expresses no such cowardly mood. On the contrary, it says: whoever has in their heart the possibility of upward progress will transform the earthly vale of tears into a place of blessing. He can draw on eternal springs even in the dreary desert, just as Christ said to the Samaritan woman that the water which he would give would spring up as a source of everlasting life. Through this the painful and dangerous pilgrimage of earthly life becomes a 'going from strength to strength' for the pilgrim.

The text is now not quite clear. It may mean 'they are seen by God in Zion' or 'they see God in Zion'. But however it is to be understood, it comes in the end to the same – the ancient mystical truth: 'I shall know fully even as I am known fully' (1Cor 13:12). The vision of God is at the same time a being seen by God. Thus the end of the pilgrimage is a 'seeing face to face'.

III

From this prospect the psalm leads back again to the feeling of 'home' in the consecrated place. Again the prayer, 'Behold us O God,' does not imply that the Omnipresent does not see everything. But the act of seeing is not felt here only from the aspect of perception. The seeing eye is not only a passive receiver of impressions, but it also sends out fine rays of light. The eye not only sees, it radiates. Hermann Beckh pointed out that just this radiance of light is expressed in the sound of the Hebrew word for 'seeing' (*ra'ah*). Thus the supplication 'behold' asks for the revelation of the divine radiance of light. To this is added the further request: 'illumine the countenance of your anointed.'

The singer of this psalm at that time may have been thinking of the King at Jerusalem, or of the High Priest. But these were both merely forerunners and representatives of him who in the fullest sense is called 'the anointed'. In the face of the Messiah, the Christ, the face of God became visible to us. 'He who sees me, also sees the Father' (Jn 14:9). The creative light of God reaches its highest revelation in the countenance of the Saviour.

Once again the psalmist is overcome by the consciousness of the infinite value of the experience of God in ritual worship: *one* day in the forecourt of the temple outweighs a thousand other days. Once again the 'Michael' note of the autumn festival is sounded in the theme of sun and shield. The words 'glory and honour' which follow are connected with concrete and distinct experiences. Man is not yet complete. 'What we will be has not yet appeared' (1Jn 3:2). There is still a cloud of unexhausted higher possibilities above our heads. What is finally to become our personal being, our inmost possession, still hovers over us. When something of this creative cloud sinks down into a person, there is 'grace'. 'Glory' (Hebrew *kabhod*; Greek *doxa*; Latin *gloria*) is a radiance that is perceptible to a higher organ of sight. In the Old Testament it sometimes actually appears as a part of the human being: 'Awake my glory' (Ps 57:8). It is something like a fine supersensory light-organism, which awakens in human beings when they share in the grace that streams into them from above.

The psalm ends with a third and last promise of blessing:

30. An Autumnal Song of Pilgrimage

Behold us O God, our shield, send us your ray of light,
    illumine the countenance of your anointed.
One day in your courts is more precious
    than a thousand others.
Rather would I stand at the threshold of the house
        of my God,
    than live in the tents of wickedness, far from him.
Yes, sun and shield is the Lord God,
    grace and glory does he bestow.
No good thing does he withhold
    from those who walk uprightly.
O Lord of the shining Hosts,
    blessed the one who trusts in you!

31

THE SONG OF THE THREE MEN IN THE FIERY FURNACE

DANIEL 3

The picture of the three men in the fiery furnace is one of the most impressive in the Bible. At the time of the captivity in Babylon, in the sixth century BC, King Nebuchadnezzar has thrown the three into the furnace for refusing to worship an idol, but the fire does them no harm. Miraculously protected, they walk about freely in the blazing fire and praise God.

Is this a crass product of a 'pious imagination' with a craving for miracles? If so, would our souls be so deeply moved by it? We feel that such a story, which charms us like a fairy tale, is somehow fundamentally true. Like all real fairy tales it has an archetypal quality.*

We find the story in the Old Testament in Chapter 3 of the Book of Daniel. Not everything is there, however. Among the so-called apocryphal writings there are two additional fragments to the story: the Prayer of Azariah and the Song of the Three Young Men. These texts are not part of the recognised Hebrew Scriptures or of the Protestant Bible. They belong to a later period than the Book of Daniel and exist only in Greek, stemming from the cosmopolitan Judaism of Alexandria.† The Greek translation as well as the much later Latin translation of Jerome, the Vulgate, included both these

---

* For further study on the background see Bock, *Kings and Prophets*.

† The Prayer of Azariah and the Song of the Three Young Men were inserted in Daniel 3 between verses 23 and 24, and in translations of the Old Testament Apocrypha are usually just one book (abbreviated Sg Thr). The Greek translation of the Old Testament, the Septuagint, came into existence in Alexandria, in the time of the Ptolemies, a Macedonian dynasty that ruled in Egypt as successors of Alexander the Great. They gave a great deal of support to cultural life.

additions as an integral part of the narrative in the third chapter of Daniel. The old Church was guided by a true feeling in acknowledging the addition, for on closer examination it proves to be intimately connected.*

First comes the Prayer of Azariah, who is one of the three (also called by his Babylonian name Abednego). He makes himself their spokesman, praying also in their name. Despite the praise it is chiefly a penitential prayer. One must imagine the terrible catastrophe that lay behind the Jews of the Babylonian exile. The flames of burning Jerusalem, the flames of the burning temple, had lighted their way into the misery of exile. All the more unusual that Azariah does not call for vengeance in his prayer, but accepts the catastrophe in humility of heart as inflicted by God; indeed, not only accepts it, but consents to it. 'You have executed true judgments in all that you have brought upon us and upon Jerusalem, the holy city of our fathers' (Sg Thr 5). The Babylonians were only tools of God's judgment. For it is 'because of our sins.' Azariah recognised in the flames of the fire the God who is a 'consuming fire', as the Fifth Book of Moses says (Dt 4:24). But by humbly accepting this fate from the hand of God, Azariah becomes acquainted with the element of fire. The fire of punishment becomes the flame of purification. Finally, within the purifying flame that burns up everything ungodly, he divines the ardour of God's love.

So the flame of sacrifice is kindled in Azariah's soul. Since the sanctuary lies in ashes, the temple rites are necessarily in abeyance, but for that reason the sacrifice has to live within human souls. 'With a contrite heart and a humble spirit may we be accepted, as though it were with burnt offerings ... such may our sacrifice be in your sight this day, and may we wholly follow you' (Sg Thr 16f) – words that have since found their way into the Offertory of the mass.

Is it for this reason that the flames of the furnace cannot harm the three, since they have kindled in their hearts the true fire, the fire of sacrifice born of the purifying, burning pain of self-knowledge?

---

* In the Roman Catholic ritual the Song of the Three Young Men plays an important part in that it appears four times in the year on Ember Saturdays, on which ordinations of priests also take place. The priest prays the song of praise of the three men, the *Canticum Benedicite,* in the thanksgiving after each Mass. In the old Gallic rite, as it was celebrated up to the eighth century, the hymn was inserted during the reading of each Mass instead of the Alleluia. *The Benedicite* is also to be found in the English Book of Common Prayer as an alternative to the *Te Deum* during Morning Prayer.

As in the Christian sacrament the sacrificial Offering is followed by the divinely effected Transubstantiation, so in the experience of the three men after Azariah's prayer of penitence and offering something yet more sublime comes. Outwardly, certainly, it seems as if things were about to get worse. Provoked by the curiously uninjured state of the three, those tending the furnace stoke the fire afresh 'with naphtha, pitch, tow, and brush' so that it burns as it were seven times hotter than it was before, and the flames leap seven times seven cubits high (Sg Thr 23f). But simultaneously with the increase of heat, the mysterious 'fourth' joins the three, the 'angel of the Lord' whom Nebuchadnezzar, who also sees it, calls 'a son of the gods' (Dn 3:25). He keeps them from destruction and lets them feel the raging, scorching fire as 'a moist whistling wind'. One is reminded of the Grimm fairy tale of The Old Man Made Young Again, who 'glowed like a rose tree' in the fire and found the blaze like a 'refreshing dew'.

And now the hymn, the Song of the Three Young Men, follows immediately. Azariah is no longer the only speaker. It is as if the appearance of the mysterious fourth had conferred on the three the ability of harmoniously uniting their different soul qualities in a true trinity. As the original text says, they began to sing 'as with one mouth'.

The content of the song of praise is wonderfully ordered. It begins by looking at the Deity himself to whom the three had first turned in the fire:

> Blessed are you, O Lord, God of our fathers,
>   and to be praised and highly exalted for ever.
> And blessed is your glorious, holy name:
>   and to be highly praised and highly exalted for ever.
> Blessed are you in the temple of your holy glory,
>   and to be extolled and highly glorified for ever.

To the Father God is added the 'name' as something in its own right – as if it were a divination of the mystery of the Son, born in eternity, in whom the Father reveals his being. Then, thirdly, the temple of glory, subsisting as it were in revealing light – here one could think of the sphere of the Holy Spirit.

In the three following verses there is a gradual descent from the innermost divine sphere of God towards the *world:* 'Blessed are you, who sits upon the Cherubim and looks upon the deeps.' There follows the picture of the throne and finally the firmament.

Up to this point the deity has been directly addressed: 'You' – 'Blessed are you ...' After something like a lower boundary of the highest divine regions is reached, the hymn turns to direct personal address to the 'works of the Lord'.

> Bless the Lord, all works of the Lord,
>   sing praise to him and highly exalt him for ever.

This verse structure, with its threefold 'bless – sing praise – highly exalt', is maintained unchanged from now on. It is repeated unremittingly through no less than thirty-two verses with the magnificent monotony of waves beating on the sea-shore.

Although the 'firmament' has been the demarcation of the lower reaches of the most holy regions, the upper regions of the earthly world now under review are seen as its immediate neighbours, and closely connected with the divine. So when attention is turned to the *heavens above,* the song calls in order upon the 'heavens', the 'angels', the 'waters above the heaven', the 'powers' of the Lord, and, in addition, 'sun and moon' and the 'stars of heaven'. These shining phenomena are therefore regarded as no other than the lowest of the vast invisible world of the spirit that as it were 'hangs down' into the visible world of the stars.

From the world of the upper heavens the hymn descends to what, in a more limited sense, can still be called the heavens, to the *atmosphere,* which mediates the transition from heaven to earth. In this realm the hymn even lingers with particularly loving minuteness of detail: 'all rain and dew', 'all winds', 'fire and heat', 'winter cold and summer heat', 'dews and snows', 'nights and days', 'light and darkness', 'ice and cold', 'frosts and snows', 'lightnings and clouds'.

Now for the first time, after lingering long over the wonders of the elemental processes of the atmosphere, the hymn 'lands' in the realm of earth. The *earth* as such is now called upon as a special and manifold sphere of existence. Since the hymn moves from above to below, the earth is first set foot upon in its towering peaks, which are still in the neighbourhood of the heavens, 'mountains and hills'. First the barren rocks, then vegetation begins: 'all things that grow on the earth'. Plant life leads to a consideration of the waters of the earth: 'springs', 'seas and rivers'.

From the plant kingdom the step is made to that of the animals. This began in the water. The story of creation describes how at first animal existence teemed in the water, how next the air was conquered, and finally how animals made their home on dry land. In the same order the hymn names 'whales and all creatures that move in the waters', 'all birds of the air', 'all beasts and cattle'.

Thus the song strides through the kingdoms of the creation. The phenomena of the world are looked at with the exalted feeling that comes from the experience of the fire. One could call it a kind of initiation. In his book, *Christianity as Mystical Fact*, Rudolf Steiner describes the experience through which an initiate goes. 'He makes the journey to Hades. It is well for him if he does not now succumb – when a new world opens before him. Either he shrinks to nothing there, or he stands as one newly transformed before it. In the latter case a new sun and a new earth lie before him. Out of the spiritual fire the whole world is born for him again.' A world born out of the spiritual fire, a new sun, a new earth that is also the content of the vision of the cosmos in the song of praise of the three in the furnace.

Why should the world arise anew for them out of the spiritual fire? Because they had found rebirth in themselves. Thus the great review of the world ends with the *human being*. Seven different calls to praise God go forth to the human kingdom. They begin with the call to the 'sons of men', which indicates the future development of humanity beyond that time. Next 'Israel', prototype of the holy people, by Christians justly understood as prototype of the Church. Then 'priests of the Lord' and 'servants of the Lord'. As priestly mediators between above and below, human beings fulfil the task allotted them by their position between angel and beast. Thus they become servants of God. In fifth place comes the significant expression, 'spirits and souls of the righteous'. Human beings are not only body and soul, but as the image of the triune God they are also threefold: body, soul and spirit. Whoever in the best sense is 'righteous', putting themselves in harmony with God and the world, are also bound to be able to live as spirit amongst spirits in the light-filled, all-embracing spiritual world.

To the 'spirits and souls of the righteous' are added those 'who are holy and humble in heart'. In the seventh and last place there finally come the three singers of the hymn themselves. And not with their foreign Babylonian names that had been forced upon them in exile and with which they otherwise appear in the story of Daniel (Shadrach, Abednego and Meshach), but with their own original Hebrew names:

> Bless the Lord, Hananiah, Azariah, and Mishael,
>   sing praise to him and highly exalt him for ever.

Thus the hymn concludes with those from whom it sprang. The three who went through the great fire experience how they inwardly reach a higher stage and consciously grasp the transformation that has come about in them. They have seen the world as reborn out of the fire, of the spirit. Now they recognise themselves as men newly born out of that fire. There follow the words: 'For he has rescued us from Hades, and saved us from the hand of death.' It is like an Old Testament divination of the great mystery that first, in full reality, entered the world in Christ – the mystery of death and resurrection.

VI

PSALMS ABOUT THE PATH OF LIFE

32

THE WORLD OF SIN AND THE WORLD OF GRACE

PSALM 36

In verses 5 to 10 this psalm contains a hymn which, in its mythical greatness and mystical fervour, may be counted among the highlights of the Old Testament. In a rare example of 'counterpoint', this hymn to God is framed in a recital of how evil in human beings becomes active from stage to stage.

I

The first verses give a concrete description of the psychology of the Fall.

> Transgression murmurs to the evil one in his inmost heart.
>   There is no awe of the divine in his eyes.

The word 'murmur' or 'whisper' is generally used in the prophetic books for the inspiration of the voice of God. Here is a sinister antithesis to such divine inspiration. The powers of the Adversary are also aware of how to instill something into human beings. Thus the serpent speaks to Eve. Thus the Devil puts it 'in the heart' of Judas to betray the Lord (Jn 13:2). The psalm knows that in the evil human impulses an objective spirit-world, outside human beings, plays its part.

After the heart comes the eye. The whisper of evil has insinuated itself into the heart; now the eyes become bold. They lose reverence for the divine. They no longer behold the glory of the divine in the material world. Their vision is entangled in the vain show of appearances,

> ## Psalm 36
>
> *Transgression murmurs to the evil one in his inmost heart.*
> *   There is no awe of the divine in his eyes.*
> *² Sin flatters him in his eyes,*
> *   and he finds himself in guilt and hatred.*
> *³ The words of his mouth are iniquity, wantonness and deceit.*
> *   He has ceased to be wise and do good.*
> *⁴ He plots trouble while on his bed.*
> *   He sets himself in a path that is not good;*
> *   he does not reject evil.*
>
> *⁵ O Lord in the heavens – your grace,*
> *   your truth – to the clouds.*
> *⁶ Your righteousness – like mountains of God;*
> *   your judgments – a great deep;*
> *   To man and beast you are a saviour.*
> *O Lord, ⁷ how precious is your grace.*
> *   Divine beings and sons of man shelter in the shadow*
> *   of your wings.*
> *⁸ They satisfy themselves on the abundance of your house,*
> *   you give them to drink from the river of your bliss,*
> *⁹ for with you is the fountain of life;*
> *   in your light we see light.*
>
> *¹⁰ Continue your grace to those who know you,*
> *   and your righteousness to those who are upright in*
> *   heart.*
> *¹¹ Let me not be trodden down by the foot of arrogance,*
> *   nor the hand of the godless drag me away.*
> *¹² There – the workers of iniquity have fallen;*
> *   they have been cast down, unable to rise.*

and with all its cleverness becomes blind to the heavenly golden ground behind the objects.

The next verse is difficult to translate. Perhaps it reads: 'Sin flatters him in his eyes, and he finds himself in guilt and hatred.' Flattery is so effective because it appeals to people's vanity. Then they find themselves in guilt and hate, falling into their realm without knowing how they do so.

32. THE WORLD OF SIN AND OF GRACE

Verse 3, passing outwards from the inner realm of the mind, now speaks of 'words'. 'The words of his mouth are iniquity, wantonness and deceit. He has ceased to be wise and do good.' The sacred character of the Word is lost, it falls a prey to the powers of lying. Wisdom and goodness are lost from our word. Cold cunning enters in their place, which with all its cleverness is ultimately foolishness before God (for in spite of all brilliant intellectuality the popular expression holds good, 'stupid as sin'). And lovelessness, even hate, follow.

It is a significant expression that someone who has gone astray 'ceases to be wise and good'. Evil is nothing primary and original, it is not a human attribute from the outset; it is, on the contrary, an 'infection', as we express with the words 'sickness of sin'. Human beings have been infected with a spirituality fundamentally foreign to them. Evil is 'inhuman'. It has come upon humans like an illness. They are in danger of completely losing their primal state, their innate divine nature. Therefore 'he has ceased', he has departed from, being truly wise and good. 'He plots trouble while on his bed.' People's sleepless hours is a theme frequently found in the psalms. It is not only in our 'nervous' age, when it has become an illness, but even earlier we find human beings passing sleepless nights, plagued by all-consuming worries, or filled by powerful emotions which keep them awake. Dealing with sleeplessness is an important part of self-training. Such exercise is found in the psalms: 'on his law he meditates day and night' (1:2), 'At night his song is with me' (42:8), 'proclaiming your loving kindness in the morning and your steadfast truth at night' (92:2). Also in the Book of Job (35:9f): 'They cry out that there is great oppression, and cry out because of the arm of the mighty, but no one asks, "Where is God my maker, who gives songs of praise in the night?"'

From the poisoning of these silent hours in which man 'on his bed' is alone, there logically proceeds the wicked deed in the light of day, 'he sets himself in a path that is not good'. Thus the evil that began with the inspiration in the heart and then found its way into the sphere of words, now penetrates into action. It is the treading of a 'path'. A path is entered, and with the first wrong deed one step follows another. All is in process of evolving, of movement. Through their power to be free, human beings can give this or that direction to their own development. Psalm 1 describes very clearly the 'two paths'.

'He does not reject evil' – people lose the natural sense of strangeness that they first feel towards evil. A healthy body instinctively rejects food that is not good for it. So are we also fundamentally equipped with a feeling for what does not suit us, is not in accord with us, for what is foreign to our nature and does not belong to us. But in the sphere of moral action, bad habits can gradually paralyse the sound instinct of rejection. 'He does not reject evil' – he loses the power of repulsing what is not of his nature.

II

A wonderful hymn to God now begins, apparently unconnected with what has gone before. Until now, we have been looking at the oppressive spectacle of how evil takes hold of human beings and with inexorable logic works itself out from the mind to the word, and from word into deed. This is depicted with penetrating observation and knowledge. We could become alarmed at these reflections. How then is this sinister process to be countered?

The psalm gives a grand and noble answer. Without concerning itself with the more obvious logical sequence of its sentences, it breaks off abruptly and speaks of something quite different, as if it wished to say: turning one's gaze resolutely to the positive and divine is the only remedy. The verses which then follow are all the more impressive through this striking contrast:

> O Lord in the heavens – your grace,
>   your truth – to the clouds.
> Your righteousness– like mountains of God;
>   your judgments – a great deep;
>   To man and beast you are a saviour.
> O Lord, how precious is your grace.
>   Divine beings and sons of man shelter in the shadow
>   of your wings.
> They satisfy themselves on the abundance of your house,
>   you give them to drink from the river of your bliss,
> for with you is the fountain of life;
>   in your light we see light.

At the beginning of this hymn the psalmist uses the name of God which holds the mystery of the I AM. And it is as if the speaking of this hallowed name leads his soul upwards in a mighty ascension.

'O LORD in the heavens – your grace.' The ardour which immerses itself in the divine is all the more powerful against the background of evil. It is like the sudden rending of a curtain. From the name of God the vision of his heavens unfolds. It is mere appearance that science and planes have got rid of 'heaven'. It is the same as if one fine day it was 'discovered' that the *Sistine Madonna* was only a painted surface, that there was in fact nothing more to it or behind it. That takes nothing away from its importance, for it is a picture. A picture which points, however, to a reality of a higher order. So too the sky we see, in its vaulted arch, in its blue, in the changes of its phenomena of light, is a picture which is given to us and which loses nothing of its value through the explanations of physics and astronomy. To surrender oneself in contemplation of the heavens unlocks in one's inner being the worlds of God's grace, which are assuredly not spatial.

For the psalmist, the heavens are the sphere in which the Godhead is utterly and entirely at home, by itself, in its own element, in which it can live undisturbed in its innermost essence. This innermost essence is known as grace.

'Your truth – to the clouds.' The clouds too belong to the 'heavens'. How much exaltation and rapture have people felt in the devout contemplation of the lofty spaces of the clouds. But still, in this second line in contrast to the first ('in the heavens – your grace') we have descended one stage and come nearer to the earth. In comparison with the starry heavens and the pure blue, the clouds are nevertheless a transition and border region in which the heavens descend nearer to the earth.

Now why should precisely the clouds be combined with the experience of truth? For us clouds are so often precisely things that veil, that conceal the view. But it was still living experience to people of old that clouds not only veiled but also revealed. Hidden forces of vision can be released in the soul by giving oneself up to the picture of the mysterious, invisible hands of God at work in the changing forms of the clouds. The truth of God as of the eternal disposing One, the forming and transforming One, reaches from the upper heavens down to the realm of the clouds. The clouds carry down the active manifestation of the living God to us beneath and make it visible. His 'immediacy' extends down as far as the clouds.

Grace and truth – we know these two significant words from the prologue of the Gospel of John. They are said of him who had become flesh, 'full of grace and truth' (1:14). What for our psalm still belongs to cosmic spaces, appeared for John for the first time in earthly form. 'Grace and truth came by Jesus Christ' (Jn 1:17). What the psalm still beholds in the 'above', removed from earth, for John actually entered the stream of historical human evolution.

The next line, the third, is again a descent: from the clouds to the mountains. And then we set foot on the solid earth. Regarded from above, the mountain summit is indeed 'earth'. But for someone in the valley, the mountain is a thing that still belongs to heaven. On mountain heights the ancients felt themselves in greater nearness to God's heaven. Someone who saw from below the sacred mountain towering upwards was reminded of the eternal. The devout experiences of past millennia, of forgotten 'fathers who have worshipped upon the mountain' (Jn 4:20), surround such an expression as 'God's mountains'.

'Your righteousness – like the mountains of God.' A comparative 'like' appears for the first time. Till now we were still in a sphere of divine 'immediacy'. Righteousness is, for the psalmist, an effect of the divine that has more connection with earthly than heavenly grace and truth. The sternness of an eternal righteousness looks down from the mountains of God upon the drifting changes below.

One more descent, a final one, follows: 'your judgments – a great deep'. Great deep, in the original text: *tehom rabah*. *Tehom* is the primal flood, with the flavour of the sinister, murky chaotic, losing itself in dreadful darkness (Greek *abyssos*). *Tehom* is the totality of all nocturnal powers of chaos, which in the form of the dragon Leviathan had to be thrust down by Yahweh in the primeval world conflict (compare Is 51:9) so that an orderly creation might arise.

Tehom rabah, the great deep, occurs significantly in the narrative of the flood. Where human beings transgress against measure and order, God punishes them by allowing the ancient powers of chaos to raise their head again, for though they were once vanquished, they were not destroyed. Then people are delivered over to the powers whose chains they have wantonly unloosed through their transgression. 'All the springs of the great deep burst forth' (Gn 7:11).

This flood, this fall of the iniquitous Atlantean magicians and 'proud giants' (Ws 14:6) is the classical example of divine judgment, the prototype of the court of justice.

Grace and truth – God in heaven. Righteousness and judgments – God on earth.

In other words, God as he can live out his true being by himself in his own archetypal world, and God as, by virtue of eternal law, he must show himself on the earth inhabited by fallen humankind. God in his light-filled freedom on the one hand, and on the other hand in his dark necessity. Only through Christ is the heaven of grace and truth carried down into the dark world which stands under judgment.

Heavens, clouds, mountains, depths of the sea. Grace, truth, righteousness, judgment. Mighty and of mythical greatness is this gradual descent from the freedom of God down to the lowest depths of necessity.

Into the sinister echoes of the flood, *tehom rabah,* some consolation is brought, reminiscent of the ark of Noah. 'To man and beast you are a saviour.' To the animals too, God's aid is promised here. Humans have drawn the animals down into the disastrous consequences of the Fall. Hence human beings must not only seek the redemption of their own soul, but must also take to heart the destiny of the creatures.

This thought of God's help forms the transition to the mystical centre of Psalm 36. For the experience of divine grace is proclaimed in anticipation of what will only be disclosed to human beings in full measure through Christ.

'Lord, how precious is your grace. Divine beings and sons of man shelter in the shadow of thy wings.'

In the original Hebrew text there is no punctuation. The word *Elohim* probably belongs to the next sentence, so that the text we use reads, 'Divine beings of the higher hierarchies [*Elohim*], and sons of man shelter in the shadow of thy wings.

A further experience of grace that goes beyond being sheltered is the sacrament of communion, the imparting of divine life: 'They satisfy themselves on the abundance of your house, you give them to drink of the river of your bliss. For with you is the fountain of life'. The house of God is the abode of his presence. Fallen man, like the prodigal son in the parable, wasted his heritage far from his father's house, and in so doing has destroyed his 'substance', falling into dire need. Divine grace calls human beings again to the table of its fullness, when in the company of higher beings (Elohim) they eat the 'bread of angels' (Ps 78:25).

The 'river of bliss' is the same as the river of Paradise spoken of in Genesis. 'Bliss' in the original text is 'Eden'. It becomes very clear here in the psalm, that in the description of Paradise one should never ask concerning its geographical whereabouts. The source of the river of Eden which represents flowing life, is 'with you'.

Life as such is not visible to earthly eyes. We see only what is filled with life, not life itself. Flowing water is its image, and all natural life, however sacred and mysterious in itself, is again but the reflection of a still higher, truly supernatural life.

It is the spirit of John's Gospel, which we meet in this psalm. While it was first the words 'grace and truth' that made us think of the prologue of the Gospel of John, we now see how 'light' is added to 'life'.

'In your light we see light.' Simple as these words may sound, there nevertheless lies hidden in them a whole epistemology. It would be impossible for human beings to have real knowledge if the world they faced was something entirely foreign to them. The light of the world outside might shine upon us ever so brightly and clearly, yet it would simply run off the surface of our nature without finding the way into our inner being. But we ourselves participate in the light. We can behold the light of the world because we can meet it with our own inner human light, light uniting with light. By our very participation in the light, we are able to see the light.

This light, which is active in human thinking, is not our own, subjective light. Even as a single individual we have a share in the divine light itself. Therefore the light of human thinking can be objectively valid for the world. 'In your light we see light.'

Similarly Psalm 18 says: 'You, O Lord, light my lamp' (Ps 18:28). Human beings have their own light, their 'lamp'. But God must illumine it for them by feeding the lamp with his own divine light. A passage in Job points to an earlier time when human beings experienced the light entrusted to them not as their own, but as still belonging directly to God. Job longs to be back in the time 'when God watched over me, when his lamp shone above my head' (Jb 29:3).

We participate in a light of vision and of knowledge because the Godhead that bears us is itself living in this light element of vision and knowledge. So says Psalm 94:9: 'Does he who formed the eye not see?'

III

This mystical centrepiece of Psalm 36 is followed by a concluding prayer which ends with an apocalyptic view of the fate of the wicked:

> Continue your grace to those who know you,
>   and your righteousness to those who are upright in heart.
> Let me not be trodden down by the foot of arrogance,
>   nor the hand of the godless drag me away.

The personal enemies and opponents of the psalmist become the symbol for the powers of evil that break in upon human beings and against which they save themselves in the divine grace.

> There – the workers of iniquity have fallen;
>   they have been cast down, unable to rise.

These lines have the character of a vision, of an apocalyptic view. 'There – the workers of iniquity have fallen!' It is the apocalyptic perfect tense: in the spirit-vision something is accepted in advance as having already happened. Thus Christ says in the Farewell Discourse – before Gethsemane and Golgotha – 'the Prince of this world has been judged', and, 'I have overcome the world' (Jn 16:11, 33). It is the same in the Book of Revelation, where the songs of victory already resound in heaven, before the Antichrist reaches the zenith of his power on earth (11:15–19). From where does this anticipation come? Spirit-vision enters a region in which the decision has in fact already been made. It is only that a little time is still needed until what has been decided in principle gradually 'arrives' below on earth.

Thus the psalmist also sees the Adversary as though already fallen. Evil is in principle already dealt with: it is judged and sentenced to death. However great the triumphs are that it celebrates, the truth of the apocalyptic vision stands.

33

THE GREAT CONFESSION

PSALM 51

I

It has been said that the greatest of evils is guilt. Adversity that meets us from without, through destiny, is, with all its pain and suffering, easier to bear than the sight of one's own guilt and its effect. All that transpires in the soul of one who has done wrong and who yet yearns and strives for the divine blessing – this is the content of the well-known penitential Psalm 51. Tradition says that it is a prayer of David after his sin with Bathsheba:

> Have mercy upon me, O God,
>   according to your steadfast love,
> according to the multitude of your tender mercies
>   blot out my transgressions.
> Wash me thoroughly from my guilt,
>   and cleanse me from my sin.

The trinity of transgression, sin and guilt is to be found at the beginning of Psalm 32: 'Blessed is the one whose transgression is forgiven, whose sin is covered. Blessed is the man whose guilt the Lord does not count against him.' The Hebrew word *pesha*, usually rendered by 'transgression' is the gravest of these three. It denotes an offence committed deliberately, a breach of trust or rebellion, whereas *chataah*, 'sin', means rather sins of passion or weakness, of missing the target.

33. THE GREAT CONFESSION

'Blot out my transgressions.' In the original text 'blot out' is a word that one can very well use for obliterating what has been written. May the transgression be effaced like the writing in a book. That is more than an ingenious image. With all that people do, feel and think, they make something like entries in an infinitely fine cosmic substance. Something is detached from us and continues in the universe beyond our reach and has its consequences.

We no longer have control over these effects of our deeds which have passed out into the cosmos. The prayer of the psalm can really only be fulfilled through Christ. He alone, by virtue of his sacrifice has the power to blot out the objective consequence of our sins for the universe, if we unite ourselves with him, as with the Lamb that takes upon himself the 'sin of the world' (Jn 1:29).

'Wash me thoroughly from my guilt.' 'Wash' in the original text is a word used for the washing of a garment. Human beings have darkened the shining of their finer nature by sin. They have sullied the vesture of their soul and lack the 'wedding garment'.

'Cleanse me from my sin.' This does not mean the washing of a garment but the direct cleansing or purifying of the body. The image of the body here refers to 'ourselves'.

With the wrong that we commit we injure ourselves. But it does not remain our private affair, since it moves out of the private sphere of our inner personal realm into the finer sheaths surrounding us and 'blackens' their innate brightness; the sin acquires an effect in the universe, for the whole of our body and soul nature is a fragment of the universe which is entrusted to us as our own. The cleansing of the body and the washing of the clothing has to do with the consequences of sins for ourselves and for the sheaths, which belong to our being and which form a kind of intermediary between our inner nature and the world outside.

But furthermore, there are effects which transcend ourselves and the fragment of the world entrusted to us and which belong to the universe outside. These are not only the changes which we have effected physically in the world through our action. What we have done in the visible world is, after all, in spite of its often dreadful reality, only a sort of image of the injury we have done to the hidden spiritual substances of the world, and which now stands as a writing in the cosmic book and looks at us accusingly.

Psalm 51

Have mercy upon me, O God,
  according to your steadfast love,
according to the multitude of your tender mercies
  blot out my transgressions.
² *Wash me thoroughly from my guilt,*
  and cleanse me from my sin.
³ *For I know my transgressions,*
  and my sin is ever before me.
⁴ *Against you, you alone, have I sinned*
  and I have done what is evil in your sight,
so that you may be found just in your word
  and be pure when you judge.
⁵ *Behold, I was brought forth in iniquity,*
  and in the realm of sin did my mother conceive me.
⁶ *Behold, you desire truth in hidden parts,*
  and you make me know secret wisdom.

⁷ *Purge me with hyssop, and I shall be clean;*
  wash me, and I shall be whiter than snow.
⁸ *Let me hear joy and gladness.*
  May the bones which you have broken rejoice.
⁹ *Hide your face from my sins,*
  and blot out all my iniquities.
¹⁰ *Create in me a clean heart, O God,*
  and renew a steadfast spirit within me.
¹¹ *Cast me not away from your countenance,*
  and take not the spirit of your holiness from me.
¹² *Restore to me the joy of your salvation,*
  and uphold me with a spirit of free will.

¹³ *Then I will teach your ways to transgressors,*
  that sinners will return to you.
¹⁴ *Deliver me from blood guilt, O God,*
  O God of my true self and my salvation,
  and my tongue will shout for joy of your righteousness.
¹⁵ *O Lord, open my lips*
  that my mouth shall show forth your praise.
¹⁶ *For you will not delight in sacrifice, or I would give it;*
  you will not be pleased with a burnt offering.

33. THE GREAT CONFESSION

> *¹⁷ The true sacrifices of God are a broken spirit;*
>   *a broken and contrite heart, O God, you will not despise.*
> *¹⁸ Show your goodwill to Zion,*
>   *build up the walls of Jerusalem,*
> *¹⁹ then you will delight in the sacrifices of righteousness,*
>   *With burnt offering and whole burnt offering:*
>   *then bullocks will be offered on your altar.*

> For I know my transgressions,
>   and my sin is ever before me.
> Against you, you alone, have I sinned
>   and I have done what is evil in your sight,
> so that you may be found just in your word
>   and be pure when you judge.

The psalmist has become fully conscious of the wrong he has done. It stands before his eyes and afflicts him. 'Against you, you alone, have I sinned.' *Tibi soli peccavi* – herein lie the true depths of his confession. First and foremost the sin is committed against God himself; it is only in the second place that it is directed to this or the other person who is concerned. We are guilty towards anyone whom we injure, but above all towards God. We also hear in the Act of Consecration that our deviations, our denials of the divine being, our weaknesses, find their way into the depths of the Ground of the World. Rudolf Steiner speaks of the pain that we cause to higher beings through our mistakes and failings. Such an indication can make this wonderful, intuitive psalm alive and real for us. 'Against you, you alone, have I sinned.'

> Behold, I was brought forth in iniquity,
>   and in the realm of sin did my mother conceive me.
> Behold, you desire truth in hidden parts,
>   and you make me know secret wisdom.

When the psalm speaks in these words of original sin this is not, as it were, pleading extenuating circumstances, but it is a recognition of hidden circumstances. Human beings, thrown out of the naivety of their matter-of-course existence by the feeling of guilt, have become sensitive to the fact that they, and the whole of their earthly human nature, are from the start incompatible with the divine world. They see themselves gripped in a vast sequence of events, fettered for thousands of years in a state of guilt and wrongdoing from which they cannot become free without divine help. They know themselves to be guilty not only of individual offences which can be named and enumerated, but they know and feel that their whole mode of life is not consistent with the divine world. To a superficial view, sin consists only in single acts, and if these had been left undone human beings would have continued 'in order'. Only a deeper wisdom that penetrates below the surface can recognise that the whole human condition from the beginning is infected by the sickness of sin.

Just as this from the start is something transcendent, something that belongs to humanity over and above the individual, so too, nothing but a divine impulse of a transcendent order can release human beings from these chains. This came about through Christ. The devout people of the Old Testament are praying in the hope of the approaching Redeemer, when at the beginning of the psalm they call upon divine grace. This grace, which enters fully into the earthly world through Christ, does not mean that God merely throws overboard the reckoning of justice and replaces it with arbitrary action. No, not that. It means he brings a new dimension into the calculation. The iron law of cause and effect is not annulled, but the result becomes different through the inclusion of quite a new power. This new factor, which gives the whole situation a new aspect, is 'grace', the Christ. This grace causes an additional force to flow into human beings, through which the consequences of evil can be carried and transformed to good.

Grace does not relieve us of our own efforts. But it must be obvious that without it, human entanglement in evil, which far transcends our own power to master it, cannot be overcome.

Psalm 51 will only become fully true and concrete in the framework of the New Testament. In Christ appears the grace which can counteract the Fall and its consequences, which have long since become too much for humanity. With the sight of the suffering God on the cross, human beings first become fully conscious of what in a sort of dreaming presentiment is expressed in the psalm, 'Against you, you alone, have I sinned.'

II

> Purge me with hyssop, and I shall be clean;
> wash me, and I shall be whiter than snow.

Here begins the actual prayer for transformation. The imagery is to be understood in reference to the rites of purification in the Old Testament. Sprinkling using a hyssop branch was commanded in the case of leprosy or contact with a corpse. We must imagine the whole dreadfulness of the disease of leprosy, where the entire body becomes rotten bit by bit. The leper decaying in the living body, the corpse which falls into decay; in both cases there is destruction of the body, and this dread of destruction was felt to be connected with the sickness of sin. The hyssop branch played a part in banishing this horror through the ritual of consecrated sprinkling. Those who have become conscious of their sinfulness feels themselves delivered up to the powers of leprosy and decay. They 'taste' death in themselves. So they pray for purification.

One should not simply dismiss the ancient rites of washing and cleansing as mere formalities. Inner and outer experiences were not so separated in those times. Bodily cleansing did not remain without effect on one's inner nature. The outer process continued to a greater or lesser degree inwardly. Even today we must not underestimate this effect. Of course outer cleanliness is not yet inner cleanliness, but it has nevertheless a conducive influence upon it.

'Whiter than snow'. Snow gives a greater experience than anything else of unearthly, shining purity. White as snow is the raiment of the Easter angel (Mt 28:3). In the Revelation, John describes his vision of the perfected saints. They are clothed in shining white raiment; 'they have washed their robes and made them white in the blood of the Lamb' (Rv 7:14). A paradoxical image, which demonstrates that through accepting what proceeds from Golgotha the whole human nature is purified and illumined. Only the 'blood of the Lamb' will bring about what the pre-Christian psalm is here imploring: 'wash me, and I shall be whiter than snow.'

The psalm passes over from the world of light to the world of sound:

> Let me hear joy and gladness.

When the human being is radiant again like fresh snow, the heavenly music of rejoicing becomes audible to the inner ear. In the parable of the prodigal son there is also the sound of singing and dancing at the great feast of reunion. It is the jubilation of the heavens when a human being, cleansed and transformed, is given back to the spheres of their origin. The theme of gladness goes through the whole of Chapter 15 of Luke's Gospel, which proclaims in three parables how what is lost has been restored. 'Rejoice with me.' 'Likewise there is joy in the presence of the angels of God.'

Consciousness of guilt takes away happiness. Anticipation of grace awakens joy. This goes through to the depths of the human being, to the bone.

> May the bones which you have broken rejoice.
> Hide your face from my sins,
> and blot out all my iniquities.

The negative element of forgiveness is expressed here once more: the turning away of the divine countenance from our sin, and thereby the cessation of the tormenting reproach that we feel when the divine gaze dwells on our faults. The following verses pass over entirely into the positive attitude. Not only are our sins blotted out, but a complete rebirth takes place through a new act of creation by God.

> Create in me a clean heart, O God,
> and renew a steadfast spirit within me.
> Cast me not away from your countenance,
> and take not the spirit of your holiness from me.
> Restore to me the joy of your salvation,
> and uphold me with a spirit of free will.

'Create in me a clean heart.' Here the word *bara* stands for 'create'. It is a word seldom used: it occurs precisely seven times in Genesis. Used here, it is to show that the transformation of fallen humanity is to be set beside the world's creation. The new creation is implanted in the innermost human heart. And as the working of the spirit belongs to the creation, so too it belongs to the new creation of humanity. In another psalm it says, 'When you send forth your breath ... you renew the face of the earth' (Ps 104:30). This renewing force of the divine spirit is to show itself here in our inner being.

It is remarkable how in Psalm 51 spirit is mentioned in a threefold manner. First it is the spirit of steadfastness, of firmness; with the creation of the pure heart, the spirit lifts us out of all vacillation and makes us come to rest on the granite of eternity. The spirit of firmness – one might call this the Father-aspect of this trinity.

Then the Holy Spirit, connected with experience of the divine countenance; through the spirit of holiness human beings are enabled to stand face-to-face with God, are enabled to know the divine as spirit-being to spirit-being. Without the spirit of holiness they must faint away before this countenance, they could not hold themselves upright in face of the personal consciousness of God turned towards them. 'Take not the spirit of your holiness from me' – the gift of the Holy Spirit can also be lost. A guilty darkening of our being can banish us from his sight. We feel the infinite preciousness, the value of this Holy Spirit, and tremble at the prospect of being again deprived of it. It is just because full holiness will only be in our complete possession at final consummation, that the beginning of our sanctification is something so delicate, so liable to attack and easily lost.

Finally the 'spirit of free-will' is connected with joy in divine aid. The word used in the original text for 'free will' in connection to the spirit also means 'noble', 'distinguished', while its root means doing good out of free will, as in making a free-will offering. Hence, 'generous' and 'distinguished', 'noble'. In distinction to the spirit of firmness and of holiness, it is here the spirit of the Son. The Son brings us the salvation of God. (The meaning of the name Jesus is 'help, rescue or salvation of God'). He helps human beings to live rightly as earthly personalities and he unseals the power which does good not by compulsion of the law, but out of freedom, generously, from one's heart as an expression of one's own nature. In this lies the true distinction and nobility of a human being as opposed to the compulsory work of a servant.

The spirit of steadfastness – the spirit of holiness – the spirit of free will. This is one of the passages in the Old Testament where the mystery of the Trinity is clearly foreshadowed.

III

If a human being has become a new creation out of the spirit, this can have significance for others, for good. As ones who have been born again and transformed, they can now also point the way to others.

> Then I will teach your ways to transgressors,
>> that sinners will return to you.

Just because we have learnt to know guilt and for this reason have gained a deeper insight into the forces of healing and transforming possessed by the Godhead, so now we can help others to find their way in life. That need not be a pretentious 'teaching'; there is no need for words. The very character of our being has its own effect.

> Deliver me from blood guilt, O God,
>> O God of my true self and my salvation,
>> and my tongue will shout for joy of your righteousness.
> O Lord, open my lips
>> that my mouth shall show forth your praise.

Those who have injured others through misdeeds can, after their rebirth, be a help to them. Through rebirth they even mean something positive for the divine world. As transgressors they served to conceal God and diminish his manifestation. Wherever something bad is present the divine is covered over and the Adversary is revealed instead. The psalm pleads that human beings may again manifest the divinity. In the long run there will be no other valid proof on earth that God exists except human beings reborn through the spirit. 'You are the light of the world' (Mt 5:14), Christ says to his disciples. People ought not to complain of the darkness and ungodliness of the world, for it is their own fault that it is dark; they are not shedding light. Humanity is the door through which God can enter the earthly world.

Generally speaking, we form a far too ordinary, vague and casual idea of what is meant by declaring praise and extolling. This is a result of a regrettable devaluing which has robbed the great words of religion of their value. To declare God's praise means to bring him to appearance, into manifestation – that is, to 'densify' his divine presence that it again becomes discernible on earth. Psalm 51 indicates that praising God is not a cheap matter. Otherwise the supplication would not have been uttered that God himself should open our lips to his praise. It is not done by opening our mouth to speak edifying words. If the outpouring of our being, of which in fact words are only a part, is to extol God, then the higher world must itself make us worthy of it and give us its blessing.

We now understand why there is again a reference in this connection to 'blood guilt'. In the original text the word blood is given in the plural, 'Deliver me from the guilty power and influence of blood-relationships.' One must not narrow this down to merely one criminal act, as perhaps David's murder of Uriah. All people are involved in a vast portentous association of guilty forces of the blood. Original sin is in the blood of the entire human race. 'Take away from me the guilty blood-forces.' This plural of blood, grammatically impossible in English, is also found in the Greek of the New Testament, where John's Gospel speaks of those 'who were born not of blood [*haimata*], nor of the will of the flesh, nor of the will of man, but of God' (Jn 1:13). The blood of Christ redeems and replaces sinful powers of human blood. Only when the blood of Christ becomes a power within us will we be able to join fully in the angels' song of praise which reveals God.

> For you will not delight in sacrifice, or I would give it;
>   you will not be pleased with a burnt offering.
> The true sacrifices of God are a broken spirit;
>   a broken and contrite heart, O God, you will not despise.

The temple ritual of the blood-offering is here turned inward. The psalm stands at the threshold of an age when the sacrifice of an animal no longer called forth an inner experience by virtue of a primitive, magical feeling of being connected with it. The inward element begins to be detached. In early times people could not sacrifice their external possession – perhaps a beast from the herd – without at the same time giving up a part of the soul. Their soul-force was objectified in this animal, streaming upward to the Godhead. This intimate connection was gradually lost. It has become fitting that a person's capacity to think, feel and will should be offered to God.

The psalmist who had this inward experience in advance of Old Testament times, had outgrown the epoch when animal sacrifices were fully justified. Their place is taken for him by the 'broken' spirit and the broken 'shattered' heart, as the text reads literally. The selfhood, formed by the Fall, always wants to shut itself off within its own narrow horizon. This exclusiveness must again and again be broken up so that we do not withdraw into our lower self and thereby shut out the true higher self which is destined for us.

> Show your goodwill to Zion,
>> build up the walls of Jerusalem,
> then you will delight in the sacrifices of righteousness,
>> With burnt offering and whole burnt offering:
>> then bullocks will be offered on your altar.

This conclusion has a strange sound after what has just been said about making the sacrifices an inward deed. It has been regarded as a later addition which was attached to the psalm lest it sounded heretical in view of the established temple worship. It has been thought that perhaps, through these final orthodox sentences, the all too bold inwardness of an individualistic religious genius was rendered harmless. This is not impossible. However these final verses may have found their way there, they are nevertheless no misrepresentation of the whole, in spite of a certain contradiction of what has gone before. In fact, they are an important and significant addition, whether they are the work of the author or of a strange hand.

These final verses uphold the truth that the shattering experiences of sin and grace are not just a matter of 'God and the soul'. After these inner processes it is salutary and compensatory that at the close, attention is drawn to great, cosmic aims. The city of Jerusalem becomes altogether a symbol in the Apocalypse of John. The 'heavenly Jerusalem' is the new, Christianised earth. Even in the Old Testament, Jerusalem begins to mean more than a geographical name. In the books of the prophets, Zion, Jerusalem, has become a symbolic concept, the epitome of a coming world of redemption and perfection. This is also in the background of the final words of this great penitential psalm. Every sin is a contribution to the building of Babylon, the city of the abyss that is established separate from the divine world.

The transformation of the sinner contributes to the building of the holy city.

And the temple offering mentioned in the last verse? The burnt offering and the whole burnt offering? They establish the truth that the inner sacrifice of a broken spirit and heart, which is pleasing to God, is not alone sufficient. Even the most pious emotions of the best of people could not release the human race from the overpowering entanglement of original sin. This could only be effected through something that allows of no comparison – the sacrifice of God, the Deed of Golgotha. The temple worship with its blood-sacrifice was the forerunner of this unique offering, which then lives on upon the altars of Christendom. In the service at the Christian altar, the inner sacrifice, the devotion of spirit and heart, then comes into its own. But the inward sacrifice of human beings is only the preparation for the fact that in the transubstantiation the sacrifice on Golgotha can live again. There is an organic union of the seemingly contradictory elements of Psalm 51 – the inward devotion of spirit and heart, the sacrificial offering of the inner faculties, and the great objective sacrifice of a God, surpassing all human possibility, the fulfilment of the ancient burnt offering and whole burnt offering.

34

IN THE PRESENCE OF ETERNITY

PSALM 90

I

Psalm 90, which bears the name of Moses, is one of the most monumental in the whole book.

> *A prayer of Moses, the man of God.*
> Lord, you have been our abode
>   from generation to generation.
> Before the mountains were born,
>   or ever you had formed the earth and the world,
>   from cycle of time to cycle of time
>   YOU ARE God.

Just as Moses is the seer who looks back, so here too the psalm opens by looking into the past. It scans the ranks of generations. The genealogy in the Gospel of Luke goes back to Adam, 'the son of God'. Here too the divine is reached in passing back through the ages.

High mountains are the representatives of eternity on the earth. They soar upwards beyond what becomes and passes away in time; throughout summer and winter they are crowned with the eternal snows. Immutable, they look down upon the ever changing human destinies in the valleys below.

Mountains, too, are subject to passing away, but it happens so slowly and imperceptibly that we do not see it or realise it; so that after all they are something relatively eternal on earth. The psalm knows that even these primal mountains were once young, they were

34. IN THE PRESENCE OF ETERNITY

once 'born', as the Hebrew has it. In far past ages the earth was not so hardened and dead as it is today where life is only to be found in the separate living creatures. The earth itself was once the living mother of these organisms. All substance was then much finer, charged with life. The earth itself, which brought forth the mountains, was also born, it once detached itself from the womb of the creative worlds of spirit.

The span of time measured by generations does not suffice for such primeval ages. The word *'olam* appears here, corresponding to the Greek *aion,* the Latin *aevum,* the English aeon. The aeon is a cycle of time. God lives from *'olam* to *'olam,* from aeon to aeon, from one cycle of time to another. The psalm says quite literally: 'And from *'olam* to *'olam* you God.' That means the same as 'you are', not 'you were'. Just as Jesus did not say, 'Before Abraham was, I was', but 'I AM'. Before Abraham entered life – I AM. That is timeless. It is removed from all sequence of time, from the state of being earlier and from the state of being later. It is above and beyond any temporal element. Here, too, in the psalm it has this meaning: 'From cycle of time to cycle of time you are.'

Out of this timelessness come the words of destiny which speak of death.

> You let mortals return to decay
>   and you say, 'Return sons of Adam!'
> For a thousand years in your sight
>   are but as yesterday that has past,
>   or as a watch in the night.

The psalm knows that in the higher worlds time is different from what it is on earth. There is no growing old, no limitation of time there, the millennia lie like an open book before the eyes of God. In contrast to the divine timelessness the transitory nature of human earthly existence is presented in three pictures. It is like the sweeping flood, like running water that cannot be held fast. It is like sleep, for earthly human consciousness is in fact like being shrouded in darkness, like sleep in comparison with supersensory, spiritual consciousness. It is like a plant soon faded away.

Psalm 90

A prayer of Moses, the man of God.

Lord, you have been our abode
  from generation to generation.
² Before the mountains were born,
  or ever you had formed the earth and the world,
  from cycle of time to cycle of time
  YOU ARE *God.*

³ You let mortals return to decay
  and you say, 'Return sons of Adam!'
⁴ For a thousand years in your sight
  are but as yesterday that has past,
  or as a watch in the night.

⁵ You sweep them away as with a flood;
  they are like a sleep,
  in the morning like grass that sprouts anew:
⁶ in the morning it flourishes and passes away
  in the evening, cut down, it withers.

⁷ For we are brought to an end by your anger;
  and by your wrath we are denied permanence.
⁸ You have set our iniquities before you,
  our hidden sins in the light of your countenance.

⁹ For all our days have passed away under your wrath;
  we bring our years to an end like a sigh.
¹⁰ The days of our years are seventy
  or even by reason of strength eighty;
yet the pride is but toil and trouble.
  for they are soon gone, and we fly away.

¹¹ Who knows the power of your anger,
  and who stands in awe before your wrath?
¹² So teach us to number our days
  that we gain a heart of wisdom.

34. IN THE PRESENCE OF ETERNITY

> ¹³ *Bring to pass the returning, O* Lord. *How long?*
>   *And have pity on your servants!*
> ¹⁴ *Satisfy us at daybreak with your grace,*
>   *that we may rejoice and be glad all our days.*
> ¹⁵ *Make us glad for as many days as you have afflicted us,*
>   *and for as many years as we have seen evil.*
>
> ¹⁶ *Let your work be seen by your servants,*
>   *and your glory to their children.*
> ¹⁷ *Let the favour of the Lord our God be upon us,*
>   *and establish the work of our hands upon us;*
>   *yes, establish the work of our hands.*

You sweep them away as with a flood;
  they are like a sleep,
    in the morning like grass that sprouts anew:
in the morning it flourishes and passes away
  in the evening, cut down, it withers.

Deep resignation speaks in these verses, resignation before the inevitability of death.

II

But the psalm does not only give way to sadness. It asks about the wherefor of this destiny, and ventures to give a clear answer to the question. The contemplation of our transitory life does not lead to a weak pessimism, but makes us face a fact which concerns the human being most deeply.

> For we are brought to an end by your anger;
>   and by your wrath we are denied permanence.
> You have set our iniquities before you,
>   our hidden sins in the light of your countenance.

If human beings were to consist of nothing more than things of a short transitory existence before then dissolving again into the universe, they would give no thought to their transience. They would pass away as a matter of course in the general passing away, without question and without trace. However, they realise that fundamentally they are more than transitory. They sense the futility of their existence as not a normal condition and feel exiled from their own setting and caught up in a way of existence that is really foreign to them.

The psalm does not merely bemoan an inexplicable destiny in this state of affairs, but confesses to an interpretation which includes human beings and their responsibility for it; it is a consequence of human sin. We are given over to transitory existence because we ourselves have failed. Our misdeeds stand in the light of the divine countenance. Ancient visionary experience survives in such a phrase. We can start from an example still to be felt today; that we are ashamed of our faults before a revered person. This is an anticipation of the experiences that await us after death. In describing the difference between earthly and supersensible consciousness, Rudolf Steiner explained that on earth we always feel ourselves to be the observer; we take our existence for granted, and inspect our surroundings; it is just the contrary over there: we experience ourselves primarily as being observed; we feel how higher beings react towards us.

Modern people are inclined quickly to dismiss such an expression as 'God's countenance' with the thought that it is only an anthropomorphism, which in a childishly naive way projects human peculiarities on to the divine. We attribute a countenance to God because we see that humans have a countenance. But the opposite is true: man is in fact an image of God. Our countenance, which we feel to be our most spiritual part, is only the reflection of an original experience in the higher world. Human beings are only on the way to having a countenance. Thus it is not a human element that is being transferred to God in an inadmissible or even childish way, but what is observed in human beings is a reflection of the reality in higher worlds.

'The light of your countenance.' The psalm knows of the power of light and from that also the judging power of the divine countenance. As the epitome of light it is at the same time the epitome of justice, it is the sun which 'brings it to light'. Because the psalm knows this countenance, it also knows sin. Sin is a religious concept. Without having a sense for the divine one cannot know what sin is.

In the First Book of Moses, Genesis, his visions include the Fall and the expulsion from Paradise into the sphere of the transitory and perishable. Why did God then make the human body die? The earthly body is something like an insulated cell in its material density. It promotes the development of an independent consciousness of self. This self-awareness in its early stages received a self-centred egotistic character through Lucifer. The material body is the stronghold of this egotistic self. If transience had not been implanted into this insulated earthly body that supports autonomy, human beings would have become immortal in this God-estranged selfhood.

As 'fallen' human beings they would have become eternal and thereby lost to the divine world. Thus it was a wise measure of Providence to ensure that human beings could only be active for a certain time in the earthly body, giving their own stamp to their personality, before being recalled through death to their home in the spiritual world for a longer period, so that they might not completely lose touch with the world of their origin. Thus human beings alternate between lives on earth, where they develop a personality between birth and death, although stamped by the effect of the Fall, and periods of dwelling in the world of their origin. In the future this influence of the Fall is to be overcome through Christ, the selfhood gained on earth made holy and redeemed to become the true self which places its free personality in the service of the divine. Then earthly and heavenly human life can be reunited.

But this cannot as yet be seen in Psalm 90 with full clarity. Our earthly existence is transitory and hastens towards death. It is recognised that this is connected with the Fall, that it is a reaction, a rejoinder of God to the Fall. To Old Testament understanding this rejoinder flows from the 'wrath' of God. 'For we are brought to an end by your anger.'

The intermingling with the Luciferic element is the reason why human beings as they have become on earth, is in conflict with the divine world. When they are called home again after an earthly life, this summons leads to difficult crises in the life after death. The dead must pay for their home-coming with painful purification. When they pass over, they find that with earthly attainments they do not straightaway 'fit' into heaven, that their presence is disturbing. Earthly human beings with their guilt realise their incompatibility with the world of their origin. They experience the wrath of God.

As Christians we may venture to say: in this divine reaction which makes human beings mortal, nothing less than divine love is active, which saves them from being made immortal in their sinful condition. Through catastrophes, through judgments, destruction and purification, God's love ever and again calls them home. Wrath is the form which divine love must assume when it meets with sinful man.

Psalm 90 sees humankind standing under wrath. At the same time this is a recognition of a history, a development. For wrath is not an original state, it is a secondary condition. There could have been no wrath at the beginning. At the beginning was love. God created human beings and blessed them. The Fall into sin put an end to this primeval state. Does this second condition remain the conclusive and final one?

Let us return to the text of the psalm, which at first pursues the motive of transitoriness.

> For all our days have passed away under your wrath;
>   we bring our years to an end like a sigh.
> The days of our years are seventy
>   or even by reason of strength eighty;
> yet the pride is but toil and trouble.
>   for they are soon gone, and we fly away.

The psalm confesses that the whole span of these few years, of whose attainments we pride ourselves, is really nothing: only toil and trouble and unhappiness.

> Who knows the power of your anger,
>   and who stands in awe before your wrath?

The psalmist feels himself to be solitary in his views and experiences. With these reflections upon God's wrath he is aware that he has expressed something that lies outside general experience. Many may have a concept of 'anger' and 'wrath', dogmatic, abstractly acquired by study and accepted. But the psalmist speaks from direct and shattering experience, 'Who knows the power of your anger?' In Rudolf Steiner's book, *A Way to Self-Knowledge,* there is a passage (p. 27) that can make this experience of wrath concrete to us. It refers to the crossing of the threshold of the spiritual world. 'As your soul is now, a task lies before it that it cannot accomplish. The suprasensory environment will not accept it in its present state; it does not wish to have the soul in its present state within it. The soul thereby comes to feel itself somehow in contradiction with the suprasensory world, saying to itself: "you are not ready to flow together with this world" ... There is something devastating to one's sense of self in this experience.' Here in modern terms, without reference to old texts, the experience is described which is called in Psalm 90 the 'wrath of God'.

> So teach us to number our days
>   that we gain a heart of wisdom.

To 'number' our days means that we should not only think about death, but altogether charge the hollow dream of our existence with consciousness, cultivate retrospection and memory and make ourselves clear as to where we stand. To number the days can also mean: to notice the inner quality of the different stages of life. Each stage in the course of this life of seventy years has its special spiritual possibilities. It is not only youth that has its character of 'once only' and 'never again'. Even if it is not so evident, each section of life has it connection with God. 'That we gain a heart of wisdom.' Wisdom of the heart will mature from such responsible communing with the years of our life.

III

The attention of the psalm now turns to the expected salvation.

> Bring to pass the returning, O Lord. How long?
>   And have pity on your servants!
> Satisfy us at daybreak with your grace,
>   that we may rejoice and be glad all our days.
> Make us glad for as many days as you have afflicted us,
>   and for as many years as we have seen evil.

Wrath cannot be the final state. It is a second state, which love assumes towards sinful humanity.

Now expectation turns to a third state; the restitution of harmony between God and humanity, the re-establishment of love. This third condition cannot come about through humans. So hopeful souls look with anticipation to God. They may change the situation through something quite new. Here the psalm becomes Messianic, although no direct reference to the Messiah is made.

The prayer for the great return is followed by the sigh, 'How long?' But just as the whole psalm shows calm endurance and composure, so, too, this 'How long?' where personal feeling comes for once to the surface, is no wild outcry; it is spoken with an understanding patience and mature calm.

'Satisfy us at daybreak with your grace.' In the Holy Scriptures we meet again and again with the mystery of the early morning. Morning is the hour when divine grace is near. Who does not feel how the whole day can be vexatious when one has begun it with a dull, heavy, sleepy morning. The resurrection of Christ happened in the early morning, still in the sphere of the night's mystery, but in the light of the dawning day. Easter is a morning event. This morning character of Christianity is significant. A new cosmic day begins with the resurrection. A new ascent is established. To use the expression of Novalis, Easter is a 'festival of cosmic rejuvenation'.

When Muslims pray they turns towards Mecca. In the same way the prayers of the psalms turn inwardly towards the approaching Christ. A quotation from Psalm 5:3 is specially instructive: 'At daybreak I will prepare it for you and look up to you.' The phrase 'prepare it' refers to the preparation of the sacrifice, but implies at the same time an inner preparation, which enables the worshippers to open their spiritual eye during the ritual of sacrifice. 'At daybreak I will prepare it for you and look up to you.'

In this psalm of Moses, the reference to 'daybreak' is particularly moving. The psalmist is the aged man, the one who has matured and grown wise. But the secret of rejuvenation, the grace of the morning, which brings about the great change, is touched upon in the last verses. They pass over from the realm of truth to a premonition of grace. If until now a calm, earnest mood of grief prevailed in the psalm, out of this very earnestness an anticipation of real joy emerges. The wisdom of age is crystallised pain. Anticipation of redemptive grace and mercy is joy. 'That we may rejoice and be glad all our days.' This joy is to be a kind of compensation for the previous sorrows.

> Let your work be seen by your servants,
>   and your glory to their children.

This is now a prayer for the deed of Christ. And even now that this deed belongs to history, the petition in the psalm has not lost its validity, for now this work should appear ever more clearly before our perception and understanding. That the splendour of glory should become visible 'to their children' points to a still more distant future, to the vision of the coming of Christ in the glory of etheric light.

> Let the favour of the Lord our God be upon us,
>   and establish the work of our hands upon us;
>   yes, establish the work of our hands.

The psalm concludes with a reference to the work of our hands. Is that not contradictory after the reflections on our transitory nature? For if everything earthly bears within it the seed of decay, is not then all activity, all working and creating, all labour of love, wasted from the outset? Did it not say earlier of plants, 'in the morning it flourishes and passes away, in the evening, cut down, it withers'? It is only possible to understand the remarkable change to a positive mood when one takes the 'great returning' seriously. It is true that it is only being prayed for. But it seems as if something of its nature had already been imparted in advance to the one praying. The morning light of Easter radiates over the close of this psalm of Moses.

The closing lines of the psalm underscore this positive affirmation of life which calls all good forces into action: 'yes, establish the work of our hands.' The Hebrew word for 'establish' also means 'confirm', 'sanction'. In the light of the resurrection our own works acquire eternal significance. They become confirmed, established through a divine 'Yes, so be it.'

The psalm sees together the eternity of God and the fate of mortal humans. But in prophetic vision it anticipates the coming salvation which will unite the two, by God's grace, and thereby give meaning to human life and work on earth.

35

'MY TIMES ARE IN YOUR HANDS'

PSALM 31

In Psalm 31, from which is taken the prayer Christ spoke as he died – 'into your hands I commit my spirit'(Lk 23:46) – we find the phrase 'My times are in your hands' (31:15). At whatever point of time something particular makes itself felt, this phrase can speak to the soul with special power.

In childhood we could not yet grasp the meaning of an idea such as 'my time'. A child will say something like, 'Now I'm four' when a birthday comes, but is as yet unaware of what it means to stand within time. Only as the personality gradually awakens do we feel the enigma that it poses: our memory of childhood becomes ever dimmer and more dreamlike, and beyond a certain point it is lost in the utter darkness of sleep. What came before our memory begins? What was happening a year before I was born? How do I experience the countless years that preceded my earthly beginnings?

Our earthly body developed from a minute substantiality into its present dimensions. But what is called 'incarnation', taking on flesh, was not only an entry into the spatial realm but also into temporality, originating from another world, an 'eternal' one above and beyond all time, and as such belonging to a quite different plane of existence. Mysterious creative powers, out of a wisdom that surpasses all human concepts, enabled the miracle of a human body to appear and to serve our I as it has gradually become more self-aware. Similarly they have given us our sense of time.

Psalm 139 gives classic expression to a pious wonder at the creation of the human body: 'I praise you that I am made wondrously [literally, that I have arisen as a miracle of development in a terribly awe-striking way] and my soul perceives this greatly' (139:14). Our entry into the spatial dimension is directly connected with our entry into a temporality assigned to us by the highest powers. Our mysterious development in the protected concealment of the womb is expressed in the words, 'Your eyes saw my as yet unformedness,' in Hebrew, 'my *golem*'. In the same verse this is followed immediately by a foreboding of the span of time allotted to this 'golem' as it configures itself into space, 'and in your book were written all the days ordained for me before a single one of them was yet to be' (139:16). This gift of time is, as it were, an entity or being in itself, appearing in the image of a book of time that contains all days that will one day be 'ours'. Accordingly, such a book is shorter or longer, configured as a particular number of pages, out of a wisdom that surpasses all human thinking. In his vision of the Last Judgment in the Apocalypse, John saw how all these individual 'books' will one day be opened for the purposes of a final judgment (Rv 20:12).

Abraham Lincoln was someone who had a highly developed sense of this span of time allotted us by divine wisdom. Shortly before he was assassinated, he had a prophetic dream of this event, which he knew to be such. With deep earnestness he readied himself inwardly for the forthcoming end of his life, believing that God would give effect to the dream 'in his own good time'. God, in the discernment uniquely intrinsic to him, will let death arrive at the time that he recognises to be the right and proper moment. 'In his own good time'; this pious acceptance of destiny is a striking illustration of the words of the psalm, 'My times are in your hands'.

The vision of the book in which all days are already inscribed before a single one of them has occurred, this perception of a divinely measured time organism that hovers in prefiguring manner over the embryonic *golem* of the unborn child: should this lead us to adopt a fatalistic outlook? Fatalism is pervaded by the sense that everything has been minutely predetermined, and that there is nothing for us to do but surrender to destiny. Here the sense is of a book whose pages are all so densely inscribed that there is no place left for anything further.

Rainer Maria Rilke once expressed in his *Book of Hours* a very particular religious experience one can have in nature: 'This is a great wonder in the world: I feel *all life is lived.*' The question arises, *who* lives it then? And it becomes apparent that 'things', that winds and waters, that plants and animals, cannot provide the answer to this question. The poet ascends from inanimate things to ensouled animals: 'Is this the warm animals as they pass / is this the birds that strangely lift themselves?' With all these creatures he senses that they 'are lived' from elsewhere and do not lead their existence under their own direction but point to higher planes where dwells the real 'subject', the conscious bearer of their existence. Having surveyed these ascending forms of being up to the animals, he asks once again, 'Who lives it then?' And, in the form of a question an intuition dawns: 'Do you live it, God, do you live life?' This is certainly a deep truth in perception of nature. But does it not overlook something very close to hand?

Between the animal and God, surely, stands the *human being*. On the one hand we certainly belong to nature too. We do not have the faintest inkling in the small, uppermost attic of our consciousness, of what occurs in mysterious wisdom in the processes of our body. This occurs without us; but it could not occur if higher spiritual powers did not live within these processes, work into them from higher levels with divine consciousness. Then, too, there are the 'givens' of destiny within which we find ourselves placed, the ways we are guided, the strokes of fate and fortune, which accrue to us without our conscious involvement.

But this is still not the whole story. Besides all that we receive in this way, that is accorded us, there is also the domain of our own, personal, conscious actions. Here the inmost I gradually works its way to the surface and experiences freedom and responsibility. We have a deep awareness that we cannot simply pass blame for the mistakes we make to our inherited, naturally-given circumstances. However great a part these may play, at the end of the day, we ourselves are also involved. We cannot approve the idea that we ourselves, like everything else in nature, are only 'lived'. In fact it is precisely our errors and misdeeds that prevent us from thinking that all our human existence is 'lived by God'. Clearly God has accorded us a realm where we can take our own actions and take responsibility for them, whether these actions be good or mistaken.

Let us now return to the question of how we should imagine the 'book' that contains our future days. Is every page pre-inscribed from top to bottom? This would be irreconcilable with human freedom. Or is it perhaps a blank book with nothing but white, completely unwritten pages, merely awaiting whatever we enter in it? That cannot be true either. We feel the prior endowments of our destiny too strongly for that, the hidden configuration in whatever fate meets us, the small beginnings of our efforts at freedom. The book is neither fully composed from the outset nor are its pages completely blank. We can say that God has partly pre-inscribed it but has left space for our own additions. God has accorded us the opportunity to be his co-worker.

The phrase in the psalm, 'My times are in your hands,' then acquires another nuance too. The piety of devout surrender applies to everything that has been divinely pre-inscribed in the book of coming days. But although these times are in God's hands, they may still be called 'my times'. It is the plural, my times, in the Hebrew original. This is not yet felt in as abstract and conceptual a way as when an intellectual nowadays philosophises about time. 'Time' is structured in its tangible vitality. In a human biography, our experience of time repeatedly grows more palpable around particular high-points, it sharpens and focuses at special moments and destiny-deciding hours. The psalm knows this: the life-span allotted to me, with its special moments, is 'my' time, entrusted to my governance, every day, every hour is unspeakably precious. We can therefore also reverse the phrase: '*Your* times are in *my* hands.' Such a sense, which can fill us with an overpowering shock at our responsibility towards this great gift we have been given, is no less humble and pious than a surrendering to what God has pre-ordained.

'Your times in my hands.' The more seriously we take this, the more it becomes apparent how all 'killing of time', all mere filling of time with trivialities or worse, is a lack of reverence for the deity who makes our time available to us and has, in a kind of consecrated act, released this time, offered it up to us. The reverse is also true: by using it rightly, by properly fulfilling it, we show that we understand this divine sacrifice, and can indeed take responsibility for it. And yet our everyday, mundane being is not capable of this. But Christ came to us, God in the form of the Son, whom we may take up in freedom in our own I, and who thereby helps us to truly 'fulfil time'. To the degree that this happens, our human life, lived in freedom, becomes 'acceptable' to higher powers. Instead of killing or misusing the time assigned to us, we can offer it up to the powers from which we originated. All such sacrificial offering by the human being basically signifies that we return in a new form to the Godhead what belongs to, but became estranged from, it. A span of human life filled with Christ can be woven by higher powers into the heavenly worlds as an enrichment of it, just as the Apocalypse looks ahead not only to a 'new earth' but also a 'new heaven'.

Thus, through the experience of 'your times in my hands', we return in a new way to the original phrase, 'My times are in your hands,' now in the sense of offering up, of bringing home again to the eternal powers of origin, a time properly filled and fulfilled.

This return to our starting point – 'my times in your hands' – now sheds a new light on that first level of experience, the surrender to a higher will. The Old Testament worshippers in a pre-Christian era felt themselves sustained in such surrender by the divine words, 'My thoughts are not your thoughts, and your ways are not my ways ... for as the heavens are higher than the earth so my ways are higher than your ways, and my thoughts higher than your thoughts' (Is 55:8f).

With Christ's appearance on earth, divine and human paths have joined together, bridging the distance between heaven and earth and opening up new horizons for future human potential. 'I no longer call you servants, for a servant does not know what his master is doing. I have called you friends; for all that I have heard from my Father I have made known to you' (Jn 15:15). Thus Christ speaks in the Farewell Discourses recorded in the John Gospel, where he also promises the advent of the Comforter, the Holy Spirit, as enlarger of consciousness who 'will lead you into all truth'.

This signifies, after all, that in the future of Christianity 'my thoughts' will increasingly shine out within 'your thoughts'. The fundamental experience of pious surrender remains, but this surrender is illumined by the granting of inmost, reverent understanding. Through Christ a higher I is gradually awoken in human beings, and remembers how, before embarking on its earthly path, it wove the tapestry of the circumstances of its forthcoming life on earth together with the wise powers of destiny. Then, during this earthly life, it will not feel blows of fate and gifts of fortune as something entirely 'alien' to it, something that 'strikes us from without' but rather as something truly appropriate for us and fundamentally belonging to us. Out of a surrender with closed eyes, a no less devout but now seeing surrender can grow. And then we find that our higher I was involved in the 'prescribing' of the book of our future days. And likewise the Godhead participates in the entries, which we ourselves inscribe upon the white spaces left in the book, in the form of the Christ indwelling us, whom we have taken into ourselves in freedom.

36

IN EXILE

PSALMS 42 AND 43

The two psalms 42 and 43 are intimately connected. Together they form a whole, as one can see from the recurring verses 42:6 and 11, and 43:5. Historically, the psalm is of a priest apparently banished from Jerusalem and living in exile in the region of the source of the Jordan. It expresses his longing for the temple worship in Jerusalem. But the psalm expresses truths which hold good far beyond this special situation of a distant life's destiny.

I

> As the a deer longs for flowing water,
>   so my soul longs for you, O God.
> My soul thirsts for God,
>   for the living God.
> When shall I come
>   and see the face of God?
> My tears have been my food
>   day and night,
> while they say to me all day long,
>   'Where is your God?'
> These things I will remember,
>   and pour out my soul into them:
> How I would go with the multitude,
>   and walk with them in procession to the house of God,
> with the voice of joy and praise,
>   with a multitude keeping the pilgrim feast.

> Why are you cast down, O my soul,
>   and why are you troubled within me?
> Hope in God; for I shall again praise him,
>   that he is the salvation of my countenance and my God.

The opening words are famous. It is the picture of the deer seeking in vain for water in the dried-up brook under the baking heat of the sun. The elemental power of this natural picture has been felt through the ages.

Desires, pleasures, pains, meet us in the animal kingdom with undiminished power: animals are completely taken up by their emotions. With humanity, the development of the intellect has, as Shakespeare's Hamlet said, 'sicklied o'er with the pale cast of thought' the naturally powerful colour of these feelings and paralysed them. The cry of an animal can go through and through us, and we can learn from it what a passionate emotion can be. Human passions seem tame and insignificant compared with such elemental outbursts.

However, this was different in past ages. When the *Iliad* describes the terrible wrath of Achilles in the image of a spreading forest fire, we get some inkling of the strength of human emotions in ancient times. However, human beings are not condemned permanently to pay for their clear consciousness by stunting the soul. This is only a transitional stage. They may be tempted by a false path to revive the full gamut of passions and emotions by reverting to the animal or even the demon within themselves. On the other hand, a healthy future possibility awaits human beings. Powerful and exciting sensations will open up in them, in the same measure as they make an active and conscious contact with the world of spirit. These sensations are no longer fettered to the darkness of animal nature, but are in harmony with the consciousness of vision. The soul feels with the spirit. It is only in the form of the intellect that spirit is an adversary of the soul.

The Apocalypse describes the Cherubim in the form of living beasts who sound forth the great song of praise. These celestial creatures 'were covered with eyes all around' (Rv 4:8). No dull blindness of instinct is seeking an outlet, but eye-faculties of the highest order are in action. Here the elemental power of passion is spiritualised, not deadened, but dedicated with all its strength to the spirit.

Psalms 42 and 43

42

As the a deer longs for flowing water,
  so my soul longs for you, O God.
² *My soul thirsts for God,*
  for the living God.
When shall I come
  and see the face of God?
³ *My tears have been my food*
  day and night,
while they say to me all day long,
  'Where is your God?'
⁴ *These things I will remember,*
  and pour out my soul into them:
How I would go with the multitude,
  and walk with them in procession to the house of God,
with the voice of joy and praise,
  with a multitude keeping the pilgrim feast.

⁵ *Why are you cast down, O my soul,*
  and why are you troubled within me?
Hope in God; for I shall again praise him,
  that he is the salvation of my countenance ⁶ *and my God.*

My soul is cast down within me:
  therefore will I remember you
from the land of Jordan and of Hermon,
  high from Mount Misar.
⁷ *Deep calls to deep*
  at the roar of your waterfalls;
all your waves and your surges
  have gone over me.
⁸ *By day the* Lord *decrees his loving devotion*
  and at the night his song shall be within me,
  a prayer to the living God.
⁹ *I say to God, my rock:*
  'Why have you forgotten me?
Why do I go mourning
  in face of the mockery of the enemy?'

¹⁰ Like a shattering of my bones,
   my enemies taunt me;
while they say to me all day long,
   'Where is your God?'

¹¹ Why are you cast down, O my soul,
   and why are you troubled within me?
Hope in God; for I shall again praise him,
   that he is the salvation of my countenance and my God.

43

Judge me, O God, and defend my cause
   against an ungodly people,
from the deceitful and unjust man
   deliver me!
² For you are the God of my strength;
   why have you rejected me?
Why do I go mourning
   in face of the mockery of the enemy?'
³ Send out your light and your truth:
   they will lead me;
they will bring me to your holy hill
   and to your dwellings.
⁴ Then will I go to the altar of God,
   to God who is my exceeding joy,
and I will praise you with the harp,
   O God, who is the God of my I.

⁵ Why are you cast down, O my soul,
   and why are you troubled within me?
Hope in God; for I shall again praise him,
   that he is the salvation of my countenance and my God.

The cry of the animal is on the one hand a reminder to us of a lost power of soul. On the other hand it is a prophecy that the human soul will one day again soar aloft on the wings of powerful emotions which are stirred by the spirit.

Thus the psalmist sees again in the longing of the deer his own longing. Thirst is in fact one of the most powerful sensations. It serves as a classical symbol of human desire, particularly in Buddhism. Buddha saw in thirst the burning subconscious longing for life and existence, which leads us again and again into the body, and hence again and again into suffering. He saw no other way of ending this suffering than to penetrate in meditation into the subconscious depths of the soul and destroy there at the roots this urge for existence.

It has only been recognised since the coming of Christ that in spite of its sufferings, earthly existence must not be regarded merely negatively. Since that time we must not regard the path to incarnation as a false path. The burning thirst which leads to earthly existence has its justification, but it must be rightly understood. We must recognise to where this thirst, this longing for existence, is ultimately directed; it must not simply seek temporary and superficial appeasement. This thirst for existence that guides us with a deep instinct into our earthly life is, after all, our longing for self-realisation, the longing to grasp our destiny and to become the bearer of the I AM. It is at the same time the longing for the God of the I AM, who, as the creative prototype of true inner selfhood, will bring about the realisation of our self. Ultimately this thirst is seeking Christ. It leads us to earthly existence because it is only on earth that we can really find Christ in his death and resurrection; without him, earthly existence and the thirst for it would be meaningless.

Thirst appears also in John's Gospel when Christ cries from the cross, 'I thirst.' It is as though with this cry he took into his divine soul the totality of the pain of human longing in order that he might fully identify himself with humanity. But by doing so he can promise human beings, 'whoever believes in me will never thirst' (Jn 6:35, also 4:14 and 7:37).

Let us return to our psalm, from which we seem to have wandered a long way, but in order really to see it in this great context.

'My soul thirsts for God, for the living God.' Here the primal emotion of thirst has become conscious of its true object. Unhappily, the expression 'the living God' has largely become religious jargon. The 'living' God is the God acting directly and spontaneously, not only working in the law, in the impersonal necessity of what he has ordained. When creation was complete the great Sabbath rest began: God ceased to create. Creation now runs along its own rails, as it were. But, behind the world which gradually became more a concealment than a revelation, where is the God who acts spontaneously, who once commanded, 'Let there be light'?

Christ brought the great Sabbath to an end. A renewal of the original powers of creation is accomplished in him. The world has detached itself to a certain degree from the creator and has become 'finished work'. But the creativity of God appears again in the I AM of the Christ. He who utters the I AM is the living God.

'When shall I come and see the face of God?' A long path of development leads to this seeing. At some future time we shall stand before God as I to I, spirit-personality to spirit-personality. As St Paul says, 'but then we shall see face to face' (1Cor 13:12).

The striving soul must for a time endure mockery, for the adversaries ask, 'Where is your God?' Those who are called to freedom must at some time have their relation to God exposed to the test of persecution, to prove that it is sustained purely inwardly, without external props and support. The scorn of the adversaries who only have eyes for the material world, and who, through what they find, come to the conclusion that there is no God – that is something that had of necessity to arise in the course of time. It is a station on the way of the cross, of the God who gave up his power for the sake of our freedom. Atheism is no accidental going off the rails, no product of special wickedness, but something that had to come for a time. The suffering of the psalmist is not only his coincidental personal misfortune but a share of the great divine-human passion.

Memories arise in this state of forlornness – 'I had it once'. The psalmist is speaking of his memories of the temple worship in Jerusalem, of solemn celebrations in the sanctuary which in those days mediated to him a consciousness of God. He speaks for humankind in general. Until now religion has largely lived by reason of such memories of a past nearness of God. The writer of our psalm pours out his soul in remembrance. He gathers all the energies of his soul into this remembering and turns it into a meditation.

We must adopt again the right technique of remembering. In the course of our life we shall all have had many more impressions of a higher reality than may perhaps appear to us today. We go about with our experiences for the most part like thoughtless spendthrifts. We could derive more from the fact that this or that has befallen us. 'These things I will remember and pour out my soul into them.'

The first section of the psalm ends with the verse which then recurs after the second and third section: 'Why are you cast down, O my soul? Why are you troubled within me?' It is part of an active religion that we are no longer so inevitably absorbed in our pains and griefs. We divide ourselves, so to speak, into the person who suffers and the one who stands by. This other one who stands by is often still very feeble; sometimes perhaps wringing their hands before their own soul when it withdraws from their encouragement. But again and again we must make the attempt to take up a position outside ourselves and from this objective standpoint call our soul to order.

The psalmist places himself similarly before his own soul, which is utterly lost in grief and cannot find its way to inner peace and calm. He offers comfort to his soul, 'Hope in God'. After each of the three stanzas the encouragement is repeated. The soul is not so quickly freed from its sorrow and restlessness; for at the beginning of the second section this reference to being cast down is brought up again, my soul is 'cast down', as if there had been no exhortation to courage. But repetition is the secret of the inner life. So the psalm again and again places spiritual comfort before the mind's eye, until it really takes root in the soul.

II

> My soul is cast down within me:
>   therefore will I remember you
> from the land of Jordan and of Hermon,
>   high from Mount Misar.
> Deep calls to deep
>   at the roar of your waterfalls;
> all your waves and your surges
>   have gone over me.

> By day the LORD decrees his loving devotion
>   and at the night his song shall be within me,
> a prayer to the living God.

The psalmist, banished from Jerusalem, lives in exile by the upper waters of the Jordan, which dash in tumbling waterfalls from the snow-covered Mount Hermon. Where the water gushes out of the rock-face a famous sanctuary was dedicated to Pan. Here, much later when it was called Caesarea Philippi, Peter was to make his avowal, 'You are the Christ, the son of the living God' (Mt 16:16).

The psalmist sees himself abandoned to the roaring waterfalls, as if the ancient dragon-power of chaos had risen up – *tehom* (*abyssos* in the Greek translation), the primal flood, not yet subdued by the God of the I AM. It has a hidden connection with the chaotic powers within the psalmist, with the inner restlessness of his soul, surging and storming without peace, which he is not able at once to control. It is as if all these waves were dashing together above his head, ignoring his painstaking attempts to take hold of himself.

The pain of exile has gripped him with all its force. Exile has been experienced and suffered a millionfold in our own time: torn away from house and home, from the familiar cherished surroundings, uprooted from one's work and profession, being dispossessed and exiled into a strange land, hostile and cold.

But with all its hardships, being exiled is also a parable of higher things. Opening our eyes in the morning in strange surroundings, have we not at times felt that this condition is known and familiar? As if one had gone through this nightmare of waking in exile in some other form? To awake in a foreign land of exile – this is the archetypal experience of incarnation, of embodiment on earth. Our soul has been displaced from its own original environment and banished into an environment not fitted for it, into the world of material things. This transplanting from the heavenly home into the material world is the archetypal experience of exile, which still trembles in the depths of every soul. The religious sense is an awakening homesickness, a dark recollection of a 'beforehand'. Religion loses this character of looking back to the past only by the acceptance of the Christ, because through

Christ the heavenly home can be carried into our earthly exile, transforming all things.

The nightly song of praise, the prayer of which the following verse speaks, are the effort to meet the chaotic mood of sorrow and unrest and to make way again for the rule of the self. It would not be right merely to say, 'I am not in the mood to pray – it cannot be expected of me today'. We must get away from these subjective surging moods. Prayer does not grow from moods, but the true mood comes out of the prayer. Here regular rhythmic repetition is a help. The regular celebration of the festivals in the Act of Consecration of Man throughout the year is something quite independent of the moods that are produced by the changing destinies of individuals. It takes hold of people, comforts them and takes them into a larger, more expansive life. The blessing rests with God; our efforts may for a time seem to bear no fruit. But a healing element lies in the very effort of observing regular ordered prayer.

So the psalmist sings his nocturnal hymn. He does not admit that pain uses up all the energy of his soul and makes it completely 'toneless'. There must always be something left over which is capable of exaltation. To take part in the times and rhythms of an ordered religious life is a great help.

The psalm carries its afflictions before the Godhead:

> I say to God, my rock:
>   'Why have you forgotten me?
> Why do I go mourning
>   in face of the mockery of the enemy?'
> Like a shattering of my bones,
>   my enemies taunt me;
> while they say to me all day long,
>   'Where is your God?'

My 'rock' – the antithesis to the chaotic flood of *tehom*. The rock, the foundation of my self, the solid ground under the feet that allows us to stand and withstand. This power proceeds from the God of the I AM.

'Why have you forgotten me?' Human beings are set free by the higher powers, who have renounced the task of guiding humans at every step. They have untied the string. Human beings are to seek their way under their own responsibility. We cannot be spared this experience of being forsaken by God. It gives us maturity to find in freedom our helper and guide in Christ.

The question, 'Where is your God?' is an added affliction in this forsaken state. In the first part it was the cause of tears; now it is intensified: it is 'like a shattering of my bones'. The pain produced by the thought that in this earthly sphere the divine can be 'called into question' affects the psalmist to the bone.

So now, for the second time, the consolation of the spirit is invoked:

> Why are you cast down, O my soul,
> and why are you troubled within me?
> Hope in God; for I shall again praise him,
> that he is the salvation of my countenance and my God.

We must summon ourselves to hope, aware that we are involved in far-reaching developments, in great plans of Providence which we are as yet unable to survey. We need to be conscious of the fact that we are in a lengthy process of becoming, which takes its time. We need a 'long-term will' which leads through the various phases of becoming with their inevitable sorrows and suffering. Such a long-term will produces then the right kind of patience, not a passive mood of letting things happen, but an active, positive attitude.

'I shall again praise him that he is the salvation of my countenance,' as the one who helps me to my true human countenance, whereas evil disfigures it. As the one who brings the human countenance into reality, he is 'my God', the god of my I AM, who is revealed in the free personality, in the true nature of the human being.

III

> Judge me, O God, and defend my cause
> against an ungodly people,
> from the deceitful and unjust man
> deliver me!

The God who will help us towards our true human countenance is at the same time the judge who makes us aware of our disfigurements and inhumanities. This judgment, however, is not aimed at condemnation but at restoration.

As we deliver ourselves to the judgment of the I-creating God – 'judge me, O God' – we gain in God the helper against our opponents. Those who shrink from the divine judgment of conscience fall of necessity into the hands of the evil powers. To become truly conscious of our faults separates us from the devil. Inward dishonesty that tries to ignore conscience leads us all the more definitely into his realm. The human enemies mentioned in the psalm are only the visible representatives of the invisible powers, of ungodliness, deceit and injustice. God himself wages war against these powers. If we do not withdraw ourselves from his judgment, then God becomes our confederate, inasmuch as he fights our battles.

> For you are the God of my strength;
>   why have you rejected me?
> Why do I go mourning
>   in face of the mockery of the enemy?'

The earlier question, 'Why have you forgotten me?' is here intensified to the more forcible, 'Why have you rejected me?' Possibilities of fearful catastrophe appear on the horizon with these questions. Since their own freedom, their good will, is counted upon in the process of their becoming true human beings, since they must themselves bring into operation through their positive attitude the grace that is destined for them, it is possible for this development to be wrecked by their own unwillingness to co-operate. Then they would be abandoned as an unfinished attempt, 'unfit to become human.' The psalmist feels himself to be 'one of the damned', he feels as if he were in an inferno. Yet he lifts his soul again to the prospect of divine grace.

> Send out your light and your truth:
>   they will lead me;
>   they will bring me to your holy hill
>   and to your dwellings.

> Then will I go to the altar of God,
> to God who is my exceeding joy,
> and I will praise you with the harp,
> O God, who is the God of my I.

Deliverance comes because God sends down to us something of his own being. It is like an emanation, an outflow of the divine essence in the direction of humanity. 'Your light and your truth.' Both words appear in the I am words of John's Gospel where Christ declares the nature of his own being: 'I am the light of the world,' 'I am the way and the truth and the life' (Jn 8:12, 14:6).

These divine essential forces 'will lead me and will make me come to the hill of your holiness' (literally). This leading is in no way a carrying, but it presupposes the participation of our own forces for progress.

The attainment of the goal, the bringing home of the exiled sufferer from the strange land to the centre of divine life, is presented in three stages. The holy hill, the dwellings or tabernacles of God and his altar.

The holy hill is in general the figurative expression for exaltation into a 'higher' world. It begins with the raising of fallen human beings to the heights of divine holiness.

If human beings have climbed the holy hill, they find there the 'dwellings' of God. Is the image of a dwelling place or tabernacles only a childish way of carrying earthly things into the divine realm? Again the reverse is true: our dwelling at a particular place is only an earthly image of the fact that the higher world too, although non-spatial, has differing realms and regions. 'In my Father's house are many rooms' (Jn 14:2). 'Your dwellings' (plural in the original) are the various realms forming the home of the higher beings in their infinitely rich and manifold differentiation, in whom God reveals himself in countless ways. In this way they are dwelling places of God.

Finally, the third and last state is in the heart of heaven, the inmost centre of the divine world, the altar of God, where his own offering brought in love is fulfilled, the imparting of his own being. All earthly altars are symbols of this mystery of the divine sacrifice. Human beings are called upon to participate in the divine cosmic service of sacrifice. As human beings they are called to the priesthood. 'Then will I go to the altar of God.' They take this step from the prompting of their inmost being. Then the divine leaders, light and truth, are no longer merely beside them, giving help and guidance. It is as though they have entered into human beings and taken part in their own decision, so that, notwithstanding all the gracious help given to them, to approach this altar is ultimately an individual's own free act.

To participate thus in the divine cosmic service of sacrifice is at the same time the highest blessedness – 'to God who is my exceeding joy.' Human beings who have received through aeons the divine sacrificial gifts, are now able themselves to give, to sacrifice, thus giving back in changed form to the world what they have received. 'It is more blessed to give than to receive' (Ac 20:35). This, speaking broadly, is the ultimate purpose of the whole of human evolution. Human 'heavenly bliss' does not consist in the indolent enjoyment of a sort of Utopia, but in being permitted to share in the creative sacrificial deeds of God.

'And I will praise you with the harp.' Human beings have now become 'resounding', all the false notes and dissonances of their nature are overcome; they are a walking song of praise. Our soul life always resounds in some way in the higher worlds, seldom harmoniously, generally quite the opposite. Christ-filled human beings must develop their soul with all its powers of resonance to become the harp of God. Thus the Apocalypse shows the redeemed as playing on the harp (Rv 14:2).

This reference to approaching the altar of God is like an apocalyptic vision of the future. But now the psalm leaves this vision of the future to the present, and at last to exorcise the despair and unrest of his suffering soul through words of spiritual consolation:

> Why are you cast down, O my soul,
>   and why are you troubled within me?
> Hope in God; for I shall again praise him,
>   that he is the salvation of my countenance and my God.

37

EXPERIENCE OF GOD

PSALM 63

'A Psalm of David, when he was in the wilderness of Judah.' The desert is part of the world that seems to have fallen away from the great organism of life, and been abandoned by the powers of creation. David experienced the wilderness in nature. People today experience it in great cities, in the domain of the death of a civilisation that makes existence lifeless and desolate. 'The desert grows: woe to him in whom deserts hide,' said Nietzsche in *Dionysian-Dithyrambs*.

Over three thousand years later the words of the psalm that was prayed in the desert of Judea can still speak to us. The psalm begins with the cry: 'O God.' All around the powers of death are triumphant – the search for God must therefore lead within. There something stirs that is connected with the living God: 'You God of my innermost being.'

'Dawning I seek you.' The word 'dawn' is contained in the Hebrew verb here. If the human self becomes conscious of its basic connection with the divine self, there is something like a dawning in the soul. Just as dawn precedes the rising of the sun, there begins to glow in the soul the feeling of a great awakening. In the world of external nature God's sun has already risen aeons ago; the innermost part of our soul is still virgin land to God. There the sun is to rise ever more in the future. This is why the start of each awakening of the soul is like a sacred dawn.

From this meeting with God in the innermost self, the psalm now turns to the life of feeling. The religious faith of the psalmist was of such an elementary nature that he could allow all his feelings and strivings, all the wishes and yearnings of his soul to converge in one mighty longing for the divine: 'my soul thirsts for you.'

> ## Psalm 63
>
> A Psalm of David, when he was in the wilderness of Judah
>
> *O God, you God of my innermost being; dawning I seek you;*
> *my soul thirsts for you;*
> *my flesh faints for need of you,*
> *in a land dry and parched without water.*
> *² So I have looked for you in the sanctuary,*
> *beholding your power and glory.*
> *³ Because your loving goodness is higher than life,*
> *my lips will praise you.*
> *⁴ Thus I will bless you as long as I live;*
> *in your name I will lift up my hands.*
> *⁵ My soul will be satisfied with rich abundance,*
> *and my mouth will praise you with joyful lips.*
> *⁶ When on my bed I call you to mind,*
> *and meditate on you in the watches of the night;*
> *⁷ for you have been my help,*
> *and in the shadow of your wings I will sing for joy.*
> *⁸ My soul clings to you;*
> *your right hand upholds me.*
>
> *⁹ But those who seek to destroy my soul*
> *shall go down into the depths of the earth;*
> *¹⁰ they shall fall by the sword;*
> *they shall be prey for jackals.*
> *¹¹ But the king shall rejoice in God;*
> *all who swear by him shall glory,*
> *for the mouths of liars will be stopped.*

Then he descends to the earthly body of flesh and blood, and is able to include that too as part of his devotion. The body does not, as so often with us, make a nuisance of itself when the soul wants to soar upwards. It is not an obstruction; even its weakness is part of the basic religious experience. Its feebleness is experienced as the need for God, as instinctive craving for God. The unspoiled human body can experience the satisfying of hunger and the quenching of thirst with devotion; so here the physical privation is experienced as desire for God.

37. EXPERIENCE OF GOD

> O God, you God of my innermost being; dawning I seek
> you;
> my soul thirsts for you;
> my flesh faints for need of you,
> in a land dry and parched without water.

The solitary desert prayer is now supported by remembrance of the experience of the ritual in the sanctuary. Ritual is arranged so that what the physical eye sees can help the visionary power of the soul. This is a further indication in the psalms of the experience of the supersensory that can arise at the sight of the holy rites.

> So I have looked for you in the sanctuary,
> beholding your power and glory.

The psalmist praying in the desert feels an awakened devotion to the divine revelation such as he has otherwise felt only when he was present in body and soul at the holy rite of sacrifice. In this experience of the divine glory, the 'love from above' comes to him and confers on him a feeling of completely new life. What he otherwise called 'his life' loses importance. When that highest goodness has shone in his heart, he may say on looking at his ordinary daily life, 'life is not the highest good.' So the psalm says, 'Your loving goodness is higher than life.'

It is to this loving goodness that 'praise' is now given. In order to feel once more the original freshness of this overworn religious word, we may consider the following. People today are predominantly critically minded. They strengthen their self-esteem by criticising, but the soul is not satisfied through this. In order to be healthy the soul needs to look up to that world which is 'better than life'. It needs to be able to be enthusiastic about something. In this way it achieves the opposite of criticism: the recognition that grows into worship. Perhaps we can understand religious praise as the positive counterpart of the critical attitude that destroys and impoverishes the individual soul. The praise of the lips goes on to become blessing: 'This I will bless you as long as I live.'

There arises quite naturally and automatically at this point the religious gesture of raising the hands. We know it from the Act of

Consecration of Man. If you raise your hands to heaven, you reach out beyond yourself. That can only properly be done 'in the name' of God as the psalm expresses it. This name stands for all that can be present of God in the one who recognises him. It grows into a true communion, an inner receiving of the divine being, which those who pray 'eat and drink', thus permeating their flesh and blood.

> Because your loving goodness is higher than life,
> > my lips will praise you.
>
> Thus I will bless you as long as I live;
> > in your name I will lift up my hands.
>
> My soul will be satisfied with rich abundance,
> > and my mouth will praise you with joyful lips.

The dawn experience then works into the hours of night. In the 'watches of the night' it proves its power. Those who watch with religious devotion during the time of sleep – we may think of the midnight service at Christmas – seek at least to reach consciously those heights that their soul otherwise enters unconsciously when it is freed from the body during sleep. What is it that the waking soul does at night according to the psalm? The Hebrew word, *hagah,* is 'meditate'. Those who piously fill the watches of the night in this way experience the security of being under the 'wings' of God.

God spreads his wings protectively over the soul. But human beings are not only the passive object of this protective care. Something in them reaches towards God – 'My soul clings to you.' The Hebrew word for 'clings', *devekut,* has become an important concept in Jewish mysticism. The Spanish kabbalist Isaac of Acre (*c.* 1300) tells the story of a student who seeks the mysteries of the inner life and is asked by his master whether he has yet achieved perfect equanimity of soul. He answers: 'Indeed, I feel satisfaction at praise and pain at insult, but I am not revengeful and bear no grudge.' That, however, does not satisfy the master. 'My son, go back to your home, for as long as you have no equanimity and can still feel the sting of insult, you have not attained to the state where you can connect your thoughts with God.'*
This story may shame many a Christian. Only above that stratum of

---

* G.G. Scholem, *Major Trends in Jewish Mysticism,* p. 97.

the soul where the pain of insult is felt lies the possibility of 'clinging to God'.

God spreads out his wings. The soul 'clings to God' – so that God can respond with a fresh deed of grace: 'your right hand upholds me.' This picture of the divine right hand holding us has something still more personal than the spreading of wings – not only protection but also support, which flows into us through this hand, giving us also power to support ourselves.

> When on my bed I call you to mind,
>   and meditate on you in the watches of the night;
> for you have been my help,
>   and in the shadow of your wings I will sing for joy.
> My soul clings to you;
>   your right hand upholds me.

But now there comes a discordant note in the pure harmony of this wonderful prayer, a typical 'Old Testament' note, in the reference to the persecutors who head for their own perdition. 'But those who seek to destroy my soul ... shall fall by the sword.' One must certainly think of what actually gave rise to this: David's flight into the Judean Desert, though the pursuers of those times can have only a purely historical interest for us today. But as the Desert of Judea becomes for us the modern desert experience, so from a religious point of view David's pursuers represent today's opposing forces, the powers of the Adversary. There is a deep inner truth in the fact that they have their place in such a song of divine love. It is an age-old experience that the closer one comes to God the stronger becomes the sensitivity to what opposes him. It is therefore just at its climax in Communion that the Act of Consecration of Man is mindful of the 'Adversary'.

It is not merely fortuitous that this passage is preceded by the verse about being upheld by God's right hand. He who feels thus upheld can now view the evil powers undismayed. In the Apocalypse, the Christian seer looks upon the adversaries, and learns that the beast from the abyss will 'go to destruction' (Rv 17:8). Spiritual observation of this creature's motivation reveals where it is heading. The seer sees that it can come to no good end.

So the psalmist sees the direction in which the servants of the enemy are heading. They are intent upon destroying his soul. 'Those who seek to destroy my soul' – this expression, once coined by David in relation to actual hostile people, is for us no longer connected with a long past feud, but acts as an appropriate pointer to certain powers. There are in fact erring spiritual powers that aim at the destruction of the human soul. Above all they are at work where 'the desert grows' – within and without. All soul destruction happens in a world that can truly be called an 'underworld'. Wherever the powers of the soul and warmth of heart die out, we are in reality no longer living in a world lit by the sun, but in a 'sub-earthly' realm.

Two further images are added – the sword and the jackal. Those who are on the way to 'the depths of the earth', to Hades, fall victim to the 'sword'. In an apocalyptic sense this is the sword of the spirit as it went forth from the mouth of the 'white rider' and overcame the Adversary. 'Prey for jackals' – this too can become an apocalyptic picture, whatever may once have been meant literally. Such noxious, carrion-eating creatures can become an image of demonic beings that feed not on the decomposing body but on all the inner elements of decay that proceed from the departing soul, beings that feed themselves as it were by means of the badness that a soul brings with it. The reference to the night-howling jackal allows a glimpse into this sinister world.

> But those who seek to destroy my soul
>   shall go down into the depths of the earth;
> they shall fall by the sword;
>   they shall be prey for jackals.

The light is all the brighter again against this gloomy background. Now comes a word that has not been heard before in the psalm, the 'king'. Again we may look beyond the person of David and regard 'king' as an expression for an exalted state of humanity – rather as the Apocalypse speaks of Christ making us 'kings and priests' (Rv 5:10). 'But the king shall rejoice in God.' For us this sounds like the Gospel of John speaking of the joy of Christ (15:11). All the religious strength of feeling hitherto expressed in the psalm – the longing for God, the seeing of God, the devotion, the sense of being fed, protected, supported – finally condenses into the 'rejoicing in God', which cannot even be extinguished in the face of the enemy.

Not so immediately accessible to the modern reader perhaps is the conclusion of the whole psalm: blessing those who 'swear by' the king, and the reference to the stopping of 'the mouths of liars'. If the psalm is read from a Christian point of view, the king is Christ himself. He bears in him the Logos, the world-creating Word. The motif of swearing indicates a mystery of the word. Someone who swears summons the presence of higher beings, the word 'under oath' is spoken in their immediate presence. Just as the Greek and Latin word for 'conscience' means a 'knowing-with' (*syn-eidon, con-scientia*) higher beings, so swearing means a 'speaking-with' the invisible. Therefore those who swear by the 'king' summon the king to speak with them, they take up into their human word something of the creative divine Word itself.

In connection with these mysteries of the divine power of the Word we can also come to a proper understanding of the last sentence of the psalm, which says that 'the mouths of liars will be stopped'. After the experience of the holy, creative word of God, the satanic character of the lie is all the more apparent. The Zarathustran religion of ancient Persia had a very strong sense that it was Ahriman, the enemy of the gods, who was active in the lie. The activity of deceitful powers is a terrible evil. The prophecy that these forces opposed to the divine Word are one day to be deprived of their power by him voices a great apocalyptic hope, and as such is a worthy conclusion to this song in celebration of man's experience of God.

> But the king shall rejoice in God;
>   all who swear by him shall glory,
>   for the mouths of liars will be stopped.

38

A GLIMPSE INTO THE SANCTUARY

PSALM 73

I

> Nevertheless, I am continually with you;
>   you hold my right hand.
> You guide me with your counsel,
>   and afterwards you receive me with honour.
> Whom have I in heaven but you?
>   And there is nothing on earth that I desire beside you.
> My flesh and my soul may fail,
>   yet God is the strength of my heart and my portion
>   forever.*

Verses 23 to 26 of Psalm 73 have always been regarded as one of the finest passages of the Old Testament, in fact of religious literature of all time. One must see them in connection with the entire psalm in order to give them their full value.

The writer of the psalm tells us at first how for a long time he was oppressed by a tormenting problem. His difficult destiny led him to the question: how is it that evil is so often successful, that so little of the divine justice appears? And on the other hand, so often the life of those who endeavour with all their power to do what is right seems insignificant and beset with trouble.

---

* More than with any other psalm, Frieling's translation is an expanded interpretation. The latter is at the end of this chapter, while here a more usual translation is given.

The first sixteen verses are devoted to the presentation of this problem. They describe in vivid and picturesque language the triumph of those who do not trouble about godly things, and then in contrast to this his own sorrowful, afflicted life. 'However much I pondered to understand this, it was too painful for me' (73:16).

He sometimes felt tempted to doubt the existence of divine justice, but something always held him back. Until one day something unusual happened to him. His honest efforts towards understanding, his steady endurance of physical pain, his struggle for purity and holiness, and assuredly also the fact that he belonged to the community of the 'Sons of God' – all this had made him mature enough for initiation.

'Until I entered into the sanctuaries of God' (73.17). This verse is the decisive passage in Psalm 73. Biblical criticism has puzzled a good deal over it. Scholars have wondered about the plural, the 'sanctuaries' of God, which would imply that it was not the temple which was meant – and yet it could only refer to the temple. It is our belief that the sentence becomes comprehensible when it is seen as a supersensible experience. We can understand the entry 'into the sanctuaries of God' only as one of those events where the 'wall' of the material world seems to open, and behind it a world is revealed which previously had been completely outside our consciousness. A world – indeed, worlds of divine life in various ranks and stages – 'the sanctuaries of God'. Actual entry into the temple and observation of the sacrificial ritual may have brought about this supersensible experience. The psalms occasionally point to this power of ritual to release supersensible vision; for the temple is the place 'where your honour dwells,' your *gloria,* your revelation of light.

A new light has been shed on the problems and questions of the one so sorely tried. He has a glimpse of things to come. He sees through the transitory nature of earthly existence. A life whose external conditions are fortunate and happy now becomes unimportant for him in view of the outcome. That an evil earthly life peters out into emptiness is henceforth deeply known by him. 'Like a dream when we awake, O Lord, when you rouse yourself, you make them worthless' (73:20).

Even the word 'awake' possesses here the peculiar colour of mystical experience. The earthly life formerly accepted as final, and taken seriously in a false way, is felt to be a dream from which one awakes into a real world. Without doubt, in the same mystical context of an awakening to higher consciousness the same expression occurs in the significant sentence of Psalm 17: 'I will see your face in righteousness; when I awake I will be satisfied with your likeness' (17:15). Even beyond the seeing of God's face the intuitive perception of the 'likeness' of God leads here to a being fed supernaturally, to a communion. The rare word used here, *temunah,* means the essential form, as it were the 'contour of the I' of God, to behold which was permitted to Moses alone (Nm 12:8). Only a most sublime 'awakening' can lead to such an experience.

After this awakening – to turn back again to Psalm 73 – the psalmist looks back at his earthly nature as it has been hitherto, seeing it from outside and feeling deeply its incompatibility with the divine. 'I was a fool without knowledge; I was like a beast before you' (73:22). It now becomes clear to the psalmist that his earlier, earthbound efforts to think remained powerless to grasp divine reality. He looks back at his uninitiated human state as something still subhuman, like an animal.

II

Only now does the psalm rise to the heights of the words quoted at the beginning. If we reproduce the Hebrew text now with our fresh understanding, it reads somewhat as follows:

> My I – for ever with you!
>> You have grasped my right hand.
> You guide me with your counsel,
>> and one day you take me into your glory.
> Who else in the heavens is the creative archetype of my I?
>> And united with you I freely stand in what is earthly.
> Then may my body pass away, and my soul also.
>> For evermore God is the rock-foundation of my heart and
>>> my fate. (73:23–26)

These verses are so unusual because they are the fruit of an initiation, a gift from the world of the 'divine sanctuaries'.

The sentence, 'I was like a beast before you,' had preceded them. Now the psalmist feels himself for the first time in his true selfhood, as a real human being. He knows that his true I is henceforth united indissolubly with God. 'My I – for ever with you!' This union with God is demonstrated in three stages. They are the grasping of the hand, wise guidance, fulfilment.

The grasping of the hand: there are Egyptian depictions of the Sun God, where the ends of the sunrays are hands. In this reference to the divine hand which grasps our hand we should not see a primitive anthropomorphism but rather consider that man is 'theomorphic', that divine secrets are revealed in the human form. This is especially the case in the marvel of the human hand. That God grasps our right hand is not accidental. We are more conscious and awake on the right side than on the left. We must find contact with God through our conscious personality.

Guidance: that grasping of the hand becomes wise guidance. The psalmist is no longer restless about his difficult destiny. An initiation does not mean that the path of life ceases to be thorny, but we can now see it in another light. The initiate trusts in the divine guidance, which has led him to his destiny with a wisdom that surpasses all human understanding.

Fulfilment: the distant aim is seen from afar – 'one day'. The original text here speaks quite simply and concisely of a taking – 'you take me'. To take is used in the same sense in the short oracular sentence in Genesis about Enoch (Gn 5:24). Because he 'walked with God', God 'took' him.

God released human beings once from their own original substance and set them free to lead an independent life. But this releasing and setting free is for the sake of union again at a higher stage. They must so shape their freedom that one day they stand with their independence not without but within the Godhead. God lets human beings go free in order to take them back again in love into his kingdom. When some day in the far future they will be utterly permeated with Christ, then in their whole being of spirit, soul and body they will be 'membered' into the heavens. This ascent into heaven was prophetically prefigured in the far past in the figure of Enoch. In monumental words Genesis says of him that God 'took' him.

There is not only the communion in which we take God into ourselves, but some day when evolution has come to an end there is to be a communion in which human beings will be received into God.

This will come about when they have utterly and entirely become ripe for eternity, when they can be received by the world of their origin without loss of substance through the survival of earthly remainders and residue. What Psalm 73 expresses as a kind of presentiment is this great 'reception' that awaits human beings. The Hebrew *kabhod* points to the *gloria,* the light of transfiguration into which human beings enter when they are received.

Psalm 49 is another parallel. First comes the impressive description of the godless in *Sheol,* in the world of the shades (*Hades* for the Greeks). 'Death will shepherd them'; and then in contrast to this, the psalm continues: 'But God will redeem my soul from the hand of Sheol; for he will take me' (49:14f). Apart from Psalm 16, which we shall still consider (in Chapter 40), Psalm 73 and Psalm 49 contain the only passages in the psalms which venture to say with such boldness that human beings shall continue to live throughout eternity.

The words, 'Whom have I in heaven but you? And there is nothing on earth that I desire beside you' are slightly different in the original Hebrew. They read, literally, 'Who to me in the heavens? And with you I desire nothing on earth.' The psalmist finds himself in the higher world, looks round on all sides and seeks among the hosts of spirits and their spheres for his special spiritual home. There in the higher worlds in creative activity the divine archetypes of the crystals, the plants, the animals are to be found. But where do human beings find the region which for them has a corresponding archetypal significance? Where is their own, their human heavenly prototype? 'Who to me in the heavens?' The dative 'to me' points simply and expressively to the nature of this divine being who is sought by human beings and who is inclined to them and allied with them. So we can translate it, 'Who else but you, the God of my I AM, is the creative archetype of my human nature?'

'There is nothing on earth that I desire beside you,' means I am no longer dependent on the terrestrial, I feel myself sovereign above earthly things. I am then no longer bound to the earth through possession and desire, but relate to the earth freely as a king. The original text does not have the flavour of turning away from the earth in heavenly bliss. Seeking God without taking account of the earth ultimately leads to an egotistical religion that is not really Christian. It is refreshing then to see that the original does not imply a lack of interest in the world, but an inner overcoming of dependence on earthly things. We can translate it as, 'united with you I freely stand in what is earthly.'

To have become independent of earthly things leads the psalmist out of the problem which embittered his former life when he still took the perishable world for the final reality and was a 'beast before God'. The freedom which has been gained is shown in the cry, 'my flesh and my soul may fail'. Inner pre-eminence lies in this 'may fail'. Linked with the God of his humanity he can look calmly on the passing away of his earthly bodily nature.

But we are concerned here not only with the 'flesh' but also with the heart. The following line, however, shows that the heart that 'may fail' is not the inmost core of the human being. 'God is the strength of my heart and my portion forever.' Only the mortal heart passes away and the life of the soul in so far as it is bound to the earthly body and is affected by the ups and downs of the bodily nature. The soul life bound to the transitory body will pass and its passing away should be borne with equanimity. The psalmist knows through his awakening that our relation to God must be anchored much deeper than in the fluctuating and changing of our daily emotions. There is a more solid anchor, independent of recurring moods. There are situations in life where people 'lose their nerve', where their emotional life is overwhelmed by catastrophic events. As Psalm 42 suggested to us, human beings must be able to stand outside these moods, these doubts and depressions, at least with part of their self. If they have found this 'outside' basis they know that though they may not always be immediately successful, they are nevertheless on the way to controlling their disturbed emotions.

The transitory nature of our body, its becoming ill and old, and hence, too, the transitory nature of a considerable part of our feelings, must all be regarded with equanimity, in view of the eternal significance of human beings.

In spite of his great experience of God, the psalmist realises that he must yet pass through deep waters. But he is no longer fettered to the world of appearances. 'God is the rock of my heart and my portion in eternity'. Here the 'heart' is not the transitory seat of passing emotions but the immortal heart, through whose powers of faith human beings find their firm foundation on the eternal rock of God. 'And my portion' – the allotted share of human life is to be God himself. Those who can speak like this have become free of fears and anxieties, heedless of whether they have their due share of earthly life, of whether life allots them the amount of good fortune, comfort and satisfaction that they think they are entitled to have. In the past God said to Abraham, 'I myself am your exceedingly great reward' (Gn 15:1). Ultimately, the value of life consists in the 'divine portion' which we carry away as our life's fruit. Anything else, joys or sorrows, pass away.

Finally, of all the problems there remains for the psalm only this one question – nearness to God or distance from God.

> For behold, those who are far from you shall perish.
> > You give non-existence to those who break the covenant with you.

It is not a revengeful act of an offended God that is at work here, rather a kind of higher law of nature taking effect. Those who give up their relation to God deliver themselves up of their own accord to a condition of nothingness.

> And I – nearness to God is my good.

The nearness of God is *the* good, the value of all values.

In this concluding verse the name of Yahweh* occurs for the first and only time in this psalm, this time intensified by the addition of *Adon* (*Kyrios* in Greek), Lord.

> I have taken my refuge with the Kyrios, the God of the I AM.

Who belongs to me in the heavens? Where is the divine background whence the true human being can proceed? The *Adon Yahweh*, the Kyrios, the God of the I AM, in truth is the God of human being.

---

* Ths sacred, unutterable name of God is usually translated as LORD (in small capital letters).

Psalm 73:23–28

²³ *My I – for ever with you!*
  You have grasped my right hand.
²⁴ *You guide me with your counsel,*
  and one day you take me into your glory.
²⁵ *Who else in the heavens is the creative archetype of my I?*
  And united with you I freely stand in what is earthly.
²⁶ *Then may my body pass away, and my soul also.*
  For evermore God is the rock-foundation of my heart and
    my fate.

²⁷ *For behold, those who are far from you shall perish.*
  You give non-existence to those who break the covenant
    with you.
²⁸ *And I – nearness to God is my good.*
  I have taken my refuge with the Kyrios,
  the God of the I AM.

39

THE PASSION PSALM OF THE REDEEMER

PSALM 22

'My God, my God, why have you forsaken me?' (Mt 27:46, Mk 15:34). With this cry, tragically familiar from the story of the passion, Psalm 22 begins in the depths of desolation. But it leads in the end to a glory all the more radiant. The psalm not only embraces death, but also resurrection and glorification.

The religious experience of a devout person of the Old Testament has been carried to such depths that it becomes archetypal. Christianity has always rightly regarded this psalm as an inspired anticipation of the passion and the glorification of Christ.

I

> My God, my God, why have you forsaken me?
>   So far away from helping me and the words of my
>   groaning?
> My God, I call to you in the day time, but you do not answer,
>   and by night I am not silent.

The psalmist who voices this cry feels the existence of God most strongly. He senses his reality, not only as that of a universal God, but as deeply belonging to himself: 'My God,' or 'You being of God in whom my innermost I rests.' But that original and natural intimate personal relationship has been lost. The soul faces an incomprehensible separation from this divine being to whom it belongs. Without the familiar presence, which in the past has been around and above them, human beings feel painfully incomplete. Left to themselves they taste bitter loneliness.

In modern times we have become accustomed to this loneliness. We accept it almost as a natural condition. We know no better. We fail to realise that our loneliness is due to being cut off from something higher which really belongs to us. So we begin to question the meaning of life. It appears senseless. At the bottom of this is a sense of loss; but no-one knows what is actually lost. The psalmist, however, does know. But he is faced with the mysterious fact that this higher divine being who sends his rays from above into the soul, and who gives fullness and depth to human life, can no longer be felt as present within him.

Try as he will, the psalmist can no longer re-establish the broken link. His cry no longer penetrates; the distance has become too great. All the same, the cry uttered from the depths of his heart is not entirely in vain. Although it cannot bridge the gulf it does recall the reassuring memory: it has not always been like this; the divine had not yet vanished from among our ancestors. All myths and sacred stories of a better, golden past witness to the original community between God and human beings. The psalmist recalls first his own ancestors. But they are at the same time the link with that universal past. The comforting picture of the ancient community of worshippers, with whom the Godhead communicated in real presence stands before his mind's eye. When the sacred hymns of old were chanted, the sounds formed a throne for God.

> Yet you are the holy one,
>   abiding in the hymns of praise of Israel.
> In you our fathers trusted;
>   they trusted, and you came to help them.
> To you they cried, and were rescued;
>   in you they trusted and were not disappointed.

II

However, this memory of the past provides only passing comfort. The glories of history are very little help in the present distress. A strident discord breaks through the echo of the ancient hymns: 'But I!' In contrast

Psalm 22

My God, my God, why have you forsaken me?
  So far away from helping me and the words of my
    groaning?
² *My God, I call to you in the day time, but you do not answer,*
  and by night I am not silent.

³ *Yet you are the holy one,*
  abiding in the hymns of praise of Israel.
⁴ *In you our fathers trusted;*
  they trusted, and you came to help them.
⁵ *To you they cried, and were rescued;*
  in you they trusted and were not disappointed.

⁶ *But I! – a worm, no man!*
  a reproach to human beings, despised by people.
⁷ *All who see me mock me;*
  mouthing insults, they shake their heads:
⁸ *'He trusts in the LORD; let him save him*
  if he delights in him.'

⁹ *Yet you drew me from the womb;*
  you made me trust in you at my mother's breast.
¹⁰ *On you I was cast from birth,*
  from my mother's womb you are my God.

¹¹ *Do not become distant from me,*
  for anguish is near, and there is none to help.
¹² *Many bulls are all around me.*
  Strong bulls of Bashan surround me;
¹³ *with gaping jaws lions*
  rage and roar.

¹⁴ *I am spilt like water,*
  and all my bones are out of place;
my heart is like wax;
  it is melted within me;
¹⁵ *my strength is dried up like a potsherd,*
  and my tongue sticks to my jaws;
  and you have laid me in the dust of death.

¹⁶ *A pack of hounds has surrounded me;*
  the adversaries encircle me;

39. THE PASSION PSALM OF THE REDEEMER

they have pierced my hands and feet –
¹⁷ I can count all my bones –
they stare and gloat over me;
¹⁸ they divide my garments among them,
   and for my clothing they cast lots.

¹⁹ But you, O Lord, do not be far from me.
   My strength, hasten to help me!
²⁰ Deliver my soul from the sword,
   my I-am-bearing soul from the hound!
²¹ Save me from the mouth of the lion!
   And from the horns of the bulls.

²² I will proclaim your name to my brothers;
   in the midst of the congregation I will sing your praise:
²³ You who fear the Lord, praise him!
   All you offspring of Jacob, glorify him!
   Stand in awe of him, all you offspring of Israel!
²⁴ For he has not despised or abhorred the poverty of the poor,
   nor has he hidden his face from him, but heard his cry to him.
²⁵ My praise of you shall arise in the great assembly.

   My vows I will perform before those who fear him.
²⁶ The poor shall eat and be satisfied;
   those who seek him shall praise the Lord!
   May your heart live forever!

²⁷ All the ends of the earth shall remember and turn to the Lord,
   and all the families of nations shall worship before your countenance.
²⁸ For the kingship belongs to the Lord,
   He rules among the nations.
²⁹ Him shall they worship who rest in the earth,
   before him shall bow all who go down to the dust,
   for him my soul shall live.
³⁰ Posterity shall serve him.
   The Lord shall be proclaimed to the coming generations;
³¹ they will proclaim his righteousness to people yet unborn.
   For he has done the deed.

to these past times the pain of being left alone on the earth is felt all the more poignantly. The overshadowing I of God has withdrawn beyond reach. And since human beings are no longer sustained from above, they are in danger of drifting into the subhuman. Their very essential nature is threatened. While the body still preserves its noble form, the inner spirit which ensouls this body fails to maintain true humanity. As Mephistopheles says when Faust dies, 'Here is the little soul, Psyche with her wings – tear out the wings and an ugly worm is left.'

> But I! – a worm, no man!
> a reproach to human beings, despised by people.

The terror caused by the distorted picture of the human being turns into an experience of being despised. Very likely the psalmist remembers the sneer of actual enemies. But these adversaries who hate him become a parable. So does he who is mocked. He is no longer just anybody who has enemies; he is the archetypal human being. The adversaries are the powers of evil, trying with satanic frenzy to tread underfoot the divine image of the human being. They are bent upon destroying the life-work of the gods: the human being. And since humanity has succumbed to the Fall, there is no lack of points of attack, nor of causes for hellish triumphs.

> All who see me mock me;
> mouthing insults, they shake their heads:
> 'He trusts in the LORD; let him save him
> if he delights in him.'

The Gospel of Matthew's report of the passion quotes these lines literally (27:43). But it is rather primitive to think that Matthew simply took over his report from this psalm. On the contrary, the psalm is an anticipation and prevision of Golgotha, when Christ in his mercy unites himself with the earthly human being, and surrenders himself to the derision and mockery of his adversaries. No doubt the style of Matthew's account has been influenced by the psalm, but in reality the psalm anticipated the future act of Golgotha.

This second wave of pain is stilled not by help from the distant past, but by a recollection of childhood. Each human being is still carried at the beginning of earthly life by the powers of God, just as humanity as a whole was borne in the arms of God at the beginning of creation. In the womb and at their mother's breast, the child is still deeply linked in complete naturalness with the divine forces of life.

> Yet you drew me from the womb;
> > you made me trust in you at my mother's breast.
> On you I was cast from birth,
> > from my mother's womb you are my God.

III

However, even this comfort which comes from the recollection of childhood is not equal to the heavy burden which is still to be put upon human beings. A third wave of pain approaches. It rises still higher than those which have gone before. It carries pain to the utmost extremity,-and thereby leads to the great turning point.

> Do not become distant from me,
> > for anguish is near, and there is none to help.
> Many bulls are all around me.
> > Strong bulls of Bashan surround me;
> with gaping jaws lions
> > rage and roar.

The 'anguish' announces a new terror. The forms of wild animals which assail humans are nightmarish visions. They are not the bull and lion of Ezekiel's vision belonging to the realm of the Cherubim. They are caricatures, distorted reflections in the nether world. In the vision of Ezekiel, bull and lion are servants of the Son of God and carry his throne. Here in the psalm they are pictures of the forces of the soul which cut themselves off in egocentric isolation. They do not serve a higher being; they turn against human beings with intent to destroy them.

From the picture of soul forces turning into beasts, the psalm proceeds to the region of the etheric forces of life. These too are affected by destruction. The water of life has run dry in the human being deserted by God. The material body is no longer adequately sustained by the forces of life. It dries up and crumbles. The bones, which in the course of evolution have gradually solidified out of the fluid and vitalising substance of life, are used as a picture to describe the dead materials which fall as sediment out of the original totality of life, and become subject to gravity. 'All my bones are out of place.' The earthly body, seized by the powers of death, deserted by life, drops away as a corpse and disintegrates.

> I am spilt like water,
>   and all my bones are out of place;
> my heart is like wax;
>   it is melted within me;
> my strength is dried up like a potsherd,
>   and my tongue sticks to my jaws;
>   and you have laid me in the dust of death.

The sensation of dying is followed by horrible spectres which rise from the underworld. Hades, the valley of the shadow of death, approaches in the picture of a pack of attacking hounds. Wild dogs falling upon a carcass, here they become the image of the forces of the underworld which threaten those souls after death that have lost their divine nature. The hound of hell in the myth of Hercules is a reality.

The sufferer sees his hands and feet transfixed. He 'can count all his bones'. He perceives himself crucified. It was a hasty conclusion on the part of certain theological critics when they tried to explain the wounds of Christ in terms of Psalm 22. The psalmist felt the stigmata in his own hands and feet and his personal suffering became a prophetic eye which beheld the future passion of the Redeemer. Christ suffered the stigmata in historical reality, as the whole passion of Golgotha is both history and mysterious super-history.

In no other form of execution is the human skeleton so emphasised as in crucifixion. The basic structure of the human form is revealed on the cross, agonisingly stretched. The sufferer on the cross has this basic structure thrust painfully into his consciousness, 'he can count all his bones'. Once again the psalm connects 'bones' and 'death'.

> A pack of hounds has surrounded me;
>   the adversaries encircle me;
> they have pierced my hands and feet –
>   I can count all my bones –
> they stare and gloat over me;
> they divide my garments among them,
>   and for my clothing they cast lots.

While the victim on the cross hears again the triumphant jeers of his enemies, he must even witness how they divide his raiment among themselves. A sensation of being finished and done with: the protective covering which has almost been part of his own being passes through strange and hostile hands. The 'liquidation' of the human being is anticipated in the psalm in a nightmarish vision. The subtle veils of the human being, woven of life and soul – these are the objects of lust of the evil one. Thus the third wave of suffering, unmitigated by any comfort, has reached its climax. From this ultimate anguish of death the bitter cry for help rings out:

> But you, O Lord, do not be far from me.
>   My strength, hasten to help me!
> Deliver my soul from the sword,
>   my I-am-bearing soul from the hound!
> Save me from the mouth of the lion!
>   And from the horns of the bulls.

The 'sword' too is a significant picture. In death the soul is severed from the body; the disembodied soul too has to face further painful separations. On earth the soul bore a varied mixture of higher and lower elements. After death it must painfully discard everything that cannot live in a higher world.

The Hebrew word *yechidah,* meaning 'the one and only', is here translated as the 'I-am-bearing soul'. The word used in the Kabbalah as the technical term for the highest faculty of the human soul in which the spiritual self, the I, rules supreme and which gives rise to unity and harmonious integration of the personality. This innermost centre is threatened by the powers of the underworld, which appear again in the image of the hound of hell.

Finally, the desperate cry from one threatened by death changes suddenly into the triumphant shout of the Redeemed.

IV

> I will proclaim your name to my brothers;
>> in the midst of the congregation I will sing your praise:

We are not told in what form the rescue came. The words of the psalm have only a pause, as it were, between the agony of death and the rescue. Only at the end do we find a hint of what is passed over here in silence. For the psalm ends with the words 'For he has done the deed.' Read in the light of the fulfilment in Christ, the pause implies the deed of Easter.

This third time, when the wave of pain has grown into the agony of death, neither the hymns of the forefathers nor the recollection of childhood can bring comfort. Only a new, unheard of, divine deed can counteract the doom of death. What we now know as the death and resurrection of the Son of God is hidden in the twilight of this prophetic psalm in oracular words: 'For he has done the deed' (in the original, only *ki asah,* 'for he did').

In the enthusiastic description of his redemption, the psalmist assumes more and more the role of the prophet. Just as Christ asked Mary Magdalene to proclaim the resurrection to his 'brothers', so Psalm 22 offers the message of joy to all humanity. The 'great assembly' is like a prophecy of the Christian Church. While in the beginning the psalm spoke of the fathers, now it speaks of the brothers.

> You who fear the LORD, praise him!
>> All you offspring of Jacob, glorify him!
>> Stand in awe of him, all you offspring of Israel!
> For he has not despised or abhorred the poverty of the poor,
>> nor has he hidden his face from him, but heard his cry to him.
> My praise of you shall arise in the great assembly.

God has identified with human beings and earthly poverty. In his joy and gratitude the psalmist promises to fulfil a vow. He invites everyone to the great sacrificial meal which, like a communion, follows the thanksgiving offering in the temple. In this picture, taken from Old Testament ritual, the sacred meal of Christ is foreshadowed, which will eventually bring the deed of redemption to all human beings. The eucharistic spirit is beautifully expressed in the wonderful sentence, 'Your heart shall live for ever'.

> My vows I will perform before those who fear him.
> The poor shall eat and be satisfied;
> > those who seek him shall praise the LORD!
> May your heart live forever!

The dynamic redemption extends further and further. The pious worshipper of the Old Testament breaks through the limitations of his Hebrew nation and reaches out to universal humanity. His poetic sentences sound like a promise of Pentecost.

The whole of humanity includes also those who have died. Eventually the vision reaches out even to them, and beyond them to the unborn souls, to the coming generations.

The psalm began with the cry 'Why have you forsaken me?' Over the second part, which praises the redemption, there is this unspoken motto: 'How you have glorified me!'

> All the ends of the earth shall remember and turn to the LORD,
> > and all the families of nations shall worship before your countenance.
> For the kingship belongs to the LORD,
> > He rules among the nations.
> Him shall they worship who rest in the earth,*
> > before him shall bow all who go down to the dust,
> > for him my soul shall live.
> Posterity shall serve him.
> > The Lord shall be proclaimed to the coming generations;
> > they will proclaim his righteousness to people yet unborn.
> > FOR HE HAS DONE THE DEED.

---

* The Hebrew of this verse is unclear. The translation follows the Greek Septuagint.

40

THE WAY OF LIFE

PSALM 16

Psalm 16 plays a special part in the history of Christianity. Together with two other quotations from the Old Testament it is quoted in Peter's address at Pentecost, the very first Christian sermon. The pouring out of the Holy Spirit released, for the first time, the power to proclaim publicly the historic deeds of Christ, the Mystery of Golgotha.

In this very first Christian message, Peter refers to three passages from the Old Testament, corresponding to the three distinct parts of his address, which are marked by the manner in which he addresses his hearers, and which expand step by step to universal humanity. 'Fellow Jews and all you who live in Jerusalem' – 'Fellow Israelites' – 'People, brothers' (Ac 2:14, 22, 29).

In the first part (2:14–21), Peter presents the outpouring of the Spirit as the fulfilment of the prophecy of Joel. In this context he speaks to begin with only of the Spirit and its effects. But in the last verse of the first part, the call upon the Kyrios, the Lord, represents the passing over to the second part (2:22–28), in which the world of the Son is described, the incarnation of Christ in Jesus of Nazareth, his death and resurrection. The third part (2:29–36), proceeds from the resurrection to the sitting at the right hand of the Father. Here Peter quotes the Melchizedek Psalm 110 ('The LORD said to my Lord, sit at my right hand') as a support for the understanding of his message. This third part leads into the sphere of God the Father sitting on his throne of majesty. It is significant that this very first Christian sermon is informed by the mystery of the Trinity.

The second part, which proclaims the fundamental mystery of death and resurrection, that is, the mystery of the Son, is supported by

Psalm 16

Preserve me, O God; I take my refuge in you.
² I said to the Lord, 'You are my Lord;
  I know of no good apart from you.'
³ He finds his glory in the saints of the earth,
  in whom all his delight rests.
⁴ The sorrows of those who run after the other shall multiply;
  their blood offerings I will not offer.
  I will not take their names on my lips.
⁵ The Lord is my chosen lot and my cup;
  you hold my lot.
⁶ The portions have fallen to me in pleasant places;
  No fairer lot could I win.
⁷ I will praise the Lord who gives me counsel;
  as in the night also my inmost life instructs me.
⁸ I see the Lord always before me;
  because he is at my right hand, I shall not be shaken.
⁹ Therefore my heart is glad,
  and my light-soul rejoices;
  my flesh also dwells in trust.
¹⁰ For you will not abandon my soul in Sheol,
  you will not allow your faithful servant to see corruption.
¹¹ You will make known to me the way of life,
  in your presence is fulness of joy,
  at your right hand is fulness of grace forevermore.

Psalm 16. Peter is communicating to his hearers the incredible fact of his message, and in order to help their understanding he quotes Psalm 16: 'For David says concerning him ...' (2:25).

According to Luke, the author of Acts, the risen Christ himself revealed to his disciples the truth of the Scriptures in his teaching during the forty days after Easter (Lk 24:44). Apart from Moses and the prophets, Luke specifically mentions the psalms in this context. We may assume that after these instructions the time-honoured sacred texts appeared to the disciples in a new light, and that these teachings of the Risen Christ inspired also Peter's Pentecostal address. We are justified therefore in regarding the original Hebrew text as potentially capable of development, open for future content beyond that of which its inspired author may have been conscious.

> Preserve me, O God; I take my refuge in you.
> I said to the Lord, 'You are my Lord;
>   I know of no good apart from you.'

This introduction is delicately coloured by the mystery of the Trinity. To start with, a reference to being preserved, to taking one's refuge – an experience of the Father. The psalm speaks of the preservation of human existence, which is threatened from all sides and left in cold isolation. It is the Ground of the World from which all preservation, all maintaining, proceeds.

But the psalm does not stop there. It is not content with preservation in the Father. The psalmist knows that man is not meant to be only 'child', but also to be 'son'. Thus he approaches God with a free act of loyalty. While the seeking for refuge was prompted by a kind of instinct of a higher order, the conscious relationship to God of the adult human being expresses itself in a definite 'word'. 'I said to the Lord, "You are my Lord".' The human being as spiritual personality meets God face to face and freely decides to follow him – a Son experience. This saying is a deed proceeding from the core of one's being, a free vow. 'You are my Lord,' in other words, 'You shall give direction to my being.'

The third sentence, 'I know of no good apart from you,' has again a different character. It implies a mental act which goes beyond standing face to face. Human consciousness surveys the whole range of values and expresses a judgment, saying, 'I know of no good apart from you.' The worth of God whom the psalmist considers as his higher self, as lord, is measured in comparison with other 'goods', and the result is: the Kyrios, the bearer of the higher self, is not only the highest good, *summum bonum,* but *the* Good. All other 'goods' deserve their name only inasmuch as they are related to this Kyrios. In these three steps: seeking refuge, free dedication, conscious judgment, we may discern the path from the Father to the Son and finally to the Spirit.

> He finds his glory in the saints of the earth,
>   in whom all his delight rests.

This is how the somewhat uncertain words of the original text may have to be read. 'He finds his glory in the saints of the earth.' We hear a faint echo of the High Priestly Prayer, 'in them I have been glorified' (Jn 17:10). The early Christians adopted the name of 'saints' although they were conscious of their human imperfections. They expressed thereby the conviction that they were touched and worked through by powers of salvation.

'In whom all his delight rests.' Again we are reminded of a great fulfilment of this saying in the New Testament, 'This is my beloved Son, in whom I am well pleased' – 'in whom I find the true reflection of my own being' – 'in whom I am truly revealed'. But in contrast to the human beings who walk the way of salvation and sanctification there is also a negative choice.

> The sorrows of those who run after the other shall multiply;
>   their blood offerings I will not offer.
>   I will not take their names on my lips.

These are the people who do not open themselves to their higher beings, but surrender themselves to demonic powers. In these demonic powers the Adversary is active, 'the other One'.

The worship of heathen Gods was a reality. Paul wrote to the Corinthians, 'You cannot drink the cup of the Lord and the cup of demons' (1Cor 10:21). In the decadent cults of antiquity a definite relationship with demons was achieved. The early Christian martyrs were rightly convinced that in making the required sacrifices they would feed the demons. For this reason they refused adamantly to do so.

However, the words of the psalm are not out of date or merely of historic interest because those ancient sacrifices no longer exist; devils and demons are a reality even today. We can feed them without special ceremony and drink from their cup. Each evil impulse of soul feeds evil spirits and makes them stronger. They settle like flies on dirt. Our blood, which registers the finest movements of our soul, is in reality the special fluid at which the devil aims. Anyone who is inwardly open to evil concedes control over their blood to those powers who oppose God. Whether knowingly or not, they make a blood sacrifice.

'I will not take their names on my lips.' This is still a valid truth today, although those rites no longer exist in which the names of demonic beings are recited in magic rituals. Evil words summon bad spirits. Swearing is in full reality a negative ritual. Not to recognise this fact is an unpardonable foolishness for people today. The psalm now takes a positive turn.

> The LORD is my chosen lot and my cup;
>   you hold my lot.
> The portions have fallen to me in pleasant places;
>   No fairer lot could I win.

In Psalm 116:13 it is said 'I will lift up the cup of salvation and call upon the name of the LORD'. This verse has been incorporated in the liturgy of the mass. It is the opposite to the sacrifice of blood and the invocation in the service of the demons.

The picture referring to 'chosen lot' is derived from the distribution of land. This distribution of land is in itself a parable. A devout person may want to settle and make themselves at home in that spiritual region where God sustains and shelters them. Then they are content with their 'lot', even if they feel that they do not have a fair share of earthly goods. Then, after the reference to the cup, the psalmist passes from the descriptive language of the third person to the direct address of the second person.

> I will praise the LORD who gives me counsel;
>   as in the night also my inmost life instructs me.

God 'gives counsel' to him, has shared his inspiration with him. At night his inmost life responds with gratitude and praise. The Hebrew word *kilyah* literally means 'kidneys'. The Old Testament frequently refers to the kidneys as the seat of the emotions. The organs hidden in the interior of the body were generally regarded as the vehicles of the inward life of the soul. In the New Testament, too, the Greek word *splangchna,* literally 'bowels' (in popular language, 'innards') signify the inwardness of soul. From this inwardness the voice of conscience is heard during the night and awakens a feeling of gratitude towards the Lord of Destiny.

Now we have reached the point where the quotation occurs which Peter uses in his Pentecostal address:

> I see the LORD always before me;
>   because he is at my right hand, I shall not be shaken.

Hitherto the psalm has spoken of turning towards God. Now it proceeds to a constant walking in the sight of God. The expression 'see the LORD always before me' refers more to a conscious mental relationship to God; the other picture of having God 'at one's right hand' refers more to the union with God through the will. The sense of the continued divine presence protects us against being moved, upset or shaken. In other words, it guarantees the solid coherence of the personality. From this deepened link with God a totally new experience of life arises.

> Therefore my heart is glad,
>   and my light-soul rejoices;
>   my flesh also dwells in trust.

The three steps contained in this verse turn the experience inside out. It begins with the heart as the centre, and reaches outwards as far as the flesh, the physical body. Between the two, the mysterious word occurs which is variously translated – my glory, my tongue, my whole being. It is *kabhod* which is also used in Psalm 8 as the Hebrew counterpart for *gloria* and *doxa*. 'My glory rejoices.' What can this mean?

In the Greek text of the address of Peter in Acts, the version of the Septuagint, the Greek translation of the Old Testament is followed. It by-passes the difficulty simply by replacing *kabhod* with 'tongue': 'My tongue was glad'. Obviously the Hebrew word was no longer understood in this context even at the time when the Old Testament translation was made in Alexandria in the third century BC. Modern translators sometimes render the phrase as 'whole being' because they assume that some such phrase must be intended.

A comparison with similar passages may be helpful. In Psalm 57:8 and 108:1 and 2 it says, 'Awake, my glory; awake, O harp and lyre.'

Kabhod is *gloria* and is normally used to express the revealing radiance or radiant revelation of God. But the human being, too, has a radiance, which surrounds the body as a subtle suprasensory part. People are not always conscious of this light which radiates from them. In their pedestrian everyday consciousness they know nothing of their subtle etheric and astral veils. It is through music that his consciousness can be awakened to these subtle organisms. Thus the awakening of harp and lyre is at the same time the awakening of the consciousness of glory. It is not unlikely that the phrase which follows, 'I will awaken the dawn' (Ps 57:8, 108:2) points to a mystical experience. In the language of mysticism, the early dawn (aurora) has always been the image of an inward process, from the Rishis of the Vedas, who 'awakened the dawn of Ushas with potent spells,' to Jakob Böhme's *Aurora, Dawn of the Day in the East.*

A further instructive passage is Genesis 49:6. The dying Patriarch Jacob blesses his sons. To Simeon and Levi, whose evil deed at Shechem he recalls, he says, 'Let my soul come not into their council; O my glory [*kabhod*] be not joined in their company.' This is said at the moment of death. Jacob is no longer thinking of a physical appearance in the assembly of his sons. He is considering the time which follows after his death when he will no longer be present in the body among his sons but will continue to influence them spiritually. When they hold council, when they assemble in solemn manner as the sons of their father, then, according to the wisdom of ancient days, the dead can be among them, not in their physical body, but in an etheric form of soul existence, in the subtle light-organism of 'glory'.

In Psalm 16, *gloria* is placed between 'heart' and 'flesh', between the core of the personality and the physical body. It can then only refer to a suprasensory reality, which was no longer accessible to the consciousness of later times. It is in the heart of human beings that the divine joy arises. In his Farewell Discourse Christ says, 'Your heart will rejoice' (Jn 16:22).

From this centre the divine joy passes over into the subtle etheric and astral organism of *gloria* – 'My light-soul rejoices' – and from there into the physical body. What has its beginning in the human inwardness eventually takes hold also of the external being. The ways of God end in the body. 'My flesh also dwells in trust'. If the impressions of the communion with God are strong and lasting, eventually not only the subtle supersensory organism, but even the physical body is affected. Other psalms also speak of such comprehensive impressions of God. 'My soul thirsts for you; my flesh faints for need of you in a land dry and parched' (Ps 63:1); 'My soul longs and even faints for the courts of the LORD; my heart, my whole body cries out in joy to God who is life itself' (Ps 84:2). Also the body shall be included in the redemption and transformation. 'My flesh also dwells in trust,' does not simply suggest that the devout person does not worry about physical well-being; it is much more an anticipation of the resurrection of the body, an expectation of that sensation which the early Christians possessed when they regarded communion as 'the medicine of immortality'.

Once again the psalm now uses the form of addressing God in person.

> For you will not abandon my soul in Sheol,
>   you will not allow your faithful servant to see corruption.

Hades, in Hebrew *Sheol,* in Greek *Hades, a-idēs* (not-seeing), is the darkness of the soul. In those days of antiquity, people still knew that death is not the end of everything; but they expected nothing but a dull and shadowy existence; a second-rate existence in an underworld which truly deserves its name. Souls had lost their native heavenly glory, their divine nature, and found themselves after death in an emaciated existence of dark shadows. A dramatic description of this is contained in the *Nekyia,* Book 11 of the *Odyssey*. These are not empty fantasies. Life after death lost its light according to the measure in which souls became absorbed in earthly existence and grew into self-centred personalities. Only Christ's descent into hell, his appearance among the dead, created a change. The Creed of The Christian Community says, 'In death he became the helper of the souls of the dead who had lost their divine nature.'

Once more we refer to Psalm 49. The souls appear like a herd which has no will: 'Like sheep they are appointed for Sheol; death is their shepherd. Death shall feed on them ... but God will redeem my soul from the power of Sheol' (Ps 49:14f).

Holy Saturday carried new light into the realm of the dead. The promise is fulfilled, 'You will not abandon my soul in Sheol.' On Easter Sunday the resurrection extends from the realm of the soul into the sphere of the body. The last enemy to be conquered is death. The reference to Sheol is followed by the sentence, 'You will not allow your faithful servant to see corruption.' Peter quotes this saying as having been fulfilled through the Resurrection of Christ. 'He [David] foresaw and spoke about the resurrection of the Christ' (Ac 2:31).

Although these are the decisive words which matter to Peter, he begins his quotation from Psalm 16 earlier, when he says 'For David says concerning him, "I saw the Lord always before me"' (Ac 2:25). Why should he first refer to these verses before he quotes the decisive sentence which speaks of the resurrection? These sentences provide the basis for the promised resurrection. The resurrection is presented not as an isolated, incomprehensible miracle, but as the final result of a gradual process, the fulfilment of a progressing evolution. It begins in the inmost centre with intimate decisions of the human heart. Then it proceeds to achieve an uninterrupted sense of the presence of God. The inward Easter radiates into the rhythm of the subtle organism, and reaches down at long last to the material body. Not only for purely external historic reasons is the resurrection described at the end of the gospels. The understanding of it can only be gained as the ripened fruit of an actual inward process of absorbing all the previous chapters, resulting in the conviction of Peter 'God raised him up, having loosed the birth pangs of death [literally in Greek] – because it was impossible that death should hold him' (Ac 2:24).

Peter continues his quotation. He adds the lines about the paths of life and speaks of the joy in the sight of God. 'Way', 'path' are old terms of the language of the mysteries describing the process of development which leads to initiation. It is significant that right at the beginning of the whole collection of psalms, Psalm 1 presents immediately the picture of both paths – the path to death and the path to life. Similarly, the Sermon on the Mount also speaks towards the end of the broad way that leads to destruction and the narrow way which leads to life. And Christ says himself 'I am the way'. He is initiation personified. When Peter quotes the sentence of the way, he emphasises once more that the resurrection of Christ is the organic fulfilment of a path and that it can become accessible to us also when we follow this path ourselves.

> You will make known to me the way of life,
>   in your presence is fulness of joy,
>   at your right hand is fulness of grace forevermore.

Thus the psalm ends in the Hebrew original with a threefold harmony. The path which leads unto life, rightly understood, includes the mystery of the passion and of the cross. The fulness of joy in the sight of God is an experience of Easter. The right hand refers to the Ascension. The fulness of grace is a foretaste of Pentecost. This last phrase, *na'iym* in Hebrew, means literally: lovelinesses, pleasantnesses, delights. The right hand of God is not a blind tyrannical will to power, although it signifies also the idea of omnipotence, but a will to create, to create beauty, loveliness in the sense of the Latin *gratia,* or the Greek *charis.* Both words mean grace and gracefulness at the same time – graceful beauty. The ascended Christ is, as the Creed says, 'the Lord of the heavenly forces upon earth, and lives as the fulfiller of the fatherly deeds of the Ground of the World.' He mediates the creative activity of the right hand of God and, being the steward of the creative forces, he sends the Holy Spirit whose outpouring is celebrated at Pentecost. Pentecost, or Whitsun, a lovely festival, is celebrated at the time in which nature shows its glorious array of colour in trees and flowers and all growing things, which are a visible parable of all that the Spirit will bring about on a higher level.

The Old Testament not only shows the severity of the divine law. Psalm 16 touches on the sphere of the Holy Spirit who graciously tends the flower gardens of a higher life. 'At your right hand is fulness of grace forevermore.'

The last word is 'forevermore', eternity. The psalm began with the prayer, 'Preserve me'. Now this preservation acquires its full and comprehensive meaning: to preserve human beings in their entirety and in the completeness of their constituent members from the threat of destruction.

The Creed of The Christian Community refers to those 'who are aware of the health-bringing power of the Christ', and it states that 'they may hope for the overcoming of the sickness of sin, for the continuance of man's being, and for the preservation of their life, destined for eternity.'

41

THE LORD IS MY SHEPHERD

PSALM 23

The psalm of the good shepherd is one of the best known. Its position in the psalter is significant. The whole psalter reflects the manifold shades of religious feeling in all the rainbow colours of the life of the soul. But this is especially true of the trio, Psalms 22, 23 and 24. Psalm 22, 'My God, my God, why have you forsaken me?' is the psalm of the suffering Messiah. It belongs to the dark side of the rainbow. The darkness of desolation grows into the blue of hope, and finally into the priestly purple of the act of sacrifice. The bright side of the rainbow shines in Psalm 24, in red and gold, the colours of resurrection and ascension. The Lord of Hosts, the king of glory, is to make his entry. The psalm of the shepherd lies between the darkness of Psalm 22 and the brightness of Psalm 24. Calm and blessing, peace and healing stream from it, as from the green in the centre of the rainbow.

In its brevity, Psalm 23 is a perfect work of art. Its short, concise sentences are all-embracing, something formulated for all time.

It belongs to the passages where the Old Testament approaches nearest to the sphere of Christ. In changed form it reappears in Chapter 10 of John's Gospel. 'I am the good shepherd.' We do the text no violence if we understand it in a Christian spirit. In doing so we put it in its proper light, as in fact so much in the Old Testament can only disclose its true depth and beauty in the light of the revelation of Christ.

> The LORD is my shepherd; I shall lack nothing.

> ### Psalm 23
>
> *The L<small>ORD</small> is my shepherd; I shall lack nothing.*
>   *² He sets me in green pastures.*
> *He leads me to fresh waters.*
>   *³ He restores my soul.*
> *He leads me in paths of righteousness*
>   *for his name's sake.*
>
> *⁴ Even though I walk through the valley of deep darkness,*
>   *I will fear no evil,*
> *for you are with me.*
>   *your rod and your staff, they comfort me.*
>
> *⁵ You prepare a table before me*
>   *in the presence of my enemies;*
> *you anoint my head with oil,*
>   *my cup runs overflows.*
> *⁶ Surely goodness and mercy shall follow me*
>   *all the days of my life,*
> *and I shall dwell in the house of the L<small>ORD</small> forever.*

A shepherd is one who bears in himself the spirit of a community. In ancient times the great leaders of humankind were called shepherds because they did not egotistically shut themselves up in a private life of their own ('Am I my brother's keeper?' Gn 4:9), but let the destiny of others live in their hearts. One who met such a shepherd felt, 'I am not coming to someone who is a stranger, but to myself. What is best and most individual in me is at home in him.'

The devout people of the Old Testament recognised their shepherd, the guardian of their eternal interests, in the God of the I AM. For this reason, Hermann Beckh translated the first verse of the psalm: 'He who speaks the I in me is my Shepherd'. This God, the true God of humankind, appears in Christ. 'I am the good shepherd.'

'I shall lack nothing.' In all 'lacking' the one great lack should be brought to our consciousness, the one from which our soul has suffered since the Fall, when it separated itself from the infinitely rich life of God. Speaking of the good shepherd, Christ says: 'I have come that they may have life and have it more abundantly' (Jn 10:10). The rest of the psalm now describes the work of the good shepherd in a classical series of pictures.

I

> He sets me in green pastures.

The soul has descended into earthly life in order to gain something there. When human beings move about on earth so that their earthly life provides nourishment for their eternal nature, then – in the profound picture-language of old – the earth becomes a 'pasture' for them. Christ too in the chapter on the shepherd, speaks of finding pasture (Jn 10:9). He leads us to the true 'abundance' of our earthly existence, where the earth offers something, where we are not starved in our deeper being. The 'green pastures' may also remind us of the green grass where Christ made the people sit down beside the lake for the feeding of the multitude.

If, however, the good powers do not guide our earthly way, the earth becomes for our eternal self a grey wilderness, a dead and stony desert. Then we are 'like a beast on a barren heath driven round and round by an evil spirit, while on all sides lies beautiful green pasture' (Goethe). These words really apply to all those who only find a materialistic relationship to the earth. That is indeed the paradox, that materialists in a deeper sense get nothing from matter, since for them it is devoid of spirit. They may live in magnificent luxury, yet their soul remains desolate and poor. When they die they have to leave all their riches behind, and over there they are truly 'poor souls'. Those who find the spirit in terrestrial things take their earthly experiences as a veritable possession with them into the realm of eternity.

II

> He leads me to fresh waters.

We in our temperate climate scarcely feel with what elemental force the sunbaked Orient feels the divine in water. Of course, on a hot summer day, after wandering long in burning heat and dust, we are also more open to the magic sound of the words 'water of life'; or we can experience something of its life-giving quality when we water thirsty flowers.

In the original text the 'fresh' water is water of 'rests' (plural), *menuchoth*. It refers to moments of rest in creation when what has been exhausted is built up again in the flow and stream of etheric forces.

III

> He restores my soul.

We know that our soul feels transformed near someone whom we revere, in whose presence we experience a kind of 'wellbeing'. So the nearness of the divine shepherd is felt through an inner enlivening. The soul is no longer a burden to itself, as happens when there is disharmony. The paralysing mood of depression disappears, and we regain our buoyancy and interest in life.

IV

> He leads me in paths of righteousness
>   for his name's sake.

The psalm, having moved from physical earth existence through the enlivening of etheric forces and the weaving of the soul, now reaches a fourth stage of human beings' inner core, the I.

'His name's sake.' God's name is I AM. In the human name God's name is to appear, in the I of human beings the I of God is to be manifest. The I name has been misused and dishonoured – the use of 'I' has come to express egotism, selfishness. Therefore we pray, 'Hallowed be your name.' Our goal is to bring to light in our self our true eternal being, and not some egotistic caricature. We are only on the way to this. We must go through our destiny for the sake of growing our true I, for the sake of the eternal name. 'He leads me in the paths of righteousness – for his name's sake.'

Our true eternal name by which God called us into existence has not yet been realised; it hovers over our earthly form. It is written in the heavens, it may be read in the stars, but not as yet upon our brow.

The star-names of all people dwell simultaneously in the name of Christ. We find ourselves when we find him, the shepherd. He leads us along the path of destiny in the light of eternal righteousness for his name's sake and thereby also ours. When the goal is reached he will write our star-name on our brow.

V

But our path of destiny 'for his name's sake' leads through the dark spheres of the Adversary, also when we are being led by the good shepherd – in fact, particularly then. No soul is spared the valley of darkness.

> Even though I walk through the valley of deep darkness,
>   I will fear no evil,
> for you are with me.
>   your rod and your staff, they comfort me.

The valley of deep darkness is a perfect picture for the material world, which prevents a free outlook and can become a nightmare. The soul whose home is in the bright realms of heaven must enter the narrow world of earthly time and space. It is gripped in a kind of claustrophobia. Born of light, the soul shivers in the sunless hollow, in the dark gorge. The cold breath of death reaches it, the hand of evil stretches out to seize it.

How many people have said these words about the dark valley in their prayers. Centuries, millennia, have poured their fears and anxieties into them.

Notice the subtle change shown in the text. From the third person ('he leads me') we pass over to the direct 'you' of the second person. While just before it read, 'He leads me in paths,' it now reads, 'for you are with me'. The reverent 'he' now becomes direct address, speaking face to face. Only when we enter into this more inward relation to the divine shepherd, can we overcome our anxieties and dangers. Only thus can we become fearless in the face of evil. The divine shepherd takes charge of our higher self.

Now the 'you' remains throughout the following verses. At the same time the psalm finally abandons the pictures of shepherd and herd and passes on to another series of images which are taken purely from human existence. The last picture relating to the shepherd is the staff. 'Your rod and your staff, they comfort me.' But just as the shepherd's staff of Moses after his calling became the powerful staff of God, the kingly sceptre, so here too in the psalm we may see in 'the comforting staff' more than the ordinary shepherd's crook. The outstretched arm is a gesture of command. If the hand grasps the staff the authoritative gesture becomes still more expressive. The Moses' staff awoke the fountain of life from the rock. Pictures in the catacombs show Christ performing the same miracle on Lazarus: his staff touches the chamber of death, and Lazarus comes forth to new life.

VI

> You prepare a table before me
> > in the presence of my enemies;
> you anoint my head with oil,
> > my cup runs overflows.

After the awakening of Lazarus, he took part in the solemn repast in Bethany: 'Lazarus was among those reclining at table with him' (Jn 12:2). Whoever has found the good shepherd as the higher being whose presence overcomes evil, is summoned to the feast of the Grail. 'He sits at the Lord's table.' But the Grail Castle is unthinkable without the opposing power of Klingsor. The feeding of the multitude by the lake takes place against the background of the death of John the Baptist, whose head lies on the charger. Judas, into whom Satan has entered, leaves the room of the Last Supper and goes out into the night. Thus also in the psalm the holy food is prepared 'in the presence of my enemies'. One cannot come to Christ without having also looked the Adversary and his hosts in the face. Without the conscious coming to grips with evil no higher development is possible.

The writer of Psalm 23 may quite well have only thought of his ordinary enemies. There is no need to set aside this obvious meaning. But our ordinary enemies are only the representatives of much more dangerous powers who can kill more than the body. We perceive the mystical depths of this psalm, which realises the fateful connection between the holy meal and the presence of the Adversary. St John's

Gospel says further of Lazarus who was at the table of Christ in Bethany, that they sought to kill him (12:10). Those who sought after his life represented the powers which would put to death the new seed of divine life.

'You anoint my head with oil.' One who partakes of the holy meal goes through a consecration, is anointed as priest and king. His head is made to serve the divine. *Christos,* the Greek translation of the Hebrew *Messiah,* means the 'anointed one'.

'My cup overflows.' To the holy meal, the mystery of the chalice is added. 'I am coming to you ... that they may have full measure of my joy' (Jn 17:13).

VII

> Surely goodness and mercy shall follow me
>   all the days of my life,
> and I shall dwell in the house of the LORD forever.

'Goodness' is the innermost force of existence itself. In 'mercy' this inner substance radiates outwards like the sun. Every human being has an invisible following which goes with them for evil or for good. The Book of Revelation says of the redeemed, 'for their deeds will follow them' (14:13).

Thoughts of eternity move through the soul of the psalmist. A presentiment of Easter shines through his words: 'I will dwell in the house of the LORD for ever'. Christians look towards the resurrection body that they are to receive, in which they will abide, dwell, survive, as in the true temple, in the house of the Lord. Human beings who are still slaves to the powers of sin must take leave of their body again and again in death. 'The servant does not remain in the house for ever' (Jn 8:35). Not until they are delivered through Christ from the sickness of sin can they dwell continuously in the resurrection body.

No doubt the psalmist means no more than a wish that it be granted him to dwell in the temple of the Lord 'to the end of his days'. We find a similar wish expressed in Psalm 27: 'One thing have I asked of the LORD, that will I seek after: that I may dwell in the house of the LORD all the days of my life, to behold the gracious beauty of the LORD and to meditate in his temple.' (Compare also Psalm 84 in Chapter 30.)

The temple was the expression of the fact that God builds a 'house'; it was a prophecy of the future dwelling of God in an earthly body. 'But he was speaking about the temple of his body' (Jn 2:21). The desire to be able to dwell in the house of God for ever was, in veiled form, the wish rising from the depths of the human being to dwell in the resurrection body, for which the 'house of God' is the prototype.

42

AUTHORITY TO TREAD ON SERPENTS AND SCORPIONS

PSALM 91

'If you are the Son of God, throw yourself down from here; for it is written, "He will command his angels concerning you, to guard you carefully; and they will lift you up in their hands, so that you will not strike your foot against a stone".' (Lk 4:9–11)

With these words the Devil shows that he too can come up with a quotation from Holy Scripture should the need arise. The verse he misuses comes from Psalm 91, and the fact that the tempter can clothe his suggestion in these particular words shows us that they must have been alive in the soul of Jesus of Nazareth. The same psalm appears once more later in the gospel when we hear a significant echo of it in Christ's own words: 'I saw Satan fall like lightning from heaven. Behold, I have given you authority to tread on serpents and scorpions, and to overcome all the power of the enemy; nothing will harm you' (Lk 10:18f).

Psalm 91 therefore plays a unique part in the conflict of Christ with the opposing powers.

The beginning is not easy to translate accurately. Some translations have: 'He who dwells in the shelter of the Most High ... says to the LORD, "My refuge and my fortress".' In the Hebrew, however, it is not 'He who dwells ... says', but 'He who dwells ... *I say*' The I is preserved in most English translations, but they have therefore found it necessary to alter the preceding clause, which in the original is never

Psalm 91

*Oh! to dwell enveloped in the mystery of the Most High,
    to shelter in the shadow of the Almighty.*
*² I say to the L*ORD*, 'My refuge and my fortress,
    my God, in whom I trust.'*

*³ He it is who will deliver you from the snare of the trapper
    and from the deadly pestilence.*
*⁴ He will cover you with his feathers,
    and under his wings you will find refuge;
    his truth is a shield and protection.*
*⁵ You will not fear the terror of the night,
    nor the arrow that flies by day,*
*⁶ nor the pestilence that stalks in the darkness,
    nor the destruction that wastes at noonday.*
*⁷ A thousand may fall at your side,
    ten thousand at your right hand;
    but it will not come near you.*
*⁸ You will only look with your eyes
    and see the retribution of the wicked.*

*⁹ Indeed, you, L*ORD *are my refuge.
    You have made the Most High your dwelling place,*
*¹⁰ no evil shall befall you,
    no plague come near your tent.*
*¹¹ For he will command his angels concerning you
    to guard you in all your ways.*
*¹² On their hands they will bear you up,
    lest you strike your foot against a stone.*
*¹³ You will tread on the lion and the venomous snake,
    the young lion and the dragon you will trample
        underfoot.*

*¹⁴ Because he holds fast to me in love, I will deliver him;
    I will protect him, because he knows my name.*
*¹⁵ When he calls to me, I will answer him;
    I will be with him in trouble,
    I will rescue him and honour him.*
*¹⁶ With long life I will satisfy him,
    and show him my salvation.*

completed; it hangs in the air without a following main clause. 'He who dwells in the shelter of the Most High and abides in the shadow of the Almighty'; now one has to sense a pause. It is as if in this unfinished introductory sentence a great and wonderful experience were dashed down in advance. It is so overwhelming, the heart is so full of it, that it cannot submit to being confined in a finished grammatical sentence. If we get the impression that something remains hanging in mid-air, that is quite right. In this way it stands like a title over what follows. One could try to include this incomplete, suspended sentence by means of the infinitive:

> Oh, to dwell enveloped in the mystery of the Most High,
>   to shelter in the shadow of the Almighty.

From this experience is born a confession of faith. From it the human I swings immediately to addressing the divine I:

> I say to the LORD, 'My refuge and my fortress,
>   my God, in whom I trust.'

The fullness and reality of the inner experience expresses itself in the variations of the divine name used. The 'Most High' (*Elyon*) – the God to whom Melchizedek, the mysterious priest-king of ancient Jerusalem, brought bread and wine was thus named. The 'Almighty' (*Shadai*), likewise called upon already in Abraham's time, was felt to be an especially potent name for the divine life force that can subjugate even the forces of death. 'LORD' denotes the power of the I within the name Yahweh – in Greek, *Kyrios*. And 'God' is the rendering of *Elohim,* which, like a rainbow, comprises the many hues of the manifold powers of the divine.

The confession of the psalmist's faith dies away into the divine silence, but out of this silence there arises a sound like an answer. A voice becomes discernible now in return, addressing him who sent his words to the supersensory world. It is not yet the voice of God himself, which speaks at the end of the psalm, but another voice from the invisible world. It is like the voice of a guardian, an angel sent before the voice of God. It says:

42. AUTHORITY OVER SERPENTS AND SCORPIONS

> He it is who will deliver you from the snare of the trapper
> and from the deadly pestilence.
> He will cover you with his feathers,
> and under his wings you will find refuge;
> his truth is a shield and protection.
> You will not fear the terror of the night,
> nor the arrow that flies by day,
> nor the pestilence that stalks in the darkness,
> nor the destruction that wastes at noonday.
> A thousand may fall at your side,
> ten thousand at your right hand;
> but it will not come near you.
> You will only look with your eyes
> and see the retribution of the wicked.

On the strength of this voice the psalmist speaks in his innermost being directly to the Godhead himself:*

> Indeed, you, LORD are my refuge.

In comparison with the first confession (my refuge and my fortress) it shows an enhancement; although there too the LORD is directly addressed, the word 'you' is nevertheless avoided. This 'you' – in Hebrew, *atah,* beginning and ending with the vowel 'a' – is like a primal utterance of wonder that there *is* the other I. The fact that I-consciousness is not the sole centre of consciousness in the world does not, as in Jean-Paul Sartre's existentialism, appear the prime scandal, but is the source of pious amazement at a divine miracle.

This second confession, which goes so far as to utter the great 'you', again actuates an inspired hearing of the mysterious 'voice'. It takes up the psalmist's statement and confirms it. It says:

> You have made the Most High your dwelling place,
> no evil shall befall you,
> no plague come near your tent.

---

* In many translations this whole verse appears as part of the words addressed to the psalmist.

> For he will command his angels concerning you
>   to guard you in all your ways.
> On their hands they will bear you up,
>   lest you strike your foot against a stone.
> You will tread on the lion and the venomous snake,
>   the young lion and the serpent you will trample
>   underfoot.

Here too comes an enhancement. The first time the voice conveyed simply a feeling of protection, of refuge, but the pious are not only to rest in the divine shelter; they are also to be sure of protection in the course of all their activities.

They have to pursue their way on earth, so they cannot be spared also encountering the adverse powers. These make themselves felt for example as 'forces of hindrance' – in our psalm the 'stone' on the path which the foot may strike. But as instruments of divine Providence angels come to the help of those who are in harmony with the divine. The mysterious 'voice' knows that this help can become so real and effective that the feeling arises of being carried as if by hands over all obstacles.

This is the Scripture the Devil has on his lips when he tempts Christ in the wilderness. As he suggests to him, he should cast himself down from the pinnacle of the temple, trusting in God. But Christ recognises the falsification of the lofty words of the psalm into overweening arrogance, and rejects 'temptation of God'.

Christ quotes more from this psalm at a later stage in his ministry when the seventy who had been sent out return from their successful mission. There he speaks of the power to tread on snakes and scorpions, in a slight variation of the text of the psalm (Lk 10:19).

The powers of the Adversary do not only throw stones in our path through life. They make direct attacks in order to destroy us – as ravening lions, as venomous snakes. The lion can also be the image of the most noble and divine qualities of the heart. Anyone who perceives the heavenly archetype in the earthly lion will be led to the sublime Christ-mysteries – to 'the lion who has vanquished'. The lion of earth, however, does not only reflect the distant heavenly archetype, but as a physical creature has acquired destructive powers and lives its life as a fierce beast of prey. This is how it is seen in the psalm. And it is from the realm of feeling, centred in the human heart stricken with the sickness of sin, that the 'bad lion' can spring with destructive violence.

Another quite different aspect of powers hostile to human beings is revealed in the venomous snake that lurks unnoticed on the path and strikes with its deadly bite. Besides lion and snake the psalm looks at another creature that no longer really exists in the natural world but has its reality in the invisible. It appears to the soul in dreams as the dragon ('serpent' in many translations).

The peculiar strength and encouragement of the psalm – one could say, its Michaelic character – lies in its being able to give confidence for life's journey despite all dangers. The dangers are clearly envisaged. We must know that they exist – lions, adders, dragons. But if there are demons and the Devil, then there are also angels. They lift us over the stone. They enable us to trample evil underfoot and carry on.

As the inspiring voice reaches these heights of revelation, it grows silent and gives place to one yet more exalted. To the two kinds of speech found so far a third is now added. Speaking himself, the psalmist said: 'I [the psalmist] and you [God]'. The inspiring voice of the angel said: 'You [the psalmist] and he [God]'. Now we hear a third voice in which the I of the Godhead himself makes itself heard, whilst the psalmist is thought of in the third person: 'I [God] and he [the psalmist]'. God's own voice says:

> Because he holds fast to me in love, I will deliver him;
>   I will protect him, because he knows my name.
> When he calls to me, I will answer him;
>   I will be with him in trouble,
>   I will rescue him and honour him.
> With long life I will satisfy him,
>   and show him my salvation.

Here, where the Godhead himself speaks, the Hebrew text resounds with the solemn and majestic word *anokhi* for 'I'. The 'love from above' can come to the rescue of the human being who 'knows' the divine 'name'. God is not 'anonymous'; with him human beings are able to know 'with whom they are dealing'. The 'name of God' is the manifestation to us of his innermost nature as it came to us, supremely, in Christ Jesus. If they have become aware of the divine name, then human beings can be 'extricated' by God above from the toils of a world forfeit to death. They become 'transfigured', changed 'from one glory to another' into ever greater glories (2Cor 3:18).

The satisfying with 'long life' at the end of the divine promise we must first translate from the Old Testament way of thinking and speaking – into which divine revelations were clothed – into a Christian way. The Old Covenant had the task of preparing the earthly body into which the Saviour could descend and become human. It was therefore in the order of things that the adherents of the Old Covenant should put a high value on their physical existence. The soul would not descend into earthly existence if it did not have a deep-rooted longing for life on earth, a kind of 'hunger'. The life on earth, then, had to fulfil this longing like a satisfying meal. In regard to the patriarchs we can have the impression that their death came at the moment when they had reached this satisfaction. They died 'old and full of days'. Apart from Abraham and Isaac, this was said only of Job, David and the priest Jehoiada.

In Christianity this special value of earthly existence was not denied but acknowledged still more profoundly. For the religious ancient Hebrews it expressed itself more quantitatively in the 'length' of the allotted lifespan, while for us the qualitative aspect is most important – that during our earthly existence we may find Christ and allow ourselves to be permeated by him. The act of redemption itself did not take place in heaven but on earth, and so it is also earthly life that offers the opportunity for becoming Christ-like. Although the human soul stems from heaven and is destined for future heavenly existence, it is here on earth that it has the decisive experience that works on into eternity. This experience satisfies the 'hunger' that leads the soul into earthly existence in order to seek the meaning of life, the 'fullness' of days.

The last sentence of God's words in Psalm 91 opens up the wider horizons of the future. The age of the Holy Spirit, the great awakening of consciousness, is announced. The knowing of 'my name' develops into an apocalyptic cosmic vision. 'I will ... show him my salvation.'

43

THE HYMN OF THE SOUL

PSALM 103

I

> Praise the LORD, O my soul,
> and all that is within me
> praise his holy name!

It is more than a figure of speech when Homer begins the *Iliad* by calling upon the muse, 'Sing to me, O muse …' The muse at that time was really an inspiring spiritual being, and Homer, a contemporary of King David, was conscious of her cooperation. Equally, the German poet Klopstock begins his epic poem, *The Messiah,* with the words, 'Sing, immortal soul, of the redemption of sinful mankind.' Homer summons the muse that is still external to him. The Christian poet can call on the depths of his own soul.

Although Psalm 103 belongs to the ancient world, it anticipates the spiritual stream which leads to Christ in the human soul. So here, too, the psalmist's own soul is to sound the praise of the Lord. The whole inner being, 'all that is within me', with all its powers and possibilities shall echo the holy name. The holy 'name' is God in so far as he is known, in so far as he manifests himself. The recognition of God and acknowledgment of his holy name in prayer, and the hymn that this calls forth, demand the full compass of the soul's powers, though it is a distant goal that all the soul's powers can echo God's name.

The spirit recognises the name of God, the soul attunes its feelings to this knowledge and merges with it fully. This feeling becomes inner music and then finally audible song. It becomes a hymn of the soul moved by the experience of such precious worth. The full significance

Psalm 103

*Praise the L*ORD*, O my soul,*
  and all that is within me
  praise his holy name!
² *Praise the L*ORD*, O my soul,*
  and forget not all his benefits,
³ *who forgives all your iniquities;*
  who heals all your diseases,
⁴ *who redeems your life from the grave,*
  who crowns you with grace and tender mercy,
⁵ *who satisfies your longing with goodness*
  and renews your youth like the eagle.

⁶ *The L*ORD *works righteousness*
  and justice for all who are oppressed.
⁷ *He made known his ways to Moses,*
  his acts to the sons of Israel.
⁸ *The L*ORD *is merciful and gracious,*
  slow to anger and abounding in mercy.
⁹ *He will not always reject us,*
  nor will he keep his anger for all cycles of time.
¹⁰ *He does not deal with us according to our sins,*
  nor reward us according to our iniquities.
¹¹ *For as high as the heaven are above the earth,*
  so great is his mercy towards those who revere him;
¹² *as far as the sun's rising is from the setting,*
  does he remove our transgressions from us.
¹³ *As a father shows compassion to his children,*
  *So the L*ORD *shows compassion to those who revere him.*
¹⁴ *For he knows how we are formed;*
  he remembers that we are dust.
¹⁵ *As for mortal man, his days are as grass:*
  he flourishes like a flower of the field;
¹⁶ *for the wind passes over it, and it is gone,*
  and its place knows it no more.
¹⁷ *But the grace of the L*ORD *is from everlasting to everlasting*
  on those who revere him,
  and his righteousness to the children's children
¹⁸ *to those who are true to his covenant*
  and remember the aims of his will to realise them.

> ¹⁹ The Lord has established his throne in the heavens,
>   and his kingdom embraces the universe.
> ²⁰ Praise the Lord, O you his angels,
>   you mighty ones who do his word,
>   carrying the voice of his word!
> ²¹ Praise the Lord, all his hosts,
>   you exalted servants who do his will!
> ²² Praise the Lord, all his works,
>   in all places of his dominion.
> Praise the Lord, O my soul.

of such related words as 'praise', 'prize' and 'precious' has largely been lost through the devaluing of words, but the meaning common to them all is connected with the experience of worth.

> Praise the LORD, O my Soul,
>   and forget not all his benefits,

People are much tempted to notice what is disagreeable, while the good they accept as a matter of course, without thought and hence also without thanks. Unless we cultivate gratitude consciously we make no progress on the path to God.

In the following lines the abundant benefits coming from God are stated one by one and placed gratefully before the conscious mind.

> who forgives all your iniquities;
>   who heals all your diseases,
> who redeems your life from the grave,
>   who crowns you with grace and tender mercy,
> who satisfies your longing with goodness
>   and renews your youth like the eagle.

The first three statements relate to a negative condition which is overcome through divine assistance: sin, sickness, death.

Sin working within is the root of all evil. The starting point for a comprehensive restoration of the whole threatened human nature is to bring the soul into order. The result of sin is sickness; the sick soul encroaches on the region of the finer formative forces and makes them 'sick'. This is not meant to imply that every illness is therefore a direct result of sin. This would be a wrong conclusion which takes no account of the complex relationships of human destiny. That an individual suffers from a particular illness may arise from quite different factors. But that disease in general is possible to humankind, that sickness and disease find access to people at all, is the result of sin.

The next step in the process by which sin becomes an integral part of the world, is death. This is why the sequence of the psalm is so organically right. It begins with the forgiving of sins, which brings the inner life into order. Then follows the healing of infirmities, just as Christ first forgave the palsied man his sins and afterwards made him whole. Finally, in the third place, comes the conquest of death. These are words which open up into future Christian times, having an enduring, even an increasing validity far beyond the life of the psalmist. They are words which become increasingly right and true with the advance of Christian development.

The word *go'el* in the original text has a special ring, 'Who *redeems* your life from the grave'. The same word occurs in the significant passage in Job (19:25): 'I know that my Redeemer lives.'

After sin, sickness and death have been disposed of, the positive side too is unfolded in a trinity of statements. The crowning 'with grace and tender mercy' has a presupposition in what was called in the ancient Orient 'the lifting of the head'. The person who was broken down now rises up with their head into the higher worlds again, whose light shines down upon them in blessing.

After the crowning of the head, which restores human dignity, the psalm turns to the heart. 'Who satisfies your longing with goodness.' The deepest longing finds its fulfilment.

The working of grace in human beings penetrates lower and lower. 'Who renews your youth like the eagle.' Ancient wisdom saw in the eagle the symbol for the transformation of the sinister powers of the scorpion. The 'scorpion' which is active in the lower human nature is a force which leads to death. When it is spiritualised, however, it turns into the eagle. John the Evangelist, who as Lazarus went through death, has the eagle as his traditional symbol. He was the first to understand the resurrection of Christ. Surviving as the centenarian of Ephesus this disciple 'whom Jesus loved' had known in himself the

43. THE HYMN OF THE SOUL

victory of renewal. 'Behold, I make all things new' (Rv 21:5). He had regained the forces of childhood on a higher level.

Isaiah also speaks of the 'eagle' with the same significance. 'Even youths grow tired and weary, and young men fall. But those who wait upon the LORD acquire new strength; they mount up with wings like eagles; they run and are not weary, they walk and are not faint.' (Is 40:30f). The natural forces of childhood and youth sooner or later fall into decline: they must be found again in the spirit. Spiritual rebirth alone rescues us from senile old age.

II

> The LORD works righteousness
>   and justice for all who are oppressed.

With these words the psalm leaves the personal sphere of individual salvation and praises the work of God on a grander scale. The interpretation of the Old Testament has frequently led to absurd difficulties, if it was all too narrowly assumed that justice is to be found within one and the same span of life; for as a rule the upright are not at first rewarded with good things and the evil punished. The fundamental intention of God's justice is, however, not refuted by this. We must view things from a wider angle by taking into account the possibility of repeated lives on earth. Only in the great panorama of all our earthly incarnations shall we be able to see how destinies are controlled in justice by the highest powers of heaven in their fullness of love and wisdom.

It was this God, ruling with his justice the great course of the world, who gave Moses insight into his ways.

> He made known his ways to Moses,
>   his acts to the sons of Israel.
> ⁸ The LORD is merciful and gracious,
>   slow to anger and abounding in mercy.

Doubtless the psalmist is remembering the unique hour which was granted to Moses as the Lord passed before him, and proclaimed to him his great Name in fullness (Ex 34:5–7). The words, 'The LORD is merciful and gracious,' are a direct quotation from this revelation to Moses.

> He will not always reject us,
>   nor will he keep his anger for all cycles of time.
> He does not deal with us according to our sins,
>   nor reward us according to our iniquities.
> For as high as the heaven are above the earth,
>   so great is his mercy towards those who revere him;
> as far as the sun's rising is from the setting,
>   does he remove our transgressions from us.

'Anger' is not the first state and will not be the last. Even in pre-Christian times, Moses knows God's willingness to forgive and to heal. Although he is a God of justice, a guarantor of the law of sowing and reaping, yet – as we saw in Chapter 33 on Psalm 51 – 'he does not deal with us according to our sins'. If there were merely a rigid, automatic justice, striking back mechanically at the doer, human beings would be destroyed by the consequences of their deeds. They would 'die in their sins'. All the wrong that they have done to the world would simply annihilate them in its repercussion.

God adds something from his own substance. He gives a great, infinitely effective divine sacrifice as a new factor though which everything takes on a different appearance. Christ does not cancel the law of cause and effect, he does not overthrow the karmic law of destiny, but he graciously brings a quite new cause into the situation by binding himself by a free deed of sacrifice to the destiny of humankind, so inserting himself into the flow of karma. The law is not thereby set aside, for precisely by virtue of this law of cause and effect the Deed of Golgotha has its own far-reaching effect.

What is said of the righteous God who nevertheless does not allow us to be destroyed by the consequences of our deeds will only become fully comprehensible in the light of Christ. The God who does not reward people according to their iniquity is no capricious sultan who arbitrarily seizes the reins of justice, but the God who is in the process of consummating the Christ-sacrifice for humanity.

And since this is so, one is not obliged to see human beings merely in their earthly aspect, as imperfect humans of earth – one would then have to give them up in despair of their future. But to the totality of the phenomenon 'man' there belongs, too, the heaven of God that arches over us, full of promise of the future. It is not credit to human beings that this is so. The universe only tolerates them for the sake of their Christian possibilities in the future. They are only 'justified through belief in Christ' because in process of becoming Christianised they will bring the great scales of eternal justice into equilibrium again.

This in no way prejudices human freedom. The high heavens of grace which wants to be realised in earthly humans are only for those who 'revere God'. One condition must therefore be fulfilled on their part before grace can be put into operation. They must be conscious of their position, they must have reverent awe. In the New Testament this one condition means that they must believe in Christ, they must turn to him. Otherwise the high heavens of grace above cannot reveal themselves, and in the last resort they must 'die in their sins'. The factor of redemption cannot then be inserted into the account of their destiny.

'As far as the sun's rising is from the setting.' We belong through our sins to a world which is going down, which is 'setting'. Grace unites us with a new dawn, the rising of the world. Through grace a different world rises in us, separated from the world of our sins by inconceivable distances.

We see the human being in great dimensions – with the high heaven of grace above that belongs to a cosmic morning, while the sins go down into a cosmic evening.

The following sentence also has a New Testament ring:

> As a father shows compassion to his children,
>   So the LORD shows compassion to those who revere him.

The Godhead who sends the Redeemer sees our frailty.

> For he knows how we are formed;
>   he remembers that we are dust.
> As for mortal man, his days are as grass:
>   he flourishes like a flower of the field;
> for the wind passes over it, and it is gone,
>   and its place knows it no more.

> But the grace of the Lord is from everlasting to everlasting
>   on those who revere him,
>   and his righteousness to the children's children
>   to those who are true to his covenant
>   and remember the aims of his will to realise them.

The 'dust of the earth', transitoriness, has entered into humans. But the Old Testament also knows of the breath which God breathed into human beings, and it tells of a creation (Gn 1:27), long before the transitory, earthly form was allotted to human beings (Gn 2:7). Through their share in the eternal, they able to make a covenant with God. Their fidelity – 'those who are true to his covenant' – to the supersensible raises them above the merely transitory. Fidelity assumes that there is a lasting element in us, it is a function of the I.

III

The psalm began with the hymn of the soul. It ends with a hymn of the universe. What began in the inmost circle is now carried out into the cosmos.

> The Lord has established his throne in the heavens,
>   and his kingdom embraces the universe.
> [20] Praise the Lord, O you his angels,
>   you mighty ones who do his word,
>   carrying the voice of his word!
> [21] Praise the Lord, all his hosts,
>   you exalted servants who do his will!

The heart's song of praise unites with the song of sacrifice of the hierarchies. The Act of Consecration of Man speaks of this at Christmas, giving the names of the nine angelic orders. The divisions of the ranks of angels is lightly touched upon, somewhat as in Psalm 104. There are first the angels who, as in the Greek *angeloi,* are simply called messengers. They bring messages from spirit to spirit. 'Mighty ones' probably indicates the middle hierarchy. They live actively in the sphere of sound and carry it powerfully into the world. The word 'hosts' *tsabaoth* carries us to the highest hierarchy. *Tsabaoth* is occasionally used for the 'starry' hosts, for instance in Jeremiah 33:22 as 'hosts of heaven' that cannot be numbered. To this highest hierarchy belong the 'exalted servants', the *liturgents* in Greek. They live in the immediate substance of the divine will. The psalm says: 'who do his will'.

Then, finally, our gaze is turned to the whole of creation:

> Praise the LORD, all his works,
> in all places of his dominion.

The concluding sentence turns back once more to the beginning. But in the meantime the soul has widened out and made the whole universe its concern. The soul's song of praise now resounds with the hymn of the worlds.

> Praise the LORD, O my soul.

VII
THE NEW SONG

44

THE FUTURE OF THE EARTH

PSALM 37

I

The psalm begins with the admonition not to waste the forces of the soul in hatred of evil.

> Do not fret yourself because of evildoers;
>   nor rant against wrongdoers!

How much energy of the soul is lost in this way! There is no doubt a great temptation to be annoyed from morning to night over one thing or another which is not what it ought to be. But righteous anger firing our energy is only useful where we can improve things. In the first place in self-discipline, dealing with our own failings. Beyond this, fretting and ranting soon becomes unfruitful. Important forces of our soul – needed in a positive direction – are used up to no purpose.

We should leave what is evil to its own unreality. At any rate, we do not share the view of some writers of the Old Testament, where it is imagined that the doom of evil must become evident in this life. We take broader views, although the early concept remains right in principle – that evil has its own judge.

The energies of the soul should flow towards the divine, not waste themselves in fruitless anger.

> Trust in the LORD, and do good;
>   dwell in the land and cultivate faithfulness.

Into this expression 'trust in the LORD' we may, as Christians, read all that our relation to Christ can be. This relationship of heartfelt confidence can also enable us to do good.

Psalm 37 circles continuously round the word *erez,* the earth, the land – to begin with, quite concretely the land of Israel, the Holy Land. Theological interpretation explains the psalm as showing the pious, the Hasidim, in contrast to those who fell away from the Yahweh religion and became subject to foreign influences. The conflict centred round the Holy Land, and which of the two parties should control it.

The psalm acquires its significance, however, from the fact that this particular conflict between two groups of people, long since relegated to the past, can be a symbol of a much greater problem. Behind the contest of the 'pious', among whom perhaps many narrow-minded fanatics could have been found, and the so-called 'godless' to control the land, there appears a much greater and more significant conflict: the fight of the good and evil powers for the future of the earth. The devout are then the people of the future who serve the Christ, and their adversaries are the powers of anti-Christ, and *erez* is then not only the land but the earth.

The actual theme of the psalm is the apocalyptic contest for the earth. That will become clearer still in what follows.

'Dwell in the land and cultivate faithfulness.' It was right for Abraham to depart from the land of his fathers and his friends. Whether someone travels to distant lands or remains at home for their whole life, differs for each individual according to their destiny. The psalm does not intend to decide this question. It is concerned with who is to possess the land. This fight for the Holy Land depends ultimately on the inner qualities, the inner character of the people. It is more than a political question, it has apocalyptic significance, 'Dwell in the land in the right way by cultivating faithfulness to the spirituality which you serve.'

This gives to the psalm its lasting importance and actual quality. Then this sentence, freed from its temporal, historical limitation, reads, 'Dwell on the earth in the right way.' Acknowledge the fact that you are not an inhabitant of heaven to whom the earth is strange, but – though of heavenly origin – you have been placed upon the earth by the wise powers of destiny. Affirm this fact! Cultivate the right loyalty to the earth and thereby serve the spiritual worlds in obedience.

44. THE FUTURE OF THE EARTH

In the end this can be fully understood only in the spirit of Christ. For Christ himself chose the earth. With the resurrection he created the seed of a transformed, spiritualised earth, which is linked with heaven in a new way. 'We are engaged in a mission: we are called upon to transform the earth.' These words of Novalis are genuinely Christian. In the idea of transformation, human beings keep faith both with heaven and earth. They bring the two together so that the great apocalyptic marriage may come about. Christians cannot simply wish 'to get to heaven': they must bring to heaven the earthly element, purified and transformed. They cannot merely wish to possess the earth, they must bring the spirit into it.

This is the theme of Psalm 37. It enjoins fidelity to the earth together with fidelity to the spirit.

II

We must not overlook the fact that the following verses, so very well known, come immediately after 'Dwell in the land and cultivate faithfulness.'

> Find your bliss in the LORD;
>   and he will give you the desires of your heart.
> Commit your way to the LORD;
>   and trust in him, and he will bring it to pass.

We are here on the sacred ground of the mystic. We see that the Old Testament does not merely recognise obedience to the law. It is also aware of the inner bliss or blessedness which is given through uniting with the divine presence.

The idea is widespread among Christians that religion has largely to do with praying to God for this or that. Many people only remember God when they need something, when they want to have something, when they want to be relieved of some affliction. This psalm is on a very different level. The psalmist knows that the first thing in religion is worship, meditation, the bliss or blessedness of gazing upon and experiencing the divine in forgetting himself. Only those who return to themselves again from a selfless adoration of the divine, may now utter their petitions. The Lord's Prayer begins by addressing 'Our Father', which rightly understood involves a contemplation of God. From this meditation the three petitions proceed which are not yet related to earthly human needs, but are characterised by 'your' – your name, your kingdom, your will. Only then, cleansed and purified by what has gone before, may we come to our earthly affairs, 'our daily bread'.

And this sentence of the psalm first speaks of the blessedness which we shall find in the Lord. Then follows the second, 'And he will give you the desires of your heart.' It can then no longer be a foolish request or egoistic desire to receive something for which we appeal to God. True prayers, worthy of being heard, come from selfless worship; only then are they really 'desires of the heart'. That is indeed a different thing from what one generally connects with the ordinary phrase 'my heart's desire'.

Christian prayer is promised fulfilment if it is uttered in the name of Christ. Of course, we need not always end our prayers with the formula 'for Christ's sake'. 'For Christ's sake' means rather that we should first completely permeate ourselves with his being. Out of this real uniting with him 'ask and it will be given to you' (Mt 7:7), for then this 'ask' has taken on a different character: then it will truly be desire of the pure heart.

A mystical experience like this is the source of the famous words which now follow: 'Commit your way to the LORD'. It is the way of destiny, to tread which you have been sent to earth by the wisdom of the higher worlds. Surrender yourself with confidence to divine guidance.

The word 'trust' (as in verse 3) is repeated. 'And he will bring it to pass.' He will act. This is no invitation to passivity. Such words must not be isolated: they are preceded by 'Trust in him'. Do good. Inhabit the land in true fidelity. Find your delight and blessedness in the divine. This all points to activity on the part of human beings. For even 'bliss', which is the state of finding delight in the spirit, is something that must be sought. Only through the inner activity of achieving quiet moments for prayer and reading can we attain true and healthy tranquillity. 'Commit your way to the LORD ... and he will bring it to pass.' He will act. We only set divine intervention really in motion through our true surrender, just as in the Act of Consecration of Man the Offertory, with our united devotion, precedes the consecration of the substances, when God 'brings it to pass' and 'acts'.

44. THE FUTURE OF THE EARTH

In Chapter 39, we met this mysterious saying that God will 'do it', in the final verse of Psalm 22, the Passion Psalm of the Redeemer.

> He will bring forth your righteousness as the light,
> And your justice as the bright noonday.

Christ says, 'Then the righteous will shine like the sun in the kingdom of their Father' (Mt 13:43). Nothing is lost that was well and truly done, even though it may seem at first to have no results. Nothing is really wasted. With all that we accomplish of real value we are building a future world. What is now inward morality will one day become nature. The right deeds that have been done on earth will one day illumine a coming world just as the sun shines upon us today. The fact that goodness will one day be rehabilitated and honoured is the wider perspective of these words of the psalm, beyond their more obvious meaning. This will come about in its most sublime form when in the future the inner light will shine forth from human beings and become world-light; for Christ's words about the upright who shine like the sun, and the destiny of his disciples to be the light of the world ('You are the light of the world' Mt 5:14) cannot be understood concretely enough.

> Be still to the LORD and tremble in anticipation of him

Be still to the Lord. Keep silent to him. Again words that let one guess at a whole world of self-training and mystical blessing. We must grasp the dative case in these sentences. Keep silence to the Lord. This silence is not a brooding in oneself, it is an inner turning towards the divine. We bring all else in us to rest and hold the soul, emptied of all other content, like a chalice to the divine, so that it may enter into this emptiness and fill it. We incline the cup of our soul to God that he may pour in his divine life – that is the meaning of this dative.

III

The psalm has such wide horizons through the fact that it weaves together the two themes of the inner state of mystical blessing and of interest in the great events of the world.

> do not fret yourself over the one who prospers in his way,
>> although his acts are devious.
> Refrain from anger, and forsake wrath!
>> Fret not yourself; it only leads to evil.
> For the evildoers shall be cut off,
>> but those who look to the LORD in expectation shall
>>> inherit the land.

We are immediately reminded of one of the beatitudes in the Sermon on the Mount, for the psalms lived in Christ. 'Blessed are the meek for they will inherit the earth' (Mt 5:5). The meek – those who by conquering their elementary passions have become master of themselves – have attained to the goal of the earth. The spirit-self is the silent power of conscience which transforms the raw material of the soul's instincts and inclinations into calm and collected humanity. Meekness is not inner slackness and weakness, but the inner conquest, the calming of the waves of passion. The meek are those who keep in check the soul-forces which want to dissipate themselves in fruitless heat and irritation, those who can actively restore silence in the soul. What is achieved inwardly produces an effect in the world itself. 'They will inherit the earth.'

The earth, *gē* in the original Greek, of the beatitude is the very word *erez* in the psalm. In the beatitude it no longer has the limited meaning of the 'land', it is the earth as a whole, the earth as a world. The inner conquests and achievements of humanity ultimately decide the destiny of the planet. Moreover the beatitudes are immediately followed by the words, 'You are the salt of the earth'. The earth itself is at stake.

In the end, the earth will not belong to those who have only made it an object of exploitation from which to derive their pleasures and desires. Such people 'receive' nothing from the earth in the true sense of the word. Basically, it is precisely the materialist who, in a deeper sense, possesses nothing of the earth. Only those who look at the earth in a spiritual way can 'inherit' it and really receive something out of it. For instance, someone may own a park without having an eye for the beauty of the trees and the green of the lawns. Others, to whom this does not belong, can open themselves to all this beauty and take it to heart. Of the two, who 'inherits' the park, who receives something out of it as the real owner? Those who have taken it into their inner being carry the earthly, spiritually transfigured, over into the other world and preserve it in their own immortality. The others only possessed it externally, and when they die they can carry nothing of it away, but must leave it behind. They have had nothing from their possession and 'on the other side' they are poor souls.

The earth as a material globe is turning to dust. But of its true nature we must carry over something into eternity. Those who would seize and grasp for themselves obtain nothing from the earth that it could actually bestow on them; they lose the earth in possessing it.

The expression 'inherit the earth', which was held worthy of inclusion in the beatitudes, is continually found as a recurring verse in Psalm 37 in manifold forms:

> Those who look to the LORD in expectation shall inherit the earth.
>
> The meek shall inherit the earth.
>
> Those blessed by him shall inherit the earth.
>
> The righteous shall inherit the earth.

We can make these four different aspects somewhat more concrete if we look at the four parts of the Act of Consecration of Man which follow each other according to the same inner law.*

The first: 'to look to the LORD in eager anticipation' – that is the mood in which we listen to the Gospel.

The second: 'the meek', literally 'those who are bowed down' – these are the ones capable of sacrificial devotion to the divine.

The third: 'those blessed by him' – the transubstantiation is the great experience of blessing, which as divine love descends upon the earthly elements and transfigures them.

The fourth: 'the righteous' – these are not the self-righteous who want to 'do works before God' and count on God for their rewards, but those into whose own being divine righteousness is poured. Those

---

* Its four main parts are Gospel, Offertory, Transubstantiation and Communion.

who receive the Communion in full reality become righteous thereby; they bring the great cosmic scales that were thrown out of balance by the Fall into equilibrium again.

The following sentence stands between the third and the fourth aspect:

> Turn away from evil and do good;
> so shall you dwell in eternity.

This 'dwell' is something similar to the Johannine 'abide'. The theme of 'earth' is concluded in the comprehensive sentence:

> Wait in anticipation for the LORD and keep his way,
> and he will exalt you to inherit the earth.

Keep his way, which, through the humility of the Offering, the blessing of Transubstantiation, and the Communion of righteousness, leads you to the inner inheritance of earth.

The beatitude of the meek has a relationship with the beatitude of the peacemakers. There is a foretaste of this in verse 37 which may be literally translated as follows:

> Preserve the perfect and cultivate uprightness,
> for a future belongs to the man of peace.

Future, in Hebrew *acharith,* means 'that which is after'. Many commentators see in this sentence only the well-known ancient Jewish hope for bodily descendants. But even if the psalmist had only meant that 'the devout man has descendants whereas the descendants of the wicked perish' (37:37f), it points to a deeper meaning.

It is true, past ages experienced the future in children, but this experience went beyond the mere continuity of the family. The children of the body are a symbol for the fact that each human being is also inwardly endowed with a future. The seed of a future development stirs within each one; it will come to light, will 'come after', when the human form in which they now appear will have passed away. The New Testament calls this true human form of the future the Son of Man, which since it has been created out of the divine, may also be

44. THE FUTURE OF THE EARTH

Psalm 37:1, 3–9, 11, 22, 29, 27, 34, 37

Do not fret yourself because of evildoers;
 nor rant against wrongdoers!

 ...

³ Trust in the Lord*, and do good;*
 dwell in the land and cultivate faithfulness.
⁴ Find your bliss in the Lord*;*
 and he will give you the desires of your heart.
⁵ Commit your way to the Lord*;*
 and trust in him, and he will bring it to pass.
⁶ He will bring forth your righteousness as the light,
 And your justice as the bright noonday.
⁷ Be still to the Lord *and tremble in anticipation of him;*
 do not fret yourself over the one who prospers in his way,
 although his acts are devious.
⁸ Refrain from anger, and forsake wrath!
 Fret not yourself; it only leads to evil.
⁹ For the evildoers shall be cut off,
 but those who look to the Lord *in expectation shall*
 inherit the earth.

 ...

¹¹ The meek shall inherit the earth.

 ...

²² For those blessed by him shall inherit the earth.

 ...

²⁹ The righteous shall inherit the earth.

 ...

²⁷ Turn away from evil and do good;
 so shall you dwell in eternity.

 ...

³⁴ Wait in anticipation for the Lord *and keep his way,*
 and he will exalt you to inherit the earth.

 ...

³⁷ Preserve the perfect and cultivate uprightness,
 for a future belongs to the man of peace.

called the Son of God. 'God's seed abides in him' and 'What we will be has not yet appeared' (1Jn 3:9 and 3:2).

It need not be a physical reality when the psalm says that the descendants of the wicked will be exterminated. But the deeper truth holds good: evil is without a real future and is humanly unfruitful. On the other hand, 'a future belongs to the man of peace'.

What promise does the Christ make to the peacemakers in his beatitude? 'For they shall be called descendants of God' (Mt 5:9). The ancient world would have said, 'For they will have sons'. We hardly need to point out that in Christianity, too, it is a high and holy human task to pass on life. In the New Testament the inner application is stressed: the 'man of peace' is to become fruitful in himself, he must progress towards his true human form as bearer of the divine forces of the future. 'For they shall be called descendants of God.'

45

'A MIGHTY FORTRESS IS OUR GOD'

PSALM 46

Luther's famous hymn *A Mighty Fortress is our God* was inspired by Psalm 46. If we consider this psalm more closely, we can see that it reaches still more deeply into the apocalyptic sphere than the stirring hymn of the Reformation. For this reason it may have a significant message for us today.

I

The word 'God' stands at the beginning of the psalm not by chance. If we desire to find a fresh relationship to the sacred ancient text, we must contemplate and worship together with the inspired poet this supreme and ultimate reality. From there a bridge is built towards us and our need. 'God is our refuge and our strength, an ever-present help in troubles.'

Out of the experience of God's gracious and ready help, these words then emerge, 'Therefore we will not fear though the earth be changed throughout, and though the mountains be moved into the heart of the seas.' This sentence has frequently been compared with a line by Horace, *Si fractus illabatur orbis, impavidum ferient ruinae* – 'If the world should break and fall on him, it will strike him fearless.' The Stoic philosophy aspired to a sovereign control of the world based on the realisation of a person's spiritual dignity. But this control could only be maintained if, on the other hand, the sensitivity for the world and its pressure was weakened. *Ataraxia* was the goal – complete imperturbability, which regards catastrophes with cool detachment.

Psalm 46

God is our refuge and our strength,
    an ever-present help in troubles.
² Therefore we will not fear, though the earth be changed throughout,
    and though the mountains be moved into the heart of the seas,
³ though its waters rage and roar,
    though the mountains tremble at its vehemence.
           Selah

⁴ A river – its branches spread delight through the city of God,
    the holy dwelling place of the Most High.
⁵ God dwells in her midst; she stands unmoved;
    With break of dawn God comes to her rescue.
⁶ The nations rage, the kingdoms totter;
    he utters his voice – the earth melts away.
*⁷ The L*ORD *of Hosts is with us;*
    the God of Jacob is our fortress.
           Selah

*⁸ Come and see the works of the L*ORD,
    who does astonishing things on the earth.
⁹ He makes wars cease to the end of the earth;
    he breaks the bow and shatters the spear;
    he burns the chariots with fire.
¹⁰ 'Desist – and know that I AM *God.*
    I will be exalted among the nations,
    I will be exalted in the earth!'
*The L*ORD *of Hosts is with us;*
    The God of Jacob is our fortress.
           Selah

The immediate, concrete experience of God underlies the psalm. With this experience the devout can afford to embrace with their feeling heart even the horrors of the world. Their feelings will not remain unaffected by calamities; they will be affected by them just as a natural, unsophisticated heart would expect to be affected. But with open eyes and open heart they can face them, because they know their inner being is supported and carried by divine powers which are stronger than all destruction. Such religious fearlessness does not arise from disdain of all terror, but from the strength which is rooted in the eternal.

Thus the vision of the psalmist can venture into the future in which apocalyptic catastrophes threaten to occur. His gaze points in the same direction as later that of St John on Patmos. Like John, he is confident that divine help can always be found, and will lead the faithful through all peril and destruction.

It has been conjectured that the psalm might have been written after the unexpected liberation of Jerusalem through the surprising retreat of Sennacherib who had laid siege to the city. Whatever may have been the historic reason, the apocalyptic vision of future oppressions and liberations on a vast scale is what matters. The psalm speaks of nothing less than the end of the world itself. 'Though the earth be changed throughout, and though the mountains be moved into the heart of the seas'. The mountains with their age-old solidity and stability seem to guarantee the security of human earthly existence; yet they are only relatively 'everlasting'. One day even they will no longer be. But when at such profound transformation even that vanishes which seemed to be lasting, the God-filled I should by then be sufficiently firm to ride out all these storms.

The raging sea has always been a picture for the unbridled forces of swirling chaos. 'Though its waters rage and roar, though the mountains tremble at its vehemence.' The Old Testament contains here and there remnants – like megalithic remains – of ancient mythological conceptions of creation. The prophets and psalms allude at times to a primeval battle which the divine Creator waged against the serpent of chaos, called Leviathan or Rahab, which appears as a sea monster. Creation is, in the last analysis, a wrestling of an organising principle with the wild forces of sheer vitality. Untamed they cause chaos. But without this 'raw-material' creation would remain lifeless.

The ancient mythologies seem to have known that the gigantic battle with the forces of chaos which occurred at the beginning of the world, would have to be fought again at the end. Comparative religion notes such facts, but refrains from asking whether they contain any truth: were these dreamers and poets perhaps true seers, do their pictures make sense?

Psalm 46 does not explicitly name Leviathan or Rahab, but waters that 'rage and roar' are clearly an apocalyptic vision. Once again the powers of the abyss will raise their head.

The Hebrew word *selah*, which may indicate a musical interlude but may also mean something like 'proceed to a higher level', marks the end of the first section of the psalm. It is repeated at the end of the second and third sections.

> God is our refuge and our strength,
>   an ever-present help in troubles.
> Therefore we will not fear, though the earth be changed
>   throughout,
>   and though the mountains be moved into the heart of the
>   seas,
> though its waters rage and roar,
>   though the mountains tremble at its vehemence.
>   *Selah*

II

In the Book of Revelation the seer beholds the souls who are united with Christ gathered in the city of God, the heavenly Jerusalem, while the old world perishes. Christian humanity continues to live thereafter in a higher, changed form of existence, as it is revealed in the mysterious picture of the heavenly city.

The second part of the psalm speaks in its own manner of this higher Jerusalem. A literal translation would say: 'A river – its branches gladden the city of God'. 'A river –' a plain and clear vision. It is the picture of the divine River of Life.

In our normal consciousness we never see life itself, only living things. For higher vision, however, this mysterious fluid which we call 'life' appears in the image of running water, a mighty river. 'And the angel showed me the river of the water of life, clear as crystal,' says St John in his description of the heavenly Jerusalem (Rv 22:1). The river of Paradise is restored. Now it flows through the holy city which is at the same time the divine world and the human world. In the physical, historic Jerusalem such a river never existed. Zechariah and Ezekiel saw the future city of God, when they saw this river rise in 'Jerusalem' (Zec 14:8, Ezk 47:1–12). Of this river also the psalm speaks.

Then the psalmist observes how the river divides into many branches, and waters the whole city. In contrast to the floods of chaos this water of life is ruled and directed by the wisdom of God. In its many divisions it is, as it were, individualised. For this life which pulsates everywhere 'spreads delight' through the city of God, it spreads joy and bliss everywhere.

It is 'the city of God, the holy dwelling place of the Most High'. The 'Most High' is *Elyon* in Hebrew. This was the name of the God whose priest Melchizedek met Abraham in Jerusalem with bread and wine, and blessed him in the name of 'God Most High'. Abraham encountered then a still higher manifestation of God than the one whom he himself served. The one who revealed himself through Melchizedek was related to Abraham's own experience of God as the sun to the moon. A ray of the future sun of Christ touched him. The God who dwells in the city which is watered by the rivers of life, is none other than this God Most High whose ritual is celebrated with bread and wine. With the word *Elyon* the ancient sacred tradition of Jerusalem is touched on. 'God dwells in her midst, she stands unmoved. At break of dawn God comes to her rescue.'

Only in this second part, in connection with the heavenly Jerusalem, does God come really close to human beings. The images of this second part only become fully transparent through their fulfilment in Christ. Of the incarnate Son of God it is fully true that 'he dwells in the midst of the city'. And the resurrection, which is an event of daybreak, is the dawn of a new world. It is in truth the fulfilment of the sentence, 'With break of dawn God comes to her rescue.'

The powers of evil are incapable of touching this world of Christ, which rises from the ruins of the perishing world. 'The nations rage, the kingdoms totter; he utters his voice – the earth melts away.' The section concludes with this shout of joy: 'the LORD of Hosts is with us, the God of Jacob is our fortress,' *Yahweh tsabaoth* is the Lord of Hosts, the Lord of stars in which the angelic hierarchies could be seen. 'With us' – in Hebrew *immanu*. This is reminiscent of the name which is given to the Saviour by Isaiah, *Immanu-El*, 'with us God'.

The God of Jacob is the God who puts human beings' strength and stamina to the test, who makes them wrestle with obstacles. He is the God to whom Jacob said, 'I will not let you go unless you bless me' (Gn 32:26).

It is remarkable how in this second part of the psalm the various names of God come together: God (*Elohim*), Lord (*Yahweh*), Most High (*Elyon*). It belongs to the mysterious quality of Christ who dwells within human beings, that the divinity is revealed in fullness and called by different names.

> A river – its branches spread delight through the city of God,
>   the holy dwelling place of the Most High.
> God dwells in her midst; she stands unmoved;
>   With break of dawn God comes to her rescue.
> The nations rage, the kingdoms totter;
>   he utters his voice – the earth melts away.
> The Lord of Hosts is with us;
>   the God of Jacob is our fortress.
>   *Selah*

III

If one considers the third part from the point of view of history, one can read it as the description of the citizens of Jerusalem emerging through the gates of the city into the open to look over the battlefield after the besieging armies have withdrawn. 'Come and see the works of the Lord, who does astonishing things on the earth.' But again, the spectacle of the broken and abandoned arms lying round about inspires a more far-reaching apocalyptic vision. The psalm speaks of the God who 'breaks the bow and shatters the spear; he burns the chariot with fire'. God's laws maintaining everlasting life will prevail. God hands destruction to the destroyers: in the end war liquidates itself, destruction destroys itself. Destructive forces meet with their own destruction. Today in the atomic age we can form a realistic picture of war reducing itself to the point of absurdity.

The vision of destruction destroyed is followed immediately by a call to awaken a higher consciousness. The original Hebrew simply says, 'desist'. It means quite concretely 'desist from warfare'. But we should not give up warfare simply for reasons of expediency or fear. The constructive action is to lift the soul to a higher consciousness. Human beings should recognise God who says 'I AM'. He can only be recognised through the human I. He will not be found in dim collective instincts, but in the very centre of the human personality which has come of age. He waits to be recognised and acknowledged freely and voluntarily by the individual human being while he sanctifies the individual I towards selflessness. He prepares it for a new and higher form of community. This God of the free I has appeared in Christ among human beings.

Apart from the ordinary word for 'I' (*ani*) the Hebrew language possesses a solemn grand form for it: *anokhi*. It is 'I AM' written in capitals. This 'I' writ large is used here. 'Know that I AM God'. With this element of 'knowing' the third person of the Holy Trinity, the Holy Spirit, is also touched upon.

'I will be exalted among the nations, I will be exalted in the earth'. The divine I AM, which to begin with is hidden to human sight in the narrow, egocentric darkness of the soul, rises up in power. The divine I AM can no longer be overlooked and ignored – it seeks to become the decisive factor in the life of humanity on earth. The development and transformation of this saying is found in the New Testament, when Christ speaks of the cross and says, 'And I, when I am lifted up from the earth, will draw all people to myself' (Jn 12:32).

> Come and see the works of the LORD,
>   who does astonishing things on the earth.
> He makes wars cease to the end of the earth;
>   he breaks the bow and shatters the spear;
>   he burns the chariots with fire.
> 'Desist – and know that I AM God.
>   I will be exalted among the nations,
>   I will be exalted in the earth!'
> The LORD of Hosts is with us;
>   The God of Jacob is our fortress.
>   *Selah*

46

'I SHALL NOT DIE, BUT I SHALL LIVE'

PSALM 118 – AN EASTER HYMN

I

It is a moving moment when Matthew's Gospel (23:39) describes how Christ bade farewell to his public ministry in order to devote the last day before his passion solely to his disciples. In this farewell to the multitude on Maundy Thursday he says: 'For I tell you, you will not see me again until you say, "Blessed is he who comes in the name of the Lord".'

His activity in an earthly body visible to everyone draws to an end. 'You will not see me again with earthly eyes.' As the Risen One, however, he is to 'come' to people in a new way and be present to them. In order to be able to perceive him in this supersensory form, people will need a new supersensory organ of vision. 'You will not see me again, until you say, "Blessed is he who comes".' *Until you say* really means: when you speak this prayer of greeting not only with your lips but from your whole being, then its words will enable you to see my coming in supersensory form. This holy prayer of greeting that makes the human soul ready to receive and perceive the coming Christ stems from the Old Testament, from the psalm which people in Christ's time clearly felt to indicate the future Saviour.

It was on Palm Sunday, as he entered Jerusalem, that the multitude first received the Saviour with this prayer of greeting from Psalm 118. Out of the dimly felt greatness of the historic moment the crowd, lifted beyond itself as if drawn up into a communal clairvoyance, had given voice to these words: 'Blessed be he who comes in the name of the Lord! Hosanna in the highest!' But the instinctive clairvoyance that burst upon souls in that special moment on Palm Sunday could not be kept alive through Holy Week – on Good Friday the 'hosanna' turned into 'Crucify him!' So in his farewell, Christ gave people these words for the distant future.

It is good therefore to look at the full text of the psalm that contains such an important saying. As we begin to read it, we are immediately caught by its joyful and elated rhythm. Old Testament scholarship sees it as a kind of festival liturgy divided between different voices and choruses. The Lord has saved the people and the victory is now celebrated with joy and thankfulness. The psalm therefore begins:

> Give thanks to the LORD, for he is good;
>   for ever his mercy!
> Let Israel say,
>   'For ever his mercy!'
> Let the house of Aaron say,
>   'For ever his mercy!'
> Let those who fear the LORD say,
>   'For ever his mercy!'

'For he is good'. The perhaps better-known Prayer Book version here says, 'for he is gracious'. In the original, however, we find in all its nobility the simple but inexhaustible word 'good', with something of what could be called finality in relation to God himself. It is the word 'good' that rushes from the lips of the rich young man in the Gospel (Mk 10:17f, Lk 18:18f) when he addresses Jesus, 'Good Teacher'. He is then faced with the searching question: 'Why do you call me good?' Has the young man discovered the full value of this word? 'No one is good but God alone.' Yet he takes Jesus for a rabbi. He would only have been able to use the word that belongs to God alone if he had seen into the divine depths of Christ's nature. It is in this primal, sublime sense, belonging only to the divine, that this word 'good' is used at the beginning of the psalm.

The jubilant confession of God's goodness seeks corroboration and confirmation through the community. It appears in three different choruses. First of all 'Israel' is called upon. Then 'the house of Aaron', the priesthood. Finally, all 'who fear the LORD', the great invisible Church of all the religious.

Psalm 118

*Give thanks to the L*ORD*, for he is good;*
   for ever his mercy!

² *Let Israel say,*
   'For ever his mercy!'
³ *Let the house of Aaron say,*
   'For ever his mercy!'
⁴ *Let those who fear the L*ORD *say,*
   'For ever his mercy!'

⁵ *From the strait of my anxiety I called to the L*ORD*;*
   *In the widths the L*ORD *gave answer.*
⁶ *The L*ORD *– to me! Nothing do I fear.*
   What can man do to me?
⁷ *The L*ORD *– to me! He is my help;*
   I look on those that hate me.

⁸ *It is good to trust the L*ORD*,*
   better than trusting in earthly man,
⁹ *It is good to trust the L*ORD*,*
   better than trusting in princes.

¹⁰ *All adversaries surrounded me;*
   *in the name of the L*ORD *I cut them off!*
¹¹ *They surrounded me, surrounded me on every side;*
   *in the name of the L*ORD *I cut them off!*
¹² *They surrounded me like bee-swarms,*
   they went out like a fire of thorns;
   *in the name of the L*ORD *I cut them off!*
¹³ *I was pushed and pushed, so that I was falling,*
   *but the L*ORD *helped me.*

¹⁴ *The Lord is my strength and my song;*
    he has become my salvation.
¹⁵ *Glad songs of victory*
    are in the dwellings of the righteous;
'The right hand of the Lord does mighty things,
    ¹⁶ *the right hand of the Lord is exalted,*
    the right hand of the Lord does mighty things.'
¹⁷ *I shall not die, but I shall live,*
    and recount the deeds of the Lord.
¹⁸ *The Lord has admonished me with admonishments,*
    but he has not given me over to death.

¹⁹ *Open for me the gates of righteousness!*
    I will go through them
    to praise the Lord.
²⁰ *This is the gate of the Lord;*
    the righteous go through it.
²¹ *I praise you who have made me humble*
    and are my salvation.

²² *A stone – the builders rejected it.*
    It has become the cornerstone!
²³ *The Lord brought this about:*
    a marvel to our eyes.
²⁴ *This is the day – the Lord has made it.*
    Let us rejoice! Let us be glad of it!

²⁵ *O Lord, hosanna, – bring us salvation!*
    O Lord, we pray, let us accomplish it!
²⁶ *Blessed is he who comes in the name of the Lord!*
    We bless you from the house of the Lord.
²⁷ *God is the Lord,*
    he is our light.
Bind the festive procession with foliage,
    to the horns of the altar!
²⁸ *You are my God, and I will praise you;*
    You are my God, I will exalt you.
²⁹ *Give thanks to the Lord, for he is good;*
    for ever his mercy!

II

In what follows the psalmist looks back again to the plight from which God has rescued him. 'From the strait of my anxiety I called to the Lord.' Many translations lack a word that conveys the confines or narrowness which would bring out the force of the imagery of verse five. Though archaic, the word 'strait' rather than 'distress' would still perhaps convey the meaning of the Hebrew most directly, as do the words 'hard pressed'. We get the picture of a gorge in which the ever closer rock walls give the feeling of suffocation. It was from this distressing sense of constriction that the cry for help to God arose. The soul once descended from the bright expanses of the heavenly worlds. Now it finds itself in the narrow, rocky gorge of earthly existence, confined by egoism, restricted by life in a hardened material body. It anxiously gasps as it were for air to breathe.

Now the imagery contrasts 'narrowness' with 'width'. The impact is lost without the contrast, that is not reflected in most translations. The human being is confined and restricted; God responds from a state just the opposite. Divine comfort comes to the troubled soul from the 'widths'. It is one of the very first elements of religion: the soul in earthly confinement calling on the divine – the divine answering from the light-filled heavenly expanses.

Following this response from the divine widths there comes the jubilant cry: 'The Lord is on my side'. In the original there is simply God's name and abruptly next to it the dative 'to me': 'The Lord – to me!' It is almost as if this were the original formulation of the dative case, that relates to giving. It is repeated: 'The Lord – to me!'

Those who experiences this inclining of the divine towards them have nothing to fear. Their enemies cannot harm them: 'I shall see my desire on those who hate me', or in many more modern translations: 'I will look in triumph on ...' This sounds really Old Testament-like. Strangely, however, the original says only: 'I will look on my enemies.' We should not necessarily understand the looking to be one of hatred and satisfied vengeance. We may fill this Old Testament expression with the Christian meaning that the gaze of truly Christian people will one day in the future disarm the Adversary.

From this arises the triumphant trust in the divine as against all deceptive and illusory repositories of our trust, such as weak people of the world and rulers.

> From the strait of my anxiety I called to the Lord;
> 	In the widths the Lord gave answer.
> The Lord – to me! Nothing do I fear.
> 	What can man do to me?
> The Lord – to me! He is my help;
> 	I look on those that hate me.
>
> It is good to trust the Lord,
> 	better than trusting in earthly man,
> It is good to trust the Lord,
> 	better than trusting in princes.

III

Once again there is an echo of the affliction undergone. The afflicters, the 'nations', translated from Old Testament into universally human terms, are the powers of the Adversary. The cry of triumph rings out three times: 'In the name of the Lord I cut them off!' It is the experience that reaches its Christian climax in the words of the sacrament at Communion: the power of the Adversary is taken from us when we shelter within the name of Christ. The name is then certainly not just a word but is that in which the presence of the divine being is recognised with full consciousness. The powers that want to bring about humanity's fall by constantly renewed temptation are put to flight by this sheltering within the holy name.

> All adversaries surrounded me;
> 	in the name of the Lord I cut them off!
> They surrounded me, surrounded me on every side;
> 	in the name of the Lord I cut them off!
> They surrounded me like bee-swarms,
> 	they went out like a fire of thorns;
> 	in the name of the Lord I cut them off!
> I was pushed and pushed, so that I was falling,
> 	but the Lord helped me.

IV

Now the rejoicing breaks out again. 'Hark, glad songs.' Only song is able to capture the soul's tremendous feeling of joy. 'The right hand of the Lord does mighty things.' The right hand is the embodiment of action. The Old Testament motif of divine acts of salvation first finds its completion in God's unique, death-conquering deed on Golgotha. Psalm 118 gains its full meaning as an Easter hymn.

This relation to the Easter joy of Christianity comes to light very clearly once more. In verse 17 we enter the Holy of Holies: 'I shall not die, but I shall live.' The psalm touches on the great mystery of life and death and expresses the certainty that human beings finally belong on the side of life, that they are destined for eternity.

In this eternal life they will not exist only for their own sake but will serve the further revelation of the being of God. 'And recount the deeds of the Lord' need not be anything to do with the spoken word. It proclaims God's deed, and the proof of it in humankind's own resurrection.

The psalmist knows full well that he has not yet reached the goal. He still needs the trials and tribulations. 'The Lord has chastened me sorely ...' But these painful blows of destiny will only awaken and chasten and so serve the higher life.

> The Lord is my strength and my song;
>   he has become my salvation.
> Glad songs of victory
>   are in the dwellings of the righteous;
> 'The right hand of the Lord does mighty things,
>   the right hand of the Lord is exalted,
>   the right hand of the Lord does mighty things.'
> I shall not die, but I shall live,
>   and recount the deeds of the Lord.
> The Lord has admonished me with admonishments,
>   but he has not given me over to death.

V

After the breakthrough to Easter certainty – as could hardly be otherwise in the wonderfully organic series of pictures – doors that were previously closed begin to open.

If one looks at the psalm in relation to its historical background, one can naturally suppose that at this point in the great festival liturgy of victory, the procession of celebrants has arrived in front of the temple and demands entry. 'Open for me the gates of righteousness!' But this does not exhaust the meaning of the sentence. The expression 'gates of righteousness' indicates that the temple doors become images of more exalted doorways. Higher worlds are about to open up.

'Righteousness' is not complacent correctness. We speak of work or material being right or correct. 'Right' is what fits like a trimmed stone in building so that one can make use of it. 'Right' is what exists in accord with the divine harmony of the universe. Therefore only the righteous can pass through the doors. 'The gates of righteousness' then become 'the gate of the Lord'. All the harmony of the universe ultimately has its origin in Christ himself.

Nor should we overlook how soon 'humility'* is mentioned after 'righteousness'. The righteous for whom these gates are to be opened are not yet fit for the divine world if they are not capable of humility.

> Open for me the gates of righteousness!
>   I will go through them
>   to praise the Lord.
> This is the gate of the Lord;
>   the righteous go through it.
> I praise you who have made me humble
>   and are my salvation.

VI

After this mention of humility there appears the puzzling image of the stone which the builders rejected that has become the cornerstone. God himself in his Messiah offers the greatest example of humility.

---

* This Hebrew *anah*, usually translated as 'answered' also means 'to be humbled'.

Here we find the presentiment that the Messiah, when he comes, does not seize power unquestioned and as a matter of course, but remains inconspicuous. So much so that he lays himself open to misunderstanding and rejection out of love for our freedom. On the Tuesday of Holy Week, Christ himself quotes these words from the psalm in direct connection with the sombre parable of the evil workers in the vineyard who kill the beloved son of the owner. Christ knew that as the rejected and condemned one, he would build the new temple in the resurrection – first the temple of his resurrection body, which is the beginning of the great and all-embracing resurrection denoted by the heavenly Jerusalem.

This word 'cornerstone' therefore contains a Christian mystery of 'building' that first becomes recognisable in the light of the Easter events. 'The LORD brought this about: a marvel to our eyes' – words with which even today Christendom can express its awed astonishment in face of the Easter event, because Easter is *the* marvel.

Through the marvel the eternal enters the temporal. Thereby time becomes something different; it takes on a content of eternity that almost breaks through it. A new 'day' shines as once the first day of creation shone in the primal divine light. Easter is this new day, which emerges as if directly from God's hands and which seeks its glorification in the radiant joy of the redeemed soul.

> A stone – the builders rejected it.
>   It has become the cornerstone!
> The LORD brought this about:
>   a marvel to our eyes.
> This is the day – the LORD has made it.
>   Let us rejoice! Let us be glad of it!

VII

The multitude felt that a true Sunday glory shone around them on Palm Sunday, the octave of which is Easter Sunday. Walking in the light of the day which 'the LORD has made' the people give voice to the verse of greeting: 'Blessed be he who comes in the name of the Lord!' The 'hosanna' that is linked to it is, like 'amen' and 'hallelujah', one of the Hebrew words that the New Testament did not translate into Greek but retained with the full force of their original sound. 'Hosanna' means 'Save us!' Together with 'hosanna', 'blessed be ...' in its Latin form, has entered into the mass and the great musical settings of the mass: *'Benedictus qui venit in nomine Domini'*. Bruckner's *Mass in F minor*, for example, shows most beautifully what a wealth of devotional Christian feeling has sprung from these words.

In the psalm there now follows an expression that in connection with the Old Testament festival procession was apparently spoken to those entering the temple precinct by the priests waiting there. 'We bless you from the house of the LORD.' One could thus conclude that the preceding sentence, 'Blessed is he', did not necessarily mean the Messiah, but was intended for the pilgrim who was solemnly approaching the temple. That sense may also have lain in the words at the time. Clearly, however, it was also felt that this sacred expression bore overtones of yet greater things. The pilgrims who solemnly made their way to the temple in Jerusalem were ultimately only the forerunners of the One who would one day truly enter his temple – the human body, of which the temple in Jerusalem was an image. The pious souls of the Old Covenant were able to divine behind the approaching pilgrims the figure of the great One who should come, the Messiah, the Christ. When later on Judaism was opposed to Christianity, it quite intentionally allowed such Messianic references in the Old Testament to fall into the background. But it is evident from the behaviour of the crowd on Palm Sunday that this verse, 'Blessed is he who comes', was once applied to the Messiah.

What, then, from our standpoint is meant by the verse: 'God is the LORD, he is our light'? Such a verse is an attestation of visionary experiences in the religious worship of the ancient past. Through true religious worship people were once able to behold the presence of the divine. At the climax came the Epiphany, the appearance of the god before the celebrants. Then gradually in the course of time these visionary faculties died out. They came to life again in a certain way in the Christian era, since up until the Middle Ages some Christians had a direct experience through the sacrament of the actual coming of Christ. Such experiences will again become possible in the future as a result of new faculties in human consciousness. Then an Old Testament expression will again find its full meaning: 'he is our light'.

'We have seen his glory' as it is expressed in the prologue of John's Gospel (1:14).

In connection with this the psalm speaks of the foliage or green branches that were carried by the participants in the sacred festival procession. This also reminds us of Palm Sunday. Through the green branches nature itself proclaims the great mystery: how from death new life arises. 'I shall live.'

> O Lord, hosanna, – bring us salvation!
>   O Lord, we pray, let us accomplish it!
> Blessed is he who comes in the name of the Lord!
>   We bless you from the house of the Lord.
> God is the Lord,
>   he is our light.
> Bind the festive procession with foliage,
>   to the horns of the altar!
> You are my God, and I will praise you;
>   You are my God, I will exalt you.
> Give thanks to the Lord, for he is good;
>   for his mercy endures for ever!

47

'SIT AT MY RIGHT HAND'

PSALM 110

For Christians, the picture of Christ sitting at the right hand of the Father has always been related to the event of the Ascension. Modern people cannot connect with this picture, because they take it in a spatial sense and so regard it as absurd. But the Ascension is not an outward process. It is a visionary experience of the apostles, who perceive that Christ is raised to a higher order of being. He now shares in a heavenly form of being in which he can, for the first time, really carry out his promise, 'I am with you always'. Now at last he can really be with us in his divine presence everywhere on earth. Similarly, Christ's 'sitting at the right hand of the Father' is also a visionary picture, which should not be taken in a physical sense. Sometimes we say about someone who acts completely in accordance with the will of another, that they are his 'right hand'. Thus the ascended Christ is 'the fulfiller of the deeds of the Father, the Ground of the World,' as the Creed of The Christian Community expresses it.

What does this mean? Christ, the Son, is at first experienced by human beings as a power within them. But he is able ever more and more to radiate outwards from within, and can finally influence the whole being of a man, even the body and blood. Our body and blood stem from very high powers who are so strong that they can carry the spiritual into the physical world. They are 'magic' forces, in the noblest and purest sense, which are able to bridge the gulf between spirit and matter; that is, they are primal, divine Father-forces. So when the Christ who has initially been experienced in a purely inward way begins to work right into the depths of the bodily organism, he is working together with the Father-forces. In that he is capable of

> **Psalm 110**
>
> A Psalm of David
>
> *Murmuring utterance of the L*ORD
>   *to him, who is my Lord:*
> *'Sit at my right hand,*
>   *until I lay your adversaries as your footstool.'*
> *² The L*ORD *extends the staff of your strength from Zion.*
>   *Rule in the midst of your adversaries!*
>
> *³ Your people – volunteers*
>   *on the day of full unfolding*
>   *they shine in sacred vestments.*
> *From the womb of the morning,*
>   *the dew of your youth will be yours.*
> *⁴ The L*ORD *has sworn*
>   *and will not change,*
> *'You are a priest forever*
>   *after the order of Melchizedek.'*
>
> *⁵ The Lord at your right hand*
>   *shatters kings on the day of his wrath.*
> *⁶ He will judge the nations,*
>   *causing many corpses.*
> *he will shatter the heads*
>   *over the wide earth.*
> *⁷ He will drink from the brook by the way;*
>   *therefore he will lift up the head.*

transfiguring our body from within, and finally of wresting it from death itself, he 'sits at the right hand of the Father'.

This descriptive phrase, which plays such an important part in the New Testament, is taken from Psalm 110. It is Christ himself who quotes this psalm, when he wishes to show the Pharisees that the Messiah must certainly be of a higher order than a mere descendant of David (Mt 22:44). In the New Testament this psalm is quoted most often. It is also exceptional in that it mentions by name the mysterious priest-king Melchizedek, who comes into the story of Abraham but does not appear anywhere else in the Old Testament.

Christ's conversation with the Pharisees shows that the Psalm 110 was applied by the representatives of Judaism to the Messiah at that time. It was possible for Christ to presuppose the view that when David, the author of the psalm, says, 'the LORD said to my Lord, "sit at my right hand",' he meant by 'my Lord', the Messiah. It was only later on, when opposition to Christianity played a part in Jewish religious life, that rabbis took up the forced interpretation that the reference was to Abraham. And it is not without interest that it was a representative of Jewish esoteric teaching, the Kabbalist Obadiah Sforno, who upheld the connection of Psalm 110 with the Messiah.*

I

The psalm begins, in a particularly solemn mood, with a word which actually means 'murmur' or 'oracular utterance', and suggests a secret, divine breathe, or inspiration.

> *A Psalm of David*
> Murmuring utterance of the LORD
>   to him, who is my Lord:
> 'Sit at my right hand,
>   until I lay your adversaries as your footstool.'
> The LORD extends the staff of your strength from Zion.
>   Rule in the midst of your adversaries!

This Old Testament way of speaking may seem strange to us at first. Can we recognise the Christ in this warlike figure of a victorious king? Does he not renounce just this, that his followers should fight for his kingdom with the sword? But in the end he does fight and conquer – only on a higher level. To deliver himself without resistance to crucifixion, and precisely through his own self-giving to win the hearts of people to a discipleship in freedom – this is his way of fighting. 'For this reason the Son of God was revealed, so that he might destroy the works of the devil' (1Jn 3:8). But he fights in his own special way. The commitment and the heroism are not less than in a 'real' war.

---

* Obadiah ben Jacob Sforno (*c.* 1470–1500) Italian rabbi and philosopher.

The picture of the victorious Messiah with his enemies under his feet is also one which must be translated out of the Old Testament. What someone overcomes is put 'beneath them'. Thus it becomes part of what carries them in life and gives them ground under their feet. What opposes gains purpose only when it is overcome.

II

The second section has a quite different ring. The strong, warlike pictures completely disappear. Secrets of the future begin to shine with a promise of blessing. But they are still veiled, and this second part has proved particularly puzzling to commentators. They are only really understandable from a Christian viewpoint.

> Your people – volunteers
>   on the day of full unfolding
>   they shine in sacred vestments.
> From the womb of the morning,
>   the dew of your youth will be yours.
> The LORD has sworn
>   and will not change,
> 'You are a priest forever
>   after the order of Melchizedek.'

The Messiah, the Redeemer, fights and conquers through sacrifice of himself. The king is also priest. His priesthood has been granted him by God through a solemn oath.

We are reminded of Psalm 2:7. There too the poet, David, is raised to a higher world where he can receive divine inspiration. 'I will declare a decree of the LORD. He said to me, "You are my son. Today I have begotten you".' It is as though the inward, divine mystery of the birth of the Son echoes in the soul of the psalmist out of the higher spiritual worlds. The emergence of the Son, in whom the Father places his 'you' over against himself, is a divine process which is above all temporality; it is a process in the timeless 'today' of eternity. It is 'the Son born in eternity'. The original text states baldly and monumentally: 'My Son – you.' The Son is enabled to reveal his I, because the Father has said 'you' to him. The background of the 'I am' spoken by the Son is the 'you are' of the Father.

Just as in Psalm 2 David hears in heaven that eternal acknowledgment of Sonship, so in the murmuring of Psalm 110 he hears the acknowledgment of priesthood: 'You are a priest for ever.' The Son, the 'you' who has emerged from the depths of the Father-being, makes the true divine use of his I-hood. He turns to the Father in sacrifice. The Son who brings the offering is the High Priest of the universe. Sacrifice is his primal, free activity, yet he does not lay claim to it as such. He feels it as given by the Father. Thus in John's Gospel (17:4) Christ speaks of the 'work which you gave me to do'. So his priestly activity rests on the foundation of this acknowledgment, 'You are a priest for ever.'

These words are described in the psalms as 'sworn' by God. When someone swears, they call upon the presence of God as a strengthening for their own words. But God cannot swear by anyone but himself. So this word sworn by God may mean that God strengthens himself in himself, in an inner concentration of his own divine being. The priesthood of the Son is founded on this powerful affirmation and concentration. God will never 'change' this oath, it is the unchangeable, eternal basis for the work of the Son, who is active in the becoming, in the offering and in the transformation of his priesthood.

'After the order of Melchizedek.' Through that high priest-king, a pure sun-ritual was once brought to Abraham in the emblems of bread and wine. With the name of Melchizedek a whole stream of human history is conjured up, which comes to its climax in the historic deed of sacrifice of the Son on Golgotha.

Christ wants to raise human beings who accept him to the same rank of his sonship. They are to grow from children to sons of God. This also means that he wishes to draw them into co-operation in his priestly activity. They are not merely to watch his deed of salvation from the outside; they are to take part themselves in the continued effect of this deed. Thus, when the sacrifice of Christ comes to new life in individual Christians, the general priesthood of all believers comes into being. In this way the 'people' belongs to the Messiah, as the psalm says in the original text, literally: 'Your people – volunteers'. The word 'volunteers' appears in the plural. Christ's people are not a 'mass' who blindly obey a dictator, but a coming together of free personalities. Roger Williams, the noble seventeenth century pioneer of religious freedom in America, spoke of 'true volunteers ... of Christ Jesus'.*

The people of Christ, who have joined together out of pure individual free will, shine forth in holy vestments. As human beings they have cleansed their supersensible aura. In the words of the Apocalypse, 'they have washed their robes and made them white in the blood of the Lamb' (Rv 7:14). The psalm knows very well that this can only become reality 'on the day of your power', at that moment when the power of Christ within human beings will come to its full unfolding.

This en-Christened humanity appears at the same time as 'youth'. 'From the womb of the morning comes the dew of your youth.' Future humankind is rejuvenated from above. It has overcome the cleverness of worldly old age in the Christian universal festival of rejuvenation, and its life is renewed as the freshness of an early dawn.

What happens within these human beings cannot be understood through mere earthly, materialistic thinking. Rejuvenation through the spirit remains a riddle to intellectual comprehension. The psalm speaks of 'dew'. When a meadow is wet with rain, everyone has seen the dark clouds from which the heavy drops have fallen. But dew comes unseen, unnoticed, in the holy hours of early dawn. The dew emerges mysteriously from the unseen. It is born as it were etherically 'from the womb of the morning'. The soul-stirring power of the aurora, the rosy light of dawn, has been deeply felt right up to the time of Jakob Böhme, and of Goethe's *Faust*. The rejuvenation of humankind comes down to the earth like dew from the heavenly supersensible world, in a new dawn.

III

The third part leads back into the rough, warlike world of the first:

> The Lord at your right hand
>   shatters kings on the day of his wrath.
> He will judge the nations,
>   causing many corpses.
> he will shatter the heads

---

* Knowles, *Memoir of Roger Williams,* p. 381.

> over the wide earth.
> He will drink from the brook by the way;
> therefore he will lift up the head.

The prophetic, apocalyptic vision is directed towards future catastrophes. As the Christ will not force people to accept salvation, but allows the full fruit of his deed of salvation to depend on their free acceptance of it, inevitably there will also be rejection. And this rejection will by inner necessity lead to catastrophes. A humanity which shuts itself off from the divine love finally rages against itself. It sets in motion the iron necessities which are rooted in the eternal being of God. Whoever sows mistrust, reaps mistrust. Whoever sows hate, reaps hate. Whoever sows death, reaps death. In so far as this law is founded on the justice of God, God brings these catastrophes; but it is human beings who 'ask for them'. The destruction which human beings bring into the world must hit back on themselves in the end, unless they find refuge in Christ. But wherever Christ's deed of salvation is not able to work through human rejection, there necessity must work. In this sense we can understand when the psalm says of God, 'causing many corpses'. This terrible vision of many dead bodies can already be recognised today much more deeply in all its horror than in David's time.

The work of annihilation also strikes back on 'kings' and on 'the heads over the wide earth'. Here we have to think less of political dictators – though perhaps these also – than on human intelligence and sovereign powers in general, which are becoming more and more the rulers of our mechanised lives. Do we not, as readers of today, recognise in 'the heads over the wide earth' the overwhelming intellectual powers of the human head?

But the 'head' is not only mentioned negatively. Certainly, the head which rules the earth in loveless, cold, and godless intellectuality will be 'shattered'. But what lives in the human head can also be included in the work of salvation. Through the power of Christ, intelligence can also turn towards the supersensible, it can be transformed from mere cleverness into wisdom. Then there comes about what the Bible calls the 'lifting up of the head'. Just because the Saviour has drunk 'from the brook by the way' – which surely means that he has bowed down deeply to the earth – just because of that, he is able to bring about 'the lifting up of the head'.

48

THE NEW SONG

PSALM 96

I

Again and again the religion of the Old Testament points beyond its own confines. Psalm 96 proclaims the message of Advent: 'He comes'. It begins by speaking of the 'new song'.

'Oh sing to the LORD a new song.' It is regrettable that this line has lost some of its freshness through ecclesiastical use. We must listen to it as if it were said for the first time, and ask for its concrete meaning. The 'new song' – 'new' signifies here more than just something different from the old. The 'new song' belongs to the same realm as 'the new covenant in my blood' (1Cor 11:25), 'a new commandment I give to you' (Jn 13:34), or 'behold, I make all things new' (Rv 21:5).

'New' has a particular relationship to Christ. It is linked with the mystery of the I AM. In the I we meet the original wellspring of a human being, the uniqueness, which is singular and irreplaceable. In each I the world is mirrored in a unique manner, life assumes a special colour not repeated anywhere else, a 'new' sound, special and unrepeatable, is heard. Through Christ, this human selfhood is purified from self-seeking and transfigured into the pattern of the creative I, the higher self, from which the divine life rises ever youthful, unspoiled, fresh and 'new'. In the en-Christened I the world is constantly re-created from the source of everlasting renewal.

It may have been inevitable that in pre-Christian ages the pessimism should be felt at times which is voiced in Ecclesiastes: 'Vanity of vanities; all is vanity.' It is not for nothing that it is followed by the saying, 'There is no new thing under the sun' (Eccl 1:2, 9). The

Psalm 96

*Oh sing to the L*ORD *a song of new beginnings;*
   *sing to the L*ORD*, all the earth!*
² *Sing to the L*ORD*, proclaim his name with blessing;*
   Declare his healing deeds from day to day.
³ *Declare his glory to the nature-worshipping nations,*
   his wonders among all the peoples!
⁴ *For the L*ORD *is great and held in much awe;*
   he is above all gods.
⁵ *The gods of the peoples are worthless,*
   *But the L*ORD *of the I* AM *made the heavens.*

⁶ *His countenance radiates the light of revelation and*
         splendour of majesty.
   Power and beauty fill his sanctuary.
⁷ *Give offerings to the L*ORD*, O families of the people,*
   *give to the L*ORD *glory and strength.*
⁸ *Offer to the L*ORD *the glory due his name;*
   Bring an offering, and come into his forecourts.
⁹ *Worship the L*ORD *in the sacred adornment of holiness;*
   stand in awe before him, all the earth!

¹⁰ *Let it be said among the nature-worshipping nations:*
   *'The L*ORD *of the I* AM *has become king!*
He has given firm ground to the world; it shall not be moved;
   He will lead the people in an upright course.'
¹¹ *Let the heavens rejoice, let the earth be glad;*
   let the sea and all its fulness roar in thunder;
¹² *Let the fields be joyful and all that they bear;*
then all the trees of the forest shall sing for joy ¹³ *before the*
      L*ORD.*
   For he is coming! For he is coming!
He will rule the earth into the order of God,
   he will show the right ways to all the world
   into the Amen-power of his truth.

two sayings belong together. Something like the negative opposite to Christianity was felt and suffered in those ages. But this, too, was part of the preparation. The Church Fathers were right when they claimed that the incarnation of the Son of God was the new thing under the sun. Only with the incarnation did life acquire meaning, and the I a creative quality. Now it is no longer true that 'all is vanity', senseless and useless, but now everything points towards the great transformation. 'Behold, I make all things new.' The 'new song' is the great hymn of transformation, the song of the renewal of the world.

The Revelation to John says of this song of renewal that it can only be sung by those who have been touched by the blood of Christ (14:3). Only those are able to 'learn' the new song.

Psalm 96, in which the sunlike being of Christ is felt, mediated as it were through the Lord Yahweh, speaks in a universally human manner of the nations (or heathens) to whom the glory of the Lord shall be proclaimed. The nations would go on with the singing of the 'old song'; they are still under the spell of the ancient religion in which the gods spoke through nature and natural events. But those who continue to seek God in the old direction, in outward manifestations, are in danger of looking for him where he is no longer to be found. God will now reveal himself in the innermost being, in the I. For this reason the psalm refers to the heathen gods as 'worthless'. But the existence of other gods is not simply denied. In the Christian conception they would be placed among the celestial hierarchies in their several ranks. But 'the LORD is ... above all gods' – who therefore must exist. Similarly, in some other psalms: he is 'the great king above all gods' (Ps 95:3), 'you are exalted far above all gods' (Ps 97:9). The sun and his glory, which the heathen worshipped outwardly in the cosmos, shall now be found in the God who speaks the I AM.

> Oh sing to the LORD a song of new beginnings;
>   sing to the LORD, all the earth!
> Sing to the LORD, proclaim his name with blessing;
>   Declare his healing deeds from day to day.
> Declare his glory to the nature-worshipping nations,
>   his wonders among all the peoples!

> For the LORD is great and held in much awe;
>   he is above all gods.
> The gods of the peoples are worthless,
>   But the LORD of the I AM made the heavens.

II

The whole of humanity is exhorted to find this God who carries the mystery of the I. The psalm knows of a ritual which is celebrated in higher worlds as a pattern and type for all ritual services on earth. While in Psalm 29, where the heavenly ritual is also known, we are shown the 'sons of God' (*bene elim*) serving as priests in the temple of God, in Psalm 96 we are taken a step further. Human beings, too, shall now grow worthy to celebrate the heavenly act. Human beings are to become priestly. Like the angels, they should reveal God with their entire being. Fallen human beings do not reveal God in their being, they obscure, they hides them, and celebrate only too often the ritual of the Adversary.

'Come into his forecourts.' Through their estrangement from God, human beings have been so much absorbed into profane and secular things that they can only gradually get used again to a living together with divine worlds and to the manners which are required: awe, devotion and reverence. It is impossible to enter straightaway from the secular world into the Holy of Holies. It is no use if some theologians, completely immersed in the modern material worldview, begin simply to talk about 'God'. There are 'forecourts' and they have their significance.

The 'sacred array' which the priestly soul wears in the 'sanctuary', is the reflection of the divine radiance mirrored in the devout worshipper. Fallen man saw that he was naked. The shame of nakedness is present wherever nothing but the material body is known, and the higher, finer, luminous members of our being are unknown, which in reality clothe us. Admitted again into the sanctuary man catches the divine splendour in the illumination of the supersensible vestments of our soul and spirit.

> His countenance radiates the light of revelation and
>   splendour of majesty.

> Power and beauty fill his sanctuary.
> Give offerings to the LORD, O families of the people,
>   give to the LORD glory and strength.
> Offer to the LORD the glory due his name;
>   Bring an offering, and come into his forecourts.
> Worship the LORD in the sacred adornment of holiness;
>   stand in awe before him, all the earth!

III

A far-off future perfection is anticipated in this vision. But before this can be achieved, something else has to be done. Human beings cannot enter the sanctuary on their own authority and volition. If they are to be saved from exile in the secular world, God must come to meet them. Before they can enter the kingdom of God, God enters the human world. This event took place in Christ. Our psalm is inspired by the expectation of the Messiah. The writer knows that a gracious development has begun, an act of grace moving towards humanity. 'He comes.' He has become king. (The Hebrew does not simply say, 'the LORD reigns,' but he 'has *become* king,' something real has happened.) His light begins to shine in the realm in which the power of the human I is destined to rule as a king.

The drawing near of the divine I AM, who wills to be active in the kingdom of the growing free personality of human beings, affects the whole cosmos. Though the new God will be received in the inwardness of human hearts, he will radiate from there into all the world and extend salvation also to the creation. The significance of Advent reaches far beyond the human world, though it can only begin in the inwardness of the soul.

The psalm finds wonderful references to nature. We sense the atmosphere of Advent and Christmas when 'the trees of the forest' are mentioned. It is as if, from the rustling of the trees, the call is born which represents the climax of this psalm and which is significantly repeated in powerful rhythms: 'For he is coming! For he is coming!'

> Let it be said among the nature-worshipping nations:
>   'The LORD of the I AM has become king!
> He has given firm ground to the world; it shall not be moved;

48. THE NEW SONG

    He will lead the people in an upright course.'
Let the heavens rejoice, let the earth be glad;
    let the sea and all its fulness roar in thunder;
    Let the fields be joyful and all that they bear;
then all the trees of the forest shall sing for joy before the
        LORD.
    For he is coming! For he is coming!
He will rule the earth into the order of God,
    he will show the right ways to all the world
    into the Amen-power of his truth.

49

ADVENT

PSALM 24

I

> To the Lord the earth and its fullness,
>   The world and those who dwell therein,
> for he has established it upon the seas
>   and founded it upon the flowing streams.

A terse and majestic style is characteristic of this psalm. 'To the Lord the earth.' This is primarily an assertion. The earth belongs to him. It belongs to him by right, for he has created it, has founded it in solidity. The earth was not always so hard and solid. The hardness of its rocks is not a matter of course. In primeval times it had still a different physical condition. From a supersensible origin it progressed through fine etheric modes of existence, becoming ever more material. The finer the substance of which the earth once consisted, the more alive it still could be. Pulsating with streams of life, imbued with the breath of divine creative impulses – that was the condition of the earth in primeval times. Like rigid ice forms out of moving water that answers each breath of wind with delicate ripples, so too did the earth become hard and rigid out of a state of flowing life to become at last really 'earth'. For its name, with deep significance, is derived from the solid element. Its densification has reached its limit, it can never become harder than stone. It is no longer the living Mother Earth of former days; the state of life that it once possessed as a whole is now continued in the separate living creatures.

The hardening of the earth came about for the sake of human beings. Called to self-reliance and freedom, they need hard resistance

> ### Psalm 24
>
> *To the L*ORD *the earth and its fullness,*
> *The world and those who dwell therein,*
> *² for he has established it upon the seas*
> *and founded it upon the flowing streams.*
>
> *³ Who shall ascend the hill of the L*ORD*?*
> *And who shall stand in his holy place?*
> *⁴ He who has clean hands and a pure heart,*
> *who does not lift up his soul to vanity*
> *and does not swear deceitfully,*
> *⁵ He shall receive blessing from the L*ORD*,*
> *and righteousness from the God of his salvation.*
> *⁶ This is the generation of those who seek him,*
> *who seek your countenance, O God of Jacob.*
> Selah
>
> *⁷ Lift up your heads, O gates!*
> *And be lifted up, O portals of eternity!*
> *The king of glory shall come in.*
> *⁸ Who is the king of glory?*
> *It is the L*ORD*, a mighty hero,*
> *the L*ORD*, a hero in battle!*
> *⁹ Lift up your heads, O gates!*
> *And lift up, O portals of eternity!*
> *The king of glory shall come in.*
> *¹⁰ Who is this king of glory?*
> *It is the L*ORD *of Hosts,*
> *he is the king of glory!*
> Selah

as the hammer needs the anvil, in order to be able to grasp themselves inwardly as an I. The forming of the solid ground for human beings was the work of the God who willed the I.

But with the solidifying of the earth another possibility arose. The world was no longer filled by direct divine life. Human beings could thus become strangers to their heavenly origin and become liable to the influence of the powers of the Adversary. Thus through humanity making itself increasingly independent of heaven, a kingdom could gradually arise upon earth of the un-godlike – in fact of the anti-godlike – to such a degree that Christ himself described the Adversary as the 'Prince of this world' (Jn 12:31). The Tempter in the wilderness had said, 'I will give you all this authority [*exousia*] and all glory, for it has been given to me; and I give it to whom I wish. If you will worship me, all shall be yours.' Lk 4:6f).

Human beings have made themselves independent on earth, and the Adversary, by way of those he has drawn into his influence, tries to gain ever surer control of the earthly world and break off the human earthly kingdom from the divine in order to make it his own. He has not yet fully succeeded, but this whole process of gradually separating a world estranged from God is at work. It is up to human beings whether the Adversary achieves his purpose or not. God has appeared anew upon earth in Christ that he may, in love for human beings, win their freedom, and through them also regain the earth for the heavens. The psalm only receives its full meaning through Christ. The sentence 'To the LORD the earth' is then no longer just a declaration that it belongs to him – it is something that must be newly brought about. The earth is to be brought back again to the divine from which it has largely fallen away, through those human beings who offer their worship to the true God and not to the 'Prince of this world'.

That the earth is no longer as clearly the property of God as the heavens are, is not a concept foreign to the psalms. In Psalm 115:16, we read, 'The heavens of the heavens belong to the LORD but he has given the earth to the sons of humankind.'

Against this background the first sentence of Psalm 24 is no longer the statement of an undisputed fact; it acquires the character of a wish. 'To the LORD the earth' becomes a dedication, a consecration, an offering. Humankind, to whom the earth was given as a 'playground', places this playground of their independence again at the disposal of God in freely resolved sacrifice. They will help through their devotion to re-establish the kingdom of God, and wrest the earthly sphere from the Adversary. All sacrifice rests fundamentally upon the knowledge that the world is God's from the beginning; it belongs to him, and yet again it does not belong to him. I use my human freedom to make him again the full possessor of his own possession in that I bring him his own as an offering.

II

Here the psalm seems to make a direct break and turn to a completely different subject with no real transition. But there is an unspoken link. If we see the sentence, 'To the Lord the earth,' as an offering, we assume that the earth no longer belongs to the kingdom of God as a matter of course, we realise that the Fall has taken place. Then human beings, filled with longing, strive once more towards the divine from their fallen state. The second part of the psalm speaks of this endeavour.

> Who shall ascend the hill of the Lord?
> And who shall stand in his holy place?

All human 'ascents' to God were initially a partial overcoming of the Fall. The mountains soar upwards as a symbol of 'exalted' human states. Many of them were therefore guarded as holy mountains, the mountains of God known to all religions. Thus Moses was able to meet God on the holy mountain and receive his revelation. Such great sages were the teachers of pupils who, following their guidance, left lower things behind and ascended to the 'hill of God' and to the 'dwellings of God' there. 'This is the generation of those who seek him, who seek your countenance, O God of Jacob.' Psalm 73:15 uses the expression, 'the generation of your children,' and in a similar way our psalm speaks of the generation of those that seek God's countenance. These people form something like a religious order. They are in reality an invisible community all over the earth, a 'communion of saints' as the early community of Christians were called.

Since the holy place of God is on the heights of the holy mountain, those who raise themselves to this experience must satisfy certain conditions: they must be purified in thoughts, words and deeds. It is not enough to find the strength to ascend. Having reached the heights they must now also be able to 'stand' before God's face – which means to withstand, endure. Without previous purification, they would be annihilated; they could not maintain their own consciousness. It is only 'in Christ' that human beings will be able fully to maintain their transmuted, Christ-permeated I in the divine world. They then possesses a consciousness of self, not only when they live on earth in the confines of the material body, but they may also carry it into their time spent as 'spirit among spirits'.

The question, 'Who shall ascend?' has a parallel in Psalm 15:1, which asks, 'O Lord, who shall abide in your tent? Who shall dwell on your holy hill?' We should remember the 'tent' of his presence, the tabernacles, is the expression for the immediate, almost densified, presence of God. With 'dwelling' is connected the being fed 'at the table of the Lord', the mystery of the communion; and the 'dwell' corresponds to the Johannine 'abide'. This is more than the temporary state of being a guest. Someone who dwells on the holy hill (Peter speaks on the mount of the transfiguration of building tabernacles) has now become a citizen of the higher world again. The Letter to the Hebrews speaks of this (12:22–24): 'You have come to Mount Zion, to the city of the living God, the heavenly Jerusalem, and to innumerable angels in festal gathering, to the assembly of the church of the firstborn, whose names are written in heaven, and to God the judge of all, to the spirits of the righteous made perfect, and to Jesus, the mediator of a new covenant.'

In these questions and answers theological commentators have rightly glimpsed an echo of the ancient ritual of question and answer at the portals of the sanctuaries. The priest as 'guardian of the threshold' gave such answers to one who came to a temple asking for admittance. In such ritualistic usage we recognise the shadow of the ancient mysteries. The answer to the question, 'Who shall ascend?' runs:

> He who has clean hands and a pure heart,
>   who does not lift up his soul to vanity
>   and does not swear deceitfully,
> He shall receive blessing from the Lord,
>   and righteousness from the God of his salvation.
> This is the generation of those who seek him,
>   who seek your countenance, O God of Jacob.
>   *Selah*

Those who satisfy the demands and are pure in thoughts, words and deeds (pure heart, no deceit, clean hands) shall receive blessing and righteousness. This blessing is the love from above that crowns the aspirations from below. The efforts for purification are answered by the light of grace from above, even as the Transubstantiation follows the Offering. The 'righteousness' referred to is obviously not an expression of the purity and moral qualities possessed by those who aspire to enter the sanctuary. Human endeavour must always await completion through the love from above. Righteousness here is endowment by grace with the very being of goodness. Experiences of purification, of 'catharsis', are concealed in the challenging words of the stern guardian of the threshold.

A particular note is sounded in the words, 'the generation of those who seek … your countenance, O God of Jacob,' coming at the end of the second part of this psalm. Those who have found the way to the holy mount and its gifts of grace no longer stand alone, but know that they now belong to a spiritual community. The old communities were formed through ties of blood, determined through the body. To 'seek' the divine and God's face – this places them in a new community, which has its bond of union in the spirit.

The psalm is still restricted to the 'God of Jacob'. But that does not prevent us, in the manner of the early Christians, from thinking of the true 'Israel' as the Christian Church, which was built on the twelve-hood of the apostles and was to include people of every kind under heaven. We may remember, too, that the God of Jacob is the God who revealed himself in the dream in which the angels ascend and descend on the heavenly ladder, and in the prayer at the scene of wrestling by the ford. ('I will not let you go unless you bless me' Gn 32:26.)

The dream was at Bethel (House of God), the fight was at Peniel (Countenance of God). Our psalm has as its theme the finding of the way to the house and to the countenance of God.

III

The concluding part now follows, and again with no apparent transition:

> Lift up your heads, O gates!
> And be lifted up, O portals of eternity!
> The king of glory shall come in.
> Who is the king of glory?
> It is the LORD, a mighty hero,
> the LORD, a hero in battle!

Commentators see in these verses a festival liturgy, perhaps an alternating chant of two choirs at the solemn reception of the Ark of the Covenant returning from victorious battle. That may have been the historical motive for the composition of the psalm. However, a more far-reaching truth is expressed in it.

The psalm celebrates the entry of the approaching God. An important apocalyptic motif is thus introduced. How can the God 'come'? Is he not already the omnipresent, filling all things? How then can he come when he is already there? Or is he perhaps after all not completely there, on the earth?

What we have said about the first part of the psalm gives the key to this question. We saw that the earthly realm no longer belongs unequivocally to the divine. This does not, of course, imply that God is not present on earth. He is everywhere. But there are degrees of his presence. His presence is, so to speak, more condensed in the heavenly sanctuaries of the higher world than on earth. Where a crime is committed, for instance, God in a certain sense is not there; for if he were completely present, not even the thought of a crime could ever arise. 'He has given the earth to the sons of humankind' (Ps 115:16). He has left it and has withdrawn his full presence from it in order that humankind might have space for its freedom. Such a thought makes it possible to speak of a 'coming of God'.

This re-entering of God into the earthly sphere which had fallen into the possession of the Prince of this world, began with the appearance of Christ. It was done in such a manner as not to impinge on human freedom. The cross is the mystery of the 'powerless God' who, through renouncing the outer power, unfolds power of another order through his sacrificial love. The power issuing from the Mystery of Golgotha does not create redemption in an automatic fashion. People are not redeemed through it whether they want to be or not. In every instance people must set this redemption in motion through their free assent; in other words, for redemption to become effective, human 'faith' is required.

The gradual re-entering of the divine into the earthly world is a process in stages. The 'coming' began with Christ becoming man. It continues with humankind becoming Christian. Gradually we are to become capable of beholding Christ's etheric light-form. He himself gave the promise that he will come again 'in glory' (Mt 25:31) – that is to say, in radiant etheric light. This coming is the ever-increasing realisation of the presence of Christ on earth. His presence will become 'denser' and more noticeable, until finally it is directly perceived supersensibly. This 'return' in the 'clouds of heaven', which begins gradually and is fully realised through long epochs of time, brings with it a judgment. As the reality of Christ becomes increasingly evident, we are more and more seriously faced with the question as to what use we shall make of our freedom, whether we shall respond with 'Yes' or 'No'; whether we shall serve Christ or the Prince of this world.

This 'coming' of God into the earthly world is foreshadowed in the Old Testament. A series of seven psalms centre round the theme of the re-established kingdom of Yahweh (47, 93, 95, 96, 97, 98, 99): 'the LORD has become King'.

It is prophesied that the divine will prevail again in the realm of the earth. So we read in Psalm 95:6–8, 'Oh come, let us worship and bow down, let us kneel before the LORD ... Today if you hear his voice, do not harden your hearts.' Psalm 96 begins with the apocalyptic motive of the 'new song' (compare Rv 5:9 and 14:3). 'Oh sing unto the LORD a song of new beginnings ... Let it be said among the nature-worshipping nations: "The LORD of the I AM has become king!"' (96:1, 10). The sentence *Yahweh malakh,* which is to be found in all these seven psalms, does not mean 'the LORD reigns' but 'the LORD has become king'. It is not a matter of announcing something that has always been there. It means rather a changing of the world situation which is prophetically represented as having already begun. Some commentators have assumed that there was a festival celebrating Yahweh's mounting of the throne, at which these psalms would have been sung. This is possible, but then this feast would in fact have had an apocalyptic character of prophetic anticipation, and the wider significance of these psalms would not be lessened thereby.

The Book of Revelation says (at the sounding of the seventh trumpet): 'The kingdom of this world are become the kingdom of our Lord and of his Christ,' and the elders fall down before the throne and say, 'We give thanks to you ... for you have taken your great power and have become king' (Rv 11:15–17). All this has only a meaning within the framework of a mighty drama in which God's rulership on earth is challenged and ultimately re-established. The time has come to recognise that this drama is not merely the mythology of childish peoples, but the only possible interpretation of the world as it really is.

It is only with this train of thought that we are in a position to do justice to Psalm 24.

'Lift up your heads, O gates! Lift up, ye portals of eternity!' (Thus literally in the original.) The gate presupposes a dividing wall. The higher world is separated as if by a wall from the hardened earthly sphere, shutting itself off in seclusion. We are not immediately able to 'see' and 'enter' the kingdom of God (Jn 3:3, 5). But there are gates through which the separated spheres do come into some relationship. We speak of the 'gate of birth' and the 'gate of death', where the threshold is crossed, both coming and going. So the psalm speaks here of the portals of eternity. The Hebrew *pithche 'olam* is, literally, 'primeval, aeon-old portals'. This does not change the sense, for the entrance to the higher worlds can be compared to age-old temple gates. These gates are to lift themselves up; a great figure wishes to pass through them.

The king of glory, *kabhod,* is the king of glorious revelation, of etheric light. In the universal symbolism of the ancient civilisations the king was the earthly representative of the divine I AM, which is the prototype of all royal bearing and dignity. 'You say that I am a king' (Jn 18:37). The king of glory who will enter our earthly realm through the portal of eternity – this is the Old Testament's prophecy of the Christ who was to come.

The proclamation of his coming is answered by the question, 'Who is this king of glory?' The question is put for the clarifying of human consciousness. It is a matter of discerning spirits. Lucifer, too, can show himself as an angel of light. There is an old phrase, *Christus verus luciferus,* Christ is the true light-bearer. In Lucifer's realm light is glittering illusion; with Christ it is the light of life (Jn 8:12). The search for discriminating knowledge lies in the question. The psalm spoke earlier of the generation of those who 'seek' him.

And the answer is 'It is the LORD, a mighty hero, a hero of battle'. The Lord who speaks the I AM, a hero of battle? Are we not still involved in the times of ancient Israel, when hoped-for victory in battle came from Yahweh? The psalmist may, in the first place, have meant this. But this does not hinder us from lifting the abiding truth from the historical background. Christ is assuredly not a fighter who uses physical power to subdue others. He did not call on destructive fire to come down on the inhospitable village of Samaria (Lk 9:54); he lets his adversaries scoff: 'If you are the Son of God, come down from the cross' (Mt 27:40). He waits for people to recognise his power as of another order, which works through sacrifice in the 'white magic' of love.

This is the nature of his fight against the Prince of this world. He does not fight in the way in which fighting was formerly imagined. He says to Peter, 'Put your sword back in its place' (Mt 26:52). And yet he is in the highest sense a fighter, a 'hero of the battle'. He confronts the brutal 'might of the Adversary' with the saving power of his love. The confronting of these two powers is the greatest battle in the world. All other conflicts are but allegory. So, rightly understood, the Christ is after all the great warrior, the Sun Hero.

In John's Gospel (16:33) he sums up his work in these words: 'I have overcome the world' (*Nenikēka,* from *nikē,* victory, conquest). This word, variously translated, occurs right through the Apocalypse. 'As I also conquered' (3:21); 'behold, the Lion ... has conquered ... and I saw a Lamb' (5:5f). Christ is the Sun Hero, the lion, but in the form of the lamb which sacrifices itself.

What follows, therefore, is fully justified: 'It is the Lord, a mighty hero, a hero in battle'.

The knowledge of the Coming One cannot be assimilated with a single proclamation, so it is again repeated as question and answer:

> Lift up your heads, O gates!
> And lift up, O portals of eternity!
> The king of glory shall come in.
> Who is this king of glory?
> It is the Lord of Hosts,
> he is the king of glory!
> *Selah*

We notice a slight alteration in this repetition. This time he is not called 'a mighty hero, a hero in battle', but 'the Lord of Hosts'. The returning Christ who becomes manifest in etheric light brings with him at the same time a new knowledge of the supersensible worlds in every detail and variety. The human consciousness opens again into the supersensible. Together with the Christ, the realms of the angels, of the hierarchies, enter again into perceptive consciousness. This is plainly expressed by Christ in his promise to return 'when he [the Son of Man] comes in his own light of revelation [*doxa, gloria*] and in that of the Father and of the holy angels' (Lk 9:26). 'When the Son of Man comes in his glory and all angels with him' (Mt 25:31). In the words, 'You will see the heavens open and the angels of God ascending and descending upon the Son of Man' (Jn 1:51), Christ promises the return of Jacob's dream of the heavenly ladder in the form of a new perception of the angelic worlds.

Psalm 24 twice makes the proclamation of the Coming One. In the parallelism of Hebrew poetry the same thing is often repeated twice or more in different words and, as we have it here, the second time can show a slight change of meaning and an advancement. The first time it is 'the hero in battle'. This is fulfilled through the deed of Golgotha, the overcoming of death. The second time it is 'the Lord of Hosts' (*tsabaoth*). This is true especially for the 'coming again' in the etheric light, which is accompanied by a new revelation of the angelic hierarchies.

We can now review the whole psalm. It consists of three apparently disconnected parts. The first part speaks of the solidifying of the earth, which involves the human problem though this is not expressly stated. It is implied in the dedication 'to the Lord the earth!' The second part speaks of human beings estranged from God and their endeavour to reach again the holy heights. 'Who shall ascend the hill of the Lord?' The third part is filled by what comes from above to meet wrestling humanity. If in the second part the movement went from humanity to God, the third is dominated by the powerful movement of God towards humanity, which at the same time is a new approach of the hierarchies to human beings as a consequence of the divine deed. The human being's search for God meets the divine search for the human being. Thus the interconnection of the three different parts is brought about as if from a hidden centre.

If we read at the beginning, 'To the Lord the earth and its fullness,' the answer is found at the end in the proclamation of the Lord who is on the way to human beings on earth, together with the hosts of heaven (*tsabaoth*).

In Psalm 8, which we considered in Chapter 1, there was the question, 'What is man?'. This question finds a complement in the apocalyptic question, 'Who is the king of glory?'

AFTERWORD

Psalms in the life of Christ

The very fact that Christ himself lived with the psalms, pondering on them and praying them, makes them worthy of our regard and reverence.

At the Jordan baptism, the divine voice – in one reading of the Luke Gospel – clothes itself is words taken from the messianic Psalm 2: 'You are my beloved son, today I have begotten you' (Lk 3:22). Soon after comes the voice of the Tempter 'disguised' in the wrongfully appropriated garb of a quote from the psalms, 'for it is written, "He will command his angels concerning you, and they will lift you up in their hands"' (Mt 4:6, Ps 91:11f).

These two inspirations, flowing from two such different sources, would not have clothed themselves in words of the psalms if they were not already within the soul of Jesus of Nazareth, as contents with which he had concerned himself, and which could therefore be used as an entry into his inner being by what here approached him.

In his disputes with his opponents, Christ often draws his arguments from the psalms: 'You are gods' (Jn 10:34) is a quote from Psalm 82.

During his entry into Jerusalem, he uses a phrase from Psalm 8 (Mt 21:16) to correct the high priests and scribes who take offence at the children's hosannas.

To substantiate that the Messiah stands higher than David, he takes words from the Melchizedek Psalm 110: 'The Lord said to my Lord, "Sit at my right hand"' (Mt 22:44).

He concludes the great speech of woes with the words, 'you will not see me again until you say, "Praised be he who comes in the name of the Lord"' (Mt 23:39), here referring to Psalm 118, from which the 'hosanna' was also taken.

In the Farewell Discourse, Christ makes the mystery of the betrayal and the groundless hatred directed at him comprehensible and utterable with two phrases from the psalms: 'But the Scripture will be fulfilled, "he who ate my bread has lifted his heel against me"' (Jn 13:18, Ps 41:9); and 'But the word that is written in their laws must be fulfilled: "they hated me without a cause"' (Jn 15:25, Ps 35:19 and 69:4).

In the words in Gethsemane, 'My soul is deeply troubled' (Mt 26:38), there is an echo of the Exile Psalm (42:5).

As at the beginning of the Jordan baptism, the psalms play an important role at Christ's death also. Two of the seven last words from the cross are drawn from them: 'My God, my God, why have you forsaken me?' (Mt 27:46) is the beginning of the Psalm of Suffering (22:1), which then closes with the eventual glorification of the sufferer and the fruit-bearing of his suffering for humanity.

The other word, 'Father, into your hands I commit my spirit' (Lk 23:46) is found (though without the address 'Father') in Psalm 31:6.

The resurrected Christ points the disciples to the meaning of the Christ prophecy of the Old Testament. This interpretive 'exposition' (Lk 24:27) extends also to the psalms, which are expressly named here alongside the law and the prophets (Lk 24:44).

Psalms in Christianity

It was natural to the disciples to read the psalms in the light of the fulfilled Christ mystery and the teachings imparted to them by the Risen One. Thus reference is repeatedly made to them in the New Testament books that follow the gospels.

Words from the psalms also became a part of Christian worship. In the Latin mass we encounter Psalms 43 (*Judica me ...* at the beginning), 141 (during the Offertory, the words about incense and the raising of hands), 26 (at the ablution). Hosanna and Benedictus come from Psalm 118, and the words about the cup and communion from

Psalms 116:12f and 18:4. In the early centuries people sang Psalm 34 at the Communion ('Taste and see...'). The mass sections, Introitus, Graduale and Offertorium are the remnants of long psalm-hymns. The psalms are also used in the priests' breviary and the monks' liturgy of hours (*Officium Divinum*). There were strict ascetic schools that prayed all 150 psalms through the night.

In the Reformed Church psalms were the only permitted singing during the act of worship. Luther loved the psalms most especially. In grave moments of his life he was comforted by the words, 'I shall not die but I shall live' (Ps 118). Psalm motifs surface in many books of songs or hymns – 'A mighty fortress is our God' (Ps 46); 'Commit your ways to the Lord' (Ps 37); 'Lift up your heads, you mighty gates' (Ps 24); 'Out of the depths I cry out' (Ps 130).

The reverberations of the psalms in culture touched by Christianity are endless and countless. In reading the psalms, a wealth of images and historical memories rise up. Here are ust a few: the hermit prays them in his cell; the monks chant them in the monastery choir; the Celtic monks put demons to flight with their loud psalm-singing. One psalm phrase ('Not to us, LORD, not to us, but to your name give glory', Ps 115:1) became the motto of the Templars. A quote from the psalms often stands as a heading to papal bulls and gives them their name. The Huguenots used the singing of psalms to fire their courage for heroic battles. Alexander von Humboldt admired Psalm 104 for its vivid images of the natural world. Herder was full of enthusiasm for the elemental poetry of the ancient Hebrews. Among the five illustrious figures which Herman Grimm believed were fundamental to western culture, he names also David – the singer of the psalms.

It is our task today to re-enliven appreciation and understanding of the world of the psalms for modern sensibilities.

Aspects of interpretation of the psalms

When we try to draw forth the meaning of ancient sacred texts, there are two ways in which we can go wrong. The first, above all if we approach the text with excessive piety, is to project too much onto it; we can overload it with significance that it does not intrinsically possess. The other possible mistake is that, in efforts to shed traditional prejudices and allow only historical and critical awareness to speak, we see the texts too trivially, failing to do justice to the depths that they actually contain.

A contestable projecting of meanings, which is absent in the text, is often the result of an intrinsically right feeling. We sense its depths, but have only a shallow and unoriginal relationship with the supersensible realities it conveys. We no longer really know anything specific about these, and are therefore unsure what the qualities are that we are seeking to express. Then it is easy to force their meaning.

This leads to the other extreme. Non-organic modes of interpretation have ended by creating doubt about the whole principle that the texts conceal deeper meaning than is immediately apparent – and so exegetes approach them in an entirely secular and critical way. But those who take this approach fail to notice (and for this reason it is not founded on true scholarship) that, though not caught up in traditional pieties, they are entangled in the prejudices and assumptions of materialism, and therefore cannot do objective justice to the texts either.

Through Rudolf Steiner's anthroposophy, a new, detailed discernment of supersensible worlds has been opened up for us. At the same time anthroposophy offers insights into evolution that enable us to understand and appreciate previous phases of cultural history. In this understanding, people originally possessed spirit vision. To ancient peoples things of the sense world were still transparent to deeper underlying dimensions, and therefore possessed true meaning. But gradually, as humankind advanced further from its origins and separated from them, a fading of this old capacity of vision became apparent. A kind of 'twilight of the gods' arose. What had once been direct perception and experience, was eventually handed down only as tradition.

In the wake of these mere echoes and traditions came the contestable mode of interpretation that imposes things upon the scriptures that do not belong to them. Ultimately the traditional echo of once living perception loses its power altogether, and a purely materialistic and intellectual mind sees only what stands in the foreground – superficially and without spiritual depth and meaning. In this 'worldview' – an expression that is scarcely apt – the mind built itself a house without windows. Transparency is at an end. But through the

Christ event, the germ of a new spirit vision is already implanted in humankind. Through the growth of this seed, through the application of the principle of redemption also to knowledge and perception, anthroposophy has arisen; and it gives us once again a worldview that is transparent for the illumined background of the supersensible.

For our relationship with the psalms, this now leads to the following. The sense of former centuries that they possess hidden depths is quite correct. But to interpret this deeper significance we first need to replenish the ideas and pictorial images of the old sacred texts. Such replenishment may appear as if we are not 'interpreting' but 'overlaying'. Yet this will be fully justified as long as we inform the texts with nothing other that what their content truly contained from the beginning. That we must re-impose such meaning is the fault of past centuries during which significance was removed and drained away.

For instance, when the word 'morning' appears, we must not abstractly decree that this has a 'deeper meaning' which bears no relation to the universal human experience of morning. Rather, it is a matter of grasping and encompassing the whole breadth of the phenomenon of morning with clarity of discernment. Then, without violating the scripture at all, we develop a relationship with, say, the morning of creation, or Easter morning. Such a relationship will not be artificially imposed or forced, but arises of itself. We need only clear away the hindrances in our own mind that obstruct this self-establishing of an organic relationship to the scripture. Thus the texts can be replenished with original significance whenever we encounter words such as morning and evening, day and night, heaven and earth, clouds, water, wind, rain, wells, mountains, countenance, hand, breath, hunger and thirst, food and drink – to name only a few. It is not a matter of fixing 'meaning' in a lexicological fashion and sticking an identifying label on it, but of recreating the primordial and original wealth of meaning such terms once invoked: in other words, to reunite what humankind sundered through the Fall by eating of the Tree of Knowledge.

Apart from this 'replenishment', the ancient texts often require a second thing of their interpreter: to bring to unfolding what is present only germinally. In the Old Testament we repeatedly find what we might call seed-thoughts that seek to grow on into the Christian dimension. Many words are 'oriented' towards the Messianic dawn that people still awaited in those days. What is to come in the future is already in some way involved in the coining of these words; futurity is active in advance of itself. But these seeds will only be perceived and further developed in the light of the Christ sun that has dawned. To elaborate in the light of Christian knowledge what is there already as prefiguring or potential is not to wrongfully 'impose' something on these scriptures.

To use another image, in the Old Testament we often encounter spiritual figures in which certain lines are only indicated as 'points'. To draw and fill out the lines of these already projected points is the task of true interpretation. This is not to impose something alien on the texts, even if their original author did not as such intend what we elaborate. It belongs to the nature of inspiration to give utterance to things that can point far beyond what speakers or writers are aware of at that moment. By no means does this imply denigrating them as mere 'mediums'. The question can only be whether what is added truly continues what is implicit in the text. If such an elaboration is organic to the context then it is not only permissible but even necessary. If one sought to prevent the potential contained in the text from unfolding, this would be something like a wrong done to its germinating life. It is also an injury to the text to keep its germinal potential frozen. A Christian interpretation of such germinal thoughts is objectively truer and more apt than a mode of historical critique which has, in fact, only a very external idea of 'history' and fails to understand the most important historical event – the incarnation, death and resurrection of Christ.

The early Christians had a better right to appropriate the Old Testament than its original possessors, who did not wish to go beyond the old covenant. Development and elaboration are intrinsic to the truly inspired Old Testament texts (it would be mistaken to assume they are all equally inspired in a general and undifferentiated way).

Christianity established the beautiful and profound custom of, as it were, 'baptising' a psalm to be used in a Christian context by adding to it the formula, *Gloria Patri et Filio et Spiritui Sancto. Sicut erat in principio, et nunc et semper et in saecula saeculorum* (Glory be to the Father and to the Son and to the Holy Spirit. As it was in the beginning, is now, and ever shall be, world without end.) Christians felt they could not adopt psalms simply as they are without further ado, but must place them into the light of Christian truth that had dawned since they were composed. Only once they are baptised in this way do they reveal what they truly contain.

It is our task today to accomplish this baptism of the psalms using the resources of the modern mind, not merely outwardly appropriating them through addition of the trinitarian formula, but by bringing to bear on them the 'Gloria', the revelatory light of the Christian mystery, with our specific and detailed discernment.

BIBLIOGRAPHY

Benz, E. *Adam: Der Mythus des Urmenschen,* Barth, Munich 1955.
Bock, Emil. *Genesis,* Floris, Edinburgh 2011.
—, *Moses,* Floris, Edinburgh 2011.
—, *Kings and Prophets,* Floris, Edinburgh 2006.
Dölger, F.J. *Sol Salutis,* Munster 1925.
Gorion, Micha Josef bin, *Sagen der Juden,* Frankfurt a. M. 1926.
Kerényi, Karoly, *Die Mythologie der Griechen,* Deutsches Taschenbuch, Munich 1966.
Kittel, Rudolf, *Die Psalmen,* Leipzig 1922 (reprint 2021).
Knowles, James D. *Memoir of Roger Williams, the Founder of the State of Rhode-Island,* Boston 1824.
Scholem, G.G. *Major Trends in Jewish Mysticism,* Schocken, NY 1946, and Thames & Hudson, London 1955.
Schürer, E. 'Die siebentagige Woche' *Zeitschrift.für neutestamentliche Wissenschaft,* 1905, pp. 1–66.
Steiner, Rudolf, *Anthroposophical Leading Thoughts* (CW26) Rudolf Steiner Press, UK 1998.
—, *Christianity as Mystical Fact,* Steiner Press, UK 1972.
—, *A Way to Self-Knowledge and the Threshold of the Spiritual World* (CW 16–17) SteinerBooks, USA 1999.
Wistinghausen, Kurt, 'Der Brunnen', *Die Christengemeinschaft,* 1931, pp. 167–72.
Zahn, Theodor. *Geschichte des Sonntags, vornehmlich in der alten Kirche,* Hannover 1878.

SOURCES AND TRANSLATORS

Sources
Chapters 1, 3, 5, 6, 8. 11 (slightly abridged), 12, 25, 31, 37, 42, 46 originally published under the title *Bibel-Studien* by Verlag Urachhaus in 1963 (some originally published in German as essays in *Die Christengemeinschaft*), published as *Old Testament Studies* by Floris Books, 1994.

Chapters 17–20 originally published in *Die Christengemeinschaft*, later in book form under the title *Von Bäumen, Brunnen und Steine in den Erzvätergeschichten* by Verlag Urachhaus in 1963, first published in English in the *The Christian Community Journal*, 1935, and later in book form in *Old Testament Studies* by Floris Books, 1994. The later German edition was considerably revised and the translation here does not reflect those revisions.

Chapter 21 originally published in German under the title *Der Sonntag: eine christliche Tatsache* by Verlag Urachhaus in 1965, and included in *Old Testament Studies* by Floris Books, 1994.

Chapters 22, 23, 24, 27, 28, 29, 30, 32, 33, 34, 36, 38, 40, 41, 43, 44, 45, 47, 48, 49 originally published in German under the title *Aus der Welt der Psalmen* by Verlag Urachhaus in 1948, first published in English as *Hidden Treasures in the Psalms* by The Christian Community Press, London in 1954, second edition in 1967.

Following chapters were originally published in *Die Christengemeinschaft*: 2 (1971), 4 (1973), 7 (1964), 9 (1973), 10 (1973), 13 (1971), 14 (1972), 15 (1972), 16 (1966), 26 (1965), 35 (1974).

Translators
Chapters 1, 3, 6, 8. 11, 12, 25, 31, 37, 42, 46: Margaret and Rudolf Koehler.
Chapters 2, 4, 5, 7, 9, 10, 13, 14, 15, 16, 17, 26, 27, 35: Matthew Barton.
Chapters 18–20: Alfred Heidenreich.
Chapter 21: Donald Maclean.
Chapters 22, 23, 24, 28, 29, 30, 32, 33, 34, 36, 38, 40, 41, 43, 44, 45, 47, 48, 49: Mabel Cotterell, Alfred Heidenreich and Eileen Hersey.

INDEX OF BIBLICAL REFERENCES

Genesis (Gn)
1:1   13, 17
1:1–2:4   18
1:10   50
1:12   50
1:16   38
1:18   50
1:20   52
1:21   17, 21, 50
1:22   19
1:25   50
1:26f   16f, 376
1:28   20, 184
1:29f   22
1:31   13, 49, 50
1:40   50
2:1   49
2:2   14, 49
2:3   14, 17
2:4   17
2:4–25   18
2:7   376
2:21f   18
3:5   35, 183
4:5f   112
4:7   113
4:9   355
4:15   113
4:22   113
5:1f   19
5:3   16
5:24   329
7:4, 10   163
7:11   274
7:16   40, 129
8:10, 12   163
9:3   22

9:6   16
11:28, 31   162
12:1, 3   37
12:5–7   127,
12:7f   150
13:16   38
13:17   126
13:18   128, 150
14:13   128
14:18   135
14:18–20   41
15:1   332
15:5f   38, 41, 129
16:9   138
16:13   135
16:14   138
18:1-33   131f
18:4   132
18:8   132
20:7   133
21:28–30   135
21:33   132, 135
22:1f   43
22:3   44
22:4f   45
22:6–8   46
22:9f   47, 150
22:11–13   47
22:12   136
22:17   38, 41
22:19   134
23:2   128
23:17   133
24:62f   138f, 222
25:11   138
26:4   41
26:12–18   139

26:19   140
26:22   224
26:25   140, 150
26:25–32   141
28:11   142
28:12f   144
28:16f   144
28:18f   145
28:19   152
29:1f   147
29:10   148
29:27f   163
31:13   150
31:42   136f
31:45f   148
31:53   136f
31:54   148
32:1f   149
32:26   396, 427
32:28   151
33:20   150
35:1   150
35:4   127
35:7   135, 150, 152
35:9, 13   151
35:14f   151f
35:19   153
35:20   152
46:1f   140
49:6   350
49:24   152
50:10   163

Exodus (Ex)
20:8   163
21:6   34
22:8f   34

– *Exodus (continued)*
22:28   34
25:40   49
26:30   49
27:8   49
31:29, 31 50
32:13   41
33:20   75
34:5–7   373
37:23   52
39–40   49–55
39:1–7   50
39:21   50
39:26   50
39:30   54
39:32   49
39:43   49
40:17–19 50
40:21, 23 50
40:24f   50, 52
40:26f   50, 53
40:29–32 50, 55
40:33   49

Leviticus (Lv)
4:3   91
8:12   91
8:30   91
9:24   75
23:6   163
23:34   163

Numbers (Nm)
6:22–27 56
12:8   328
22:5f   63
22:20–35 64
23:3, 6 66
23:21   68
24:1f   67f
24:15f   68
24:17   69, 94

Deuteronomy (Dt)
4:24   261

Joshua (Jsh)
24:26   128

Judges (Jg)
6:11–24 71
6:14   72
6:19   74
6:22   75
6:23   81
6:24   76
9:37   128
13:5–8   78
13:9   77, 79
13:11, 15 79
13:19   77, 80
13:20   75, 81
13:21f   81
13:23   82
14:12, 17 163

1 Samuel (1Sm)
28:13f   34
31:13   163

1 Kings (1K)
7:14–46 114
8:12   208
8:53 (LXX) 208
8:65   163
11:36   92
15:4   92
18:38   75
18:46   224

2 Kings (2K)
8:19   92

2 Chronicles (2Ch)
2:13   114
4:16   114
7:1   75
21:7   92

Job (Jb)
3:8   89
9:13   86
19:25   372
26:12f   86
29:2f   32, 276
34:14f   198
35:9f   271

38:7   31, 233
41:18–21 85
41:34   85

Psalms (Ps)
1:2   271
2:7   412
4:1   223
5:3   298
8   **175–85**
8:2   179
15:1   426
15:4   437
15:19   223
16   **344–53**
17:15   328
18:28   276
19   **201–12**
19:6   224
22   **334–43**
22:1   436
23   **354–61**
24   **422–33**
25:8   258
27:4   360
29   31, **241–46**
31   **300–305**
31:6   436
32:1f   278
33:6   30
33:9   29
35:19   436
36   **269–77**
37   **381–90**
41:9   436
42   **307–18**
42:5   436
42:8   271
43   **307–18**
45:6   34
46   **391–97**
49:14f   351
51   **278–89**
57:8   349f
63   **319–25**
65   **247–53**
69:4   436
73   **326–33**
73:15   425

INDEX OF BIBLICAL REFERENCES

– Psalms (continued)
74:13f	87
77:6	226
78:2	226
78:25	23, 276
80:10	194
82	34
82:6	35
84	**254–59**
89:5–8	245
89:9f	86
90	**290–99**
91	**362–68**
91:11–13	90, 185, 435
92:2	271
94:9	276
95:3	418
95:5	192
95:6–8	429
96	246, **416–21**
96:1, 10	429
97:9	418
103	**369–77**
104	**186–200**, 376
104:30	285
108:1f	349f
110	**409–15**
110:1	344
115:1	437
115:16	428
116:12f	348, 437
118	**398–408**
118:5	223
119	**220–30**
121	**213–19**
132:17	92
136	180
139:14	301
139:16	301
141:2	53
145:16	199
147:4	39, 180
148	**231–240**
148:3	180

Ecclesiastes
1:2, 9	416

Isaiah (Is)
6	245
6:1	99
6:2	100
6:3	101
9:6	80, 238
11:6	238
27:1	89
40:26	39
40:30f	373
43:7	27
51:8f	87, 274, 304

Jeremiah (Jer)
33:22	377

Ezekiel (Ezk)
1:1	104
1:5, 8	105
1:13–28	106–8
3:12	108
4:3–5	109
10:13	106
10:20	105
11:22f	109
43:7	109
47:1–12	395
48:35	109

Daniel (Dn)
3	**260–65**
7:1	117
7:2, 7	113
7:9–11	115
7:13	113, 116
7:14	117
7:15	111
7:19	113
7:27	117
7:28	111, 117

Amos (Am)
9:3	88

Haggai (Hg)
1:6	93
1:14f	93
2:6	93
2:8	97

2:9	94
2:21–23	94

Zechariah (Zec)
2:5, 13	95
3:1, 8f	95
4:6	96f
4:7–10	97
4:14	96
6:11	97
9:9f	96
14:8	395

Malachi (Mal)
1:11	119
4:2	118f, 167
4:4f	120

Tobit (Tb)
12:15	80

Wisdom of Solomon (Ws)
14:6	275

Song of Three Youths (Sg Thr)
5, 16f	261
23f	262

Matthew (Mt)
1:6	92
4:6	435
5:5	386
5:9	390
5:14	286, 385
5:48	35
7:7	384
13:43	385
16:16	313
17:2	120, 167
18:10	178
20:16	249
21:15f	179
22:44	410, 435
23:39	436
25:31	428f
26:38	436
26:52	431
26:64	117
27:40	431

– Matthew (continued)
27:46   334, 436
28:1   165
28:3   283

Mark (Mk)
2:27   169
10:17f 399
15:34   334
16:2   165f

Luke (Lk)
1:19   80
3:22   435
4:9–11 362
9:26   432
9:54   431
10:18f 362, 366
10:23   228
15   284
18:18f 399
22:17   199
23:46   300, 436
24:1   165
24:27   436
24:44   345, 436

John (Jn)
1:13   287
1:14   208, 274, 408
1:17   274
1:18   59
1:29   279
1:51   432
2:21   94, 109, 361
3:3, 5 430
3:29   207
4:14   310
4:16   78
4:20   274
6:35   310
6:46   101
6:55   23
7:37   310
8:12   89, 317, 430
8:56   89
9:5   167
10:9f   356
10:11   354

10:18   30
10:34   35, 183, 435
12:2   359
12:10   360
12:32   397
12:41   99, 104
13:2   269
13:18   436
13:34   416
14:2, 6 317
14:9   59, 258
15:1f, 5 21
15:11   324
15:15   304
15:25   436
16:11   277
16:14   60
16:22   350
16:33   277, 431
17:4   413
17:10   347
17:26   239
18:37   430
20:1, 19 165
20:26   164

Acts of the Apostles (Ac)
2:14–21 344
2:22–28 344
2:24f   345, 352
2:29–36 344
2:31   351
4:32   19
15:20   164
20:7–11 165
20:35   318
26:13   167

Romans (Rom)
4:11   37
8:32   43, 136

1 Corinthians (1Cor)
3:21   166
10:21   347
11:25   416
13:12   249, 257, 311
15:41   180
16:2   165

2 Corinthians (2Cor)
3:18   15, 368
4:4   15
12:2   178, 233

Ephesians (Eph)
2:14   76

Colossians (Col)
1:15   15
1:16   115

1 Timothy (1Tm)
6:16   101

2 Timothy (2Tm)
4:7   206

Hebrews (Hb)
1:8f   34
7:3   129
11:19   136
12:9   20, 33
12:22–24 426

2 Peter (2Pt)
1:4   36

1 John (1Jn)
3:2   42, 258, 390
3:8   411
3:9   36, 390

Revelation (Rv)
1:9   111
1:10   165
1:16   167
2:10   183
2:27   114
3:11   183
3:20   132, 249
3:21   117, 431
4:6   112
4:8   307
5:5f   68, 135, 431
5:9   429
5:10   324
7:14   283, 414
10:3   244

– *Revelation (continued)*		14:3	418, 429	21:5	373, 416
11:15–19	277, 429	14:13	360	21:24–26	166
12	83	17:8	88, 323	22:1	395
12:5	114	19:15	114	22:8	111
13:1	112	20:12	301	22:16	70
14:2	318				

INDEX

Aaron 55f, 91
—, blessing of 56–60
—, sons of 56f
Abednego (Azariah) 261f, 265
abide 388, 426
Abimelech, Philistine king 134f, 140f
Abraham 37–48, 125–33, 134–36, 141, 146, 162, 368, 382, 395, 411
—, name changed from Abram 130
abyssos (Greek: depths) 274
acharith (Hebrew: that which is after) 388
Achilles 307
Act of Consecration of Man 23f, 54, 387
activity (third stage of creation) 191
Adam 16, 18f
adam (Hebrew: human being) 176, 182
Adam, Old 182
Adam qadmon (Hebrew: Adam before Fall) 227
adamah (Hebrew: earth) 176
Adon (Hebrew: Lord) 332
aeon 225f
aevum (Latin: aeon) 291
agriculture 193
Ahriman 192, 325
aion (Greek: aeon) 291
Alexandria 260
alphabet, Hebrew 220f
altar (for burnt offering) 53
—, building of 126–29, 150
Amen 41f
anabaseis (Greek: way upwards) 257
anah (Hebrew: answer, humility) 405
Ancient of Days (name of God) 114–16
angel(s) 33, 72–75, 77–79, 144, 149, 233

angelos (Greek: messenger) 33
anger 374
ani (Hebrew: I) 397
anokhi (Hebrew: great, emphatic I) 120, 367, 397
anthropos (Greek: human being) 175, 177, 179
apocalyptic perfect tense 277
Apollonius of Tyana (Greek magician) 160
Apostles, Council of 164
Aquarius (Waterman) 105
Aristotle 233
arze-el (Hebrew: cedars of God) 194
Ascension 353, 409
ascent 257, 425f
asensiones (Latin: way upwards) 257
ass, donkey 64f
assiah (Hebrew: made) 26
astra (Greek: star) 195
astral, astrality 52f, 195f
atah (Hebrew: you) 365
ataraxia (Greek: imperturbability) 391
Atlantis 88f
atmosphere 237, 263
Atziluth (Hebrew: emanation) 26f, 29
Augustine, St (Church Father) 110, 162, 168
awe 228f
Azariah (Abednego) 261f, 265
—, Prayer of 260f

Babylonian exile 261
Balaam 63–70, 94
Balak, Moabite king 63–67
baptism (of Jesus) 110
bara (Hebrew: create) 16f, 26, 234, 284

Bathsheba 278
beatitudes (of Sermon on the Mount) 257, 386
Beckh, Hermann 258, 355
Beer-lahai-roi (Well of Him who Lives and Sees) 138
Beer-Sheba 132f, 134f, 138–40
Beethoven, Ludwig von 251
Behemoth 84f
being (first stage of creation) 191
belief (in Old Testament) 41
ben-adam (Hebrew: son of man) 182f
bene elim (Hebrew: sons of gods) 31, 419
bene elohim (Hebrew: sons of the gods) 233, 245
Benedicte, Canticum 261
Benedictus 436
Benjamin (Jacob's son) 152
Benz, E. 19
Beriah (Hebrew: creation) 26
Bethel 142, 145–47, 150–52, 427
Bethesda, Pool of 72
Bethlehem 153
Bismarck, Otto von 171
bliss (Eden) 276
blood of the Lamb 283
Bock, Emil 9f, 146
body, material 295
Böhme, Jakob 350, 414
bones 340
book 301–3
Branch (*tsemach*) 95, 97
bread 194
breadth, broadening 223–25
bridegroom 207f
bronze 113f
Bruckner, Anton 407
Buber, Martin 10, 222
Buddha 147, 310
bull 104f

Caesarea Philippi 313
Cain 112–14
calendar reforms 171f
Calvin, John 171
Carmel, Mount 75, 224
Catacombs 359
cedars of Lebanon 194

Chaldean planetary week 158f
charis (Greek: grace, beauty) 353
chataah (Hebrew: sin) 278
Cherubim 51, 98, 105–7, 307
children 178f
chosen (person) 249f
Christ 59f
— becoming man 428
—, second coming 428f
Christos (Greek: anointed one) 360
Clement of Alexandria 168
cloud(s) 51, 98, 273f
Comforter (Holy Spirit) 304
Communion (fourth part of Act of Consecration) 387f
confessio (Latin: radiance of being) 189
Constantine (emperor) 167
cornerstone 405f
countenance of God 294
creation 83f, 234
— of human being 14–24
Creed, Nicene 32f
crocodile 85
Cyril of Jerusalem (Church Father) 101
Cyrus, Persian king 92

Daniel 98, 111–15
dassie (rock hyrax) 195
dative 402
David, King 278, 287, 368
dawn 298, 319, 322
day 204
Delitzsch, Franz 10
descendants 388, 390
desert 319–21, 323
devekut (Hebrew: cling) 322
dew 414
diapsalma (Greek: selah) 256
Dio Cassius (Roman historian) 160, 162
Dionysius the Areopagite (or Pseudo-Dionysius) 100f
Dölger, F.J. 165
Domitian (emperor) 165
donkey, ass 64f
Dostoevsky, Fyodor 223
doxa (Greek: glory, light of revelation) 258

dragon, serpent 83, 86–90, 236f, 367
dust of the earth 38
dwelling of God 425

eagle 104f, 372f
earth 386f, 422, 424, 428
Easter 298f, 342, 404–6
ecce homo (Latin: behold the man) 108
Edda 87
eikon (Greek: image) 15f
El-Bethel (God of Bethel) 135
El-Elohe-Israel (God who is God of Israel) 149
El-Elyon (God Most High) 135, 364, 395
Eliezer (Abraham's servant) 138
Elijah 75, 120, 224
Elohim (God, gods) 32, 99, 275f, 364
Elohim (Hebrew: gods, plural) 15
elohim (Hebrew: assembly of judges) 34, 238
elohim (Hebrew: the dead) 34
El-Olam (Everlasting God) 135f, 140
El-Roi (God of Seeing) 135
Emmaus, disciples at 79
Endor, witch of 34
Enoch 329
Ephrath 153
erez (Hebrew: earth, land, Holy Land) 382, 386
Esau 149
Esek (well of contention) 140
eternity 203, 225, 353
euthys (Greek: straightaway) 207
evil 218f, 271f
exomologēsis (Greek: radiance of being) 189
Exousiai (angelic hierarchy) 100
eyes 213
Ezekiel 98, 104–10, 111, 395

Fall, the 123f, 295
Father God 59
feet 216
finished work (fourth stage of creation) 191
firmament 203, 263
flattery 270

flood, the 163, 274f
forecourts 419
forgetting 221f
Francis of Assisi, St 65, 100
freedom 54
Freya (Germanic goddess) 158
Friday (origin) 158
furnace, three men in 260–65

Gabriel 80
galgal (Hebrew: whirling wheel) 106
gates 430
gē (Greek: earth) 386
genealogy (in Luke) 290
Gerar, herdsmen of 140
Gideon 71–76, 81
Gilead (Transjordan) 149
Gitthir 254
gloria (Latin: glory, light of revelation) 245, 258
glory 349f, 430
God of Jacob 425, 427
go'el (Hebrew: redeem) 372
Goethe, Johann Wolfgang von 40, 48, 141, 210, 215, 224, 234, 414
gold 211
golem (Hebrew: unformed embryo) 301
good, goodness 199, 346, 399
Gorion, Micha bin 137
Gospel (first part of Act of Consecration) 387
grace 273–76, 288, 375
graciousness 373f
Grail 359
gratia (Latin: grace, beauty) 353
Gregorian calendar 172
Gregory XIII, Pope 172
Grimm, Hermann 437
guardian of the threshold 426f
guilt 278f
Gunkel, Hermann 10

hadar (Hebrew: splendour of majesty) 183, 189
Hades 330, 351
hagah (Hebrew: meditate) 322
Haggai (prophet) 93
haimata (Greek: blood) 287

halal (Hebrew: praise) 231
hallelujah 231
Hamlet 307
Hananiah (Shadrach) 265
hand 217, 329
—, right 353, 404, 409f
Haran (city Chaldea) 125, 148
Hasidim 382
heart 224f, 331
heavens 178, 201, 233, 273
Heliodromos (Greek: Sun Hero, Sun Runner) 206, 224f
help, need for 213
Herculaneum 160
Herder, Johann Gottfried von 437
hero 206f
Herodotus 89
Hezekiah, king 92
hierarchies, celestial 33, 376
high priest(hood) 91, 93
hippopotamus 85
Hiram (king of Tyre) 113f
Hittites 133
hod (Hebrew: radiance of being) 189
Holy Land 382
Holy of Holies 51
Holy Spirit (Comforter) 19, 60, 117, 146, 149, 209, 262, 304
home 254, 256, 258
Homer 369
homo (Latin: man) 175
homoiosis (Greek: likeness) 15f
honey 211
Horace (Roman poet) 161, 391
horn (or ray) 239
hosanna 398f, 406f, 436
Huguenots 437
humanus (Latin: human being) 175
Humboldt, Alexander von 437
Hymir (Norse giant) 87
hyssop 283

Ignatius of Antioch 165, 170
Iliad 307, 369
image (*eikon*) 15f
Immanu-El (Hebrew: with us God) 396
incense offering 53
initiation 265

interpretation of psalms 437–41
iron 113f
Isaac 41, 130, 132, 134–41, 222, 368
—, Fear of 136
—, sacrifice of 43–48, 136
Isaac of Acre (kabbalist) 322
Isaiah 98f, 104, 111, 238, 373
Israel
— as Christian Church 427
—, new name of Jacob 149, 151
—, Stone of (name of God) 152

Jabbok, River 149, 151
Jacob (patriarch) 127, 140, 142–53, 163, 350, 396
—, given new name of Israel 149, 151
—, well of 139
Jehoiada (priest) 368
Jerome, St 167, 260
Jerusalem 395f
Jerusalem, heavenly 109, 288, 394f
Job 32, 88, 368
—, Book of 84
Joel 344
John the Baptist 118
John the Evangelist 36, 104, 170, 393
—, Gospel of 210
Joseph (Jacob's son) 163
Josephus, Flavius 128, 161
Joshua (Israelite leader) 128
Joshua (high priest) 93–95
joy, rejoicing 284
Judas 359
judges 238
judgment 274f
Julian (the Apostate), Emperor 40
Julian calendar 172
Julius Caesar 172
Justin Martyr 166, 168
Juvenal (Roman poet) 161, 169

Kabbalah 26, 28, 110, 341
kabhod (Hebrew: glory, light of revelation) 183, 245, 258, 330, 349f, 430
Kautsch, Emil 10
kerem (Hebrew: horn, ray) 239
Kerényi, Karl 31

ki asah (Hebrew: for he did) 342
kilyah (Hebrew: kidneys) 348
Kimchi, David 183
kings 238
Kiriath-Arba 128
Kittel, Rudolf 10, 207
Klingsor (evil magician) 359
Klopstock, Friedrich Gottlieb 369
kokhab (Hebrew: star) 180
Koran 224
Kyrios (Greek: Lord) 215, 332, 346, 364

Laban (Jacob's father-in-law) 149
ladder to heaven (Jacob's dream) 144, 432
lamb 69
Lamb of God 135
landscape, human effect on 126
Last Judgment 244
Last Supper 21, 30
laylah (Hebrew: night) 204
Lazarus 359f
Leah 148
Leo (Lion) 105
leprosy 283
Levi (Jacob's son) 350
Leviathan 83–90, 197, 274, 393f
light 222f, 276, 286, 317
lightning 190
likeness (*homoiosis*) 15f
Lincoln, Abraham 301
lion 104f, 366f
— of Judah 68
loneliness 335
Lord of Hosts 395f
Lord's Day 165
Lord's Prayer 211, 383f
love 215, 228–30, 296f
Lucifer 35, 183, 185, 295
Luther, Martin 171, 391

Machpelah, cave of 133
Mahanaim 149
makarios (Greek: blessed) 257
Malachi 118–20
male-female human being 18f
Mamre, oak grove of (at Hebron) 128f, 132f

Mamre, owner of oak grove 128
man (English word) 175
manifestation (second stages of creation) 191
Manoah 75, 78–81
maqom (Hebrew: place) 45, 127, 142f
marriage, mystical 19
Martial (Roman poet) 161
Martin of Braga 168f
Mary Magdalene 342
matsevah (Hebrew: stone pillar) 148
Maximus of Turin (bishop) 167
Mecca 298
meditari (Latin: meditation) 222
meditating 222
Melchizedek 41, 91, 129, 134f, 146, 364, 395, 410, 413
Melech, Salomon ben 183
Mensch (German, human being) 175
menuchoth (Hebrew: waters of rests) 357
mercifulness 373f
Meshach (Mishael) 265
meshamah alyonah (Hebrew: higher soul) 183
meshoreth (Hebrew: servant, minister) 190
Messiah, anointed one 360
—, coming of 69
—, kingship of 91–97
—, priesthood of 91–97
Michael (archangel) 89
Midgard snake 87
Mishael (Meshach) 265
Mithras mysteries 224
Monday (origin) 158
monotheism 31, 35
moon 195f, 217f
Moreh, oak of (at Shechem) 127
Moriah, Mount 45, 134, 136
Moses 41, 49f, 55, 120, 374, 425
—, staff of 359
mountain(s) 237, 264, 274f, 290, 425
murmur, whisper 269, 411

na'iym (Hebrew: grace, beauty) 353
name of God 234, 322, 357, 369
Name, divine 177f, 185

narrowness 402
natsar (Hebrew: preserve) 222
Nebuchadnezzar, King 260, 263
nephesh (Hebrew: soul, life) 218
new 416, 418
Nicaea, Council of 172
Nietzsche, Friedrich 54, 237, 254, 319
night 204
nikē (Greek: victory) 431
Noah 40, 129, 162
nourishment, daily 22f
Novalis 36, 137, 298, 383, 244

Odyssey 351
Offering (second part of Act of
    Consecration) 387
Ogyges, oak of 128
oil 194
'olam (Hebrew: aeon) 226, 291
Olives, Mount of 109
Ophrah, oak of 71
ordering 235
Origen (Church Father) 110
overshadowing, shade 217
Ovid (Roman poet) 161

pachad (Hebrew: fear) 137
Palm Sunday 398f, 406, 408
Pan (Greek god) 313
Passover 163
pastures 356
path, way 352
Paul (apostle) 37, 43, 76, 166, 178,
    206, 233, 347
Peniel 149, 151, 427
Pentecost 165, 353
— address 344f
— flames 75
pesha (Hebrew: transgression) 278
Peter (disciple) 36, 313, 344f, 351,
    431
Philo of Alexandria (Jewish philosopher)
    91, 161
pilgrimage 213, 257
Pisgah, Mount 67
pithche 'olam (Hebrew: aeon-old portals)
    430
planets, seven 159f

Plutarch 32
Pompeii 160
practice, religious 220
praise 371
prayer, praying 314, 383f
principium (Latin: principal) 27
Pseudo-Dyonisius 100f
purification 283, 426f

qedem (Hebrew: long ago) 226f
qol Yahweh (Hebrew: voice of the Lord)
    241–43

ra'ah (Hebrew: seeing) 258
Rachel 147f, 152
—, grave of 152f
Rahab 86, 393f
rain 234, 251
rainbow 245
Raphael (archangel) 80
ray (or horn) 239
Rebekah 138f, 147
Redeemer 372
Reformation 391
Reformed Church 437
Rehoboth (well of broad places) 140, 223f
Rembrandt 81
resurrection 352
— body 360f
right hand 353, 404, 409f
righteousness 274f, 405, 426f
Rilke, Rainer Maria 301
river 394f
rock 314, 331
rock badger (rock hyrax) 195
ruach (Hebrew: spirit, breath) 198
running 224

Sabbath 161, 163
—, great 311
sacrifice, animal 288
—, human 34
salvation 228
Samaritan woman at well 78
Samson 77, 163
Samuel (prophet) 34f, 91
sanctuaries of God 327
Sanctus 101

sand of the seashore 38
Sarah 130, 133
—, name changed from Sarai 130
Sartre, Jean-Paul 365
Saturday (origin) 158
Saturnus (Roman god) 158
Saul, King 34, 91
Schiller, Friedrich 88, 235
Schmidt, Werner H. 10
Scholem, G.G. 322
scorpion 366
selah (Hebrew: unclear meaning, break?) 256, 394
Seneca the Younger (Stoic philosopher) 161
Sennacherib 393
sepher (Hebrew: book) 201
Septaguint 175, 260
Septimus Severus (emperor) 160
Seraphim 98–101, 190
—, theology of 101
serpent, dragon 367
Seth 16
seven 159, 170
sexes, division of 18
Sforno, Obadiah ben Jacob 411
Shadai (Hebrew: the Almighty) 364
shade, overshadowing 217
Shadrach (Hananiah) 265
Shakespeare 307
shalom (Hebrew: peace) 249
Shechem 125–27, 149f
shemaim (Hebrew: heavens) 178
Sheol (Hebrew: Hades) 330, 351
shepherd, good 354–59
Sheth, sons of (chaos) 69
shewbread 52
Simeon (Jacob's son) 350
sin 278, 281f, 288, 371f
—, original 287
—, sickness of 271, 282
Sitnah (well of feud) 140
skēnē (Greek: tent) 208
sleep 216f
sleeplessness 271
snake 366f
snow 283f
Solomon 208

Son of Man (Christ) 116f
son of man 182f
Song of Three Young Men 260
sōteria (Greek: salvation) 228
sphangchna (Greek: bowels) 348
staff 75, 359
star(s) 69f, 94, 129, 180–83, 195, 233, 263
—, numberless 38f
Stark, Willy 10
Steiner, Rudolf 20, 28, 35, 115, 171, 223, 264, 281, 297, 438
Stoic philosophy 391
stone(s) 142–53, 366
—, standing or pillar 142, 145, 148
Suetonius (Roman historian) 161
sun 195f, 206–9, 225
Sun God 329
Sun Hero 206f, 431
Sun of Righteousness 118–20, 167
Sun, Day of 166f
Sunday, in Christianity 157–71
—, origin 158
Sun Runner (*Heliodromos*) 224f
swearing 325, 348, 413
sword 431
syneidon (Greek: conscience) 325

tabernacle 49–55, 75, 426
Tabernacles, Feast of 163
tamarisk tree 132, 135
taninim (Hebrew: dragons) 236
Tatian the Assyrian (Christian writer) 169
Taurus (Bull) 105
tehom (Hebrew: deep, flood) 191, 197, 237, 274
tehom rabah (Hebrew: great deep) 274f
Templars 437
temple of Solomon 75, 100, 108f, 113
—, curtain of 30
—, dedication 163, 208
—, destruction 109
—, rebuilding 94
temple of the (resurrection) body 94, 109, 360f, 406
temporal, time 204, 225, 300–5
temunah (Hebrew: essential form) 328
tent 208, *see also* tabernacle

Tertullian (Christian writer) 167
Theodosius (emperor) 168
theorion (Greek: beast) 112
third day 45
thirst 310, 319
Thor (Norse god) 87, 158
Three Young Men, Song of 260
throne 107, 115f
Thrones (celestial hierarchy) 115
Thubal-Cain (son of Cain) 113
thunder 241–45
Thursday (origin) 158
Tiberius (emperor) 161
Tibullus (Roman poet) 160
time, temporal 204, 225, 300–5
tithe 146
Tiw (Germanic god) 158
Tobias 80
Torah 222
tracks, paths 252
transgression (*pesha*) 278
Transubstantiation (third part of Act of Consecration) 387
tree(s) 125–33
—, sacred 71, 125
Tree of Knowledge 132
Tree of Life 133
Trinity 15, 59f, 130–32, 285, 344–46
truth 273–76, 317
tsabaoth (Hebrew: shining hosts) 256, 233, 376f, 395, 432f
tsemach (Hebrew: Branch) 95, 97
Tuesday (origin) 158

Ur (city Chaldea) 125
Uriah 287
Uzziah, king 98f

vanity 416, 418
Vienna Genesis 40f
vine, I am the true 21
vow, religious 247
Vulgate 260

Wagner, Richard 222
water 234, 356f
Wednesday (origin) 158
—, eight-day Roman 159
—, five-day 172
—, Jewish 160–63
—, six-day 172
—, ten-day 172
weekend 171
well(s) 134–41, 147
wheels (in vision) 106, 115
whisper, murmur 269, 411
widths 402
Williams, Roger 413f
wine 194
winepress 254
Wistinghausen, Kurt von 137
Wodan (Odin, Germanic god) 158
wondrous (name of angel) 80
worship, altruistic 214
wrath 296f

Yahweh (LORD) 32, 57, 99f, 332, 364
—, as Christ 215
Yahweh malakh (Hebrew: LORD has become king) 429
Yahweh-Elohim 18
yechidah (Hebrew: one and only) 341
yeshuah (Hebrew: salvation) 228
Yetzirah (Hebrew: formation) 26
yom (Hebrew: day) 204

Zahn, Theodor 170
Zarathustran religion 325
Zechariah (father of John the Baptist) 80
Zechariah (prophet) 65, 94–97, 395
Zerubabbel, King 92–94, 96f
Zipporah 147
zodiac 105
zōon (Greek: living creature) 111f

You may also be interested in...

The Complete New Testament Studies

Rudolf Frieling

In this collection of essays, Rudolf Frieling draws on his deep knowledge and insight to make the events of the New Testament more understandable to modern readers. He returns to the Greek text to uncover the meaning and power of the original language.

Frieling's masterful analysis surpasses the dry concepts and conventional explanations of many biblical commentaries and brings the events of the New Testament vividly to life. The result is a work that continues to be important for understanding the New Testament today.

florisbooks.co.uk

The New Testament

A Version by Jon Madsen

Many translations of the New Testament tread a challenging line between scholarly accuracy and living, spirit-filled words which will inspire a general reader.

This unique version balances the two in such a way that something of the Holy Spirit, working in the early church, can become part of a reader's experience.

Madsen draws on other translations, including Emil Bock's seminal German translation, as well as the sacramental language of The Christian Community, to present a singular version which uncovers the living wisdom of the Gospels. Beautifully bound in hardback with eye-catching dust jacket, this gift edition will remain a wise companion for years to come.

Also available as e Book

florisbooks.co.uk

Paths Into the Book of Books
New Biblical Translations through the Festivals of the Year

Elsbeth Weymann

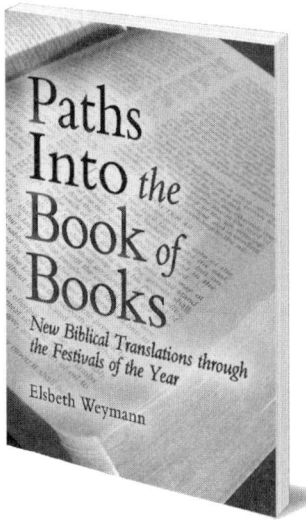

In this insightful book, Elsbeth Weymann, an expert in Greek and Hebrew, has selected biblical passages which take the reader through the festivals of the year – from Advent and Easter to Pentecost and Michaelmas. Each passage has a fresh translation and in-depth commentary. For instance, in the story of Pentecost, she highlights the use of the unusual feminine form of the word 'spirit', which points to a feminine aspect of the Holy Spirit.

Weymann's study of specific words and grammar also shows how the living presence of the Old Testament is evident in the New Testament. This book is for anyone looking for deeper meaning in the Bible.

florisbooks.co.uk

Christianity and Reincarnation

Rudolf Frieling

Reincarnation – by which human beings return to live on earth – is a concept most often associated with eastern philosophies rather than Christianity. Yet in this challenging book, Rudolf Frieling makes the case for the integration of reincarnation into a Christian world view.

He shows how an esoteric Christianity was brought to life again through the thinking of Rudolf Steiner, arguing that theology around the 'end of days' has shown how a gap exists between death and resurrection on the Last Day.

Presenting the essence of Christianity, Frieling shows how it harmonises with reincarnation, and examines the relationship of reincarnation to the Bible.

florisbooks.co.uk

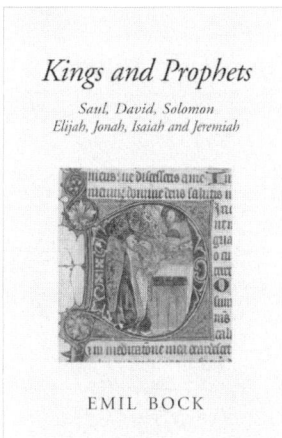

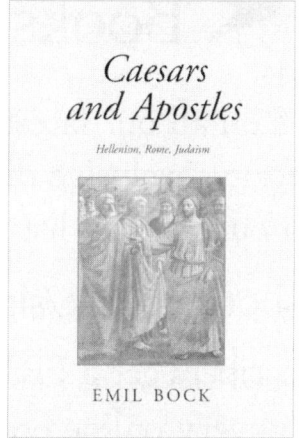

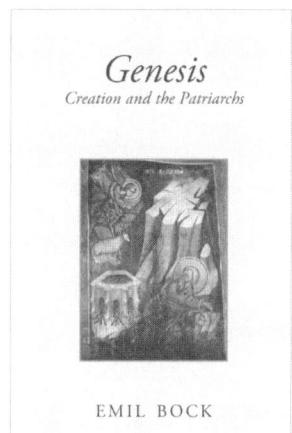

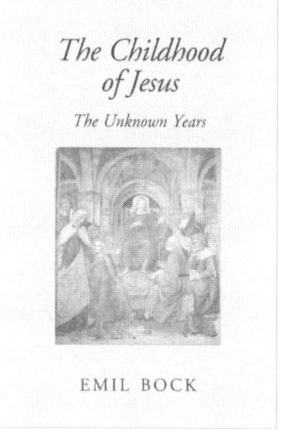

florisbooks.co.uk

For news on all our **latest books**, and to receive **exclusive discounts**, **join** our mailing list at:

florisbooks.co.uk/signup

Plus subscribers get a FREE book with every online order!

We will never pass your details to anyone else.